AF527806

THE CONGRESS PARTY AND GOVERNMENT
Policy and Performance

THE CONGRESS PARTY AND GOVERNMENT
Policy and Performance

B. B. MISRA

Completed under the auspices of
the Centre for Policy Research

CONCEPT PUBLISHING COMPANY, NEW DELHI-110059

ISBN 81-7022-221-4

First Published 1988

Published by
Ashok Kumar Mittal
Concept Publishing Company
A/15-16, Commercial Block, Mohan Garden
New Delhi-110059

Photo-composing by
Microtech Advance Printing Systems Pvt. Ltd.
New Delhi-110015

Printed by
Taj Press
3024, Gali Ahiran, G.B. Road
Delhi-110006

Preface

This study is essentially an attempt to understand, in the context of British imperial legacy, the class character of the Congress Party and its Government in terms of its economic policy and political behaviour. As the presence of imperialism imparted to the Congress a national complexion, its class character remained blurred in the early stages of development as a movement. Even so, the movement-party dichotomy could not altogether be suppressed. Though basically devoted to an understanding of the Congress economic policy, the coverage of this work tends consequently to be wider in some chapters so as to include the related considerations of politics and problems of policy implementation.

I was invited to undertake this study by Mr. L. P. Singh, a retired member of the Indian Civil Service and former Governor of Assam and Nagaland, who initially discussed with me its subject matter and, as one of the founders of the Centre for Policy Research, introduced me to its Director, Dr. V. A. Pai Panandikar, a reputed and recognized scholar in the field of empirical research, who encouraged the pursuit of this study.

Though aware of my limitations to handle a subject in the field of economic history calling for a certain degree of professional and conceptual competence to which I could hardly lay any claim, I readily accepted the invitation on the strength of the experience of research I had acquired in such allied fields as politics, public administration and political institutions. In fact, I viewed it as an opportunity to educate myself by an extension of my earlier span of inquiry to find out the kind of relationship that developed between the controllers of business and the country's economy on the one hand and the political leadership of the Congress Party on the other. I am glad to find that the choice I made was not without avail. The two entities are closely related to each other, the latter being a function of the former.

I am grateful to Mr. L. P. Singh who, as Home Secretary to the Government of India, had earlier permitted me the use of some archival material, relevant not only for purposes of administrative research, but also for industrial policy and economic organization. Mr. Singh has, in fact, been a source of great help to me in my scholarly pursuits. I am also indebted to Dr. Pai Panandikar and his Centre for Policy Research for the financial assistance given to me for completing this work. I shall be failing in my duty if I omit to record my sense of obligation to the Indian Institute of Public Administration, more especially to Professor S. K. Goyal and his Press Clipping Section which made available to me the relevant source material, including documents relating to Congress policy published as part of the Special Independence Number of 1972 in *Young Indian*. To Dr. Pai Panandikar and Mr. Bisht of the Federation of Indian Chambers of Commerce and Industry I am no less obliged for the permission to use some of its archival material which provided an insight into the political role of business to safeguard its own vested interest, an interest which counteracted the regulatory measures of the State based on a policy of control. Mr. Duli Chand of the National Archives of India and Mr. B. M. Lal of Shyam Lal College, Delhi, are two other persons to whom I am deeply indebted. While the former helped me ungrudgingly in the selection of files on the subject of industrial policy and foreign trade, the latter not only saw to it that I was in no way inconvenienced but also helped me in the supply of published material.

I shall be failing in my duty if I omit the name of Professor S. R. Maheshwari of the Indian Institute of Public Administration, New Delhi, who has always been extremely helpful to me in the conduct of my researches in the field.

B. B. MISRA

Contents

ONE

Congress as an Elitist Movement Politico-Economic Development to 1920

The Indian National Congress came into existence at its first session held in Bombay from December 28-30, 1885. It was a political organization intended initially to advance the case of educated Indians in the superior civil service of the country. But as an elitist body it was natural, and even necessary, that it should have that interest raised to a higher national level, manifestly representative of the interests of all classes and communities.

Except for the First Would War period of 1914-18 which saw the emergence of a new competitive class of Indian capitalists, the emphasis of the Congress during 1885-1920 remained, on the whole, political, a question of the country's constitutional relationship as part of the British Empire itself–a question embodied in the vague concept of *swaraj* interpreted differently by different leaders without any attempt to define it in socio-economic terms. It was Dadabhai Naoroji who alone raised the question of India's poverty in the course of his presidential address to the Congress in 1906, and related it to the political principles of *swaraj*, vaguely understood as self-government within the British Commonwealth.

In sociological terms, B. G. Tilak doubtless represented culturally what might be described as an antithesis of elitism and thought in terms of the lower middle class or mass interest. Rooted in the soil as genuine nationalists, some of his adherents even contributed to the growth of left politics. But since Tilakites were in general influenced by the Hindu tradition laid down earlier by Shivaji, their approach to politics could not be said to be altogether free from a communal bias. This chapter is intended to throw light on the Congress policy-performance gap which arose not only from considerations of communal and cultural variations, but more especially from an adherence to the politics of power to promote the middle-class elitist interest which became allied with that of the emerging business Houses, for the most part Hindu in social and cultural terms.

Elitist v. National Interest

The existence of a gap between the Congress being professedly envisaged as "the germ of a Native Parliament" and its actual elitist aim of advancement in the covenanted civil service was first brought to light by Sir William Wedderburn, an erstwhile Civilian who presided over its fifth session in 1889. In the course of his presidential address he traced the origin of the Congress to a "movement" directed against Lord Lytton's policy which had led to the lowering of age for open competition from 23 to 19 years and the introduction of nomination for recruitment to the Statutory Civil Service created for Indians in 1879. The Indian Association, organized by Surendranath Banerjea, was an expression of this movement which rose in open protest against Lytton's policy and marked the beginning of the Indian National Congress.

Though recognizing, in general terms, that "the movement which has now culminated in the Indian National Congress" was "the natural and healthy fruit of higher education and free institutions freely granted to the people of India", Sir William did not omit specially to emphasize that "looking back to the history of the movement" there doubtless was one critical time in its development. That was almost 10 years ago (1879). The leaven was then actually at work, though the purpose of the movement was not then so well defined, and it was unwisely sought to deal with it by a policy of repression.[1]

The issue initially involved in the origin of the Congress as a political movement was thus in the main an issue of recruitment to the country's superior civil service. There was in law no racial bar to entry, although difficulties arose in practice. These led to the politics of employment which sought to raise the elitist civil service issue to the level of national importance. It was considered by the very first session assembled in Bombay with 72 "self-elected" representatives got together with the exertions of a few leading men of influence interested in the promotion of what they called public interests of an all-India nature. As W. C. Bonnerjee pointed out in his presidential address, the object declared was to develop friendly intercourse among earnest workers for a common cause of national unity forming part of the British Empire. He confessed that judged from the standard of the House of Commons the Congress was of course not representative of the people of India. But if community of sentiments or community of wants could enable anyone to speak on behalf of others, it might justly claim to be representative.[2] This in fact was an attempt to cover up the gap between the declared goal of national unity and the reality of the elitist class interest.

Official Support as Main Source of Initial Strength

The period of tribulation arising from the civil service controversy was, however, cut short by the viceroyalty of Lord Ripon. He fulfilled the aspirations of the educated middle class. The political recognition he extended to this class in fact imparted to its rising movement a national identity. In other words, its demand in respect of the civil service, howsoever limited to elitism, was sought to be treated as part of a national demand. The middle class itself appeared as identifiable with the nation.

Doubtless, Lord Dufferin who succeeded Ripon held quite a different view. He treated the Indian middle class as representing a mere sectional interest, not the interest of Indian society as a whole–an interest which the bureaucracy claimed to represent by virtue of the monolithic constitution of British rule. Moreover, the educated elites, who dominated the Congress, were known for their selfishness and, as Dufferin said, their instincts "in nine cases out of ten" were to promote their own interests "at the expense of those of the bulk of our subjects".[3] This impression was formed on account of their sustained opposition to land reforms based on the extension of occupancy rights to tenants under the various tenancy enactments[4] intended to provide relief to the bulk of agricultural population.

Admittedly, the Congress was of course a middle-class organization. It was dominated by men of note and influence belonging to the professions of law and education, trade and industry, banking and insurance, journalism and medical practice, social and religious reforms. This became clear from an occupational analysis of the classes to which the representatives of the very first session of the Congress belonged. It was further confirmed by Sir Auckland Colvin's survey of its Allahabad session held in 1888.[5]

Dufferin's reluctance to recognize the Congress as a "party" invested with the exercise of power on behalf of the "people" of India as a whole was therefore quite understandable. It was not without reason. For he said: "To hand over the Government of India either partially or otherwise to such a body as this (the Indian National Congress) would simply be to place millions of men, dozens of nationalities and hundreds of most stupendous interests under the dominance of a microscopic minority ... there are signs that the Native Princes, Magnates and Landholders are becoming seriously alarmed at the thought of a small class of Barristers, Native Newspaper Editors, and university students intervening between them and ... the British Government."[6]

Even so, Dufferin himself had earlier invited to a garden party the members of the Congress attending its second session held in Calcutta in 1886. In a letter of September 24, 1888, he later even pointed out to his Secretary of State that several government servants acted as agents of Congress propaganda "using their official position to collect money on its behalf".[7] The practice continued under Lansdowne also.[8] Even Lord Curzon appointed Congressmen as judges of High Courts.[9] The case of N. G. Chandravarkar was specially significant. Prior to his appointment as judge of the Bombay High Court he had been President of the Lahore session of the Congress held in 1900. Writing to Lord George Hamilton, Secretary of State, Curzon justified his action as an attempt to keep the Moderate group in the Congress on the side of the British Government and to prevent them from assuming "an attitude of hostility and revenge".[10]

Obviously, there seemed to be an identity of interest between the Congress and the Government of India. While the former wanted an official recognition as a national political organization to rise in social scale for the fulfilment of its middle-class elitist and bourgeois interest, the latter needed a non-official political organization to act as a barometer of public opinion in the formulation of public policies. That perhaps was the reason why Dufferin, who differed from Ripon, thought in terms of a popular link within the framework of a bureaucratic despotism. Being "the acknowledged representative of the legally constituted bodies" established under the Viccroyalty of the Marquis of Ripon, he wrote to his Secretary of State, they might "speak with great weight of authority" because of their "continual contact with large masses".[11]

The Moderates who dominated the Congress spared, on their part, no pains to prove their loyalty to the British Crown and Parliament, not only in political and constitutional terms but also in terms of cultural deportment. Addressing the representatives of the very first session of the Congress, W. C. Bonnerjee, for instance, assured that there were no more thoroughly loyal and consistent well-wishers of the British Government than he himself and the friends of the Congress gathered around him. Dadabhai Naoroji who presided over the second session of the Congress in Calcutta was even far more exuberant in his praise for British rule than his predecessor. "Let us speak out like men", he said, "and proclaim that we are loyal to the backbone, that we understand the benefits English rule has conferred upon us, that we thoroughly appreciate the education that has been given to us, the new light that has been poured upon us, turning us from darkness to light and teaching us the new lesson that kings are made for the people, not people for their kings; and the new lesson we have learned amidst the darkness of Asiatic despotism only by the light of free English education"[12] Speaking of the Congress, therefore, Naoroji assured, with a solemn voice, that it would be "another stone in the foundation of the British Government to ensure its stability".[13]

By the time the fifth session of the Congress was held again in Bombay in 1889 divisive forces had started raising their head at the call of Sir Syed Ahmed and Raja Shiva Prasad who formed the anti-Congress United Patriotic Association which charged the Congress with sedition and disloyalty against the British Government. In the course of his welcome address Pherozeshah M. Mehta not only refuted the charge, but boldly asserted and reaffirmed loyalty to the

Government by a steadfast appeal to the authoritarian record of the Congress in terms of its words, thoughts and deeds. "We of the Congress", he emphasized, "are more loyal than Anglo-Indians themselves".[14] Sir William Wedderburn confirmed it in his presidential address.

Movement-Party Dichotomy

The growth of suspicion against the Congress in official circles or even elsewhere as part of a communal development was, however, not without reasons. It proceeded from a dichotomy involved in the double role of the Congress functioning simultaneously as a movement as well as a party. As a movement, it acted as a national body to deal with an alien government, politically sovereign and different in race and religion. Its declared aim was in that capacity to ingratiate itself with all classes and to mobilize them to bring pressure to bear upon the British Government for a gradual transfer of power to Indians, irrespective of any class consideration. As a party, on the other hand, it was interested in how best to make use of that power in the promotion of its own dominant class interest. While the one widened its operational sphere and made it a socially heterogeneous body, the other conduced to the formation of a central core or caucus of its middle-class leadership controlling both the movement and the party.

The formation of the caucus with the sole object of arrogating to itself the exercise of the whole power gained through the cumulative efforts of a movement, comprising all the elements of a plural Indian society, became in course of time the main cause of suspicion among government officials who pleaded for the interest of all classes as well as the minority communities who feared the inevitability of a caste-Hindu caucus born of the Congress movement, especially in the case of its revivalist culture kind. This movement-party dichotomy, which had from an early period developed an element of contradiction, actually came to the surface even on the partial admission of the Congress demand for a representative government in 1892. It was recognized as a concrete achievement and the seats given to Congressmen in the Legislative Councils enhanced its position, not only with the Government, but also with those who did not belong to its social categories. Though representing the interest of a small section of Indian society, it appeared as a political force to reckon with, claiming, as it did, the loyalty of even those classes whose interest clashed with its own. The strength so gained came to the Congress as a party, although it flowed from its growing strength and influence as a movement. In the words of Lord Lansdowne: "Although there is a good deal of jealousy against this class there is every reason to believe that many of the Chiefs and leading men do and regard its proceedings with disfavour, but are giving it secret assistance and encouragement. Even some of those who are ostensibly hostile or neutral are, for reasons not difficult to fathom, maintaining amicable relations with the leaders of the progressive party".[15]

The Congress as a party had thus been gradually gaining on its achievement as a movement for national status. This in fact was as much the work of the Moderates as of the Government who did not deny the benefit of its official recognition from considerations of policy. This perhaps was responsible for the financial support the Congress received as a professedly national body from all classes, more especially from certain chiefs and zamindars who wanted to be popular with the Congress leadership from motives of self-interest, an interest which, in the absence of a developed industrial culture and highly monitized economy, differed but little in qualitative terms from that of the landowning professional classes and traders in the Congress. Its early supporters thus included the Maharaja of Darbhanga, the Rana of Vizianagaram, the Raja of Ramnad in Madras, Maharaja Sir Jotindranath Tagore, the Gaekwar of Baroda and some others who viewed the Congress as an alternative source of power and influence.

Rise of New Forces

The Congress thus kept on growing in strength as a movement. The dichotomy in question, however, did not disappear. That too kept on growing with increasing devolution of power to the legislature, both central and provincial. The rise of cultural nationalism as a new political force was of course important because of indigenous business enterprise as an economic force was basic in terms of an alternative source of financial support which in course of time dispensed with the necessity of governmental recognition or patronage. Both the developments became noticeable in the wake of the partition of

Bengal in 1905.

The revivalist cultural trend in national politics was an expression of reaction against the liberalizing modern influences proceeding from the higher Western education and monitized capitalist economy, a rule-bound administrative system as well as a foreign political control which was believed to have shaken the cultural foundation of the country's tradition-bound caste order based on status rather than social change or mobility.[16] Though socially backward-looking, the trend was politically radical, giving rise to revolutionary and terrorist movements, inimical to parliamentary institutions and constitutional methods advocated by the Western-oriented leaders of the Moderate group in the Congress who dominated it.

However, it was cultural orientation or religious approach to politics that marked the beginning of a mass orientation in its movement. According to the vernacular tracts circulated at the Madras Congress of 1887, for example, it envisaged "village-to-village preaching of the doctrine that the Congress is to be the remedy for all grievances... that the Collector (European) must be got rid of, and that then the ryot will get off his assessment. Give us, the educated classes, power, and you, the uneducated, will be freed from oppression as you used to be years ago".[17] Under the influence of its radical group the Congress, instead of the earlier practice of memorializing the House of Commons, proceeded to appeal to that element of the British electorate which, after the labour franchise of 1884, showed an increasing tendency to support socialism.[18]

Because of its anti-imperialist overtone, the new political force conduced to the emergence of what later became known as revolutionary communism forming part of the Left in general terms. The Nau Jawan Bharat Sabha and the Hindustan Socialist Republican Association of the 1920s could be classed along with some others as a pattern of revolutionary organization intended to promote the cause of socialism and national freedom.[19] The various shades of political non-conformism, however, formed part of the Congress itself as a movement. It flowed in the first instance from religious revivalism which regarded political freedom as a necessary condition for its promotion. In other words, the revivalist leaders believed that religion and politics were indistinguishably intermingled. The one could not flourish without the other. The most distinguished among the early non-conformists were men like B. G. Tilak, Lajpat Rai and Bepin Chandra Pal. The political conspiracies and acts of violence that occurred in the 1920s were perhaps comparable to Tilak's recognized norms of political behaviour. In the context of the Russian Revolution of 1917 the anti-imperialist revolutionary trends turned for the most part to Leftism without caring to shake off their revivalist hang-over.

The political radicalism of cultural nationalism came to the notice of the Government during the Madras session of the Congress in 1887. The revivalist group had through its own organization circulated in Tamil and Hindi certain secret tracts which, among other things, emphasized demands for representative government by converting the Congress into "an Indian Parliament". They also advised popular agitation against the British Government until nomination was replaced by an elective principle in the Constitution of the Legislative Council. Dufferin had this extremist group in mind which led him to believe that the Congress might prove to be a "mischievous organization" because of its being connected with what he broadly viewed as a "Home Rule Party in India" or " Advanced Native Party", demanding representative institutions as a panacea for all ills. This rabid group in the Congress was headed by Tilak himself.[20] A. O. Hume, a great supporter of the Congress, admitted the existence of this radical group and regretted the manner in which the Home Government was sought to be maligned by it, although he held that it was after all a small group of individuals who did it, not the persons professing to be Congressionists.[21] The fact, however, remained undisputed that it was the radical anti-imperialist, though small, group in the Congress that pressed for the acceleration of political advance for an ideology which, though initially cultural, conduced to a mass movement, a prelude to the lower orders of society being involved for a higher socio-economic goal, not the ruling caucus interested in its own monopoly of power and all that flows from it.

1905-20 : Widening of Policy-Performance Gap Leading to Congress Split

As discussed above, the element of the movement-party

dichotomy, which necessarily developed in the functioning of the Indian National Congress, was the basic cause of a gap between its profession and action. The gap so caused naturally tended to increase with the extension of power to the legislature, both central and provincial. This period was marked by two main features. While the Surat Split (1907) brought into focus the importance of defining the political goal of *swaraj*, the imperialist war (1914-18) raised for the first time the vital issue of Indian economic development both calling for a devolution of power from London to New Delhi.

It was in respect of the progressive decentralization of legislative authority that the political radicalism of cultural nationalism had its own importance insofar as the analysis of the Congress policy-performance gap was concerned. For it was this radicalism that emphasized the political issue of its demand and strongly pressed for the introduction of an elective principle in the constitution of the legislative authority under the Indian Councils Act, 1892. A gap appeared on the surface. For the Moderates were in their attitude too soft to put up any fight for political advance. But, as suggested before, the Government came to their rescue. The Congress of the Moderates was sought to be credited with the concession of the demand for policy's sake. Even so the crisis was not over. As the radicals had resolved in their secret circulars, the Moderates in the Congress could not accept any revivalist suggestion for the downward filtration of the political process of a mass movement. As Naoroji said in 1906, the radicals were after all a small group, hardly recognized as "Congressionists". But as subsequent developments showed, they nonetheless constituted a Brahmanic political force to reckon with. Revivalist politics had in fact come to stay. It was this radical group in the Congress itself which was known as the "Advanced Party"–a party opposed to blind imitation and responsible for pressure being brought to bear upon the British Government to concede the representative principle in the organization of legislative councils.

The Nationalists

Constituted for the most part of the lower middle classes, the radical elements in the Congress were in the earlier period to remain satisfied with subordinate positions for want of an able leadership.

But while the elitist section chose to remain cool after the constitutional advance of 1892, the radicals became organized into a separate group known as the "Extremists" led by B. G. Tilak, Lajpat Rai, Khaparde and B. C. Pal. The Moderates, who still dominated the Congress, came to be known as "Liberals" operating within a constitutional framework in cooperation with the Government. Both the groups were heading towards an open clash in respect of their ideologies as well as their methods of attainment. It was precipitated at the Calcutta session of the Congress in 1906, and, though averted for a time through the intercession of Gokhale and Naoroji, could not long be put off. The Surat Split of 1907 came as its actual consummation.

The Moderates were in fact faced with a dilemma which arose from the declared policy of the Extremists in the Congress being far more advanced over their own. For, the latter not only pressed for *swaraj*, a vague term for self-government, which later became a bone of contention on ideological grounds, but also insisted on the inclusion of *swadeshi*, boycott and national education as part of the Congress programme for the attainment of *swaraj*, interpreted as real self-government or independence in opposition to the Moderates' choice for dependence within the framework of a mere self-governing colonial constitution. The idea of *swadeshi* or incentive to indigenous manufacture and boycott of British goods appeared to the elitist mind not only inexpedient, but even inspired by the revolutionary cult arising from the partition of Bengal in 1905 and functioning outside the Congress without any legal sanction.

As regards the Liberals, including even G. K. Gokhale, their ideological commitment to *swaraj* was in fact more formal than real. It was in practice watered down by their emphasis on gradualness. In his presidential address to the Banaras Congress in 1905 Gokhale, for instance, had clearly pointed out that the attainment of self-government within the British Empire would necessarily be gradual, "for the proper exercise of the political institutions of the West can be acquired by the Eastern people through practical training and experience only".[22] He believed that Indians must be "renovated, purified and perfected before India could be the master of her own destiny".[23] S. P. Sinha, an important leader of the Moderate group in the Congress and the first Indian Member of the Viceroy's Executive

Council, held even a more conservative view. In the words of Lord Minto, the Viceroy, Sinha "thought British Government the best adapted form of government for India and that it is no good speculating as to the future as British administration must continue at any rate for two or three hundred years".[24]

Ideological Crisis and Surat Split Analysed

Obviously, the reason for a clash between the Moderates and the Extremist groups in the Congress was not only their difference of ideology and mode of operation, but also a clear want of the former's commitment to its own declared policy to work for **swaraj** even in terms of its own interpretation. What tended to precipitate the crisis of confidence which led to the Surat Split was this noticeable gap between the declared intention and the actual performance of the Moderates, the ruling caucus who controlled the Congress. The Calcutta Congress, it is true, marked a complete triumph of Tilak's group, for his resolutions on swaraj, swadeshi, boycott and national education were all passed by it. But the Congress which so emerged from Calcutta meant no business in operational terms. Tilak realized this in the course of a campaign he organized in support of his "New (Nationalist) Party". The Liberals were all out to blame him for his inaugural speech at Calcutta on January 2, 1907, when he made it clear that his Nationalist "Party" would seek an answer to India's economic and political problems not in petitioning but boycott, not in mendicancy but in withholding all assistance to the British Government in the administration of the country.[25]

The Surat Split of 1907 was a logical sequence to these developments. It resulted in the main from two immediate causes: first, the attempt of the Moderates to omit from the agenda any discussion of swaraj, swadeshi, boycott and national education; and secondly, the refusal of the Nationalists to accept Dr. Rashbehari Ghose[26] as the Congress President at Surat, the choice of the Reception Committee dominated by the Moderates. Besides being a clash for the control of leadership, the Surat Split was an expression of polarized interests and ideologies.

Ideologically, the Indian situation of 1905 and immediately after that called for a change in keeping with the extent of advance in education and public opinion. An official despatch of March 21, 1907, for instance, shows that in the course of 20 years after 1885 English education and newspapers had nearly doubled, but employment in the public services on a salary of Rs. 75 and above did not show any increase beyond 6 per cent.[27] This too was limited to the lower ranks of government service–a situation that reflected on India's national status.

There were other developments causing social and political unrest. These included, for instance, the rise in prices, the growing tension of race relations, the rigidity of the bureaucracy and, above all, the political policy of the Government of Lord Minto who, instead of recognizing the aspirations of the rising middle class of educated Indians, sought to apply a counterpoise to it by means of special electorates provided under his projected constitutional reforms.

There was, in addition, a serious development which, though of local importance to start with, assumed a national dimension. This was the Partition of Bengal which Lord Curzon effected in 1905, an administrative measure which led to terrorist activities and revolutionary movements.

Involved in the assassination of Europeans as well as Indians, the "Revolutionaries", who operated outside the Congress, were separate and distant from the "Extremists" in the Congress. But the Nationalist Party which emerged in the context of the Surat Split contained both. In 1908, Mrs. and Miss Kennedy were killed by Khudi Ram Bose who had flung a bomb at Kingsford, the District Magistrate of Muzaffarpur, then in Bengal, but missed him. Nandlal, the sub-inspector who had arrested Khudi Ram Bose, was murdered, as also Narendra Gosain, the approver of the Alipore Conspiracy Case where Aurobindo Ghose was defended by C. R. Das who had earlier defended B. C. Pal involved in a sedition case but later acquitted in 1909, although many others were awarded heavy sentences, including transportation for life. In 1909 itself, Ganesh Savarkar was sentenced to transportation for life on a charge of writing inflammatory verses; and Ashutosh Biswas, Public Prosecutor, was shot dead, while leaving the court in Calcutta. On July 1 of the same year, Madan Lal Dhingra had shot dead Sir Curzon Wyllie in London. Among the banishments in 1907 were those of Lala Lajpat

Rai and Ajit Singh of the Punjab and of B. G. Tilak who was in prison in Mandalay from 1908 to 1914.

The Nationalist Party thus represented a force directed against the dominance of foreign rule in the country. It was obviously a political force. But the basic source of its motivation was a concern to revive and promote Hindu religion and culture by means of a struggle to win swaraj or "Home Rule", capable of resisting the infiltration of Western influences.

As the Age of Consent Bill (1891) showed, the Nationalists aimed directly at the exclusion of European cultural influence in matters of Indian social legislation. But since their leadership was essentially Hindu, they could not but be viewed as anti-Muslim in socio-religious terms. Though partially inclined later to get attuned to the Left, their revolutionary elements could not completely shake off the core of their legacy. Even so, it was the nationalists who constituted the main force behind the Indian political movement, leading not only to constitutional advance of 1909, but also to the revocation of the partition of Bengal in 1912.

Continuing Control of Moderates

The Moderates were, for all practical purposes, a party of petitioners. But their main source of strength was the backing they received from the Government. They lent their support to the enactment of repressive measures intended to put down the activities of the "Extremists" and Revolutionaries. These measures, for instance, included the Prevention of Meetings Act (1907), the Criminal Law Amendment Act (1908) and the Press Act (1910).

Indeed, the Moderates became the Congress Party. They provided a well-structured and formal Congress constitution in 1908 and took exclusive advantage of the Morley-Minto Reforms introduced in 1909. Earlier, the Congress had continued to be weak organizationally. There had of course been some Standing Committee, but nothing like a formal organization before 1899, when a hierarchical build-up arose for the first time with an All-India Congress Committee on the top, the local standing committees at the bottom and the Provincial Congress Committees in between. But as its object did not go much beyond a mere expression of a vague ideal to promote the well-being of the Indian people, the organization remained for the most part unrelated to anything like a well-defined goal beyond an oft-repeated call for representative councils, which had already been met in 1892.

Following the Surat Split, the Liberals assumed for the first time a rigid attitude against the Nationalist Party in the same way as the Government. They met in a Convention to which no dissidents were to be invited. The Convention adopted colonial self-government as its goal which was to be attained strictly by constitutional means. It appointed a Committee with Dr. Rash Behari Ghose as President and Gokhale and Wacha as Joint Secretaries to perfect the Constitution of 1899 so as to make sure that no dissidence was allowed against the declared policy of the Congress. The Committee met at Allahabad on April 18, 1908. Its hierarchy was completed by the constitution of Congress committees at district, sub-divisional and tahsil or taluka levels, with provision for such other associations or public bodies as had the recognition of the AICC. Its main principle was in fact centralization. On subjects like the election of the President, the rules of business or any other important issues, for instance, final decisions were in all cases vested in the AICC, although subordinate committees were given a voice. The constitution so designed excluded the Nationalists altogether. The Moderates, now known as the Liberal Party, remained in exclusive control of the Congress machinery from 1908 to 1915.

No Congress Commitment to Declared Goal

The goal declared at the Moderate Convention of 1908 was the attainment of colonial government. But the means employed did not go beyond moving resolutions or asking questions in the legislature. After the exclusion of the Nationalists the Congress even dropped "swaraj" and "boycott" and watered down "swadeshi" and "national education". On the contrary, it was full of praise for the Morley-Minto Reforms which, in Minto's own words, had been designed to provide a "counterweight" to the Indian middle classes. The Congress placed on record "Its sense of high statesmanship which had dictated the action of the Government in the matter".

The Congress representatives in the Legislative Council cooperated with the Government irrespective of official response to its resolutions. During 1910-17, for example, as many as 168 resolutions were moved. Of these the Government accepted only 24. The remaining 144 of the resolutions were either withdrawn or rejected altogether. Those which were rejected were of immediate relevance to national education and self-governing institutions. They included, for example, Gokhale's resolution on elementary education, Surendranath Banerjea's resolution on the separation of executive and judicial functions, the abolition of the Press Act, the expansion of the Local Self-Government and the election of the chairmen of district and local boards. Their cooperation with the Government was in fact so complete and unconditional that 59 per cent of the Bills were passed without any discussion whatsoever.[28] To all intents and purposes the role of the Liberal Party was one of collaboration, concerned with the exercise of power without any popular backing or sanction.

Nationalists Readmitted to Congress, Liberals on Road to Exit

Tilak's release in 1914 after a sentence of six years in prison marked the emergence of a new political situation which jeopardized the prospects of the Liberal Party to continue in power ad infinitum. What shook this Party to its foundations was a series of developments that followed his release. These included, for instance, his own tactical rapprochement with the Moderates to re-enter the Congress, his Home Rule League established in 1916 with a change of attitude in favour of responsive cooperation with the British Government and the joint Congress-Muslim League Scheme of Self-Government formulated at Lucknow in December 1916 itself. The ovation with which Tilak was received at Kanpur on his return from the Lucknow Congress led the Lieutenant-Governor of U.P., Sir James Meston, to acknowledge the popularity of the Home Rule League in a secret Note addressed to the Viceroy. He said: "The cult of the Nationalists has gone to very great lengths. You see disconcerting photographs in quiet village homes and in every student cubicle. The reception of Mr. Tilak at Cawnpore on his return from the Congress was an eye-opener to people who continue to delude themselves on this score."[29]

In his attempt to seek understanding with the Moderates Tilak's strategy was in fact to use his popularity to capture the Congress. A subsequent report of the Government of India thus made it clear that when his "seceding group sought and obtained readmission, it was as an invading body whose aim appeared to be not reunion so much as annexation. After this reunion the influence of the Moderate Party in the politics of the old Congress steadily declined".[30]

An Indian Home Rule League was first sought to be organized by Mrs. Annie Besant who mooted the proposal at a meeting held in Bombay on December 27, 1915, just before the annual session of the Congress. The subject was, however, postponed till the Congress and the Muslim League had presented their joint report on the prevailing question of self-government. This postponement was against the wishes of the Hindu nationalists who, at a conference held earlier at Poona, had already appointed a Committee for the purpose. At its meeting held at Belgaum on April 28, 1916, this Committee recommended the formation of an Indian Home Rule League representing a synthesis of radical nationalism and liberal constitutionalism. Its object was self-government within the British Empire to be attained by constitutional means.[31] The Bombay Provincial Conference, which met just the next day with Khaparde as President, adopted the recommendations of the Committee, which were in keeping with the understanding already reached with Moderates. Tilak's Home Rule League thus forestalled that of Mrs. Besant, which came into existence in the September of the same year. Her Home Rule League which was followed by her election as President of the Calcutta session of the Congress in 1917 signified a further victory of the Nationalist Home Rulers in a situation which was preceded by the famous policy announcement of August 20, 1917.

The Montford Report that followed in 1918 appeared to the Moderates as a dilemma. They were called upon to choose between two alternatives: to submit or to secede. They finally chose to secede, because they did not believe that the Nationalists would adhere to strict constitutional means in case the extremist demand for greater provincial autonomy was not conceded. The Moderates in fact feared that they, by their cooperation with the Nationalists, would close a prospect of increased share in the Government held out by the Montford Reforms. So they did not attend the special session of the Congress held in Bombay on September 1, 1918, to determine its line of action. They held, on the contrary, a convention of their own in Bombay on November 1 and 2, 1918, and formed themselves into a separate party which in 1919 became known as the National Liberal Federation. Unlike the Congress, it declared the Reforms of 1919 as a great constitutional advance even in its original form and extended its full cooperation to the government to make it a success. Though founders of the Indian National Congress originally, the Moderates had to quit because of the compulsions of a new situation.

War and Rise of Indian Capitalism : A New Politico-Economic Force

The main cause of a change in the national policy was the First World War which created a new situation involving an interaction between the radical politics of cultural nationalism and the exigencies of rapid industrial development conducive to the emergency of Indian capitalism as a new politico-economic force.

A confidential communication from the Government of India to the Secretary of State in the Department of Commerce and Industry (No. 51 of November 26, 1915) shows that demands for State aid to Indian industries were being pressed forward ever since the start of the swadeshi movement "which summed up the universal desire to see India a manufacturing country". The movement, as the letter said, "was a failure owing to the lack of technical knowledge and business aptitude on the part of its leading participants" who were for the most part "politicians and literate public" in addition to manufacturers. But the desire which gave birth to it remained undiminished. It expressed itself again and again "in the form of resolutions and questions in the Imperial and Provincial Councils, of resolutions in the Indian National Congress and at public meetings, and of articles in the Press.

What immediately led to a recognition of demands for State aid to industry were, however, "the special conditions created by the war", conditions which called for "the prohibition of imports from enemy countries" and offered "an opportunity for the replacement of the manufactures of these countries by articles produced in India", the pivotal centre and line of military supply in Asia. Connected immediately with the rising class of Indian capitalists was even a more important consideration of future economic policy which could by no means ignore their claims to recognition as a force entitled to State aid. The letter thus pointed out: After the war India will consider herself entitled to demand the utmost help from her Government to enable her to take her place, so far as circumstances permit, as a manufacturing country. This desire, if thwarted, will certainly turn, and already shows signs of turning into an insistent request for a tariff penalizing the import of all articles from abroad, British or foreign, and the demand for fiscal protection will inevitably be intensified and will become increasingly difficult for the Government to rebut without laying itself open to the charge of neglecting Indian interests. A definite and accepted industrial policy was therefore sought to be initiated on the principle of State aid to industry. The appointment of an Industrial Commission under the Government of India Resolution of May 19, 1916, was the first step taken in this direction.

The importance of Indian capitaliam apart, there was a still more pressing consideration for State participation to secure rapid industrialization. As the Confidential A. Proceedings (Nos. 7-22) of the Government of India in the Department of Commerce and Industry, 1919, pointed out, this consideration related to defence strategy that flowed from the experiences of the war itself. It was clearly brought out and put in perspective under the most important recommendations of the Indian Industrial Commission 1918. The Government agreed with the Commission in respect of the three main postulates laid down by it.

It was taken for granted, in the first instance, that "there must be in the immediate future a great industrial development in India. It has commenced already, and even if there were no indications of public sentiment in its favour (which, of course, there are), it would have to be forced on the country if only for Imperial military reasons". For it was realized that "with the rapid and certain development of aeronautics and submarinism", it would be well-nigh "impossible for the Empire to rely as heretofore on sea-communications in times of war". It was necessary that "each part of the Empire must therefore be, as far as possible, self-supporting" in order to make sure that the whole was not endangered. It was thus suggested that for special reasons "India must become the arsenal of the East". For "military reasons", as the Government emphasized, "an industrial revolution is necessary; and not only necessary but urgently necessary. There is no time to be lost".

It was also taken for granted that no industrial development was possible without the active assistance of the Government. It is true that State aid to industry clashed with free-trade principles. The view now taken by the Government was that "the old laissez-faire doctrine is as dead as Queen Anne".

The third postulate of the Indian Industrial Commission called for the pursuit of a coordinated all-India industrial policy by the Government of India. It was in fact accepted right when the proposal to appoint the Commission was mooted. "The whole basis of the decision to have a Commission at all rested upon the fact that isolated attempts of Local Governments to assist industries had for the most part been ineffective because of the want of a central policy". It was considered that if the control of industrial development was to be left entirely to Local Governments, the only thing that might follow would be "industrial chaos". This question was finally decided by the Indian Constitutional Reforms of 1919 under what came to be known as "transferred subjects", or Provincial Department of Industry set up in addition to the Imperial Department of Industry. The whole development was summed up in due sequence in the Government of India despatch (No. 15 of June 4, 1919) to the Secretary of State in the Department of Commerce and Industry.

The necessity of State aid as an instrument of industrial policy was thus fully recognized, more especially from the point of view of defence preparedness. But since the State itself was under the control of an alien Government, its policy, even though sound in principle, remained subject to misunderstanding for lack of confidence arising from an all-pervasive influence of European firms. While cultural politics continued to retain its attitude of resistance to foreign dominance in both political and economic fields, the indigenous industrial interest sought to ally itself with that politics in quest of political support for success against foreign competition.

The rise of Indian capitalism proceeded in fact from both contexts, the war and cultural nationalism. While the first created conditions for the growth of indigenous manufactures, the second provided a political element for a spirit to fight against foreign competitors. Sir James Meston, who was Lieutenant-Governor of U.P. during 1912-18 and Finance Member in 1918-19, pointed out that a new India was fast emerging in the course of this war because of the rising ambition of the Indian merchant community to participate in the political life of the country to secure the promotion of industrial development. Sir Dorabji Tata, for example, advocated in 1915 at the Industrial Conference in Bombay that both politics and industry should be yoked together to force the Government of India locally to organize the production of everything needed for the prosecution of the war as well as for the encouragement of Indian industries.[32] As a result of the political pressure so exercised, the Government of India, by a resolution passed on May 19, 1916, appointed its first Indian Industrial Commission to report on the expediency of government participation and direction in India's industrial development–a step which the Government had scrupulously avoided before in keeping with the principle of laissez-faire.

The Commission regretted that in spite of India being rich in raw materials, she had in the past remained poor in her manufacturing accomplishments, more especially because the exponents of laissez-faire considered the Government ill-qualified to undertake industrialization by direct action. Besides, the Government too acted under an erroncous belief that with their fertile lands and trying climatic conditions tropical countries were more suited to the production of raw materials than manufactured goods. It was India's success in the manufacture of textiles as well as iron and steel that dispelled this mistaken view. What the war did immediately was to bring into focus the exigencies of defence which dictated the necessity of creating in India conditions for industrial self-sufficiency for defence and allied purposes, for it was no longer possible to rely on the importation of goods or even to keep intact the normal lines of regular military supply.

It is true that the difficulty of importing machinery and skill in the course of the war had rendered it well-nigh impossible to start new enterprises. But the capital accumulated during the war led to huge floatation immediately on its termination. The magnitude of this development is clear from the fact that while the number of companies registered in 1918-19 was 198 with a capital of pound sterling 4.5 million, the number for the year 1919-20 totalled 906, with an aggregate capital of pound sterling 183 million.[33] According to the industrial census reports, the number of industrial establishments, both registered and unregistered with 20 persons or more employed in each, increased from 7,113 in 1911 to a little over 15.000 in 1921.[34]

The fact that India had by the second decade of the present century entered a new era of industrial advance as a consequence of the war and policy reorientation is reinforced by increasing imports of machinery and mill-work. The following figures, which are based on the *Statistical Abstract* for relevant years, make the point quite clear:

Imports of Machinery and Mill-Work
(Rs. Crores)

Year	Value of machinery and mill-work	Value of railway plant and rolling stock
1873	1.00	0.43
1882	1.34	1.11
1892	2.11	1.48
1912	5.41	6.40
1921	34.25	18.91

Modern industrial development in India in fact began with the laissez-faire or colonial economy formally introduced under the 1833 Act which permitted the settlement of Europeans for the promotion of trade and industry on the principle of free enterprise and mass production to meet the growing urban demand. It was a revolutionary step which immediately called for the import of capital and technology, a development which was accelerated by the great trading ports of Bombay, Calcutta, Madras and Karachi, with some up-country market towns at important railway junctions. These new centres not only offered incentives to European and local entrepreneurs, but also became exposed to foreign competition. What the European Managing Houses did in organizational terms was to promote the development of foreign markets which they initiated and sustained by virtue of their extensive international contacts. The result was that the two most successful industries, namely, cotton and jute, in pre-1914 India kept on growing swiftly even without tariff protection.

By far the most important of the engineering and metal industries organized and developed even before the war was the Tata Iron and Steel Company established at Jamshedpur in 1907. It grew during the war and by 1929 employed about 28,000 workers.[35] A considerable growth of factories took place in other industries, both textile and non-textile, perennial and seasonal.[36]

Area of Indian Industrial Interest : Indian capitalist interest in modern industry developed far more rapidly in Bombay than in Calcutta which was dominated by Europeans, with their industries centred in Hooghly, its vicinity. With the establishment of the first cotton mill in Bombay in 1851, the Bombay Presidency, and especially the island of Bombay and Ahmedabad, maintained the lead. Kanpur (Cawnpore) in U.P. came next in order of importance. Accounting for the industrial superiority of Bombay, the *Report of the Indian Industrial Commission* which came out in 1918 thus commented:

"If the cause be sought, some indication may be found in the fact that Indians have held a large and important share in the industry of Bombay since the city first came into English hands. The Mohamedans of the west coast, especially, traded by sea with the Persian Gulf, Arabia and East Africa from such earlier times. The Parsees and Hindus from the northern Bombay coast districts are recorded, in the beginning of the British occupation, as taking, with the Mahomedan sects of Khojas, Memons and Bohras, a most important share in the trade of the port as contractors, merchants and shipbuilders, and have throughout shown themselves little, if at all, inferior to the English in enterprise, and usually in command of more capital.[37]

According to Dr. M. M. Mehta who has in his *Structure of Indian Industries* made a statistical study of certain Indian business communities, the British played a dominant role in India's industrial activity up to 1911, except in the western sector where the Parsis, Jews and Gujarati Hindus held the ground quite firmly. Foreign interest was in no sense weak in the western sector also. But it held a virtual monopoly of Eastern trade and industry before the First World War. This was specially so in Bengal, including Assam, where British and Scottish interests exercised an almost exclusive control of tea, jute and coal.

The Indian interests made a noticeable progress in the course of the war. Of the Indian communities, the Marwaris emerged by far the most outstanding. The Parsis, Gujaratis and Bengalis were ahead of them till 1911. But the Marwaris took full political advantage of the swadeshi and swaraj movements of the subsequent period and stole a march over all of them. While the number of Marwari companies rose from nil in 1911 to 96 in 1951, the number of their directors rose to 146 in 1931 and then again to 618 in 1951. It is they who stood next to British interests, with their companies in 1951 being 382, while their directors 865. The most important of the Marwari interests were the Birlas who were closely associated with the activities of M. K. Gandhi. They were known for their support to the Right in the Congress.

Concentration of Economic Power : Historically, the basic source of concentration was the Managing Agency System which developed with the development of free enterprise and large-scale production as part of India's colonial economy. From considerations of managerial integration and centralized financial control, a managing agency firm held the bulk of interest in several industrial units whose administration it controlled through a system of multiple directorship which conduced to economy and efficiency not only in administrative but also financial terms. Capital and management both remained with the managing firm.

The organizational model of the Managing Agency system, which developed in the peculiar Indian context of entrepreneurial and financial inadequacies, acted as a powerful instrument of capitalist economy, European as well as Indian. Dr. M. M. Mehta's study on the *Structure of Industries* (p.281) shows that a group of Managing Agents in 1911 controlled and managed as many as 189 industrial units. Of these, 93 units were controlled and managed by the "Big

Five" of the Managing Agency Houses of Calcutta. These were Messrs. Andrew Yule, Bird, Shaw Wallace, Duncan and Begg, Dunlop and Company. They were all foreign-owned and operated. With the exception of Tatas, there was at the time no Indian Managing House which controlled or managed more than five industrial units. A number of Indian Managing Agents had, however, just started emerging in the western sector. They belonged, for the most part, to Jewish, Parsi and Gujarati communities. The enterprising Indian industrialists so emerging included Sassoons, Khataus, Cowasjees, Thackerseys, Jeejeebhoys and Wadias. In the eastern sector, the only Indian firm of any importance was Messrs. N. C. Sarkar and Company who managed five big collieries. As said above, it was the First World War forces that boosted the interest of the Indian industrial concerns on any major scale.

Conditions Conducive to Left Politics : The first imperialist war not only contributed to the growth of Indian capitalism, but also created its antithetical labour force which organized itself as a central focus of Left politics into an All-India Trade Union Congress established in December 1920. While the war led to the growth and expansion of Indian industries, the consequent emergence of a concentrated population of factory workers lent itself to Leftism in political propaganda to an extent far greater than the widely scattered peasant population of rural areas. This new economic force expressed itself in unprecedented industrial strikes of 1920, which, as the following table shows, occurred over a wide area, although Bombay happened to be by far the most seriously affected :[38]

Province	No. of operatives involved
Punjab	1,000
Burma	1,431
Central Provinces	6,000
Bihar & Orissa	10,370
United Provinces	41,371
Bengal	49,965
Bombay	181,595

These strikes had earlier been preceded by the Russian Revolution of 1917 which encouraged ideological incentives to Leftism in Indian politics. It was virtually a revolutionary trend born of conditions created by the war, more especially in a colonial situation. In a letter to the Viceroy the Secretary of State, Sir Austen Chamberlain, described Indian developments as in fact influenced by all the world being "in a state of revolution". The ferment of new ideas, he said, "is working everywhere and in India as much as anywhere. Opinions cannot but be excited by the Russian Revolution, by congratulations showered upon the revolutionaries, from England and elsewhere, and by the constant appeal to the spirit of liberty and nationality which are the groundwork of most of the public declarations of the time".[39]

It was in the wake of the Russian Revolution, more especially towards the close of the war, that Indian revolutionaries abroad started shifting their operational headquarters from Berlin to Moscow. They were fast coming under Bolshevik influence which induced them to go in for a peasant and proletarian revolution as the basis of Indian struggle for freedom. Even a staunch Hindu revolutionary like Har Dayal came to switch over to European social democratic parties which, as he came to recognize and believe, not only identified themselves with the cause of socialism at home but also with colonial freedom abroad.[40]

The Communist International established in Russia in 1919 provided at the time an institutional support to the socialist conviction of the Indian revolutionaries functioning abroad. For its object was to overthrow all capitalist and colonial governments (including the British Government in India) by means of strikes and armed revolution. Its whole approach was a resort to mass action as by far the most effective instrument of class war to end the exploitation of the poor by the rich. It therefore emphasized the organization of workers' and peasants' parties, of Youth League and Students' Union, of Communist cells and Nationalist movements. The Indian revolutionaries therefore viewed it as a source of strength and organized international support not only for political freedom but also for a new social and economic order based on freedom from exploitation.

Congress Capitalist Policy Approach–1915-20

As shown above, the Moderates who were the Congress till 1915 were forced to secede and form their own separate party in 1918. The Congress was left primarily with the Home Rulers, the erstwhile Nationalists of Tilak's group, and the supporters among the Moderates of M. K. Gandhi who, after his successful passive resistance movement in South Africa, had returned to India early in 1915. While the former insisted on a policy declaration to concede Home Rule or colonial "self-government" as a condition for responsive cooperation with war efforts, the latter cooperated unconditionally with the recruitment of volunteers for the army. What was common to both Tilak and Gandhi, however, was their adherence to religion and culture as the cornerstone of political organization and public life.

The Nationalists of Tilak's brand in the Congress had in the course of 1915-20 mellowed down in political terms, a development which had brought them nearer to the Moderates. But their commitment to cultural nationalism was so deep that it not only continued unabated but left its mark on a number of leading Congressmen, including M. K. Gandhi, Rajendra Prasad and some others who were by no means identified with the creed or political ideology of the Home Rule movement. In their religious and cultural appeal the Nationalist group in the Congress in fact compared well with the Hindu Mahasabha first established in 1915 at Hardwar. The Subjects Committee of the Mahasabha so organized included, among others, men like M. K. Gandhi and Munshi Ram, later known as Swami Shradhanand, an Arya Samajist leader, who inaugurated the Indian Trade Union Congress established in 1920, with Lajpat Rai, a nationalist leader, presiding over it. The All-India Committee of the Mahasabha included, on the other hand, such men as Sir Tej Bahadur Sapru, Lala Hans Raj, Asutosh Mukherji, Sir Gangadhar Chitnis and Motilal Ghose.[41] Pandit Madan Mohan Malaviya, a Nationalist leader, actually presided over the Mahasabha session of 1916. The Committee which the Mahasabha appointed in 1924 to report on the Hindu-Muslim problem comprised, among others, such Nationalist leaders of the Congress as Lajpat Rai, Rajendra Prasad and Jairamdas Daulatram.

Thus although the growth and expansion of Indian industries and the consequent development of capitalist economy with its antithetical labour force called for a secular class approach to policy-making at a national level, the pervasive influence of Hindu cultural nationalism caused an obsession which blurred the attributes of rationality and discrimination, more especially in the presence of a foreign rule opposed to a socialist order of society. Doubtless, the industrial strikes of 1920 symbolized the existence of strained relations and distrust between millionaires and workers, an expression of class antagonism in pure economic terms. But the remedy applied was, surprisingly enough, a resort to an appeal to religious and cultural sentiments. That perhaps was the reason why Swami Shradhanand and Lajpat Rai, two of the Arya Samajist leaders, were invited respectively to inaugurate and preside over the Indian Trade Union Congress organized in 1920. Religion acted as a cover of vested economic interest–an interest which, for all practical purposes, was owned and controlled by Hindu business communities under Congress patronage.

Hindu Dominance in Indian Business Houses : Beginning of Religio-Political Development

Traditionally, the Hindus were a race of people who controlled the lever of economic power and influence. The Mughal conquest of the country, which was of special significance in terms of a highly centralized polity, did not interfere with that power, more especially in the field of trade and commerce, industry and finance. They acted as monopolists and financiers for the government. James Grant's *Political Survey of the Northern Circars* points out that while the village communities had the virtual control of the rural economy, the feudatory status of Hindu zamindars remained unaffected in spite of periodical dislocations caused by the movement of armies. The *Ninth Report of the Parliamentary Select Committee* of 1783 also confirmed that the Muslims had not generally engaged in trade and commerce, nor had they disappropriated the ancient Hindu status or proprietors whom they conquered. Their chief, if not sole, support was share in the civil and military offices of government, especially in its police and judicial departments.[42] The Department of Revenue was, even under the Mughals, manned almost exclusively by Hindus who continued to dominate the district staff of Warren Hastings' Amini Commission.[43]

The rise of British power in India came as a blessing in disguise for the Hindus whose growth over a century in terms of both business enterprise and employment in the public service was distinctly marked and noticeable from Plassey in 1757 to the Mutiny in 1857.[44] It was a century of decline for the Muslims because of a loss of their political power and influence.

Starting from a position of "gomastas", agents and junior partners of Europeans, the Hindus, more especially in Bengal, rose to the status of free merchants under the administration of the East India Company which induced Bengalis and Parsis to engage in joint-stock businesses on the model of the English Houses of Agency designed to pool European skill and capital without any prejudice to Indian trade and industry. They received training in European methods of business organization and set up their own firms on joint-stock principles. The Agency Houses in fact acted as means to introduce what was European without destroying what was Indian.

This development was slow in the beginning because of the Company's interest in preserving India's traditional artisan production which, from its cheapness and excellence, brought considerable profit to it in its home as well as European markets. However, it was the Company's rule that accounted for India's being spared the inconveniences of large-scale colonization, which also saved the Indian merchants and bankers from undue European competition. The Indian agents of the Company and its European servants as well as those employed by the European houses of agency were the class of people who stood to gain by the constraints imposed on free colonization. The Indian entrepreneurs took advantage of the Company's rule and organized their own joint-stock business on the models of the European houses of agency.

The abolition of the Company's rule in 1858 created a new situation, prejudicial to Indian entrepreneurs. It led to a steep and steady rise in the influx of British capital and skill, which raised the level of competition to an extent far beyond the capacity of Indian businesses to match. What it did was immediately to increase capital resources for industrialization; but more than that was the contribution of the political system set up under the Government of India Act (1858). It provided for the payment of loans on government account incurred for the construction of railways, irrigation and other public works. It obviously meant State's participation in the provision of technological facilities as well as an infrastructure for the industrial development.

The whole approach of the new political system was imperio-colonial. It introduced a new pattern of industrial organization called the managing agency system which contributed to the concentration of economic power in both financial and administrative terms, a system which shaped the character of India's economic development in keeping with her highly centralized polity coming down from an early period of British rule.

The managing agency system differed from the old agency houses of the Company's period in two ways. In the first place, the capital of these houses was mainly in Indian rupees forming part of the savings of the Company's public servants, and, secondly, the managing agents, especially in the beginning, were for the most part representatives of British companies operating with sterling capital as owners and not as distributors which the agency houses had, in the main, been in the past. When these parent British firms floated new companies from the profit they earned, the new companies so floated enjoyed a legal and functional independence, contributing to the horizontal expansion of more and more new industrial units, while at the same time preserving their vertical integration, under the direction and management of the pioneering firm. A limited number of managing agents thus came to control the bulk of the country's economic power. The financial integration restricted the growth of the Indian industrial entrepreneurial class, while the administrative integration reduced the number of the superior executives, especially directors, functioning on the principle of multiple directorship under the centralized control of the managing agent of the parent company or firm.

The Indian managing houses that emerged, though only slowly, were for all practical purposes Hindu with the exception of the Tatas, the leading Parsi concern. The British dominated the field right up to 1911. It was the introduction of a liberal protective tariff policy that contributed to the rise of the Tatas, the Birlas, the Dalmias, the Thapars, the Gujarati Hindus and the Jews. But the Muslims hardly figured anywhere.

The Europeans continued to dominate the Eastern sector. But even in the cotton textile industry which developed originally with the initiative of Parsi and foreign capital, the Muslims had hardly any hand. The *Report of the Royal Commission on Labour in India*, which came out in 1931, pointed out thus :

"The industry is in Indian hands. In Bombay, Parsees, who were responsible for its initiation, and Gujarati Hindus have the biggest interests and the latter class control nearly all the mills in Ahmedabad. Europeans control some mills in both these centres and they and Hindus of various provinces are responsible for most of the mills in the smaller centres. Musalmans control some mills in Bombay, but few, if any, elsewhere. A considerable number of Englishmen, drawn mainly from Lancashire, are employed in the mills as managers or heads of departments throughout the industry; but there are now many mills where the whole of the managing staff is Indian".[45]

The Parsis in the cotton industry were in the 1930's overtaken by the Gujarati Hindus and the Marwaris.[46] Of these, the Birlas, who just began to emerge in the early part of the 1920's, rose to prominence with Congress support. They bought a number of concerns and came to hold a major interest in sugar industries also.

The conclusion that arises from this brief analysis of the main trends in modern economic development in India is a steady concentration of economic power in the hands of Hindu business communities. Socially, it meant a steady decline of Indian Muslims in material economic terms, more especially because the Indian business houses differed from their European counterparts in respect of their personnel administration. The Hindu or even Parsi managing houses doubtless adopted the European model in structural terms, but they added to it, in other respects, regional and caste prejudices affecting the appointment of directors and managers, secretaries and engineers, personal staff and experts. This naturally perpetuated the Indian tendency to limit the selection of persons belonging to the caste or community controlling the business concerned. Unless reduced to public control, industrial administration was bound to be an exclusive sphere of influence of traditional business communities, prone to use religion as the main pillar of their vested economic interest. This became noticeable when, as a result of the First World War, they first started emerging as competitors of British concerns in the beginning of the 1920's with commerce and industry being transferred to popular control in the provinces. By the 1930's they had in fact become a force to reckon with. The industrial backwardness of Muslims in general egged them on to a resort to politics for power to revive.

Educated Employment and Electoral Politics
Further Policy Problem

Educated employment in the public services under British rule, as we all know, became pretty weighted on the side of the Hindus who took full advantage of the British system of education which repudiated the medieval monopoly of learning and recognized the principle of competition as the best test of merit and ability. The Indian Muslims generally stood aloof from English education which from Macaulay's minute of 1835 and onwards came to be the sine qua non for government service. In their approach to Western education, as the Bengal Government said, they were for several decades guided by "religious repugnance to make terms with modern thought".[47] Whatever the reasons for the gap, it became a cause for grievance and therefore a policy problem.

In a memorial presented to Lord Ripon on February 6, 1882, the National (Central) Muhammadan Association (Calcutta) pointed out the causes which had in their opinion led to the decadence of Muhammadan learning as well as to the impoverishment of the Muhammadan population in Bengal, especially in Eastern Bengal where the bulk of the population happened to be Muslim.

The memorialists stated that although the East India Company had come to be vested with sovereignty under its Mughal Diwani grant of 1765, the interests of the Muhammadans remained unaffected because of the virtual continuance of the Mughal system of administration, more especially in its police and judicial departments. The Permanent Settlement and the administrative reforms of Cornwallis doubtless interfered with Muhammadan prosperity to an extent. Even so, they continued to enjoy the largest share of State patronage until the time of Lord William Bentinck. It was his administration that not only abolished Persian as the official language and replaced it by English and the local vernaculers of the several porvinces in the conduct of judicial and other proceedings, but also enacted resumption laws, "ruining the educational system of the Mahomedans, which was almost entirely maintained by rent-free grants". Together, his measures, it was alleged, "threw out of employment a considerable body of Mahomedan subordinate officers who depended on Government pay for their livelihood".[48]

The memorialists further contended that although under the new administrative policy all aspirants for public services were expected to know English, no order was passed making a knowledge of English obligatory for government or for entering the profession of law. The result was that right up to 1864 candidates for the post of munsiffs or for admission to pleaderships were allowed to pass their examinations either in Urdu or English. A sudden change, however, came about when under the orders of the Calcutta High Court English alone was recognized as the medium of examinations for the post of munsiffs, while a university degree in law was made obligatory for a higher grade of judicial posts and pleaderships both under Act XX of 1865. Because of their blind adherence to Islamic beliefs the Muslims were in general shot out naturally from Government employment.

In a letter of October 14, 1882, addressed to the Government of India, the Bengal Government, it is true, admitted that "the Muhammadans of Bengal have fallen behind in the race and yielded place to the Hindus". But the cause of decadence, it was emphasized, "is to be sought neither in great administrative improvements nor in light and righteous assessments of public taxation, which fall on Moslems and Hindus alike but to failure on the part of the Mahomedan population to read the signs of the times, and to take the advantage of the opportunities afforded impartially to all subjects of the British Government".

In its approach to the memorial of the National (Central) Muhammadan Association, the Government of India did not allow itself to be influenced by any consideration other than merit and justice. It was studied carefully by all provincial governments before the Government of India passed its Resolution as part of its Home

(Education) A Proceedings of July, 1885. While explaining its position, its Resolution made it clear that admission to all superior services in every province, including Bengal, was generally regulated either by public competition or by possession of qualifications altogether independent of the race or caste of candidates.

However, the fact of Muslim lag in English education remained indisputable, although Sir Syed Ahmed and his Anglicist supporters did their best to make it up. This lag was clearly reflected in the Government appointments of 1903 under Lord Curzon on a monthly pay of Rs. 75 and upwards. [49] The Indian Muslims figured mostly in the lower and subordinate ranks of the public service. The Europeans and Anglo-Indians dominated the superior services, while the Hindus came next to them. Apart from the nature of economic development, the situation so created from disparity in the distribution of State patronage involved an additional, though major, policy issue for the National Congress, a dominantly Hindu body in social terms.

To these major issues of policy must be added a third problem of even greater importance, namely, the politics of electoral institutions which in principle emerged in course of time from the creation of a separate legislative authority with the appointment of Macaulay, a non-official, as law or Legislative Member of the Governor-General's Council–a development which preceded, in a logical sequence, the provisions made under the Indian Councils Act (1861) for the appointment of "Additional Members" invested with legislative function.

The introduction of electoral institutions in the 1880's, which formed part of local self-government at the district and municipal levels, marked the beginning of a revolutionary process designed to provide in stages political links between the different levels of government for the settlement of grievances. The electoral principle so introduced in the 1880's extended to the constitution and progressive expansion of central and provincial legislatures in India. Indeed, it envisaged and called for the transfer of sovereignty from London to New Delhi, a sovereignty signifying, under that principle, the rule of numbers which meant a majority rule, where Muslims, being a minority community, had no choice but to submit. Electoral politics was naturally viewed as a serious obstacle to Muslim advance. Speaking of the electoral politics of local bodies, the Muslim address which was presented to Lord Minto on October 1, 1906, made it clear, for example, that "it is most unlikely that the name of any Mahomedan candidate will ever be submitted for approval of Government by the electoral bodies as now constituted, unless he is in sympathy with the majority in all matters of importance, nor can we in fairness find fault with the desire of our non-Muslim fellow subjects to take full advantage of their strength and vote only for members of their own community or for persons who, if not Hindus, are expected to vote with Hindu majority on whose goodwill they would have to depend for their future re-election". A resort to nomination and creation of a separate Muslim electorate was therefore suggested from considerations based not on mere Muslim population, but on their "political importance" and "the position which they occupied in India little more than a hundred years ago, and of which the traditions have naturally not faded from their minds".[50] The All-India Muslim League was established in 1906 itself to keep those "traditions" fairly fresh in Muslim minds. The Morley-Minto constitution too was supposed to be a help in the same direction, its object being a "counterpoise" and "constitutional autocracy" for clipping the wings, as it were, of the rising middle-class nationalists, for the most part Hindus.

The Morley-Minto scheme of reforms, however, failed to accomplish the object of its enactment. While the result of elections held under the 1909 Act showed hardly any movement towards political mass mobilization on communal lines, the lever of control remained with lawyer representatives lacking in any real connexion between the primary voter and the members who sat in the legislative councils. Moreover, a new situation arose with the outbreak of the First World War, which imparted to legislative debates a racial twist because of the Muslim State of Turkey being involved on the side of Germany, the arch enemy of the British Empire. Instead of creating any division among Indian elected members this racial twist stifled their differences, if any, and drove "them to a league against the Government, into which the nominated Indian members also tend to enter".[51] This was a trend towards Indian political unity resulting from international developments. It was an expression of downright failure of the Morley-Minto plan to alleviate Muslim grievances by providing a middle-class counterweight. A Bengal Government Resolution of August 3, 1916, showed that there was in the secondary schools of the province "only one Muhammadan teacher to every four Hindu teachers".[52]

The Indian Business Reaction Politico-Economic

Pragmatic in their approach to developing war conditions, the reaction of Indian entrepreneurs was clearly politico-economic, not religio-political. Speaking of the emergence of a new spirit in India, Annie Besant, President of the Indian National Congress in 1917, pointed out that "the awakening of the merchants into political life is perhaps most potent and the most pregnant with happy possibilities". It was they who had pressurized the Government in 1915 to hold in Bombay an Industrial Conference where Sir Dorab Tata emphasized the necessity of "yoking together of politics and industry", for hitherto the merchants had remained immersed in their own occupations, and realized the importance of politics only when they found that those very occupations were threatened with disaster by the attitude of the Government towards such industries as earlier "had been connected closely with German trade", but "were menaced with ruin by the war".[53]

The basic cause of grievance against the Government was its refusal financially to help Indian business to manage and run the German factories which, it was feared, were being sought to be absorbed by the English companies. The copra and coir industry on the west coast which had passed into German hands was, for example, happily rescued and acquired by the firm of Tata & Sons. But there were mica mines, undressed hides, monazine, an ingredient of munitions, and other industries which Indian businessmen wished to own and manage but could not do so without financial and import facilities. Indeed, the Government of India would rather go in for English firms who were supposed to have the first claim to official patronage for the acquisition of German industrial interest and property in India. It was here that the importance of the political dimension of business enterprise was fully realized by the Indian merchants who were determined to aid Indian politics to win freedom for the advancement of their own interest. Their thinking was reasonably in keeping with the capitalist principles of political economy. The Indian Home Rule movement of 1916-17 proceeded in the context of this war-time politico-economic development. Its whole emphasis was on politics. But obviously, the object was to secure the promotion of the Indian capitalist interest emerging as a competitive force.

Left and Right Emerging Side by Side
Problem of Choice

As said above, the growth of a concentrated population of workers proceeded naturally with the development of the large-scale factory industry initiated and sustained in the first instance by the European Managing Agency Houses with their extensive international contact and control over foreign trade. The strength of factory workers in cotton textiles, for example, increased from 113,000 in 1892-93 to 327,000 in 1922 while jute recorded even a greater increase from 66,000 to 320,000 during the same period. Engineering and metals as well as other industries were likewise known for a progressive increase in the size of their operatives.[54] The industrial unrest that followed between the millowners and their workers was marked by a series of strikes which called for the establishment of the All-India Trade Union Congress in 1920–an organization which symbolized the rising trend towards the Left.

The War, which marked the emergence of Indian capitalism as an independent and conservative Right force, witnessed the rise of its antithetical Left force also. Ideologically, however, the line of distinction, in terms of class dichotomy, had still remained more or less heavily blurred. The result was that the tie between the two forces was sought to be resolved by reference to two of the nationalist leaders, Swami Shradhanand and Lajpat Rai–associated essentially with the Arya Samaj, a religious organization of the Hindus.

This development was, on an international plane, comparable, for political reasons, to collaboration between Muslim and Hindu revolutionaries operating abroad, especially in Germany where they had established, in Berlin, their Indian Independence Committee with Muslims being in majority in 1914. The bond of unity was in the main political, arising from Turkey's involvement in war against Britain. The economic or mass basis of unity had not yet engaged the attention of revolutionary leaders, Hindu or Muslim. Political considerations enabled even a staunch Hindu revolutionary like Har Dayal to overcome his anti-Islamic prejudices and assist Germany in its design to use the "Holy War" slogan and its pan-Islamic appeal in mobilizing the Muslim world against Britain.[55]

A new situation developed when on the termination of the War the Indian Independence Committee shifted to Moscow, the headquarters of the Bolshevik Revolution of October 1917 and the Communist International established in 1919, with a declared goal of socialist world culture cutting across the religious and even national barriers recognized by the capitalist principle of socio-economic order. The growth of science and technology came as an immediate help to the dissemination of a knowledge of socialism and the influence it exercised on government and society. Naturally enough, India could not for long resist the new ideological invasion directed from the land of its origin. The culturally oriented Indian revolutionaries abroad, who were the first to be influenced by the socialist mission of world peace and colonial freedom, acted as instrument and agency for purposes of disseminating the new political philosophy, secular and socialist in its content and approach to relations among classes in society.

Doubtless, the series of industrial strikes that took place in the wake of the imperialist war was an expression of communist influence operating in India through the agency of the Workers' Welfare League linked up with an industrial communist revolutionary movement.[56] It formed part of the international communist movement.

The League so operating as an antithesis of Indian capitalism and emerging as a rearguard for a socialist movement in India, however, did not signify any rebuttal of the nationalist Home Rule movement which, in the presence of imperialist rule, was viewed as a matter of primary political importance. The Communist International itself was in favour of nationalist forces being strengthened as an instrument of colonial freedom, the first step towards a Socialist State and economy. But care was at the same time to be taken to see that no member of Mrs. Besant's capitalist Home Rule movement should have any connection with the labour organization. Capital and labour were to be treated as separate and mutually exclusive categories to be treated as separated and mutually exclusive categories in terms of ideology and interest. The Bolsheviks were soft towards religion and culture, but not prepared to make any compromise with capitalism. This perhaps was also a factor why Shapurji Saklatvala, the Indian Bolshevik in England, advised cooperation with Lajpat Rai who, as stated above, presided over the All-India Trade Union Congress representing an organized force of the Left.[57] Whatever the reasons, the first imperialist war created a situation which brought into focus the dialectics of dichotomy between the Right and the Left.

Mohandas Karamchand Gandhi : His Approach to Indian Developments

As said above, the main feature of Indian developments to 1920 was political, involving a contentious question of India's relationship with the British Government within the framework of swaraj, a term which lent itself to a variety of interpretations in terms of autonomy or self-government. What tended to impart to the dominantly political content of swaraj an economic dimension was the emergence, in the course of the First World War, of a competitive force of Indian capitalism as well as its antithetical Left counterpoise fed internationally on the Bolshevik Revolution of 1917 and indigenously on the movement of revolutionaries born of British policy of repression and colonial bias. The involvement of the Indian business communities in the politics of the country was in fact a new development which proceeded from their resolve to have political pressure used in the promotion of their economic interests. It started off initially from an Indo-British competition for the acquisition of German industrial concerns in India, a competition where Indians stood no chance of success without the power of politics, which involved an active support to the nationalist movement in its fight for swaraj or self-government.

However, the establishment of the Communist International in 1919 posed a new threat to Indian capitalism. It was feared that its war-born industrial force against imperialist rule might seriously be prejudiced by the international agencies of communism operating in the country itself. The formation of the Federation of Indian Chamber of Commerce and Industry later in 1927 was intended to fight against both imperial preference and communist interference.

Gandhi as a Moderate in Indian Politics

On the advice given to him by G. K. Gokhale, the leader of the Moderates in the Congress, M. K. Gandhi, returned from South Africa, landing in Bombay on January 9, 1915. The person who organized a public reception for him on January 12 at Mount Petit was Sir Pherozeshah Mehta, one of the founders of the Indian National Congress and its President in 1890 and then again in 1909, when the Congress had become no more than an exclusive concern of the Moderates, B. G. Tilak, the nationalist leader, being already sentenced to imprisonment for six years in 1908.

A perusal of the antecedents of M. K. Gandhi shows that he had been a loyalist from a much earlier period, having received the Boor War Medal for his services during the Boer War (1899-1900), the Zulu War Medal in South Africa for his services as Officer-in-Charge of the Indian Volunteer Ambulance Corps in 1906, and the Kaisar-i-Hind Gold Modal for the services in the course of the Great War (1914-18). The "loyal cooperation" he had rendered to the British Government was duly acknowledged in a letter addressed to the Viceroy on August 2, 1920.[58]

Naturally, Gandhi lent his full support to the first resolution of loyalty to the British Government moved by the Gaekwar of Baroda in the course of the Imperial War Conference held at Delhi on April 29, 1918, a conference which was attended, among others, by the rulers of Gwalior, Bhopal, Bikaner and such leaders of public opinion as Srinivas Sastri, Surendra Nath Banerjea, Madan Mohan Malaviya and Hasan Imam. Speaking partly in Hindi, Gandhi supported the resolution on loyalty "with all his heart" in a manner marked by public "applause".[59]

It is true that the importance of Gandhi as a national leader came into focus in the course of his movement against the indigo planters of Champaran in Bihar who forced the peasants against their will and interest to cultivate indigo in certain fixed portions of their land. My *Select Documents on Mahatma Gandhi's Movement in*

Champaran, 1917-18, however, makes it clear beyond doubt that his agitation against the planters did by no means signify any loss of his faith in the Government. For the Government of Bihar as well as the Government of India allowed him full freedom in the conduct of his inquiries into what he called the "economic" grievances of peasants.

Gandhi, it seems, had in fact implicit faith in the integrity of the British Government and, like the Congress, his initial rise to eminence flowed not a little from the recognition extended to him by the Government in return for the services he willingly offered himself to render. Unlike B. G. Tilak who argued that the British Government must first concede the Indian demand for swaraj and grant equal rights in the army and other matters before the Indian people should be asked to rescue it from the threats to which it was exposed in the course of the war, Gandhi went ahead unconditionally with the recruitment of volunteers for the army. He did not even seem to be clear about the constitutional implications of the term *swaraj*. What he emphasized was the importance of standing by the Government in the hour of its dire need. "My opinion", he said, "is that in anything that we demand by way of swaraj, we should agitate to get it as a matter of right . . . and, simultaneously, stand by the Government and help it".[60]

Gandhi considered the Montford Scheme "to be good in conception", although there was room for "modification". In a letter addressed to Surendra Nath Banerjea on August 10, 1918, he therefore said : "I should like a party in the country that would be simply pledged to these two propositions, helping the Government on the one hand in the prosecution of the war and enforcing the national demands on the other." He did not want anything like "a patched-up truce between the so-called extremists and the so-called moderates, each giving up a little in favour of the other".[61] He recognized that the "enslavement of the nation is thorough". Even so, he held that the Englishmen have not deliberately meant it. "I only cling to England", he reiterated, "because I believe her to be sound at heart and I believe that India can deliver her mission to the world better through England." [62]

Gandhi's speeches and writings recorded after his arrival from South Africa make it clear that far from the economic issues being raised to any position of importance, even the immediate political goal of swaraj remained well-nigh undefined, with opinions moving like a pendulum between "responsible" government and "self-government", Gandhi himself being disposed, unlike "many of the leaders", to devote all attention "exclusively to recruiting" in order to gain " "responsible government".[63]

Organizationally, the Congress itself had at this period been waning as a political force. The Liberals were on their way out. The erstwhile radical elements of the Congress had at the same time created their separate spheres of influence as Home Rulers. It is true that these elements did continue to fight for recognition as part of the National Congress. But both Tilak and Annie Besant functioned separately as leaders of their respective Home Rule Leagues. They were doubtless one in their demand for immediate self-government. But their Home Rule Leagues remained organizationally separate and distinct, not only from each other, but also from the Congress.

Politically, the only sign of unity that appeared was a pact concluded at the Lucknow session of the Congress with the Muslim League in 1916. This Congress-League Pact was a reinforcement of British decision to maintain separate communal electorates first introduced under the Indian Councils Act of 1909 for the representation of Muhammadans. The pact recognized the communal principle of separate electorates and provided for Muslim representation in provincial councils on a proportion much greater than the percentage of Muslims in the total population of the provinces. As for the Central legislature, the Pact laid down that one-third of the Indian elected members should be Muhammadans elected by separate Muhammadan electorates in the several provinces. Obviously, the Pact so concluded proceeded from an immediate Muslim concern for Turkey, a Muslim country, involved in war against Britain which at the time was confronted with the Indian demand for the grant of swaraj, a demand which Gandhi, as said above, interpreted later as amounting even to "responsible government" envisaged by the Montagu-Chelmsford Scheme.

A new situation emerged from the defeat of Turkey and the consequent danger to its territorial integrity. The Indian pan-Islamist

Muhammadans who, along with the advanced group of the Muslim League Party, had already started coming increasingly closer to the National Congress and cooperating with the nationalists in their demand for self-government, sought to make a common cause with all such elements as they considered hostile to the British Government. The object was to mobilize a mass movement to save the Caliphate from disintegration, a movement which contained in its ranks and leadership men of diverse political persuasion–nationalists, revolutionary nationalists and even Bolsheviks who were united in their common hatred of British rule, although the Khilafatists were in the main guided by an immediate desire to restore Islam to its original political vigour by an attempt to overthrow British rule and bring India under the influence of an adjoining Muslim country.[64] The developing situation necessarily called for the enactment of a legislative measure known as the Rowlatt Act which, in spite of the opposition of Gandhi and the Home Rulers, was passed on March 21, 1919. The object was to preserve law and order, although the manner in which it was enforced led to the Amritsar tragedy at Jallianwala Bagh–a development which followed the Satyagraha or passive resistance organized by Gandhi with the help of some Home Rulers in the second week of April.

Indeed, the change that had come over India in the wake of the First World War expressed itself in two main directions, namely, the growth of industrial capitalism with its emphasis on self-government which in the peculiar Indian conditions lent itself to a reinforcement of religion as the basis of politics, and the rise of the Left as an economic proletarian force wedded to Bolshevism and the Communist International established in 1919. What Gandhi did was to cast his weight on the side of pan-Islamic Muslims who used the religious slogan of *jehad* or holy war against the English to defend the cause of Turkey. His support to the Khilafatists expressed itself in his declared stand to resist the Rowlatt legislation with the help of Mrs. Besant's Home Rule League which was converted into a Satyagraha Sabha to organize civil disobedience in April 1919. This was, however, soon called off, and the idea of satyagraha was not revived until Tilak's death which occurred on August 1, 1920.

Gandhi's approach to the developing Turkish problem, it seems, was purely political, the question of restoring the Congress to a position of strength in organizational terms and with it the question of his own leadership which remained cramped before the radicalism and intellectual predominance of B. G. Tilak. He converted, as said above, Mrs. Besant's Home Rule opposition to the Rowlatt Act into a Satyagraha Sabha and used the Khilafat agitation as an instrument to invigorate the Congress which had since 1915 been steadily on the decline. He sought to emerge as a leader of national importance by an attempt to collaborate with the leaders of the pan-Islamic Khilafat movement in conjunction with his non-cooperation movement started on August 2, 1920, with an emphasis on a demand for swaraj signifying an organized move to resist the reformed Constitution of 1919. It was contemplated that the steps so conceived would, above all, save India from Bolshevism. For a Confidential Government Note of May 1921 clearly pointed out:[65]

"In June 1919 the Government of India received intimation that Mr. Gandhi contemplated a renewal of civil disobedience unless circumstances altered his plans. The experiences of the preceding two and a half months, he stated, had convinced him that nothing save satyagraha, of which civil disobedience was an enlarged part, could save India from Bolshevism–and even a worse fate. He added that the exhibition of anti-British feeling during the second week of April was due, not to the satyagraha movement, but to pre-existing causes and that the Rowlatt legislation was the *causa causans* which he hoped would be withdrawn."

In his anti-British posture of politics Gandhi was thus guided by a policy to save India from Bolshevism, a revolutionary cult of proletarian dictatorship, a politico-economic force of the Left. His in fact was a tactical move to strengthen the National Congress as an organized force of the Right. This he sought to do not only using the resources of the Home Rulers for what was called swaraj, but also exploiting the religious sentiments of pan-Islamic Muslims of the Khilafat movement whom he brought as part of the National Congress, though only for a time, under his own leadership. His non-cooperation and Khilafat agitation in fact sought to weaken the forces of Bolshevism, inimical to both imperialist and Indian capitalist interests.

It was perhaps the fear of Bolshevism that led to imperial and national interests being reconciled to an extent under the reformed constitution of 1919. While commerce and industry became "transferred" subjects to be administered by Indians under that constitution, a policy of discriminating protection was recommended by the Fiscal Commission of 1921. Accordingly, a number of Indian industries like iron and steel, cotton textiles and sugar, matches, paper, etc., received the benefit of protection and made considerable progress, although the policy was restrictive and the conditions of eligibility happened to be "very stringent".[66] Evidently, the Indian big business and the Government were both united in their resolve to check the Bolshevik invasion of India. The protective tariffs of 1921 was an expression of compromise between the imperialist and the national capitalist interest.

The compromise so effected was in the nature of a joint effort to avert the usual trade depression or the crisis inherent in the capitalist system itself. Imperialism, which is after all an enlarged form of the same system, was equally subject to it. In the pre-war period Indian business enterprise was more in the nature of trade and commerce than independent and distinct entities concerned with manufactures on capitalist principles. The approach of the country's political leadership, too, was in general vague, academic and elitist, influenced more by considerations of agriculture-based industries and a search for their protection rather than the development of factory industries for the production of capital goods. Factory industries had, of course, been growing and called for protection for increasing growth. But the imperialist government did hardly respond.[67] The resolutions of the National Congress remained in the main limited to demands for the Indianization of the civil service, the reduction of military expenditure, an overall introduction of the permanent settlement and encouragement to the swadeshi movement which meant no more than an emotional appeal for the promotion of indigenous manufactures. It was in the course of the First World War that the Indian business communities emerged as a distinct class of capitalists using the compulsions of the war as a sanction to advance the interest of Indian industrialists as a matter of right and not as a class to subserve British imperial interests. The sanction so created by the exigencies of the war was sought to be reinforced by a suggestion to have industry and politics yoked together–a suggestion which involved a clear demand for self-government to secure India's industrial advance as a competitive force. The reformed constitution of 1919 and the protective tariff concessions of 1921 were a partial fulfilment of the goal envisaged by Indian industrialists at the Industrial Conference of 1915.

The political principle which Sir Dorab Tata emphasized and sought to link with the development of industry had earlier been suggested by Dadabhai Naoroji in the course of his presidential address to the twenty-second session of the Indian National Congress in 1906. He related this principle to social reforms and industrial progress, each being influenced by the other. Though inter-related, the political principle was recognized by him as the root of India's strength and hope, which were all summed in self-government, the chief remedy for the millions of the Indian people who died of poverty and starvation.

The Report of the Industrial Commission which came out in 1918 brought into focus the importance of an active role which the Government must play in the promotion of industrial development, a task which called for encouragement to Indian capital and enterprise, the setting up of advisory boards in consultation with Trade Associations and Chambers of Commerce, the establishment of commerce colleges and relevant faculties of science and technology in the universities. The Report contained a well-reasoned and comprehensive minute by the Hon. Pandit Madan Mohan Malaviya, a nationalist leader who was an advocate of heavy and large-scale industrialization.

The politics of self-government with its close link with economic development was, however, not that simple. It not only involved the question of relationship with the British Government, but more immediately of escalating the communal problem arising from the progressive advance and dominant position of Hindus in both business enterprise and public service. Then, there was the question of a choice between the economic growth of the country on the Western model of capitalist economy and the Soviet model and its communist pattern. As self-government did not at this period signify any negation of British sovereignty, the choice was made in favour of the Western capitalist model. India's sterling balance accumulated in the course of the war was accordingly used partially to facilitate the import of machinery and mill-work, which showed a steep rise from Rs.5.41 crores in 1912 to Rs. 34.25 crores in 1921, the year when the protective tariffs were also imposed in the interest of Indian industrialists. The value of imported railway plant and rolling stock likewise increased from Rs.5.40 crores to Rs.18.91 crores in the same period.[68]

The results of the industrial censuses of 1911 and 1921 showed that the number of industrial establishments, both registered and unregistered, with 20 persons or more employed in each increased from 7,113 in 1911 to a little over 15,000 in 1921.[69]

The "sterling resources", it seems, continued to be drawn upon in the "sectional interest" of the Indian "capitalist" class, to which certain eminent economists like K. T. Shah, C. N. Vakil and B. P. Adarkar were in principle opposed even as members of the Federation of Indian Chambers of Commerce and Industry established in 1927. G. D. Birla, one of the leading industrialists and President of the Federation in 1929, viewed this attitude as in fact a move on the part of "the so-called economists" to capture the Federation from the hands of the "bona fide merchants". Birla thus complained, "I understand that it has been suggested by some economists that the sterling resources should not be used for any sectional interest. God alone knows what they mean. The plan seems to be to confuse the whole issue and create an impression as if the industrialists have some ulterior motive."[70] Whatever the motive, the academic community had started suspecting the bona fides of the capitalist modus operandi.

Congress Policy Inconsistency

Prior to the emergence of M. K. Gandhi as the spokesman of the Congress, it believed in the Western methods of production and distribution. Its Calcutta session of 1901, for example, appointed a committee to review the problem of economic depression, a committee which included B. G. Tilak, Madan Mohan Malaviya, Ranade, Bhupendra Nath Dutta and some others. The most important economic question which engaged its attention was that of organizing a sound capital and credit system in "villages, towns, provinces and the country" in order to improve "our economic condition". The Congress not only stressed the importance of mineral resources and currency legislation, but also suggested soon after in 1902 the necessity of an economic survey for the collection of a comparative body of data for purposes of economic development on the pattern of foreign countries.[71]

Later in 1918 when the Report of the Industrial Commission came out the Indian National Congress welcomed its recommendations about industrialization on the lines of Western countries and made its own suggestions to ensure progress in that direction.[72]

In 1920, however, the Congress assumed a contrary position, a position opposed to Western capitalist methods. Its Working Committee adopted a "Khaddar Scheme" and asked all provincial committees "to stimulate the production and consumption of hand-spun and hand-woven Khaddar on a sound organized basis". It expressed itself against all kinds of technical assistance and loan or financial liability for purposes of modern industrial development. Under the Khaddar Scheme, as the resolution of the Working Committee said, the Congress repudiated "the authority of the legislatures that have been or may be formed by the Government in spite of the national boycott of the said institutions in future to raise any loans or to incur any liabilities on behalf of the nation, and notifies to the world that on the attainment of *swarajya* the people of India, though holding themselves liable for all debts and liabilities rightly or wrongly incurred hitherto by the Government will not hold themselves bound to repay any loans or discharge any liabilities on and after this date on the authority or sanction of the so-called legislatures brought into existence in spite of the national boycott".[73] A special department was, in keeping with this principle of policy, sought to be organized under Seth Jamnalal Bajaj to help the provinces by way of loans and technical advice for the production and sale of khaddar.

The incongruous policy trend so introduced proceeded from the influence which Gandhi came to wield on the Congress after the death of B. G. Tilak on August 1, 1920. It was perhaps a consummation of Gandhi's publicly declared belief in the conceptual unity that must exist between economics and ethics, or, in other words, between material and moral progress–a unity, as Gandhi alleged, was rarely perceptible. For, his contention was that economic progress even clashed with "real progress" which he identified with morality in terms of religion or faith in God, a clear evidence of an obsessive mind.

Indeed, Gandhi first expressed this view of economic progress in the course of a meeting of the Muir Central College Economic Society which was presided over by Pandit Madan Mohan Malaviya on December 22, 1916. Although admittedly unaware of books on economics by such well-known authorities as Mill, Marshall, Adam Smith and a host of such other authors and advised to read these works before experimenting in matters economic at the expense of the public, Gandhi made bold to observe: "I venture to think that the scriptures of the world are far safer and sounder treatises on laws of economics than many of the modern textbooks".[74]

The *swadeshi* movement, which had the full support of the Congress as well as of Gandhi, was by no means a negation of factory industries. In his speech on swadeshi at a Missionary Conference in Madras on February 14, 1916, Gandhi attributed the poverty of the Indian masses to the departure from swadeshi which he wanted the country to adopt as an article of faith, not as a boycott movement undertaken by way of revenge against Lancashire. He wanted India to be self-sufficient. For he stressed that "India cannot live for Lancashire or in fact for any other country before she is able to live for herself".[75] Obviously, India could not manage to live for herself without an Indian counterpart of Lancashire in industrial terms. It was precisely with this end in view that Indian industrialists had been anxious to use politics to promote their business by means of tariff restrictions to reduce foreign competition. Gandhi was in for it, though not by way of revenge.

The Khaddar Scheme of the Congress and its simultaneous support for swadeshi as a counterpoise to foreign goods seemed to be apparently enigmatic, though not mutually exclusive. While the former had a popular symbolic appeal, in socialistic terms, for the dying handloom industry in the interest of poor weavers, the latter was viewed as an instrument to secure the fulfilment of the indigenous capitalist demand for protective tariffs. The well-to-do upper middle-class leaders of the Indian National Congress appeared under these conditions as meant to be representative of the poor, though essentially belonging to a position in the Indian social hierarchy which called for an alliance with the rich and the privileged. Whatever the case might be, this approach to economic policy benefited the Congress as a political organization which doubtless became strong under Gandhi's leadership because of its identification with the masses in cultural terms. This was not so with the anglicized leadership of the earlier generation.

Though a strong supporter of the swadeshi movement, Gandhi, in fact, was in principle opposed to unlimited competition. He of course believed that India could live for herself only if she produced or was helped to produce "everything for her requirements within her own borders". But, as he said, she "need not be, she ought not to be, drawn into the vortex of mad and ruinous competition which breeds fratricide, jealousy and many other evils". He was, however, fully conscious that he could not "stop her great millionaires from entering into the world competition.[76] It was this ambivalence of Gandhi and his want of clarity on economic issues that later accounted for confused thinking and delay in the formulation of a sound industrial policy.

Though by nature, education and culture a moderate given to peace and non-violence, Gandhi was by conviction and mental habit a "nationalist" to the core, wedded to religious belief like Tilak but prone to liberalism like Gokhale. The nationalist in him was, however, more powerful than liberalist. That perhaps was why in the course of his speech at the opening ceremony of Benares Hindu University on February 6, 1916, he made a reference to the "misdirected zeal" of "the bomb-thrower", but indirectly attributed to it the revocation of the Partition of Bengal under Lord Hardinge who presided over the inaugural function. Mrs. Annie Besant, who was present on the occasion, asked Gandhi abruptly to "stop it". But Gandhi went on and said, "Let us frankly and openly say whatever we want to say to our rulers and face the consequences if what we have to say does not please them".[77] It was this strong and religiously upheld nationalist urge in him that took the Congress forward in the direction of an anti-imperialist Non-Cooperation Movement, while the Liberals not only seceded from it, but formed a separate party of their own to cooperate with the Government in working the Montford Reforms. The expediency of using the Khilafatists as part of that movement to strengthen the Congress with their collaboration on the Turkish issue was of course a debatable question. But the fact that the advanced anti-imperialist nationalist forces with a tendency towards the Left arose from within the Congress itself in the context of the Bolshevik Revolution could not by any reason be denied.

Summing up the whole development to 1920, it would be clear that the Congress by and large retained its elitist character. During the first 20 years of its existence it raised no basic claim for self-government in any form. Its oft-repeated demands were for simultaneous examinations for the ICS, in England and India, representative government and protective tariffs. The early Moderate leaders were anxious to see some Indian members on the Council of the Secretary of State and the Viceroy's Executive Council. The Congress in fact rose into importance because of the recognition extended to it by the Government for policy's sake.

It was only in 1906 that Tilak and his group in the Congress pressed for the acceptance of swaraj as its national goal. But it was not long before they were forced to quit in 1908. The Moderates alone ruled the roast till 1915, when the compulsions of the First World War dictated the exigencies of "responsive" cooperation with the Government even on the part of Tilak.

Tilak's cultural approach to politics, which was potentially prone to mass movement, was, however, symbolic manifestly of a Hindu revivalist force, liable to be identified as representing a communal trend forming part of the Congress, a national organization. His Nationalist Party, formed after the Surat Split of 1907, was inclusive even of the terrorists and revolutionaries who reinforced it informally with their anti-British links established abroad. It was the political radicalism of revolutionary nationalists that heralded the socialist movement in India in the wake of the Russian Revolution of 1917 and the Communist International established soon after in 1919. This was on a direct political level related to the activities of academics, educated elites and university students.

A more important and stable source of strength to the nationalist forces was the rise of Indian capitalism as a competitive economic force in the course of the First World War (1914-18). At the Industrial Conference held in Bombay in 1915, the Indian industrialists resolved for the first time to "yoke" together politics and industry as an instrument to win self-government in order to ensure India's industrial advance by exclusion of foreign competition. Naturally enough, there developed an identity of interests between the Indian business enterprise and nationalist politics, both being in the main though influenced, at the initial stage of Indian capitalist development, by considerations of religion and philanthropy rather than class interest in economic terms.

Industrial strikes were, doubtless, many towards the close of the war on account of rise in prices without a corresponding increase in wages. But as there was yet no political movement on the basis of socialism or the conceptual basis of a working-class movement, a nationalist leader like Lajpat Rai, who was an outsider, presided over the first All-India Trade Union Congress established in 1920. The whole approach could at this period be philanthropic, actuated by a commitment to national political interest. Even so, the rising capitalist development had by then reached a stage where the nationalist politics could not but respond favourably to it. The role of capitalist entrepreneurs and business enterprise, though really significant and powerful as an organized pressure group and source of financial assistance to politics, remains for the most part unseen and unacknowledged by scholars of history, although it was this informal body of business entrepreneurs who set the pace of India's industrial advance and held the key to political change also. It was made clear by the Report of the Industrial Commission (1916) and the official steps that followed soon after.[78]

Appendices to Chapter I
Notes Excluded

APPENDIX "A"

Government of India, Department of Commerce and Industry, Industries A. Proceedings, May 1917, Nos. 1 to 31 (confidential)

APPOINTMENT OF A COMMISSION TO EXAMINE AND REPORT UPON THE POSSIBILITIES OF FURTHER INDUSTRIAL DEVELOPMENT IN INDIA

No. 589-D
No. 7

GOVERNMENT OF INDIA.

DEPARTMENT OF COMMERCE AND INDUSTRY.

From

A. H. LEY, Esq., C.I.E. I.C.S.

Joint Secretary to the Government of India,

To

ALL LOCAL GOVERNMENTS AND THE HON'BLE CHIEF COMMISSIONERS OF THE CENTRAL PROVINCES, ASSAM, NORTH-WEST FRONTIER PROVINCE AND DELHI.

Dated Delhi, the 7th December 1918.

Sir,

I am directed to address you on the proposals made in the Report of the Indian Industrial Commission for the establishment of an Imperial and Provincial Department of Industries. The report covers a wide range of subjects and includes a number of incidental recommendations which, though important in themselves, can be reserved for separate consideration in due course. The basis of the main proposal, however, may be summed up in the following three general propositions:-

(1) That the improvement of Indian Industries is of vital importance to the future of the country; that it will throw on Government many new and serious responsibilities, and requires a consistent and co-ordinated effort for its achievement. These considerations appear to necessitate the creation of a special department of the Government of India to formulate and direct the new policy:

(2) That for obvious reasons the actual execution of the policy must mainly be effected by authorities under the control of Local Governments:

(3) That, in view of the past history of Indian Industrial development and of the present conditions of industrial success in other countries, no real progress can be expected without an expert study of industrial possibilities and expert advice and assistance in undertaking the solution of industrial problems, and that the necessary staff can be best obtained and most advantageously employed by the creation of organised services.

2. With these three basic propositions the Government of India are in general agreement; but the principles on which the function of the imperial and the provincial departments should be correlated require some further discussion in the light of considerations arising out of the report on Indian Constitutional Reforms. The Government of India do not wish at the moment to commit themselves to any definite view as to the exact division of functions between the Imperial and Provincial Governments. It appears to them obvious, however, that in certain directions the Government of India will not be able to divest themselves of responsibility. Industries, for instance, the development of which is necessary in order to secure national safety; industries, again, which though not perhaps essential from the point of view of national safety, yet affect materially such

wide economic interests that their development in any particular direction is a matter of more than provincial importance; possibly industries for which no form of assistance will be of real value which does not involve serious financial responsibility, or industries which can only be developed by the employment of a wide range of technical staff; these suggest themselves as matters which may have to be regarded as of imperial concern.

3. While, however, the Government of India feel that they cannot divest themselves of the grave responsibility which is entailed by the decision to accept the policy of attempting the improvement of the industries of the country on the widest possible scale, they fully recognise that the actual development of industries must in the main be carried out by local authorities. It is particularly, therefore, with regard to the proposals contained in Chapter XXI of the Report, on provincial department of Industries, that I am now to address you. It will be realised that a volume of work, which will be extensive, will, in any case, even from the beginning, have to be entrusted to Local Governments, to many of whom the problems to be dealt with will be entirely new, and the work will entail on them responsibilities which cannot be performed without the assistance of a wide range of technical advice and experience.

4. In some provinces the nucleus of a provincial department of industries already exists; in others this still remains to be created; in all alike, as it seems to the Government of India, there is great scope for fresh activities and an urgent necessity for the employment of a considerably extended staff. Without at the moment discussing the precise proposals for the organisation of a provincial department which have been made by the Commission, I am directed to draw your special attention to the recommendation that the staff employed should form part of an Indian Industrial service which will in the main be composed of men whose training has qualified them as mechanical engineers. There appear to the Government of India to be three possible methods of recruiting the men required for the work of industrial development in the provinces:

(a) They may be casually recruited on terms special to themselves;
(b) they may form part of an organised provincial service; or

(c) they may form part of an organised all-Indian service.

Casual recruitment will, in the view of the Government of India, unquestionably entail unnecessary expenditure, while at the same time it will fail to afford sufficient incentive to the training of Indians in the higher forms of scientific and technical education. It is likely, moreover, to give rise to discontent on the part of officers in regular services who would in general be employed on a lower rate of pay than men recruited on terms special to themselves. These objections would be partially, but not wholly, removed, if there could be in each province a separate organised industrial service. On the other hand, it seems clear that even the most advanced province could not provide for more than a small expert cadre, which would afford inadequate scope and insufficient prospects to ensure the recruitment of the right type of men at a reasonable cost; while in any event there would have to be a nucleus of experts employed under the Central Government. The Government of India are provisionally of opinion, therefore, that the most promising line of advance will be found in the direction of creating in the beginning a well-equipped central organisation and decentralising its functions as rapidly as the progress made and the experience gained will permit.

5. The Commission's scheme for an industrial service contemplates the recruitment of its members into an all-India service, and their employment mainly under Local Governments. There would, however, be some experts, who would either be lent for particular pieces of work to Local Governments, or retained directly under the Government of India for researches in which more than one province may be simultaneously interested. The men employed under the Local Governments would ordinarily be retained by them, as is usual in the case of the Agricultural, Forests and other Imperial Services; but Local Governments would be entitled to ask the Government of India to replace men who were not found suitable for the work required of them, and the Government of India might equally find it necessary to ask occasionally for the surrender of men to meet the needs of other provinces or to fill higher posts under the Central Government. It must be remembered that in the interests of the staff no less than in that of the work itself scope must be provided for the promotion of men whose experience and qualifications render them suitable for higher responsibilities than the con-

tinued performance of mere laboratory work; a purely provincial service may not be able to provide such opportunities without unjustifiable expense, while to withhold them will lead to discontent and waste of power. Some such system appears prima facie to the Government of India to afford the form of organisation most suitable to the growing industrial requirements of the country as a whole.

6. Much the same remarks apply to the Commisssion's proposal to create an Imperial Chemical Service. The Government of India do not contemplate interference with the activities of Local Governments in research work, but they consider it important to provide an agency by which Local Governments can be assured that the officers engaged in research are keeping up to the required standard. They believe that a properly equipped central research organisation will be of great value in the advice and assistance which it will be able to afford to Local Governments, and that the waste which the duplication of equipment and the overlapping of research work on some questions involve, when carried to an extent which results in the neglect of others, affords substantial reasons for the creation of an effective agency for securing a full and free exchange of information and the correlation of results.

7. An important part of the Commission's recommendations relates to an alteration in the existing system for the purchase of Government stores. The suggestion for a central purchasing department has been made before, even in the period prior to the war, while, since the war broke out, the functions of such a department have in fact been exercised in a large measure by the Indian Munitions Board. It may be urged that the existence of a central purchasing department in this country may lead to increased delays in obtaining stores from England. On the other hand, it may reasonably be anticipated that with the encouragement and development of industries in this country there will be a great reduction in purchases from England, while the advantages of central control in securing economy by amalgamating indents and purchasing in bulk–advantages which have been proved beyond question under war conditions–seem to outweigh any of the reasons which may be urged in favour of a continuance of the system existing prior to the war, by which individual officers indent on the Stores Department of the India Office for

stores required from England. The Government of India believe the Commission's recommendation to establish a central organisation in India for the purchase of Government stores (a recommendation which was also made in the Report of the Public Works Department Re-organisation Committee) to be one of the most valuable of their proposals for the development of Indian industries. The Commission at the same time contemplate considerable decentralisation from the Central Stores Department to provincial agencies, which will be a necessary part of the provincial departments of industries, and propose that the degree of decentralization should be examined by a small expert committee.

8. It will be observed that among the subsidiary activities of the Provincial Department of Industries the Commission include the collection of local commercial and industrial intelligence. In this respect their proposals seem to be generally consonant with the views of Local Governments expressed in reply to Mr. Enthoven's letter No. 5256-5264–10, dated the 29th of June 1914, on the subject of the re-organization of the Commercial Intelligence Department.

9. I am now to ask for an early expression of the views of His Excellency the Governor in Council, His Honour the Lieutenant Governor in Council of your views on these general proposals, viz. :

(a) Whether Provincial Departments of Industries should be created, or developed, on the lines suggested by the Commission;

(b) whether the responsibilities of these Departments should include

(1) the local purchase of Government stores, subject to such degree of centralisation as may be decided upon after consideration of the report of a special committee, and

(2) the collection of local commercial and industrial intelligence;

(c) what arrangements are most suitable for utilising the officers of the proposed Indian services, industrial and chemical, in order to combine the advantages of a common system of recruitment, and central criticism in wider questions of research, with the control which Local Governments must necessarily exercise in executive and administrative matters and to secure the fullest utilisation by the Local Governments of their own staff on local problems; and

(d) what generally should be the relations between the Imperial and Provincial Departments.

The Government of India trust that the views of the Local Government may be forwarded to them not later than March next.

10. If the principle of Indian industrial and chemical services is accepted, questions will arise with regard to the manner in which specialist, already employed under the Government of India or under Local Governments, are to be brought into the services, as well as with regard to the staff to be recruited in the near future, the method of recruitment and the status and emoluments of individual officers. For the immediate purpose of an answer to this letter these matters need not be discussed, though, no doubt, the local Government/you will begin without delay to take them into consideration. The immediate intention of this reference is merely to obtain the general views of the Local Government on the main principles involved. Meanwhile the Government of India intend to work out a scheme for giving such effect to the principle of an Imperial Department of Industries as can be given without an immediate alteration of the law governing their constitution. It will be the duty of this Central Department, as soon as it is formed, to consult the Local Governments on the numerous incidental proposals made by the Commission, which, however important in themselves, it is unnecessary to discuss for immediate purpose of coming to a decision on the proposal to establish Provincial Departments of Industries. Such are the proposals in Chapter X on technical and industrial education, those in Chapter XX on industrial finance, the suggested increase of the Forest Department by the addition of forest engineers, the proposals regarding the inspection of Government mining rules, suggestions with regard to the acquisition of land on behalf of industrial concerns, the welfare of labour, the transfer of the preventive work of the Northern India Salt Revenue Department to the Local Governments concerned, and sundry other matters.

I have the honour to be,

Sir,

Your most obedient Servant,

A. H. LEY,

Joint Secretary to the Government of India

No. 590-D.

Copy forwarded to all Departments of the Government of India.

By order, etc.

G. S. HARDY,
Under Secretary to the Government of India.

Viceroy to Secretary of State.

Telegram P., No. 2370, 10th December 1918. (Despd. for C.&.I. Dept.) No. 8.

No. 667-D. Report of the Industrial Commission. The proposal to create a new Industries Department with the Government of India has our approval, and we are anxious that this proposal should be carried out with as little delay as possible. But the number of Members of Council cannot be increased without legislation, and we are not prepared, for the special purpose of creating an Industries Member, to ask for this. Until readjustment of portfolios consequent on the Reform Scheme has been settled, the question whether an additional Member will be ultimately required cannot be determined. It is important meanwhile to start with the least possible delay new industrial organisation at centre, and it is proposed by us to convert Munitions Board into Industries Board. We propose that Sir Thomas Holland should be created head of the new Department under Viceroy's special charge, and receive a personal salary equivalant to that of an ordinary Member of Council, subject of course to his pension remaining in abeyance during his tenure of post. When industrial questions are involved, he would take part in meetings of Council, but without power of voting. Your sanction to this proposal as temporary measure is requested. Though we hold the opinion that an organisation at centre is essential to supply necessary stimulus, especially at the outset, we intend that the actual work of developing industries should be done chiefly by provincial effort and under provincial control. We shall ask for sanction subsequently to more precise proposals for staff and emoluments of new Department when these can be worked out. If the proposal mentioned above be sanctioned as a beginning, Sir Thomas Holland will at an early date take short leave to consult India Office and note recent developments at home. As Sir Thomas Holland will be completing his private arrangements for resigning commission and leaving India on demobilisation, we should like to receive early orders.

No. 15 of 1919

GOVERNMENT OF INDIA.

DEPARTMENT OF COMMERCE AND INDUSTRY.

INDUSTRIES.

To

THE RIGHT HONOURABLE EDWIN MONTAGU,

His Majesty's Secretary of State for India.

Simla, the 4th June 1919.

Sir,

In our despatch No. 51 (Industries) dated 26th November 1915, we set forth the reasons which led us to propose the appointment of the Indian Industrial Commission. The Commission submitted their report on the 29th October last. Their recommendations were unanimous, except for the dissenting note of one member. The few definite suggestions that emerge from his note are, however, not of a nature that we can accept, and have therefore not been dealt with by us in this despatch, though his arguments against some of the Commission's proposals which we support are generally covered, we believe, by our statement of the case.

After the issue of Mr. Ley's letter No. 589-D, dated 7th December 1918, to Local Governments (annexure I), inviting their views on the main principles laid down in the report, we deputed Mr. Low, Secretary in the Department of Commerce and Industry, who had been a member of the Commission, to visit Local Governments, in order that their attention might be focussed, by free and informal discussion of the somewhat complex questions involved, on the main points at issue, and their replies might be expedited.

2. There are four cardinal points which require to be settled before definite progress can be made in giving effect to the Commission's recommendations : viz. the proposals :-

(1) to constitute provincial departments of industries;

(2) to constitute a central department of industries;

(3) to create all-India scientific and technical services;

(4) to create an agency for the purchase and inspection of stores in India.

We shall place before you in this despatch our views on each of the above points, and ask for your general approval of our proposals in each case. The replies of the Local Governments whom we consulted on the above points, are annexed to this despatch.

PROVINCIAL DEPARTMENTS OF INDUSTRIES.

3. In paragraphs 303 to 306 of their report the Commission recite their reasons for proposing the creation of provincial departments of industries, and we need not repeat them here. The duties of the provincial departments as suggested by the Commission in paragraph 306 of their report are as follows :-

"(a) The direct encouragement of industries, including a large share in industrial research work, the provision of technical advice and assistance to industrialists, the examination of applications for special concessions, and the grant of loans to small and cottage industries.

"(b) The collection and distribution of commercial and industrial intelligence; the work of passing Government indents and of purchasing and inspecting certain classes of Government stores; the organisation of markets for local products; the conduct of special enquiries and industrial surveys; the holding of industrial exhibitions and the management of commercial and industrial museums.

"(c) The control of technical and industrial education. This would necessitate the training of staff for, and the inspection of, industrial schools; the organisation and inspection of apprentice classes attached to large works, and the provision of the staff for the necessary theoretical teaching. The Director would also have to take his share in the control of the higher institutions for technical training. Funds for technical and industrial education would be provided from his budget.

"(d) The control of the staff employed for the local administration of the Electricity, Factories and Boiler Acts; and the furnishing of advice to Government on the industrial and commercial aspects of the Mines Act and of the rules for mining leases and prospecting licenses."

The Commission also drew attention to the necessity for some means of exchanging information regarding the experience gained in different provinces. Even in respect of cottage industries they considered this to be necessary.

The provincial department would thus be the mechanism through which the motive force contained in the technical, scientific, educational and financial proposals of the Commission would be applied in the way in which they can be most effective; viz. through an agency under the complete control of Local Governments. Promising results, though necessarily on a most inadequate scale, have already been obtained from the operations of such local departments of industries as already exist in the Central Provinces, the United Provinces and especially in Madras, in spite of their lack of technical equipment and of the absence of a correlating central agency. The organisation proposed by the Commission follows the existing lines of these provincial departments, but strengthened in such directions as experience has been able to suggest. It is with confidence that we invite your approval of the proposal to institute provincial departments of industries on the general lines laid down by the Commission subject to such further applications for detailed financial sanction as the powers which may be exercised by the Government of India or the Local Governments, respectively, may necessitate, and to such further consideration in points of detail as may be found requisite. The principle has been supported by all Local Governments, although certain of the Commission's detailed proposals are not unanimously accepted, and the Burma Government make certain suggestions for the control of the department of industries and its co-ordination with the departments of agriculture and co-operative credit, that are dependent on a scheme of provincial reforms which they are about to put forward. These proposals will however receive further consideration on receipt of your reply.

AN IMPERIAL DEPARTMENT OF INDUSTRIES.

4. The necessity for a central agency to co-ordinate and supplement the efforts of the local departments is obvious. Industry follows economic, not provincial, boundaries; individual undertakings compete for their raw materials, and for the sale of their products, within areas limited only by the cost of transport; information regarding the nature of raw materials and of industrial process is of far more than provincial application; some of the raw materials required for the completion of industrial operations in one province are often derived from another, industrial labour now moves more and more freely from one province to another. If the Government organisation for the development of industries work in water-tight compartments, or depend for the exchange of information solely on spontaneous and undirected co-operation, progress will be limited by the comparatively small power of the local agency; and much even of that small power will be wasted.

A central co-ordinating agency is thus clearly needed. It will fulfil its responsibility by keeping closely in touch with the work being done by provincial departments; by offering from time to time its advice, based on the opinions of appropriate specialists, regarding the conduct of that work; and by ensuring that the experience of the more progressive provinces is placed freely at the disposal of the more backward ones. Personal discussion between Local Government and the higher officers of the central department of industries, men who have built up business and administrative experience in handling technical subjects, on a basis of technical knowledge, will be invaluable in supplementing the inevitable deficiencies in experience, qualifications and equipment that will characterise most, if not all, of the provincial departments of industries for a long time to come. Several of the Local Governements, it will be noticed, specifically mention the advantages which they hope to derive from the creation of a central organisation capable of creating such relations with Local Governments. A central agency is also needed to supplement certain inevitable deficiencies in provincial departments, in respect of special research problems that have a bearing on the development of industries, in the laboratory or experimental factory.

5. It was true that we propose to leave entire freedom to Local Governments, subject to a few restrictions of very limited scope, in respect of the above functions. But various considerations will in practice prevent Local Government to concentrate on exploiting the results of research, while much of the actual work of research will be left to the central Government. That Government, dealing in one or other of its departments with matters like the manufacture of munitions, the Geological Survey, the proposed purchase and inspection of stores in India, at any rate on behalf of the large central consuming agencies, and the production of salt in Northern India, will be compelled in any case to maintain a far larger staff of technical experts and scientists than any Local Government. In addition to this, it must have a large share in the administration of central institute for research and for professional and technical training. It is of paramount importance to recollect that specialisation is the key-note of all modern science and technology, and without a far higher degree of specialisation than has hitherto been attempted in India, research work will be infructuous and attempts at development wasteful and dangerous. We must proceed in future on an entirely different principle, and the qualifications, numbers and organisation of the staff must be adjusted with reference to the work to be done. It is obvious that no Local Government can afford more than a fraction of the equipment required; and though the Commission contemplate the services of scientific specialists being placed freely at the disposal of Local Governments, the technical side of their work must even in such cases be assisted by an expert central agency.

6. There will be many industries of which the possibilities will have to be investigated on a minimum commercial scale before private enterprise is willing to come forward and undertake their further development. Such investigations, sometimes., involve considerable expenditure for longer or shorter periods. Local Governments have to carry on a number of minor industrial activities, such as the en-

couragement of cottage and small local industries, as well as industrial and technical education, matters which in the aggregate involve large amounts of recurring expenditure, and render local resources relatively less elastic than those of the Government of India. Financial limitations, therefore, will often render it impossible for Local Governments to undertake the more expensive and ambitious lines of development. Reference to Appendix E of the report, for instance, shows the variety of specialists necessary in glass manufacture and explains the consistent series of failures that in their absence have followed the attempts to manufacture glass in India. On the other hand, no individual undertaking could be worked on a scale which would recoup a private concern for the initial expenditure of so general an investigation. Moreover, it is necessary, when factors of national safety are involved, and very desirable, when the question is merely one of high economic importance, to secure the development, on a suitable scale and at the right time, of each link in a chain of inter-dependent industries, instead of, as in the past, relying on imports to fill the gaps. The links of such a chain will often have to be located in different provinces; and in any case the necessity of any particular link is not always clearly visible or specially urgent from any one provincial point of view. There should be a central agency, in a position to create or encourage, failing adequate action by Local Governments, industries needed to fill such gaps. This principle is generally accepted by the Local Governments. As the Bombay Government remark, research, experiment and demonstration undertaken within their Presidency will have to be supplemented by further research and experiments either within or without that Presidency, in the general interests of India.

7. One of the most potent instruments for the encouragement of new undertakings is the guarantee by Government of the purchase of manufactured products for a term of years. It is obvious that in hardly any instance would a single Local Governments be in a position to give a purchasing order large enough to be of the slightest assistance to a big undertaking. Not only are the individual requirements of Local Governments small, but the large purchasing departments which use manufactured articles, such as the Army, the Railways, the Post and Telegraphs, are all under the Government of India.

8. There is a further reason why a central agency is needed. The commission enumerate in paragraph 324 of their report certain subjects, in addition to their two headings 9 and 10, which relate directly to the encouragement of industries by Government, as suitable for inclusion under a central department of industries. These are at present all dealt with by departments of the Government of India.

1. Geology and Minerals (including the Geological Survey of India and the administration of the Indian Mines Act).
2. Salt.
3. Indian Explosives Act and the Indian Petroleum Act.
4. Stationery and Printing.
5. Inventions and Designs.
6. The collection and distribution of commercial and industrial inttelligence.
7. The supply of stores.
8. The Indian Factories Act.

11. The administration of the various Acts relating to steam boilers.
12. Electricity.

In addition to these the inclusion of two additional subjects is suggested, if it be decided to place them under the control of a civil department.

13. Ordnance Factories.
14. The inspection of Ordnance manufactures.

Though the Committee for the Division of Functions recommend that one or two of these heads should be definitely placed under the control of provincial Governments, subject to all-India legislation, this proposal will affect the existing practice but little. Subject to the above qualification all of these heads have been recognised by the Committee for the Division of Functions as falling within the proper sphere of the Central Government, and they can be controlled more appropriately by a central agency which is concerned with industrial matters, than by the un-specialised departments to which they at present belong.

9. Finally, the Imperial Government cannot divest itself of respon-

sibility for the industrial progress of the country, and for its economic and military safety, so far as the latter can be secured by the supply of munitions and stores. It will in any case maintain almost exclusive control of the tariff policy, shipping, foreign trade relations, ports, waterways and railways, matters of which industry throughout the country can never be independent, and it will retain certain important responsibilities in respect of minerals, the property of the State. Moreover, the fact that Government are embarking on a new and very important line of policy postulates the necessity of a sufficient degree of central co-ordination to ensure that the whole resources of the country are, as far as may be, utilised in the pursuit of that policy. It is in the first few years that the success of the policy will be determined; and it is in those years that the task of the central agency will be the heaviest, and the necessity of its existence strongest.

10. We will now explain our reasons for holding that, during at any rate the initial stages of our new industrial policy, the proposed central agency must be a special department of the Government of India in charge of a separate Member of Council. On this point we are in general agreement, though some of us hold that the development of industries will always require to be a separate charge. We may point out, in the first place, that the Commerce and Industry Department is at present, and for some years to come, at any rate, will be, so heavily overburdened with work, as to render it incapable of undertaking such important additional responsibilities; while the nature of these responsibilities and the character of the personnel required for their performance, is, in most cases, in no way akin to the personnel employed under the Department of Commerce and Industry, or to the functions that it exercises. The relief afforded to the present Department of Commerce and Industry by the transfer of heads 1-11 mentioned in paragraph 8 above, will reduce the number of receipts dealt with by it by less than one-seventh; and we do not consider that, even with the very small amount of devolution in respect of the remaining subjects dealt with in that department which has been proposed by the Committee on the Division of Functions, the remaining work will be less than that department, as at present constituted, or the Member in charge of it, can properly undertake.

11. We may exemplify our reasons for not entrusting the carrying out of the new policy to the Department of Commerce and Industry by a reference to the position in the United Kingdom. There the newly established State agencies for research are not placed under the Board of Trade, but under a special Committee of the Privy Council. This work in India, in the utter absence of private or commercial agencies for research, will fall for a long time almost entirely upon the State.

In addition to this, two still more important classes of activity have to be undertaken by the Indian Government, for which in England the necessity and even the occasion are almost entirely absent, namely the stimulation of private enterprise and the exploitation of the great State properties. The present unsatisfactory position in India is almost entirely due to the lack of private enterprise; this has to be built up and encouraged by the provision of technical information, the training of consultants, technologists and artisans, the offer of Government orders, concessions and guarantees, and by the creation of a system of finance which will afford to industries the facilities which have hitherto been concentrated on trade. In England most of these advantages have long existed; they have been created by private enterprise and in turn they have reacted on it, and extended its scope. In the next place, the Indian Government possesses and is responsible for the economic utilisation of a very potent instrument of aid to industries, which to England is lacking; viz. the State ownership of extensive forest areas, mineral and water rights. But to make this instrument effective, it will have to be wielded with far greater skill and purpose than heretofore, and must therefore be directed by an agency which is designed to stimulate and assist industries, rather than by one which is well adapted, indeed, to assist commerce, but whose relations with industries have hitherto been mainly restrictive.

The Department of Commerce and Industry was, it is true, intended to benefit industry as well as commerce. But the absence of a definite industrial policy has left that department without the expert staff which could alone effect the latter object. Even if that deficiency were supplemented, the additional load of responsibility would entail the risk of paralysing an already over-burdened department.

12. It is indeed possible to bring forward a further reason for separating the functions of Government in relation to trade from those which concern industry. The future economic policy of India will be affected by two forces, which will often be in opposition; the wish to protect home industries by fiscal measures, and the necessity of maintaining the free movement of trade and of securing to the consumer goods at a reasonable price. It would be, we think, a serious mistake to confuse the issue by placing the interests of industry and commerce, which respectively represent these two conflicting forces, under a single representative. Each interest should have its own line of action clearly before it; in any case where these lines diverge, the course must be settled after a full and clear consideration of all the factors in that case and should not depend on whether the Member who may be at the time in charge of both interests happens to favour protection or free trade.

13. In forming a decision on the necessity of a separate department popular sentiment and expectation cannot be ignored. As the Industrial Commission have said in paragraph 320 of their report, the duties of a central industrial agency "are sufficiently important and sufficiently correlated, both in themselves, and in the public mind, to justify special treatment, and they involve interests which deserve separate representation in the Viceroy's Executive Council". This view was anticipated in paragraph 340 of the Report on Indian Constitutional Reforms. The importance to India of a definite policy for the improvement of her industries is based on the strongest economic, political and military reasons; for years past it has been prominently in the public mind and is now urged still more forcibly by all classes of Indian opinion as an indispensable condition of the future political progress of the country. Anything short of the creation of a central department of industries will be generally considered an inadequate expression of that policy. Popular opinion will look to the central department of industries for the fulfilment of India's hopes for a great industrial future; and will regard it, in fact, as the pre-eminently swadeshi department.

For these reasons we agree that a central department of industries is, at any rate, during the initial stages of the new policy, the necessary and appropriate agency for stimulating, guiding and coordinating all forms of Government effort for the development of industries and to this view we ask you to give your approval in principle.

14. The proposal of the Commission is that the Member-in-charge should be assisted by a board. We do not wish to be understood as endorsing this particular proposal as the ultimate constitution of the new Department. It is probable that the initial organisation of the Department will have to be on somewhat informal lines, depending for its success as it must do more on men than on mere system. The Member-in-charge will require the help and advice of officers with various qualifications and experience. Whether these officers can be most helpful as heads of subordinate departments, as secretaries, or as members of a board, can be most fittingly determined by actual experience.

15. If you approve in principle of the necessity of a separate department of industries, we propose to begin with a short-time interim scheme.

It will in any case be impossible to create, without amendment of the Government of India Act, 1915, a new post of a Member of the Governor General's Executive Council. Legislation has recently been undertaken in connection with the scheme of Constitutional Reforms, which is designed to delegate to the Government of India power to modify the number of members of that Council. It would be impossible to submit before that date detailed proposals for a department exercising such entirely novel functions, but we think that a few months' *interim* experience with the temporary organisation which we explain below, should enable us to form a much more accurate idea than is at present possible of the establishment required; and we hope to be in a position, if our present proposals are approved in principle, to submit a detailed scheme for sanction in a few months' time.

We propose on receipt of your sanction to hand over to the Indian Munitions Board, which may be appropriately renamed "The Board of Industries and Munitions", the subjects and subordinate departments enumerated in paragraph 324 of the Commission's report, except Nos. 6 and 14, regarding which we reserve our opinion.

Some of this work has hitherto been undertaken under war conditions and for purposes connected with the war, by the Munitions Board. This organisation has throughout been in more intimate touch with the industries of the country than any department of Government has ever been before; and with a little re-adjustment can do what is needed for the present, while winding up the remains of its war work. The department so constituted should retain the powers at present possessed by the Munitions Board, but answerable through its President direct to His Excellency the Viceroy, as previously proposed in our telegram No. 667-D of 10th December 1918.

To do this in addition to its existing task of closing its war commitments will necessitate the employment of certain establishment, and the incurring of certain expenditure to initiate work on various schemes which have been considered by the Munitions Board for some time past, for which we shall, when necessary, request your sanction.

16. To recapitulate, we ask you–

(1) to approve in principle of the creation of a Department of Industries, to be placed under the charge of a Member when a vacancy occurs or can be created, in order to deal, generally speaking, with the subjects recommended by the Commission;
(2) to agree that the Indian Munitions Board should, for the present, carry on the initial work of organisation, and in particular, should frame proposals in detail for the new Department.

RELATIONS BETWEEN PROVINCIAL AND IMPERIAL DEPARTMENTS OF INDUSTRIES

17. We shall now explain what in our opinion should be the relations between the central and the provincial departments of industries. In paragraphs 3 and 5-9 of this despatch we have generally indicated what we think should be their respective duties. But we desire to leave the fullest liberty to the Local Governments in respect of the functions and responsibilities to be exercised by their departments of industries. They should, we think, be free to conduct any form of research or experiment, to initiate any industries on experimental

lines, or to encourage the starting of any industrial undertaking, by any means that lies within the general financial and other powers that may be conferred on them from time to time. The various possible methods of encouragement are more particularly indicated in Chapter XIV and XX of the Commission's report; and though some of the proposals set forth in the latter chapter will need further consideration and perhaps further reference to yourself, we wish to state here that, whatever conclusion may be reached regarding their adoption, we do not propose to restrict the employment by the Local Governments of any particular form of authorised assistance or to reserve any such form for the exclusive use of the Government of India.

It is therefore necessary, as we explained in paragraph 116 of our despatch on the Report of the Committee on the Division of Functions, that the duties and activities of Local Governments and of the Government of India must in some respects be concurrent, but we do not think that this should give rise to difficulties which, indeed, are not anticipated by Local Governments, who fully concur in the above general proposals. We assume that there will be a free exchange of information regarding the activities of the respective agencies. In considering the steps to be taken for the development of any important industry, the advice and aid of the central department's experts are certain to be invited while they will be, it must also be assumed, fully aware of any important industrial inquiries that Local Governments may be carrying on. The relative advantages of imperial and provincial action will be thoroughly discussed from a technical point of view before definite proposals are presented to the Governments concerned; the abilities of Local Governments will be limited in respect of financial resources and staff; and it should seldom be difficult to come to a conclusion as to which authority should undertake the work.

As an alternative, such operations might be undertaken jointly on the lines indicated in paragraph 23 of Annexure V to the Functions Committee's Report, "as a business arrangement with a Local Government by which it will take a subsidy from central funds for carrying on some work in which the central and provincial authorities are interested".

The few cases of overlapping that will actually occur in practice will not necessarily mean a waste of money, and are in any case not too high a price to pay for the only satisfactory solution of a very real difficulty, a solution which, as we have said, is generally accepted by Local Governments.

18. The above proposals are, however, necessarily subject to certain reservation. In the first place cases may occur in which the action of Local Government, in initiating or assisting any industry, is likely to come into conflict with other important interests in the rest of India. In these cases, which, though important in principle, are not likely to occur often in practice, we desire to reserve to the Government of India power of veto. We have in mind the danger to Indian interests which would arise if a Local Government proposed to encourage a form of industry which entailed the disposal of a raw material limited in quantity, in such a way as to deprive the rest of India of the advantage arising from its manufacture in the country. Supposing, for instance, the Government of Burma thought fit to encourage the export of its zinc sulphide ores, the only adequate Indian source of sulphuric acid, or their reduction by a process which would involve the waste of the whole of their sulphur contents, then we think the resulting injury to the rest of India from the loss of an indigenous supply of this vitally important chemical would be so serious as to require the interference of the Government of India. We have given as an instance the possible misuse by a Local Government of the monopoly of a raw material; but we consider that the same considerations should apply to the misuse of monopolies of sites which could produce large quantities of water power at exceptionally low cost; such sites would necessarily be very few and the application of the resulting power must be a matter of national policy.

The necessity of the Government of India retaining a power of interference in cases like these is specifically recognised by those Local Governments which have dealt with this point, and is accepted by the Government of Burma, for so long as that province forms a part of the Indian Empire.

19. Apart from cases where actual interference by the Government of India may be necessary in the general interest, cases will doubtless occur where the interests of two or more Local Governments in the

establishment of rival industrial undertakings are at variance, and our intervention would be required, in order to avoid needless competition and loss.

20. We do not consider it necessary for Local Governments to submit their schemes for the approval of the Government of India, merely that the latter may assure themselves that the schemes do not contravene any of the above criteria. Such submission, as the Governments of Bombay and the United Provinces point out, would cause undesirable delay; and the Government of India can place themselves in a position to interfere in the rare cases where interference will be necessary, by regularly receiving information from Local Governments regarding the schemes they have in hand, an arrangement which will indeed be necessary to enable the country generally to pool its knowledge and to secure the necessary co-operation between the central and local organizations.

21. The above restrictions on the liberty of action otherwise possessed by Local Governments are particular applications of the general principles laid down in paragraphs 5 and 6 of our despatch on the report of the Committee on the Division of Functions.

THE SCIENTIFIC SERVICES

22. The third of the main proposals refers to the constitution of scientific services and of an industrial service. The Commission draw attention to the extreme importance of research under modern industrial conditions, and to the especial needs of India, in view of her vast unexpected resources in raw material and of the paucity of her scientific workers. They criticise the complete lack of organisation among scientists employed by Government, and describe the difficulties, both administrative and technical, to which this gives rise. The Commission recommend as a remedy the creation of a similar mechanism to that through which the Central and Local Governments have hitherto carried out almost all their most important activities, especially those requiring technical knowledge, viz. all-India services; and they discuss the basis on which these services should be constituted. The Commission propose the creation, not of scientific departments, but of scientific services, an essential distinction which has been clearly brought out in the replies of Local Governments,

though it has not been so clearly apprehended by critics of the proposal. The Commission contemplate the recruitment of officers into separate scientific services, such as a chemical, botanical or zoological service for employment under imperial and provincial departments, such as Forests and Agriculture, which deal with the application of a number of separate sciences. They propose that scientific officers in the employ of Government, instead of being recruited in small numbers or single units into the different services which happen to require them, should be recruited as experts in their several sciences, into scientific services, each with its appropriate conditions of qualification, pay, pension and promotion. Although the services will be distinct entities for the above purpose, yet the only members of those services that will not be actually employed under various departments that require their services, will consist of a central staff, engaged under such officers, for instance, as Deputy Chief Chemists at research centres, in scientific work. This central agency will also serve as a reservoir to meet the demands that may be put forward by other departments or by Local Governments for men to undertake temporary special investigations, to fill new posts or leave vacancies, or for the replacement of existing officers.

The head of each scientific service would thus exercise an influence over the members of his service in matters scientific by the check of scientific results and by the provision of advise and criticism on scientific work, whether for Local Governments or for research workers. It is not, we understand, proposed by the Commission, nor do we ourselves contemplate, that he should actually control research work in the sense of ordering definite problems to be taken up by officers serving under Local Governments, or should turn his department into a gang of hack researchers. We rely on constant correspondence between scientific officers of the same caste and periodical conferences as sufficient to correlate research programmes.

23. With the Commission's view of the very unsatisfactory nature of the present position as set forth in paragraphs 116 and 117 of their report, we are in complete accord.

Local Governments and heads of departments find the greatest difficulty in forming an opinion of the work done by scientists employed under them; or of the probable value of lines of research proposed by their officers. Should the administrative authority consider the results obtained by a scientist unsatisfactory, it is almost impossible to obtain an authoritative opinion on his work and qualifications; or to say whether he might not do better in another post; or to find such a post for him. The difficulties arising from the existence of isolated specialists in a department are in fact notorious. Local Governments constantly find themselves saddled with unsatisfactory men for long periods. The Chief Commissioner of the Central Provinces, for instance, specifically alludes to his own experience of these difficulties.

The impossibility of applying any common measures in determining the respective claims to promotion of a botanist, a chemist, an engineer and a political economist have been recognised in the existing services by creation of separate posts on a time scale. But this does not get over the difficulties already indicated, nor supply the proper incentive to the research worker, not afford scope or prospects for men of more than average ability. The absence of such prospects is bound to militate against our chances of obtaining good recruits, to render our staff discontented, and to prevent our securing the best work from the best men.

Moreover, so long as students of particular science are recruited sporadically on behalf of different departments as vacancies occur, Government will have to accept the men that happen to be left over, whatever their qualifications, after other and more regular demands have been supplied. The prospects of regular annual recruitment will enable the Government of India to fill its future demands for scientists, as it has hitherto done for engineers, forest officers and medical men.

24. The present system, under which the only chemists employed by the State are scattered through numerous departments without any organisation that can marshal the chemical forces of the country to attack problems of national importance, can give no help towards an active industrial policy.

We might quote as illustrating the inspiring value of a central co-ordinating authority the work undertaken by the Munitions Board through its chemical adviser. The report of the conference of chemists at Lahore, which we append to this despatch, shows that even our isolated and scattered chemists can be moulded into one team for the purpose of suggesting new lines of research and means for turning the results to practical account, without overlapping and consequent waste of effort.

This experience, in the light of the magnificent results obtained in England by the Research Committee of the Privy Council, show clearly how much may be expected from a system which provides a permanent organic connection between all chemists in Government employ.

25. The importance of a common system of recruitment and a common service has recently been recognised by the Council of the Institute of Chemistry in the United Kingdom, (vide proceedings of the Institute of Chemistry, 1918, part IV, page 14), in a representation submitted by them to all Government departments in which chemists are employed; they state their opinion that "the time is opportune for taking steps to secure for the provision of Chemistry a position corresponding to that occupied by the learned profession, and they feel that much would be accomplished towards the attainment of that end if, in the first place, adequate and uniform conditions of appointment were accorded to chemists directly engaged in the service of the State. The necessity for a definitely organised chemical service (both in peace and war) for all purposes of the State on which the science of chemistry has a bearing, has long been recognised in the chemical profession."

Conditions in India render services of chemists employed under Government of even greater relative importance than in England. India is far more deficient than England in the knowledge of its raw materials and of the appropriate industrial processes; consulting chemists and chemists in private employ are almost entirely absent here, and this deficiency is not likely soon to be remedied. Research institutes with special reference to a particular industry in England, it would seem, will usually be financed and controlled by the industry itself, with a Government grant-in-aid, whereas in India the position will be precisely the opposite, and the industry will rely primarily on State chemists. We therefore agree with the Commission that the advancement of industries in India must depend for scientific assistance almost entirely on State-employed men and these men will be far more concerned with initiation of important new lines of development and research and far less with merely routine work, than is the case in England. "The need of organisation is the greater, in that the functions of Indian State chemists are more important to the country; while their greater isolation and the consequent absence of a scientific atmosphere furnish an additional argument. The case for a State chemical service is thus even stronger in India than in England.

26. We are much influenced by the prospects which the proposed system affords of increasing the number of Indians in the scientific services. An Indian appointed to an isolated post, or as an assistant to an isolated professor in a country where the scientific atmosphere is non-existent, or at the best, exceedingly attenuated, lacks guidance and the stimulus of his fellows in the pursuit of scientific knowledge. His ambitions tend to become limited to the improvement of his pay and prospects rather than of his professional attainments. His membership of an all-India service, based on the pursuit of a common science, will increase the prestige of that science in his eyes and in those of the Indian public; the existence of the proposed imperial nucleus of scientists under a distinguished chief will provide him with an incitement to excel, with assistance in his studies and with opportunity for training if he desires it.

27. The Commission propose that, if the principle of scientific services is approved, committees should be appointed to formulate proposals for the permanent organisation and the terms of employment of each such service, and for the location and equipment of research laboratories. We support this recommendation, subject to the condition that the terms of reference to each committee should include a direction to report as to the advisability of constituting all-India services for each well-defined science.

28. Without anticipating the conclusions of the proposed committee, we think it desirable, in view of criticisms which have been expressed in some of the annexures to this despatch, to indicate certain principles in the general administration of these services, which should govern the relations between the members of the scientific services

and the heads of departments and Provincial Governments, under whom many of them will be employed.

We do not think that members of scientific service should be seconded by the method which the Commission propose, viz. by deputation for periods of 5 years at a time; but we consider that, as in the case of other services, an officer when once placed permanently under the orders of a Local Government, should remain with that Government for the rest of his service, unless the Government under which he is serving itself desires his transfer; or unless his services are required in a higher post or in a post requiring special qualifications outside the province, in which case the Local Government will recognise that the Imperial Government have a claim on them. This is the system which exists at present in respect of all similar services.

Local Governments would have complete liberty to appoint, after consulting the head of the service, to any post in their industrial or scientific cadre, any available members of the respective services; they would also be at liberty, in the special circumstances arising during the initial stages, to appoint to such posts men outside service; but the subsequent admission to the all-India service of men so appointed would be entirely controlled by the Secretary of State. The Local Governments universally support the proposed scheme of scientific services, and though the Governments of the Punjab, the United Provinces and Bombay and the officers and public bodies consulted by them put forward certain criticisms of the scheme, especially with reference to the position of scientists in the Education Department, these criticisms are, we think, fully met by the foregoing explanation of the lines on which we think the proposed services should be administered.

29. We desire, however, to add a few remarks with special reference to the case of science teachers. We fully recognise that much is required of a scientific professor in a college, outside his scientific work. He must look on himself as a member of the body responsible for the tone of the college and for its general success. It will, therefore, we agree, be most undesirable that such a man should continuously have in mind the possibility of promotion outside his own department. We think, however, that this difficulty will be obviated

by the general principle laid down by us above, viz. that members of scientific services serving under the Department of Education should not be removed from that department, unless at the request of the educational authorities, or for posts requiring high administrative capacity, or special scientific qualifications.

The advantage to the Education Department of a system of scientific services will still be very considerable. In the first place, we consider that, though University and college science workers should be by no means entirely divorced from technical research, their main sphere of activity should lie among problems of pure science. The proposed central scientific organisation should afford a means whereby such problems arising in the course of technical research can be referred to University and college laboratories.

Such co-ordination, both in respect of pure science problems and technical problems, can be most readily effected in cases where the educational researchers are themselves members of a scientific service. This policy will doubtless stimulate the interest in research work taken by students and professors. Officers who have entered the educational service as teachers may be in some cases expected to develop as research workers. The existence of all-India scientific services will afford a ready means for accommodating men whose aims in life have thus been diverted from one form of work to another. In the next place, the present system of recruitment of scientists into the Educational Service is capable of improvement, and far better results could be obtained with the aid and advice of watchful central agencies in India. The absence of a scientific atmosphere again has been particularly injurious to scientific officers in the Educational Service and has led to great stagnation in respect of research work. This atmosphere will in future reach individual officers by the numerous channels of communication which will be created between them and the central agency on technical subjects, whether by way of correspondence, conferences and scientific publications, by the central staff's tours of inspection, or by officers spending some portion of their vacations at research institutes. The case of scientists at present employed under the Department of Education will obviously require careful treatment; such men should not be allowed to join the scientific services as a matter of course, but each case will have to be considered on its merits and there may still be classes of appointments for which men will have to be recruited independently. Further, the whole question, so far as it affects the employment of officers with scientific qualifications in colleges and universities, will have to be reviewed in connection with the proposals of the Calcutta University Commission regarding recruitment.

30. In addition to the opinion expressed in the letters received from Local Governments, two important conferences of chemists have recently put forward their views on the Commission's proposals. A record of their discussions is appended. A full meeting of the Sectional Conference of Agricultural Chemists at Pusa in February passed the following resolution:-

"That this Conference considers that, in view of the intense local knowledge required for effective work for agricultural improvement by chemical methods, it is not desirable that the chemists in the Agricultural Departments should be formed into a service apart from the ordinary agricultural service in which the bond of union would be the science rather than its application. On the other hand, in addition to agricultural chemists attached to the Provincial Departments, this Conference is definitely of opinion that a strong central body of chemists should be maintained by the Imperial Department of Agriculture from whom Provincial Departments could draw for the investigation of special problems."

The main objection taken was, it will be observed, based on the idea that men would usually be transferred after 5-year periods. We have explained already that such an idea forms no part of the system which we contemplate. It is also significant that the same resolution declared the necessity of a strong central body of chemists for the department of agriculture; and it may be added, the same meeting pointed out the desirability of equipping the agricultural research organisation to deal with certain industrial problems arising out of agricultural research. The sum of these conclusions seems to point to the desirability of supplying some agency which can correlate chemical research with agricultural and industrial problems, and of avoiding the needless expense of creating separate research nuclei for dealing with each separate class of chemical problems.

A conference of chemists was convened in Lahore in January 1918 by the Indian Munitions Board. It included not only Government officers, but also chemists attached to missionary colleges and employed under private firms. The Conference passed no formal resolution, but strongly supported the proposed system of scientific services.

THE INDUSTRIAL SERVICE

31. The position in respect of the proposed industrial service is somewhat different. In the first place, there are few, if any, existing officers, who correspond to the class of men whom it is proposed to recruit into the industrial service. In the second place, the question is here not of a science, but of a group of professions, among which that of mechanical engineering and its various specialised forms greatly predominates. The advantages to be derived from an expert central agency do not exist in the case of an industrial service to the same extent as in that of a scientific one; though the proposed central institutes of technical research will no doubt be of help to industrial officers of all classes. The advantages claimed for the proposal are mainly administrative, and will be best perceived by an examination of the disadvantages of any alternative system. The officers filling the higher posts must possess administrative capacity and business qualifications, built up on a basis of technical knowledge. These necessary qualifications can only be obtained by training and experience in the lower ranks of the service, where the work will be mainly technical, but where there will be ample opportunities for the acquisition of business and administrative experience.

The alternatives to a service are, the engagement of men on short-time contracts, or the creation of a number of separate appointments; unconnected, unless possibly in small provincial departments of, at the most, half a dozen officers. In the case of the first system, though it is appropriate enough to engage highly qualified men on short-time contracts for specific enquiries, or other isolated pieces of work, it is clearly unwise to offer such terms to men who are to be engaged on duties which involve the application of a progressive and consistent policy over a long period, and the existence of close acquaintance and personal confidence between the public and Government officials. The first two or three years of an officer's career are spent in making himself familiar with local conditions; if he departs at the end of a five-year agreement, Government loses a trained man and has to replace him by an untrained successor. With regard to the second course, we can state definitely from experience of applications for employment already received, that the best candidates greatly prefer an all-India service to a system of isolated posts. Such a system will labour under most of the administrative disadvantages which, we have already pointed out, attend the employment of isolated scientific officers. It will, in fact, practically mean a perpetuation of the admittedly unsatisfactory ad interim scheme proposed by the Commission, under which men will have to be sought wherever they may be found, with many probable failures; and it will be very much more expensive than a service, since, in the absence of settled prospects members of the industrial department, unless retained by very high salaries, will be continually tempted to take up private employment. The institution of an industrial service seems to us also the best, if not the only means of training Indians of the right type to fill the higher industrial posts, whereas the alternative system of employing temporary experts must necessarily perpetuate the employment of Europeans.

The Government of the United Provinces dissent from the Commission's proposals, which are, however, accepted by all other Local Governments, notably by that of Madras, whose comparatively advanced experience in the actual working of a department of industries renders their opinion of special value, and by that of Burma, subject to the proviso, which they apply also to the case of the chemical service, that Indian members of such services should not be posted to Burma.

32. The arguments given by the Commission for the constitution of an all-India industrial service will be found in paragraph 330-334 of their report; and those arguments have our concurrence, except that, though we agree that a training in some form of mechanical engineering will be in most cases the best basis of recruitment, we should not make this the absolute rule. We think it may prove convenient to include in some cases men with other technical qualifications, who cannot appropriately be engaged on short-term contracts, but may possess or acquire business or administrative aptitude that may fit them for higher promotion. We also contemplate the neces-

sity of engaging consulting experts on short-term agreements for definite pieces of special work. The position of members of the industrial service employed under Local Governments should be in our opinion as nearly as possible analogous with that already suggested by us for members of the chemical service.

We do not desire to formulate the conditions of the industrial service, untill we have discussed the matter with Local Governments and received their proposals for their provincial establishments. By that time we hope to be in possession of the recommendations of the committee on the chemical service, which will doubtless afford a useful analogy. We wish, however, meanwhile to be in a position to offer and to allow Local Governments to offer the prospects of suitable posts in the future industrial service to recruits, most of whom will have, as recognised by the Commission, to be brought in at first on special terms; the engagement of such men will, it is presumed, be as a rule subject to some probationary period, by the expiry of which we hope to be in a position to include in the industrial service those of them who prove satisfactory.

AGENCY FOR THE PURCHASE AND INSPECTION OF STORES IN INDIA

33. The remaining point, viz. the purchase of stores in India, may be more briefly dealt with.

The present system under which the only specific organisation for the purchase of stores required for the use of Government is situated in London, has long been the subject of serious criticism both by politicians and by business men in this country. It is alleged, and not without reason, that this system discourages the purchase of Government stores manufactured in India and thus tends to perpetuate itself by withdrawing an important form of stimulus from nascent industries. We agree that this is not the spirit or intention of the rules, which give considerable scope for the purchase of Indian made articles. But in actual practice the absence of an expert buying and inspecting agency in India makes indenting officers unwilling to take the responsibility for the purchase of locally made articles, and inevitably leads to their placing their orders with the only Government agency properly equipped for purchase and inspection, viz. the

Stores Department of the India Office. A departure from this system is urgently and universally demanded; and its continuance would be looked on as an instance of the alleged economic selfishness of the British nation who, it will be said, are prepared to give away political concessions, but to part with nothing that touches their pockets.

The history of the past three years has shown some unexpected capabilities of India for local manufacture, even in the face of the lack of expert workers and of essential plant arising out of war conditions; it has also shown the beneficial effect of Government purchase and inspection in encouraging Indian industries and inducing them to improve their methods and strike out fresh lines. A rough and ready system of purchase and inspection by expert officers, so far as these were available, was created, and will serve as a useful guide in working out the details of the future system which the Commission propose. Several provincial Governments, in particular those of Burma and the United Province, have pressed for a considerable degree of independence in respect of the purchase of stores. The former Government, indeed, ask for complete freedom from any control by the central Stores Department in India in respect of their power of purchase of Government stores for provincial use, and liberty to deal direct with the purchasing agency of any other Local Government. We doubt whether Local Governments in the absence of actual experience in these matters, fully realise the waste of money that is bound to result from a system of isolated purchases by separate and therefore competing Government agencies without expert market knowledge; and the absolute necessity of an expert and specialised inspecting agency, not only for finished articles, but in many important cases, for raw material and processes of manufacture. At the same time we fully appreciate the desire of Local Governments to encourage, as far as possible, their own local industries, and the necessity for the greatest degree of decentralisation that is practicable and economically safe, in this as in other matters. Some system of compromise is necessary; but the ultimate decision must depend largely on the relative extent of imperial and provincial demands for the different classes of articles, and of their production in the different provinces. We trust we may receive your approval of the general principle of purchasing and inspecting agency in India for goods manufactured in India, when we propose at once to appoint a committee to work out a detailed scheme.

You will doubtless, when the probable effect of the new system has become apparent, consider the desirability of a reduction of the staff of the Stores Department of the India Office; and we shall probably also address you at a later stage regarding the desirability of including members of the technical personnel of some of our consuming departments in that staff.

COLLECTION OF COMMERCIAL AND INDUSTRIAL INTELLIGENCE

34. In our letter No.589-D to Local Governments, dated 7th December 1918, we consulted them regarding the Commission's scheme for the collation and dissemination of commercial and industrial intelligences, which had a certain bearing on the important question of the relation of the central and provincial departments. No Local Government raises any objection to the scheme; but we do not put it forward for your approval at this stage, since it is not of the same importance or urgency as the four matters already dealt with; and we have not yet decided finally on the structure of the proposed agency, nor as to the department which should control it.

CONCLUSION

35. We cannot conclude without placing on record our appreciation of the very thorough treatment accorded by the Commission to the difficult and highly technical subjects dealt with in their report. Many of them fall entirely outside the range of ordinary official work, and could not have been discussed save by persons with special qualifications and experience, who had made a prolonged and careful study of the subject. We esteem ourselves fortunate in having been able to secure the services of gentlemen with an extensive range of Indian business experience, who were ready to devote much valuable time to the work, and have brought into the enquiry a wholly fresh atmosphere. We think that the labours of the Commission have resulted in well considered and practical proposals for an active industrial policy, for which the report abundantly proves the necessity.

36. Our proposals for the present are, shortly:-

(1) that your approval in principle be accorded to the proposed

provincial departments of industries, on the general lines set forth by the Industrial Commission, but subject to further consideration in respect of details and to sanction in respect of particular proposals, whether by yourself or by the Government of India, that may be required;

(2) that your approval in principle be accorded to the proposed Imperial Department of Industries on the general lines set forth in this despatch, subject to the submission of detailed proposals later on. The relations of the Imperial and Provincial Departments of Industries should be on the lines indicated in this despatch;

(3) that for the present, and until a vacancy occurs or is created in our Council, the development of the scheme be made over to the Indian Munitions Board, modified as may appear necessary, and placed under the direct control of His Excellency the Viceroy;

(4) that your approval in principle be accorded to the creation of all-India scientific services, and of an all-India industrial service; of an organisation for the purchase and inspections of stores in India; of the appointment of a committee to consider the lines on which an all-India chemical service should be constituted; and of a Committee to work out the detailed organisation for an Indian Stores Department.

37. Nearly all the most important recommendations of the Commission depend on the main principles to which we request your approval in this despatch. There are, however, certain proposals which can be taken up independently, and with these we are proceeding as rapidly as possible. The statement appended (Annexure 5) will show the extent to which action has already been taken, either while the Commission were sitting or since their report has been received.

We have the honour to be,

Sir,

Your most obedient, humble Servants,

CHELMSFORD.
C. C. MONRO.
C. SANKARAN NAIR.
G. R. LOWNDES.
W. H. VINCENT.
T. H. HOLLAND.
R. A. MANT.
H. F. HOWARD.

APPENDIX 'B'

Government of India, Department of Commerce and Industry, Industries, A. Proceedings, June 1919, Nos. 7-22 (Confidential)

VIEWS OF THE GOVERNMENT OF INDIA ON THE MAIN PRINCIPLES ON WHICH THE MOST IMPORTANT RECOMMENDATIONS OF THE INDIAN INDUSTRIAL COMMISSION DEPEND.

CONFIDENTIAL

No.1.

No. 51 OF 1915.
GOVERNMENT OF INDIA.

DEPARTMENT OF COMMERCE AND INDUSTRY

INDUSTRIES

To

THE RIGHT HONOURABLE AUSTEN CHAMBERLAIN

His Majesty's Secretary of State for India.
Delhi, the 26th November 1915.

Sir,

We desire to place before you certain proposals on the subject of the policy which should be pursued by the Government of India in respect of the State encouragement of industries. There are many reasons why we feel it necessary at this juncture to bring to your notice our views on this important question, which has now for some time been receiving our earnest consideration. It is becoming increasingly clear that a definite and self-conscious policy of improving the industrial capabilities of India will have to be pursued after the war, unless she is to become more and more a dumping ground for the manufactures of foreign nations who will be competing the more keenly for markets, the more it becomes apparent that the political future of the larger nations depends on their economic position.

2. The attitude of the Indian public towards this important question is unanimous, and cannot be left out of account. Manufacturers, politicians, and the literate public have for long been pressing their demands for a definite and accepted policy of State-aid to Indian industries: and the demand is one which evokes the sympathy of all classes of Indians whose position or intelligence leads them to take any degree of interest in such matters. As far back as 1906, the opponents of the partition of Bengal found a rallying cry that united all sections of the community in the word "Swadeshi" which summed up the universal desire to see India a manufacturing country as well as a mere exporter of raw materials, and experessed the duty which lay on every patriotic Indian to help on the consummation of this end, whether as a consumer or as an investor.

3. Although this movement was a failure, owing to the lack of technical knowledge and business aptitude on the part of its leading participants, the desire which gave birth to it has been no way diminished. The people have recognised their inability to carry out their programme without the help and guidance to Government and confine themselves for the most part to pressing their demands for assistance from the State, and for a policy of tariff discrimination against foreign imports. Public sentiment has again and again expressed itself in the form of resolutions and questions in the Imperial and Provincial Councils, of resolutions in the Indian National Congress and at Public meetings, and of articles in the Press. In Bombay particularly, where Indian commercial opinion is relatively more highly educated and has been stimulated to greater keenness by foreign competition, the movement in the direction of enlisting Government sympathy in an active propaganda of industrial expansion has been most marked for some years past. This movement which has acquired considerable political significance in India generally has followed two particular lines of expression. In the first place, there is the constant asseveration that the British Government in India have with malice intent or, if not with malice, by their attitude of indifference, allowed indigenous industries to be overwhelmed by foreign and especially by British competition. The

second charge is that the British system of education has confined the energies of educated young men to literary pursuits and the learned professions and has created among them a demand for employment limited to Government service, the law and medicine. It is to the overcrowding of these avenues of employment that much discontent and unrest are attributable. These contentions emphasise one aspect of the need for an industrial policy which will enable technical education in India to produce its best results and which will lighten the pressure on purely literary courses and reduce the excessive demand for employment in the services and callings to which these courses lead up.

4. Finally, we would draw attention to the special conditions created by the war. The prohibition of imports from enemy countries during the war has been generally welcomed as offering an opportunity for the replacement of the manufactures of these countries by articles produced in India, in spite of the difficulties which must occur at such a time as the present when capital is timid and skilled industrialists are lacking. After the war India will consider herself entitled to demand the utmost help which her Government can afford to enable her to take her place, so far as circumstances permit, as a manufacturing country. This desire, if thwarted, will certainly turn, and already shows signs of turning, into an insistent request for a tariff penalising the import of all articles from abroad, whether British or foreign; and the demand for fiscal protection will inevitably be intensified and will become increasingly difficult for Government to rebut without laying itself open to the charge of neglecting Indian interests, unless it is able to put forward an alternative policy for the promotion and development of industries in this country.

5. In view of these facts, we have been led to a careful examination of the facilities which we possess for attempting the policy demanded of us. We find that though isolated attempts have been made by some Local Governments to aid indigenous industries they have not attained any marked degree of success, owing to lack of technical equipment, of co-ordination, and most important of all, of any general guiding principles. The question of such a policy has never been considered for India as a whole: and the Government of India have consequently had to deal with the industrial proposals of Local

Governments without any general principle to guide them, without any accepted experience or authoritative advice on which to rely, and with feeling that they were to a large extent debarred from accepting certain classes of proposals, which the history of industrial progress in this and other countries has shown to contain some promise of success.

6. The greatest industry in India is and will for long be, that of agriculture. We may, then, perhaps refer to our agricultural policy for an analogy to help us in the discussion of the present question. Here we see that in spite of the numerous failures that had to be recorded before the isolated efforts of Local Governments were coordinated by a generally accepted policy, which involved the external employment of expert assistance, the Departments of Agriculture under Local Governments are now pursuing, with varying degrees of efficiency, but on the whole with remarkable success, the lines laid down for them some ten years ago. The need for a considered central policy is, in some respects, more urgent in the case of the manufacturing industries than in that of agriculture. So far as agriculture is concerned, it is unnecessary for us to take into account either the competition of Government farms with private producers or the competition of local areas inter se. With regard to industries, on the other hand, account must be taken not only of the competition with private enterprise, but also of competition with similar industrial pioneering efforts in other parts of India. Without such coordination, two industries might find themselves forced into close competition with disastrous results to either or both. These, then, are the general postulates of such a policy as we propose: and if these are duly fulfilled, we may entertain good hopes that the development of a general policy of State-aid to the manufacturing industries in this country, though the difficulties are undoubtedly greater than in the case of agriculture, may be attended with better results than have been attained by the somewhat haphazard methods hitherto pursued. In order to give some idea of the difficulties experienced by the Government of India in their attempts to frame a policy, we will proceed briefly to describe the steps which have hitherto been taken in that direction.

7. These steps have hitherto been along one or other of the following lines:-

(a) Technical and industrial education.
(b) Instruction and advice.
(c) Financial assistance to new and nascent industries.
(d) Demonstration factories.

8. (a) **Technical and industrial education** :- Though this subject is important and is perhaps the one line in which any approach has been made to a definite policy, it cannot be said that it has had any marked effect on the development of Indian industries. The various forms of technical education, whether of the nature of workshops, industrial schools, technical colleges or institutes, have, in some cases, produced artisans; in the case of Bombay, where Indian industrial development had already made considerable progress, they have evolved men, who, after a few years' work in existing factories, have become successful engineers, weaving and spinning masters and even factory managers; but even in Bombay there is no instance in which they have created or appreciably extended an industry. It was at one time undoubtedly expected that they would bring this about, apparently on the mistaken analogy of Japan. where, however, the first step taken towards State industrial aid was by starting demonstration factories under European control. Technical institutes, we understand, were not set up there till after these factories had been in progress for some time.

(b) **Instruction and advice** : In the United Provinces a sugar engineer has been appointed to assist an industry of considerable importance; it has, however, since proved necessary to erect a small experimental sugar factory to work out certain problems and bring the results to the notice of the public. The insufficiency of mere technical advice without some form of demonstration has here been clearly felt. In Madras the "Pumping and Boring" Department has worked successfully as an advising agency. The advantages of irrigation being fully recognised by the people, the Pumping and Boring Department has been in a position to help in the introduction of the most suitable type of pumping plant, and to inspect it and keep it in order afterwards until an indigenous agency was evolved. It extended its functions to the provisions of power plant for rice hulling, flour milling, and other forms of industry, all of them, be it noted, on a small scale. It must be remembered, however, that all these industries had already been accepted as commercial possibilities, and the need for demonstration was thus very small. A few experts in various lines, such as handloom, weaving, dyeing and tanning, have been appointed in several provinces, mainly with a view to the improvement of cottage industries. Assistance of a similar kind for purely agricultural objects, such as well-boring, and cotton-ginning with a view to seed production, have been carried out in Bombay, the United Provinces and the Central Provinces, and this form of assistance to industries is now generally recognised and approved. As has already been indicated, its scope is distinctly limited for it is a datum of industrial development in this country that Indian capital, outside the highly modernised community of Bombay, is timid and uneducated, and will not venture on what it has seen with its own eyes as an actual working success.

(c) **Financial assistance to new or nascent industries.** : The following cases only have come under the notice of the Government of India:

(1) A small loan free of interest to a dairy in Shillong, given in 1900.

(2) The grant of Rs. 30,000 to an Indian sugar manufacturer in 1912 to enable him, with the assistance of the Government sugar expert, to remodel a badly designed factory.

(3) A loan of 7 lakhs to a firm of European planters at Babhnauli to start a sugar factory on modern lines.

(4) A loan of Rs. 37,500 to an oil mill at Cawnpore to enable it to modernise its plant.

In the second and third cases, the condition was imposed that advice of the Government Expert should be followed in the purchase and erection of the plant, and the factory should always be open for inspection by persons interested in the industry.

There may be other cases in which Local Governments, under the financial powers possessed by them, have taken similar action, but such cases have naturally not come to the notice of the Government of India, and there is reason to believe that they must, in any case, be few and unimportant.

In passing orders on the proposals for these loans or subventions, we have always found ourselves confronted by the following difficulties. We had no accepted policy, and no technical advice to guide us, nor had we any information available regarding the degree of success attained by similar measures in the past. Similarly, the recommendations of the Local Government do not seem to have been based on any general principles. This defect is especially dangerous in the case of proposals for financial assistance by way of loans where the grant of one request is certain to lead to others which it becomes difficult to refuse without creating a suspicion of unfair treatment. The whole question requires careful examination with a view to discovering the lines on which such assistance can best be given, under what conditions and within what limits.

(d) **Demonstration factories** : The first attempt to organise a pioneer industry was the development of aluminium hollow-ware manufacture by the Madras School of Arts. This was begun in the year 1898, and in 1903 the business was sold to the Indian Aluminium Company, an imitator and rival, for Rs. 2,09,600. The School of Arts never actually showed a profit on its aluminium work, as surpluses were mostly spent on experiments; but the Indian Aluminium Company thought, and thought rightly, that the manufacture of aluminium hollow-ware had been shown to be a profitable venture. The Company, though it has several imitators, small and large, in various parts of India, is now making a profit, which sometimes exceeds, and seldom falls short of 10 per cent. It pays a monthly wage bill of Rs. 5,000; and in addition to its European Business Manager employs an Indian works manager, a B.E. of the Madras Engineering College, on Rs. 500 a month and commission. The benefit to the country generally from the demonstration of this particular industry has been appreciable; and the foreign aluminium producer, who could with difficulty have imported his light and bulky manufactured ware to compete with locally manufactured brass and copper, sold Rs. 25.51 lakhs worth, or 35,809 cwts. of aluminium to India in the year 1912-13, against Rs. 1.05 lakhs, or 890 cwts., in 1904-05. Before the Madras School of Arts took up the business, the import was infinitesimal.

Prior to the experiments undertaken in Madras by Government, chrometanning was always thought impossible under Indian climatic conditions. The process was started in Madras on a commercial scale; and in 1910, after 7-1/2 years' working, the factory was sold. The results of working were as follows:-

		Rs.
Capital Cost		69,596
Cost of Working		4,86,814
	Total	5,56,410
Receipts		4,04,780
Sale of factory and stock		96,272
	Total	5,01,052

Objections were lodged by private traders on the ground that the State was competing with private interests and operations, in consequence, were gradually restricted with injurious effects on profits, and ultimately the factory was sold. But Mr. Chatterton, who was responsible for the working of this as well as of the aluminium factory, claims that, at a cost of Rs. 55,000, the practicability of chrome-tanning in India has been proved and a large and flourishing industry rendered possible. The lead thus given by Madras was followed by the United Provinces Government whose demonstration chrome leather factory is mentioned in the eleventh paragraph of this despatch. Private chrome-factories are now in existence in Cawnpore, Calcutta, Cuttack and Bangalore.

After the war started, the Madras Industrial Department considèred the idea of taking over and managing a glass works in Madras, a paper works, a pencil factory and a match factory, on an experimental basis, and it is understood that the pencil factory has started working and that some progress has been made with the other proposals, but nothing is known as to the terms on which these factories are being taken over. The Director of Industries is also arranging to set up an oil-expelling plant. No definite degree of success can, it is understood, be claimed as yet in respect of any of these ventures. A grant of 2 lakhs was assigned by the Madras Government for these and other purposes.

Certain steps have been taken by the United Provinces in respect of pioneering new industries which are worthy of note. In view of the opening which appeared to exist for the manufacture of cottonseed oil in India, Sir J. Hewett decided to start a factory for the purpose of experimenting in, and demonstrating the possibility of, this process which was at that time thought to present special difficulties in view of the peculiarities of Indian cotton seeds. The United Provinces Government accordingly set up a cotton seed oil factory at Cawnpore at a cost of Rs. 55,000. The mill was run by Messrs. Begg, Sutherland on a monthly remuneration, on the condition that all losses should be recouped by Government. The seed was pressed undecorticated and the cake did not find a ready market. The Local Government closed down the venture in 1911, in consequence, we understand, of certain orders of the Secretary of State which will be alluded to below. No official reference on the subject was made to the Government of India. There are now in India two fairly large and successful cottonseed oil mills financed by Indian capital which were started, it is stated, largely as as result of this demonstration factory.

9. The establishment of pioneer factories was not approved by Lord Morley; and a discussion took place between the Government of India and your predecessors, the history of which will be given in greater detail below when we come to consider the causes which have led to our present difficulties. It must be admitted also that criticism has not been wanting in India itself of the policy of pioneer factories. There is always the temptation on the part of an enthusiast to extend operations in the hope that this may turn a deficit into a credit balance, forgetting that the larger the operations of the factory, the greater are often the difficulties in ultimately disposing of it and the greater the probability that private traders will protest against its extending activities. The retail boot and shoe business, attached to the Madras chrome leather factory in the hope of enabling it to show a profit, caused an amount of ill feeling in commercial circles quite disproportionate to the modest additional gain brought by it to the financial side of the undertaking. If again, the concern proves successful, objections are often raised by the official manager to bringing the venture to its logical conclusion and handing it over

to private enterprise. Moreover, dissatisfaction has been freely expressed at the fact that, though the primary object of a pioneer factory is to show that a particular industry is financially profitable when conducted on a commercial scale and on business lines, the accounts are seldom presented in a way that commands the confidence of business men. It is clear then that though undoubted success has been obtained by pioneer factories in certain instances, there is a considerable element of doubt whether the degree of success has been sufficient to warrant the acceptance of the principle of State demonstration of industries on a commercial scale, and, if accepted, what are the circumstances under which it should be adopted and the conditions, under which it should be carried on. Here, too, we feel ourselves in need of disinterested and skilled advice based on a thorough consideration of such local data as are available, and of the experience of other countries where a similar policy has been tried.

10. We have hitherto assumed that it is open to the Government of India to attempt all or any of the methods above described, and we have enlarged only on the difficulty that we felt in deciding which of them is the most promising and what are the conditions under which it can most suitably be brought into operation. We shall proceed, as we have already indicated, to put forward proposals in this despatch for an enquiry by a Committee of qualified experts and business men into these questions. But before doing so, we must solicit your assistance in the removal, at any rate provisionally, of a preliminary obstacle. In order to explain the nature of this obstacle, it is necessary for us to recount, in some detail, the history of the discussion which took place between the Government of India and Lords Morley and Crewe between the years 1909 and 1912 on the subject of direct State-aid to industries.

11. The first expression of opinion by the Secretary of State on the policy of Government pioneer factories is to be found in Lord Morley's despatch No. 110-Public, dated the 30th July 1909. The proposal was nominally for a "chrome leather tanning" school in the United Provinces to which a school for teaching boot and shoemaking with improved tools would be attached. This was evidently of the nature of a pioneer factory for the United Provinces Government spoke of the possibility of "selling it to private capitalists" later on and described the articles it would manufacture. The fact that the

demand for chrome leather for agricultural purposes would have to be worked up was given as a reason why Government should undertake the enterprise. Lord Morley raised no objection. His despatch states: "The chrome leather tanning school and boot and shoe factory is said to be the only branch of industry which the Lieutenant-Governor at present desires to pioneer. It also follows lines already developed in Madras, and is intended to furnish agriculturists with improved waterbags and buckets; and if the experiment proves successful there would, it is stated, be no difficulty in selling the business to private capitalists. The proposed carpentry school at Bareilly is intended to develop an existing industry; and the engagement of a button maker to be attached to the Lucknow Industrial School requires no special justification.

"All these branches of the scheme appear to me to be useful and promising experiments, and I shall have no difficulty in agreeing to their being undertaken whenever the Lieutenant-Governor is in a position to provide the necessary funds. While I recognise fully the necessity of giving a fair trial to any schemes of industrial development which local responsible opinion considers useful, I would also lay stress on the necessity for the prompt abandonment of an experiment which is failing, and for incurring as small an initial expenditure on buildings as is compatible with an adequate trial of the scheme."

Lord Morley appears to have changed his ground, however, when on being confronted with the larger Madras proposals, he realised the extent of the policy to which he was being asked to commit himself. The proposals of Madras, which were throughout merely general in nature in favour of pioneering industries, are found in paragraph 6 of Madras letter No. 4291-A.-08-1, dated the 3rd March 1909. "On the general and cardinal question whether State intervention is desirable or necessary in fostering industrial development in a country in which private industrial effort has hitherto been either spasmodic or practically non-existent, the opinion of so representative a body as that which assembled at the recent Conference is entitled to great weight. Resolution No. 5 of the Conference which relates to this matter represents the opinion of 35 out of the 38 gentlemen who composed the Conference. This Resolution lays down that, subject to the restrictions therein specified, the Government may undertake, as a pioneer, the introduction of new industries or industrial processes for the purpose of training students or apprentices or for demonstrating that such industries will be commercially successful. His Excellency in Council is in entire agreement with the position taken up in this Resolution and he believes that when Government action is so directed, private enterprise has nothing to fear, while it may have much to gain, from the association of the State in the work of promoting industrial development. His Excellency in Council has accordingly approved the recommendations of the Conference (Resolution No. 1) that there should be a special department under a special officer to deal with industrial questions and (Resolution No. 3) that this officer should be styled the Director of Industries. He considers also that to this officer should be entrusted the control of industrial instruction as defined in the 14th Resolution of the Conference, that is, instruction in the performance of definite operations not necessarily involving the teaching of general principles, but only of their applications. Technical education as defined in the 13th Resolution of the Conference will continue to be in the charge of the Director of Public Instruction."

Lord Morley in Reply (Rev. No. 50, dated the 29th July 1910, paragraphs 6 and 7) expressed himself strongly against the proposal. "I have examined the account which the Madras Government have given of the attempts to create new industries in the Province. The results represent considerable labour and ingenuity, but they are not of a character to remove my doubts as to the utility of State effort in this direction, unless it is strictly limited to industrial instruction and avoids the semblance of a commercial venture. So limited, interference with private enterprise is avoided, while there still remains an ample and well defined sphere of activity. The limit disregarded, there is the danger that the new State industry will either remain a petty and ineffective plaything, or will become a costly and hazardous speculation. I sympathise with the Conference and the Madras Government in their anxiety for the industrial development of the province but I think that it is more likely to be retarded than promoted by the diversion to State-managed commercial enterprises of funds which are urgently required for the extension of industrial and technical instruction.

"The policy which I am prepared to sanction is that State funds may be expended upon familiarising the people with such improvements in the method of production as modern science and the practice of European countries can suggest; further than this the State should not go and it must be left to private enterprise to demonstrate that these improvements can be adopted with commercial advantage. Within the limits here indicated it appears to me that the objects which the Industrial Conference had in view can all be accomplished by means of technical and industrial schools; it is in such schools that a knowledge of new industries and new processes can be imparted, that the use of new implements can best be taught, and the technical skill of the artisans most readily improved. In a leather school the method of chrome tanning can be demonstrated and taught; in a weaving school the indigenous hand-loom can be improved and the advantage of the improvement demonstrated. If the schools are properly managed they will supply the private capitalist with instructed workmen and with all the information he requires for a commercial venture. To convert the leather or weaving school into a Government factory in order to demonstrate that articles can be manufactured and sold to the public at a profit goes, in my view, beyond what is desirable and beyond what is found necessary in other provinces. My objections do not extend to the establishment of a bureau of industrial information, or to the dissemination from such a centre of intelligence and advice regarding new industries, processes, or appliances, provided that nothing is done calculated to interfere with private enterprise.

"I have not overlooked certain remarks in my Public despatch No. 110, dated 30th July 1909, which might be read as assenting to schemes for pioneering new industries in the United Provinces. I understand that no steps have been taken in that province in this direction, and I desire that in it and in other provinces the instructions of this despatch may be observed."

We now have to see to what extent the policy laid down in Lord Morley's despatch has been modified. In his despatch No. 24-Revenue, dated the 15th March 1912 Lord Crewe seems to have diverged somewhat materially from Lord Morley's original line. "The creation of a separate Department of Industries in the Madras Presidency must turn on the question of the functions proposed to be assigned to it. As regards the latter, I must re-affirm my predecessor's decision against the extension of its activities to trading on commercial lines. I have no doubts as to the wisdom of that decision. At the same time I desire to point out that the Government of Madras appear to have placed too limited a construction upon the orders given in my predecessor's despatch of 20th July 1910. The policy which he then sanctioned was that State funds might be expended upon familiarising the people with such improvements in the methods of production as modern science and the practice of European countries could suggest. This need not be interpreted as confining instruction sulkily to industrial schools. I am prepared to recognise that in certain cases instruction in industrial schools may be insufficient and may require to be supplemented by practical training in workshops where the application of new processes may be demonstrated; and there is no objection to the purchase and maintenance of experimental plant fcr the purpose of demonstrating the advantages of improved machinery or new processes and for as certaining the data of production. I have, for example, in view the experiment which the Government of the United Provinces is now carrying on with a small sugar plant. Such an experiment does not exceed the limits within which the Government of Madras may promote the industrial development of the Presidency."

While objecting to 'trading on commercial lines', Lord Crewe's despatch admitted the desirability of workshops for training, fitted with experimental plant, where the data of production might be ascertained. Presumably the workshops would have to dispose of their products: and the distinction between the industrial workshop approved of by Lord Crewe and the pioneer factory condemned by Lord Morley seems to be that the primary object of a pioneer factory is to show that a manufacture can be carried on at a commercial profit, and its secondary one is to train workers: while a workshop of the type above described has education for its primary object, while experiment in the possibility of commercial production is a consequence rather than an object of its operations. Lord Crewe stated in addition that he was prepared to sanction the constitution of a Department of Industries on the lines laid down by Dr. Morris Travers, which are reproduced in the Madras Government order of the 1st April 1914 cited below.

The Madras Government, after some preliminary correspondence, accepted these dicta and put forward a series of conditions under which Government demonstrative workshops might safely be started. These conditions, which the Government of India recommended for acceptance by the Secretary of State, were as follows:-

1. that no such undertaking shall be engaged in without prior consultation with an Advisory Board representing both Indian interests and the leading commercial and trading industries in the Presidency;

2. that no such undertaking for the purpose of demonstrating the commercial value of any process shall be engaged in unless enquiry has shown that no private capitalist is willing to enter upon it;

3. that the fullest publicity shall be given to the details of the working of any such undertakings; and

4. that the Government shall withdraw from any undertaking entered upon in order to demonstrate the commercial advantages of any process as soon as such advantages have been demonstrated.

After the limitations suggested by Lord Crewe had been accepted by the Madras Government, they reconstituted their Industrial Department which is now being conducted on the following lines (Madras Government Order No. 368, dated 1st April 1914).

"The functions of the Director of Industries will be:

i. to collect information as to existing industries, their needs and the possibility of improving them or of introducing new industries;
ii. to carry out and direct experiments connected with such enquiries;
iii. to keep in touch with local manufacturers, to bring the results of his experiments to their notice and to obtain their notice and to obtain their co-operation in the conduct of operations on a commercial scale;
iv. to supervise the training of students; and

v. to advise Government with regard to technical matters involving legislation."

The question of pioneer factories was again taken up in connection with the proposals of the Government of Eastern Bengal and Assam for a technical institute at Dacca, and in their Finance Department despatch No. 252, dated the 26th October 1911, paragraph 6, regarding the above proposals, the Government of India explained their attitude in the following terms:-

"Difficult questions arise in connection with demonstration factories at the Central Institute and the establishment of pioneer factories. We have already, in our Financial despatch No. 227, dated the 21st September 1911, on the Madras industrial scheme, indicated to Your Lordship our views upon the general question, and have indicated the conditions under which we recommend the establishment of such institutions experimentally in view of the great difficulty experienced in India in getting practical training. We need only add that these factories, if instituted and maintained on a sufficiently small scale, will aim at demonstration rather than at commercial enterprise. And, if lessees can be found, the institutions might, at an early stage, be handed over on lease for a term of years." The Secretary of State in his despatch No. 12-Public, dated the 19th January 1912, did not attempt any criticism of the scheme but asked for its reconsideration in view of the redistribution of the Bengal Provinces.

12. Except so far as indicated in the above correspondence, both the Local Governments concerned and the Government of India have abstained from putting forward any proposals of a nature which appeared to contravene the orders in Lord Morley's despatch of 1910. The result has been a distinct setback to the progress which had up to that point been achieved in Madras, and a considerable modification of the scheme for a Department of Industries which has since been accepted for the United Provinces. The main lines of Lord Morley's despatch became known to the Indian public and have frequently formed the subject of protest and of adverse criticism. The view was often expressed, however unfairly, that the veto formed part of the plan of stifling Indian industrial development, which is often made a charge against the British Government in India. Lord

Crewe's despatch of 1912, while it went some way towards relieving us of the disabilities imposed by Lord Morley, still leaves the Government of India in a considerable degree of doubt as to the precise lengths to which they are justified in going when dealing with proposals for demonstration plants, financial assistance, and other forms of direct aid to industries. In view of the uncertainty in which we find ourselves regarding the extent to which, and the circumstances in which, these as well as other forms of State-aid may profitably be employed, we desire to examine the whole question ab initio with the help of a specially selected Committee. It is necessary, if the investigations of its members are to bear full fruit, to allow them as far as possible an unfettered discretion in respect of the methods of State-aid to industries which they would be at liberty to investigate and recommend. For this reason we would ask that, for the purposes of their investigation, the Committee, if you approve of its appointment, may be permitted to consider, as open to free discussion and examination, all questions of direct State-aid to industries, which do not involve a modification of our existing fiscal policy, and that their enquiry may not be restricted by any rigid interpretation of the rulings laid down in the despatches of Lords Morley and Crewe quoted above. The desirabilitty or otherwise of maintaining these restrictions can then be considered afresh in the light of the Committee's findings which will, we confidently anticipated, form the basis of our future industrial policy.

13. At present, however, we do not desire to ask for more than your approval in principle of the appointment of a Committee, under the conditions explained in the preceding paragraph, composed of a suitable number of officials, business men and experts, some of whom should be acquainted with Indian conditions, some with industrial progress in other countries where similar objects have been pursued, and others with industrial problems generally and their business side. It will, we recognise, be difficult, if not impossible, at the present juncture, to secure a properly constituted Committee of the requisite type, while the disturbance of trade and industry created in India by the war will obscure the conditions which will need to be examined in the field of enquiry itself.

We are on all grounds desirous to proceed as rapidly as possible in laying what we consider the necessary foundation for our future industrial policy by the initiation of a thorough investigation on the lines we have indicated; and we shall, if you approve generally of our proposals, forward our detailed suggestions for the constitution of the proposed Committee and its terms of reference for your sanction as soon as we think circumstances are sufficiently favourable. But we recognise that it is no less important to obtain the best possible men to conduct the enquiry and to ensure that they are in a position to do so under the most favourable conditions, and we therefore anticipate that it will in all probability be impossible for the Committee to begin its work till after the close of the war.

14. We briefly recapitulate our proposals. We have been led to recognise the paramount necessity, both on political and economic grounds, of framing a policy of State-aid to Indian industries. We have been confronted by the difficulty that, although numerous isolated efforts have been made in this direction by Provincial Governments, there is considerable diversity of opinion among those best qualified to form one regarding the value of the different methods which have been suggested or attempted from time to time. The proposed Committee would be the best agency for examining the various kinds of uncoordinated action taken by the several Local Governments and the experiments which they have made, with a view to ascertaining both cause of failure where there has been failure, and the degree of success attained where some success has been reached. We desire therefore your approval to our proposal that a properly qualified Committee should be appointed as soon as circumstances permit, to examine the whole question; and that, in order to enable them to do so to the fullest advantage, they should not be precluded from a consideration of the methods of which disapproval was expressed by Lord Morley and in a lesser degree by Lord Crewe.

We have the honour to be,

SIR,

Your most obedient, humble Servants,

HARDINGE of PENSHURST,
BEAUCHAMP DUFF,

SAIYID ALI IMAM,
W. H. CLARK,
W. S. MEYER,
C. H. A. HILL,
C. SANKARAN NAIR.

No.3403. GOVERNMENT OF INDIA

No. 37

DEPARTMENT OF COMMERCE AND INDUSTRY.

(INDUSTRIES).

RESOLUTION.

Simla, the 19th May 1916.

The Government of India, as announced by Sir William Clark when speaking on Sir Ibrahim Rahimtoola's Resolution in the Legislative Council on 21st March 1916, have decided that the time has come when the question of the expansion and development of Indian manufactures and industries should be taken up in a more comprehensive manner than has hitherto been attempted. India possesses two notably successful manufacturing industries in the two great textile industries of cotton and jute, and there are others which have also reached some degree of importance; but it remains none the less true that she is still in the main a producer of raw materials. The Government of India have strong hopes, however, that it may prove possible to place the industries of this country on a much firmer and more extended basis than at present, and they consider that no means should be left untried which hold out a reasonable hope of effecting this end. They are aware of the eager desire of a large number of the people of India for the industrial development of their country, and with this desire the Government of India fully associate themselves.

The efforts of Government in the past towards this end have disclosed the existence of numerous difficulties. Indian capital is timid and unenterprising; skilled labour is lacking; and there is a want of practical information regarding the commercial potentialities of India's raw products. All these difficulties require full examination by men of technical experience and high business standing. The Government of India have therefore decided to appoint a Commission, some of whose members will be acquainted with Indian conditions, some with industrial progress in other countries where similar objects have been pursued and others with industrial problems generally and their business side in particular. The Government of India are well aware that there are especial difficulties in the way of such an enquiry during war time, but after full consideration it has been decided to appoint the commission at once in order that, when after the close of the war the financial position is once more established on a normal basis, the Government may be able without further delay to take such action as may seem suitable after considering the Commission's recommendations.

2. In framing the terms of reference it has been found necessary to exclude two matters from the scope of the Commission's labours. In the first place, any consideration of the present fiscal policy of the Government of India has been excluded from its enquiries. When introducing the Financial Statement in the Legislative Council, the Honourble Finance Member, it will be remembered, stated, in connection with the question of the cotton duties, that the general fiscal relationship which exists between the various parts of the Empire and other countries must in the opinion of His Majesty's Government be reconsidered after the war, and that in the meantime they wish to postpone any action that would tend to raise such questions. The same considerations apply with even greater force to any proposals involving the imposition of duties for the specific purpose of protecting Indian industries, a policy which would very directly affect the fiscal relations of India with the outside world. In the next place, it is not proposed that the Commission should re-examine those aspects of technical and industrial education which have recently been dealt with by Committees working in England and India whose reports are at present under the consideration of the Government of India.

3. Subject to the above qualifications, the Commission will be instructed to examine and report upon the possibilities of further industrial development in India and to submit its recommendations with special reference to the following questions:-

(a) whether new openings, for the profitable employment of Indian capital in commerce and industry can be indicated;

(b) whether and, if so, in what manner Government can usefully give direct encouragement to industrial development;

(i) by rendering technical advice more freely available;
(ii) by the demonstration of the practical possibility on a commercial scale of particular industries;
(iii) by affording, directly or indirectly, financial assistance to industrial enterprises; or
(iv) by any other means which are not incompatible with the existing fiscal policy of the Government of India.

The Government of India trust that the Commission will find it possible to place their report in the hands of the Government of India within 12 months from the date of its assembling in India.

4. The Commission will consist of the Following gentlemen:-

PRESIDENT.

1. SIR T. H. HOLLAND, D.C.I.E., D.Sc, F.R.S.,President of the Institution of Mining Engineers.

MEMBERS.

2. MR. ALFRED CHATTERTON, C.I.E., B.Sc., A.C.G.I., A.M.I.C.E., M.I.M.E.,
Director of Industries and Commerce in Mysore.

3. THE HON'BLE SIR FAZULBHOY CURRIMBHOY EBRAHIM, KT.,
Messrs. Currimbhoy Ebrahim and Company, Bombay.

4. MR. EDWARD HOPKINSON, M.A., D.Sc.,
Managing Director, Mather and Platt, Manchester, and Deputy Chairman, Chloride Electric Company.

5. THE HON'BLE MR. C. E. LOW, C.I.E., I.C.S.,
Secretary to the Government of India, Department of Commerce and Industry.

6. THE HON'BLE PANDIT MADAN MOHAN MALAVIYA, B.A., LL.B.,
   of Allahabad.

7. SIR RAJENDRA NATH MUKERJI, K.C.I.E.,
   Messrs. Martin and Company, Calcutta.

8. THE RIGHT HON'BLE SIR HORACE CURZON PLUNKETT,
   P.C., D.C.L., LL.D., F.R.S., K.C.V.O.

9. THE HON'BLE MR. F. H. STEWART, C.I.E.,
   President, Bengal Chamber of Commerce.

10. SIR DORABJI JAMSETJI TATA, KT., J.P.,
    Messrs. Tata, Sons and Company, Bombay.
    The Secretary will be appointed later.

ORDERED that a copy of this Resolution be forwarded to all Local Governments and Administrations, with the request that the Commission men be given any assistance which they may require and that any applications for information which may be made by the Commission may be complied with.

ORDERED also that a copy of the Resolution be forwarded to all Departments of the Government of India, to the Director-General of Commercial Intelligence, to the President and Members of the Commission, and that the Resolution be published in the Supplement to the Gazette of India.

C. E. LOW,
Secretary to the Government of India.

REFERENCES

1. Zaidi (ed), *The Encyclopaedia of the Indian National Congress*, Vol. 1, p.428.
2. Ibid., p.45
3. I.O. MSS. Eur. E.243(25), Enc. 2 in Dufferin to Cross, November 17,1888, p.180a.
4. Misra, B.B.,*The Indian Political Parties*, p.72.
5. Ibid., p.47-48.
6. I.O. MSS. Eur (Cross Papers) E.243 (25), p.179b, November 11,1888.
7. Ibid., p.91b.
8. Lansdowne to Cross, June 23,1890, Ibid., p.3.
9. See *Hamilton Collection*, I.O. MSS. Eur. D. 510/2, XIV, 67.
10. Ibid. MSS. Eur. D.510/7, p.160-1. See also Misra, *The Indian Middle Classes*, p.352-53.
11. Cross Papers, I.O. MSS. Eur. E-243 (25), p.177b (November 11, 1888).
12. Zaidi (ed.), op. cit., Vol.1, p.125.
13. Ibid., p.124.
14. Ibid., p.425-6.
15. Lansdowne's Note on the Home Dept. Despatch No. 67 1888, I.O. MSS. Eur. E. 243 (26), p.176(16), May 4,1898.
16. See Misra, B.B., *The Indian Middle Classes* which discusses in some depth the nature of Indian society and the instruments of change conducive to mobility in social space.
17. Enc. 3 in Dufferin to Cross, June 29, 1888, I.O. MSS. Eur. 243 (24), p.12-13.
18. See Misra, *The Indian Political Parties*, p.56.
19. Ibid., p. 258-59.
20. Tilak was a great admirer of Wasudeo Balwant Phadke who believed in violence and had established a secret society where young men were given training in shooting. See Selections from Desp. to India (Public) no. 148 of Dec. 16,1897, and (Education) no. 19 of 1897. See also Dufferin's view in Misra, *The Indian Political Parties*, pp.49-50.
21. See Enc. IV in Dufferin to Cross, Oct. 29,1888, I. O. MSS. Eur. E. 243 (25), pp.150a, 151b, 163b-165b.
22. Gokhale's Speeches, p.698.
23. Ibid., pp.708-9.
24. Minto to Morley, I.O. MSS. Eur. D.573 (21), xv, p.86b.
25. See R. R. Srivastava, *The Speeches of Bal Gangadhar Tilak*, pp.189-93.
26. Ghose was a frontline Liberal politician whom Minto described as "a nice old gentleman", a member of the Viceroy's Legislative Council having "an addiction to drink, which every now and then incapacitated him". See Minto to Morley, June 11,1905, I.O. MSS. D. 573 (16), k,pp. 18-19.
27. See Minto to Morley, March 21, 1907, I.O. MSS. Eur. D. 573, para 2.
28. See B.D. Shukla, *History of the Indian Liberal Party*, p.176-7.
29. I.O. MSS. Eur. AC 22/91 (Feb. 7,1917), para. 3.
30. NAI, Appx. 1 to Home (Pol.) B. Progs., Jan. 1920, K.W. Nos. 283-92.
31. Home (Pol.) B. Progs., May 1916, Nos. 577-80.
32. See Philips (ed), *Selections*, pp.204-5.
33. See *Moral & Material Progress Report*, 1919-20, p.78.
34. See *Census of India*, 1911, Vol. 1. Pt.2, p.332;1921,i,292.
35. See *Report of the Royal Commission on Labour in India*, 1931, p.9.
36. Ibid., pp.6-9.
37. Para 102; see also para 135.
38. See Home (Pol.) B. Progs., April 1920, No. 189.

39. Chamberlain Papers, I.O. MSS. Eur., AC.22/91, para 3.
40. See Horst Kruger, *Har Dayal in Germany*, paper read at XXVI International Congress of Orientalists, 1963, The Indian revolutionaries abroad were earlier functioning from Berlin in the hope that Germany would help them to win freedom against Britain.
41. See Indra Prakash, *A Review of the History and Work of the Hindu Mahasabha and the Hindu Sangathan Movement,* 2nd edn.(1952), p18.
42. 9th Rep. Sel. Com., H.C., 1782-83, p.56a.
43. 6th Rep. Sel Com., H.C. 1782-83, appx. 15, p.943.
44. See Misra, *The Indian Middle Classes*, Part II.
45. pp.7-8. See appendix to this chapter giving a list of managing agents in Bombay in 1927. Muslims did not count for much even in Bombay.
46. Mehta, op.cit., p.311.
47. See Home (Education) A Progs., Nos. 51-58 of July 1885 (Muhammadan Education in British India and their employment in the public service generally), containing Bengal Govt. letter to the Govt. of India dated Oct. 14, 1882.
48. See Home (Education) A Progs., Nos. 37-41, March 1882. The memorial was signed by Mahomed Farrukh Shah, President; Meer Mahomedally, Vice-President; and Ameer Ali, Secretary.
49. See Misra, *The Administrative History of India, 1834-1947;* also see *The Bureaucracy in India: An Historical Analysis of Development up to 1947.*
50 Philips (ed), *Select Documents*, iv, p.191.
51 *Montford Report*, p.56.
52 Philips (ed), *Select Documents,* p.197.
53. See Ibid., p.204-5.
54. See *Report of the Royal Commission on Labour in India,* 1931, Chapter II.
55. See Misra, *The Indian Political Parties*, pp.148-51.
56. See Home (Pol.) Deposit Progs., Aug. 1920, No. 110, pp.13-14. See also *An Indian Communist Manifesto in the Glasgow Socialist*, Ibid., p.2. It was published under the signatures of M.N. Roy, Abani Mukherji and Santidevi.
57. Misra, op. cit., p.171.
58. See Home (Pol) Deposit Progs., Aug. 1920, No. 38.
59. *The Indian Annual Register*, 1919, pp.122-23.
60. *The Collected Works of Mahatma Gandhi*, XV, pp.1-3 (Speech at Surat, Aug.1, 1918).
61. Ibid., p.15.
62. Ibid., p.16.
63. Ibid., p.15 (Letter to Sir Surendra Nath Banerjee, Aug. 10, 1918).
64. See Foreign-Political (External) B. Progs., Nos. 138-142, Oct. 1921 (B. 361).
65. See Home (Pol.) Deposit (Print) Progs., May 1921, No. 43 (The Rowlatt Bill and the Passive Resistance Movement).
66. FICCI, *5 Decades of Progress,* p.18.
67. See Sneh Mahajan, *Imperialist Strategy and Moderate Politics*, Chapter VI.
68. See *Statistical Abstract of British India,* for relevant years.
69. See *Census of India*: 1911, vol. I, pt. 2, p.332; 1921, I, 292.
70. H. Venkatasubbiah, *Enterprise and Economic Change: 50 Years of FICCI*, pp.19-20.
71. Zaidi (ed), *The Foundations of Indian Economic Planning,* pp. 32-36.
72. Ibid., pp. 44-45.
73. Ibid., p. 49-50.
74. *The Collected Works of Gandhi*, Vol. XIII (Publications Division), p. 313.
75. Ibid., p. 222.

76. Ibid.
77. Ibid., p.215.
78. See Appendices A and B to Chapter I on British industrial policy in India.

TWO

The Contradiction of Congress Politico-Economic Policy : 1920-47

To lay down policy direction for the Indian National Congress, an all-India political organization seeking to be recognized as the only alternative to British sovereignty in India, was not a simple task, especially in terms of her plural society where, apart from dominance in the public services and the learned professions, the Hindus had, in the course of the First World War, emerged, along with the Parsis, as a competitive economic force equipped with capital and material resources for potential control over commerce and industrial enterprise. Of the problems that beset the task of policy-making, the presence of imperialism in the country or, in other words, the existence of foreign rule to which her entire economy was directly linked up, was by far the most intricate, involving, as it did, not only political issues, but also socio-economic.

Indeed, broadly speaking, the colonial situation which had since 1834 developed in India under British rule, with the Congress emerging initially as an organized body of collaborators on a limited scale, raised in course of time the problems of politics as a means to control the economy. While the plurality of Indian society led to communal politics which created Pakistan as a separate sphere of Muslim interest, the Indian industrial interest which was in the main Hindu organized itself in the Federation of Indian Chamber of Commerce and Industry in 1927. It influenced the politics of the Congress-majority provinces and, in its fight against the imperialist regime for an over-all control over the Indian economy, collaborated politically with the Congress.

But as the Congress itself was, since the Russian Revolution of 1917, known for heterogeneity in its approach to social and economic policies, its response to the Federation tended naturally to be double-faced, openly talking for the Left, but actually acting for the Right. This was a case of infirmity in policy-making arising, as it did, from nationalism being itself called upon to play the dichotomous roles of an anti-imperialist national movement and a class-based political party. What enabled the Congress to tide over the contradiction of movement-party dichotomy was the generally recognized belief that freedom from colonial rule was a necessary precondition for socialism. The importance of an all-out movement for political freedom thus reduced to subservience the call for an emphasis on defining the goal of the State. This goal, towards the end of this period, was lost sight of in the midst of a mutually acceptable political settlement for the transfer of power in which the business communities, both Indian and European, were immediately interested in operational terms. They favoured a united India not only for the sake of security in the pursuit of a free and joint capitalist enterprise in the sub-continent but also for purposes of defence involving the Indian Ocean area in the interest of the Commonwealth countries. As the bulk of the British capital investment existed at the time in the Congress-majority Provinces, British business and defence considerations both dictated the expediency of a pro-Congress line of policy in terms of a united India, a policy which Sir Claud Auckinleck, Commander-in-Chief, recommended for acceptance by the British Cabinet.[1] His proposals did not materialize. India was divided because of the insistence of the Muslim League. But the thinking of businesses in India was quite understandable.

Congress Politics : 1920-37

The main feature of development during 1920-37 was the beginning of mass involvement in politics arising from political, economic and religious considerations. While the political element, which involved relations with the imperial government, was a common factor leading to the downward filtration of politics with extended franchise in the organization of legislative authority, the economic and religious approaches to public affairs acted antithetically to each other in behavioural terms.

Politically, the British policy announcement of August 20, 1919, was by far the most important event in the immediate background to 1920, which marked the end of one epoch and the beginning of another–an announcement which promised parliamentary government within the framework of British sovereignty as its goal and assigned to the Home Government and the Government of India the responsibility of judging the extent and the manner of each advance towards the attainment of that goal. The Government of India Act (1919) that followed actually provided for responsible government in the provinces and bicameral legislature with elected majority at the Centre. The political system so inaugurated, though much below national expectations, encouraged the formation of political parties with their own Press and other means of propaganda conducive to mass movement.

The non-cooperation and civil disobedience movement which followed in the context of the Amritsar Massacre of 1919 was not the result of any agitation against the reformed constitution of that year, for M. K. Gandhi, who was later responsible for that movement, asked the delegates to the Amritsar Congress, December 1919, to cooperate with the Government and work the constitutional scheme of the 1919 Act which had received the assent of the Crown before the Congress session. And this he did as one of the members of the committee of inquiry set up by the Congress to go into the circumstances leading to the Amritsar atrocities which he knew well.

Even a staunch nationalist leader like B. G. Tilak had, by the end of 1919, turned a "responsive"[2] cooperator, and in a telegram of December 25, 1919, communicated to His Majesty the loyal thanks of his Home Rule Party for the general amnesty granted to those involved in the Punjab disturbance.[3] The Revolutionary Party too had by 1920 become "quiescent".[4] The associations supporting it had practically broken up and become reconciled to political autonomy. There were, in addition, communal parties, both Hindu and Muslim. But these and other religion-based political elements were all acting as barriers to the general recognition of the new economic approach to politics proceeding from the development of indigenous capitalism and international communism. Religion in fact acted as a cover to vested interests.

Pan-Islamic Sentiments of Indian Muslims used by Gandhi to Strengthen Congress

It is clear that the reformed constitution of 1919 gave no cause for Gandhi's non-cooperation movement against the British Government in India. As shown earlier (in chapter I), British economic policy too had started taking Indian industrial interest into active consideration. The cause was therefore his own policy or choice to use the pan-Islamic sentiments of Indian Muslims on the Turkish question to strengthen the Congress which had been waning since the scessionist trends of the Moderates and the Home Rulers. As indicated earlier, he was in his decision also guided perhaps by considerations of his own leadership, for he came out with a declaration for non-cooperation only after Tilak's death on August 1, 1920. It was in his letter addressed to the Viceroy on August 2 that Gandhi first pointed out that "the scheme of non-cooperation inaugurated today" was essentially "in connexion with the Khilafat Movement" and that the Punjab question was a mere "additional cause" which at the time no longer existed in the context of the general amnesty already proclaimed. The letter contained no reference to any demand for swaraj.

It was in March 1920 that Gandhi came in close contact with Muhammed Ali and Shaukat Ali, two of the prominent leaders of the pan-Islamic movement who had during the war years been interned for their open support to the Turkish cause and persistent intrigue with the enemies of the British Government. Gandhi was being gradually involved in the proceedings of the Central Khilafat Committee which had, in its conference held in Madras on April 17, 1920, urged Indian Muslims to surrender titles, to resign from government service and to refuse payment of taxes.[5] In a subsequent conference one of the Khilafat Committee leaders, Hasrat Mohani, went still further and "promised to join any Afghan army that might invade India to drive out the British", the object being not to win swaraj, but "in the interest of Islam".[6]

This inner political ambition underlying the outer religious cover of the Khilafat movement was later confirmed by a secret memorandum of the Political Branch of the India Office in London, which was submitted in the context of the activities of Muhammad Ali, the Indian Khilafat leader, who visited Europe at the head of a delegation which interviewed the British Prime Minister on March 19, 1920, seemingly to plead the case of Turkey. The Memorandum made it clear that the sole or even the principal object of the Indian Khilafatists was not limited to procuring the *status quo ante bellum* for Turkey. It was to restore Islam to its political glory by creating a Muhammadan India and uniting her by means of "a revived Islam" with Muslim countries situated along her frontiers.[7]

After the June Conference of the Central Khilafat Committee at Allahabad, men like Malaviya, Motilal Nehru, Tilak and Lajpat Rai persuaded Gandhi to desist from being led into the Khilafat tangle. Lajpat Rai even made it clear that although the Hindus would be prepared to help the Muhammadans in every way, they would do so only for "the political betterment of India". He stressed the importance of Hindu-Muslim unity", the core of Gandhi's argument. But this, as he cautioned, could last only so long as there was no danger of "foreign invasion". He warned that this unity "would break up as soon as they (the Hindus) felt that the Afghans were making a move towards India".[8] His, in fact, was a kind of apprehension which was later confirmed by the secret memorandum of the intelligence agency of the Indian Office. Even so, Gandhi remained unaffected.

Obviously, there was a lack of insight and clarity in policy direction, a kind of confusion proceeding from Gandhi's religious approach to Congress politics. It was intended not only to strengthen it but also to reinforce his own leadership with Muslim support. But what could be his object in so "strengthening the Congress". As pointed out earlier, on the basis of a Confidential Government Note of May 1921, it was recognized that a strong Congress alone could, through passive resistance, "save India from Bolshevism–and even a worse fate".[9] Bolshevism was to Gandhi a much greater danger to India than anything else. And this could not by resisted except by the organized force of a strong Congress representing both Hindu and Muslim interests in religious terms. A Hindu-Muslim alliance, though a matter of convenience in terms of religion, was considered a political reality intended to act as a show of national unity in the interest of both the Khilafat movement and the Congress. The situation was aptly described by the Viceroy in a telegram addressed to the Secretary of State on March 1, 1920, a time when Gandhi was establishing close contacts with the Pan-Islamic leaders like Muhammad Ali and Shaukat Ali. The telegram thus said:[10]

"The Hindu-Mahomedan alliance is principally an alliance of political leaders–the Mahomedans hoping thereby to reinforce their position as to the terms of peace with Turkey and the Khilafat question, the Hindus in order to present the appearance of a great national unity. The alliance does not go very deep and breaks down whenever the touchstone of concrete differences is applied."

This was a correct appraisal of the situation which was confirmed by an official Note of August 4, a couple of days after Gandhi, in his letter of August 2 to the Viceroy, had declared his decision to non-cooperate with the Government and join the Khilafat movement. The results of his speeches, as the Note said, "have not been very serious. The non-cooperation movement is almost dead, if not quite". The hartal of August 1 which Gandhi had declared had turned "in reality a fiasco". The Note therefore said that "it would be a great mistake to take any serious notice of these furious outbursts".[11]

What converted Gandhi's non-cooperation into a mass movement was, however, not the limited political objective of the pan-Islamic Indian Muslims. It was, in ideological terms, a formal acceptance of swaraj as the political goal of the Congress, adopted at its Nagpur session in December 1920 along with a provision for the use of Khaddar or handspun and hand-woven cloth made obligatory for all its members as part of its policy to promote cottage or rural industry. From an official communication to the Secretary of State it appears that promises were made not only to win swaraj within a year's time but also to provide for rent-free land, free railway passes, cheap clothes and cheap food.[12] These promises created widespread agitation among the peasantry and unrest among the labour, the result of a combination of political, religious and economic forces.

The popular fervour created in favour of Khilafat non-cooperation, however, could not be sustained for long. It led to serious riots in several places, the disturbances at Chauri Chaura, a little village in the United Provinces, being by far the most inhuman.

The peasants there had stormed the police station and burnt it in a manner resulting in the death of 22 policemen. Gandhi took immediate steps and hastened to convene on February 12, 1922, a meeting of the Working Committee, which decided to end not only the mass civil disobedience, including non-payment of tax, but the entire anti-British campaign itself. The alternative substituted by the Bardoli resolution was the "constructive" programme of spinning, temperance, social reform and educational activity.

By far the most important of the steps taken was a reiteration of the rights of zamindars who dominated the rural economy in keeping with Congress policy itself. While the cultivators were asked to pay all taxes to the Government, Congressmen and organizations were advised "to inform the ryots (peasants) that withholding of rent payment to the Zamindars (landlords) is contrary to the Congress resolutions and injurious to the best interests of the country". The Working Committee further assured the Zamindars under its Bardoli resolutions "that the Congress movement is in no way intended to attack their legal rights, and that even where the ryots have grievances, the Committee desires that redress be sought by mutual consultation and arbitration.

Growth of Leftism in spite of Congress Right

Whether Gandhi's dream of strengthening the Congress by an active involvement in the politics of the pan-Islamic Khilafat movement was, actually or even partially, realized is a debatable question which calls for a much deeper investigation that is beyond the scope of this study. What immediately followed the suspension of the movement is, however, known to history. While the settlement of the Turkish question dispensed with the necessity of Hindu support to the Khilafat, the educational and economic backwardness of the Muslims in the Punjab, in spite of their being in majority, created a state of tension with the Hindus who dominated both education and business. It led to a series of communal riots. The Hindu-dominated bourgeois Congress did not remain unaffected. Its annual sessions and those of the Hindu Mahasabha were held simultaneously at Gaya (1922), Benares (1923) and Belgaum (1924), the attendance at the Mahasabha meetings consisting for the most part of the delegates elected to the annual Congress meetings. They also organized a *Shudhi* movement to reclaim Hindu converts to Islam and a *Sangathan* movement intended to organize the Hindu community as a whole. Since the Congress was in its composition predominantly Hindu, the leadership of the Mahasabha and the Arya Samaj continued to influence it, although Leftism was not far behind to counteract their influence.

As said earlier, the Muslims had a good case in both educational and economic terms. But their blind adherence to religious bigotry was not only a serious impediment to progress but a handle to Hindu business communities to uphold the cause of religious reaction as an instrument of their vested economic interest. The attitude of educated Muslims, it is true, was known for its prudence and perspicacity. But as an official analysis of the post-noncooperation period shows, they too had begun "to reflect more deeply on the implications to their own community of the swaraj programme under such conditions as the non-cooperation movement had created. On their reflection there emerged "a clearer appreciation of the danger to their community latent in any unregulated political advance and a greater insistence on the production of substantial guarantees for its protection in both the political and administrative spheres".[13] Though aware of the importance of a closer cooperation with the Government, they determined to sustain themselves by their own strength and resources. The Muslim League was therefore revived after the Belgaum Congress of 1924. The Congress-League tangle so created in the wake of the non-cooperation had its cultural and, more especially, economic roots. The country's partition which later followed was the result of a failure to adjust differences on the footings of rationality which demanded a recognition of reciprocity as the basic principle of politics. The pressure group of the predominant Hindu business communities in Congress politics was perhaps not prepared to give in.

However, the growth of Leftism proceeded from within the Congress itself as a national organization which became subject to external influences, more especially of the Communist International, the basic source of Indian scientific socialism. Surprisingly enough, it was some pan-Islamic and revolutionary nationalist elements who, after the "general amnesty" proclaimed in 1919, chose to enter the Congress as part of the non-cooperation movement. Indeed communism in India helped them in the early 1920s when Moscow-trained Indian emissaries were sent out to spread the new ideology. As the frequency of correspondence on the subject between the Secretary of State and the Government of India showed, the awareness of the potential danger of communist propaganda first became noticeable towards the closing months of 1922.[14] It was in fact in 1921 that the Communist International first determined to establish a branch organization in British India and an "appeal" was actually issued on December 1, 1924, in the name of the "Communist Party of India"–a leaflet distributed among Congress delegates to the Belgaum session, the object being to promote communist aims from within the Congress itself. The communist new line of policy which was highly critical of the Congress Bardoli resolutions became the basis of the Kanpur Bolshevik conspiracy case in which Sripad Amrit Dange, Shaukat Usmani and Muzaffar Ahmad were found to have been involved. M. N. Roy with his more secular and world view of communism issued an identical, though separate, appeal to the Congress delegates at Belgaum but, in his conclusive paragraph, advised the erstwhile revolutionary nationalists as well as the workers and peasants in India to develop closer relations with the advanced proletariat of the world.

On the basis of the oral and documentary evidence placed before the Allahabad High court, including the admissions of the accused persons involved in the Meerut Conspiracy Case (1929), it appears that those who acted under the direction of the Moscow-based Communist International aimed at the establishment of a world social order founded on Marxian economic theory as interpreted by leading communists and supported by the pronouncements made from time to time by the Communist International. This theory, briefly speaking, was an antithesis of capitalism based on private property and profit motivation in competitive terms. Organizationally, it was condemned as an instrument of exploitation of the poor by the rich, of the weaker sections of society by those who held the reins of power. What the Communists aimed to do throughout the world was to fight for the cause of the proletariat and the peasantry against the capitalist and the landlord. And this they sought to achieve by means of an armed revolution or revolutions to overthrow all the existing governments or political systems based on capitalism, and considered to be the basic cause of most human ills. The remedy was to go in for Soviet Republics on the Russian model. And, as imperialism was viewed as a more developed form of capitalism, the Communists involved in the Meerut Conspiracy Case aimed at the overthrow of the imperialist power over British India, the active expression of which power was the sovereignty of His Majesty, the King Emperor.

According to the judgement delivered in 1930, the methods adopted as a programme of work for the revolution in India included incitement generally of antagonism between Capital and Labour; the creation of Workers' and Peasants' Parties, Youth Leagues and Trade Unions organized and run by Communists; the introduction of fractions in the existing trade unions, political bodies and the like with a view to capturing them in communist interest; encouragement of strikes, hartals and similar demonstrations; propaganda by speeches, newspapers, articles, letters, celebration of anniversaries and "days"; and utilization of any other movements hostile to the Government, such as Bardoli, Independence League, etc.[15]

The goal aimed at and the methods employed by the communists to achieve it were thus both directed towards the overthrow of the foreign imperialist rule–a political objective which could not be accomplished except by means of collaboration with the Congress, the national body dominated in the main by upper class landed and industrial interests. According to Jawaharlal Nehru, eight of the 32 communists accused in the Meerut Conspiracy Case thus happened to be members of the All India Congress Committee.[16] While the Congress gained ideologically by being connected politically with the Left, the Communism as a class-based socialist movement had to lose because of the repressive measures to which they were later subjected.

The communist influence on the Congress, though feeble in the beginning, became perceptible after the suspension of the non-cooperation and civil disobedience movement. A confidential report of 1923 gives a list of several revolutionaries who had links with the Bolshevik and joined the Congress to reorganize their party by fresh recruitment and financial assistance from abroad.[17] Subhas Chandra Bose, too, had contact with Bolshevik revolutionaries in those days.[18] M. N. Roy was in fact one who had been sent out to India even earlier in 1922. Writing to Roy on October 12, 1922, Bolshevik Usmani informed him of his Benares Centre and supplied to him in cipher the names of his "Party" members, including Sampurnanand, then an influential man in the Congress circle, who served as a link with Jawaharlal Nehru and submitted to him for his consideration a *Memorandum on the Congress Programme*, a criticism of Gandhi's emphasis on non-violence, which contained most of the views of M. N. Roy to revitalize the Congress for a more revolutionary programme on Bolshevik lines.

Communist influence on the Congress increased after the arrival in 1927 of Philip Spratt, a member of the Communist Party of Great Britain, who organized the Workers' and Peasants' Party of Bombay. For instance, when S. A. Dange was released from jail on May 24, 1927, a meeting was held in his honour at Congress House, Bombay, where he was, in the presence of Spratt, congratulated for being one of the pioneers of socialism in India.[19] Towards the end of 1927 and early in 1928 that influence became even deeper. It made the Congress, for the first time after Bardoli, look ideologically anti-imperialist, secular and representative of the weaker sections of society.

Indeed, it was a steady growth of Leftism that imparted to the Congress the character of a mass movement. This was in spite of Gandhi and his supporters. What immediately marked a sudden upsurge and tide of working class advance in 1928 was the arrival of the Indian Statutory (Simon) Commission in February. It was the arrival of this commission that placed the militant trade unions for the moment in the vanguard for the national struggle for independence. Their membership in Bombay which during 1923-26 had only advanced from 48,669 to 59,544 reached 75,602 by 1927 and then lept forward to 95,321 by March 1928, and to 800,325 by March 1929. Foremost among these was Girni Kamgar (Red Flag) Union of the Bombay mill-workers. Their strength, which stood at only 324 at the beginning of 1928, rose to 54,000 by December of that year, and 65,000 by the first quarter of 1929. It was this growth of Communist influence during 1928-29 that led the *Bombay Chronicle* in May 1929 to join the national Press outcry of "Socialism in the air". The Public Safety Bill was in these circumstances introduced in September 1928, and, though turned down by the central legislature, was issued as a special ordinance. The Meerut Communist trial was conducted under this Ordinance.

The Congress publicly condemned the Public Safety Bill designed to secure the deportation of certain foreign communists like Philip Spratt and B. F. Bradley as also to check the flow of foreign money transmitted to India for promoting communism.[20] Commenting on the growth of communist influence on the Congress, a secret official analysis of its Calcutta session thus pointed out:[21]

"The rapidly growing influence of the Communists is reflected in the proceedings of the recent session of the All India National Congress of Calcutta ... Resolutions condemning the Public Safety Bill and the Trade Disputes Bill were passed, and it was decided that the Congress should take up the organization of workers and peasants as part of its future programme of constructive work for non-cooperation. Some Communists have secured places on the All-India Congress Committee. Similarly, the Communist groups in Bombay were remarkably successful in the municipal elections; and in other public bodies throughout the country, they are gradually gaining footing."

It is clear that the Congress was under communist pressure or influence obliged to adopt a socialist programme as part of its own organization which, in social and economic terms, consisted of elements with interests basically opposed to those of workers and peasants. As its compulsions were obviously political, its commitment to any socialist programme was bound to be formal or ephemeral, not real or lasting. A gap between its declared policy and actual performance was but naturally inevitable.

Politically, too, it was the continuing pressure of the Left in the Congress and outside that resulted in the Lahore resolution of the Congress passed in 1929 in favour of complete independence. It was under communist influence that the Calcutta session of the Congress had even a year earlier in 1928 pressed for independence and a constitution drafted by the Congress, not by the British Government, although on Gandhi's compromise resolution the matter was shelved and referred to the Subjects Committee. The leftist influence was in fact being induced at this period by Jawaharlal Nehru, General

Secretary of the AICC, who, on his return from his internationalist and communist connexions in Europe, acted as a link between the Right in the Congress and the Leftists.

Indeed, the Congress had in the existing political situation no choice but to go in for complete independence as its goal and civil disobedience as its means. This was especially so in the context of the Great Depression which had in the course of 1929 started raising its head with increasing educated unemployment and the consequent loss of faith in the existing form of government and moderate politics.[22] The arrest and conviction of important communist leaders under the Meerut Conspiracy Case doubtless created a vacuum. But the revival of revolutionary nationalist and terrorist movements which provided the material for the emergence of different shades of Indian socialism in the wake of the Lahore Congress resolution of 1929 created a situation in no way less serious in both political and economic terms. The Congress could not go back on it. It was considered necessary for sustaining its credit as a national party.

Even so, "Gandhi himself was very anxious to avoid doing anything definite". For "men of substance of all kinds (were) greatly concerned with the reddening colour of the Congress creed, and (were) appreciating the importance of organizing themselves and taking part in public life with a view to preventing such development".[23] The Congress itself was of course divided. But the combination of Left and Centre in the party became so formidable that Gandhi could not resist the pressure. Civil disobedience became inevitable. It started with his Salt March to Dandi (seashore) in February 1930 along with his hand-picked followers, a step to manufacture contraband salt, which developed into a mass movement, involving not only Congress supporters but all shades of leftists, not excluding terrorists.[24]

The mass movement so developed was, however, not in keeping with the interest of the learned professions or the business magnates of large cities. The Gandhi-Irwin Pact of March 5, 1931, was therefore sought to be arranged to secure Congress participation in the second Round Table Conference in the hope of a compromise. But since the communal question remained unresolved in the absence of the politico-economic understanding of Indian developments, that participation ended in smoke. While Gandhi returned empty-handed and frustrated, Willingdon who succeeded Irwin took to repressive measures which had earlier been scrupulously avoided to see that Gandhi did not "pass out of the picture".

The Meerut Communist prisoners who were, in due course released, helped to swell the ranks of civil resisters and created a situation when Gandhi found himself helpless to control the movement. In July 1933, he sought an interview with the Viceroy who refused it unless civil disobedience was finally ended. The Congress leadership replaced mass civil disobedience by individual civil disobedience. The Government reacted by intensifying its repressive measures. In August, Gandhi was arrested again, but soon released for reasons of fast. The final end came in May 1934 after Gandhi's statement issued on April 7 stopping the movement altogether without any reference to the Working Committee or the AICC. The Government allowed the AICC to meet at Patna for the unconditional withdrawal of civil disobedience. As directed by the Home Department the right wing of the Congress was sought to be "disentangled" from its "revolutionary elements" and encouraged to build its strength to get into power by a resumption of "constitutional courses".[25] The AICC met at Patna in June, ratified Gandhi's statement of April 7 and, in addition, passed a resolution to form a parliamentary board for purposes of contesting elections to the legislatures as a political party. The Government then lifted the ban on the Congress and declared the Communist Party of India as illegal. The October Session of the Congress in Bombay gave its seal of approval to the decisions of the AICC taken at Patna. It excluded all but the duly recognized and permanent Congress Party members from the privilege of contesting elections on its ticket under the revised constitution. In a letter of September 22, 1935, Gandhi made it clear to Nehru that "the present policy of the Congress" was in the main of his own "shaping" and that it was not "one of drift".[26]

Why did Gandhi stop the movement? Whose interest was there in his mind that induced him to withdraw it unconditionally on his own? Obviously, as said above, it was for "men of substance of all kind" who viewed with concern the "reddening colour of the Congress", not for the poor peasants and workers, the basic elements of a mass movement which all considered necessary for any political advance or concession in the presence of a foreign rule. But while big business was ever ready for a compromise to obviate the risk of "reddening", the left chose to go in for a national revolution as a pre-condition for the establishment of a Socialist State. The exigencies of mass support were thus common up to a point for both the right and the left. But since their goals were antithetical, a split in the national organization became a matter of course. Gandhi cast the weight of his influence on the side of the right as soon as he saw the prospect of constitutional advance resulting from the civil disobedience movement. He even resigned from the Congress to register his protest against the Socialists being allowed to gain ascendancy in it. They were obliged in fact to get out and form a separate Congress Socialist Party of their own.

The anti-imperialist movement of Gandhi's shaping was thus obviously a means to acquire a degree of political advance from where the Indian big business could bargain advantageously with the British and the bourgeois elites should have greater scope for the exercise of power and patronage. The declared goal of the Congress mass movement to fight against the facts of poverty was yet a daydream. Its promise-performance gap was clearly reflected in an intercepted letter of August 14, 1934, which Jawaharlal Nehru wrote to Gandhi when he was permitted parole for two days to visit his ailing wife at Allahabad. He pointed out that the knowledge of the suspension of civil disobedience had given him "one of the biggest shocks". It was to him a "spiritual defeat", not an ordinary setback. What pained him most was, however, the rise to prominence of those who, during the civil disobedience movement, had cooperated with anti-revolutionary elements.[27]

"The leading figures in the Congress suddenly became those people who had obstructed us, held us back, kept aloof from the struggle and even cooperated with the opposite party in the time of our direst need. They became the high priest in our temple of freedom and many a brave soldier who had shouldered the burden in the heat and dust of the fray was not even allowed inside the temple precincts. He and many like him had become untouchables and unapproachable and if he ventured to raise his voice and criticize the new high priests, he was shouted down and told that he was a traitor to the cause because he spoiled the harmony of the sacred precincts. And so the flag of Indian freedom was entrusted with all pomp and circumstance to those who had actually hauled it down at the height of our national struggle at the bidding of the enemy, to those who had proclaimed from the house-tops that they had given up politics (for politics was unsafe for them) but who emerged with a jump to the front ranks when politics became safe."

The Congress in Nehru's own words had actually become a "caucus" where nothing but "opportunism flourishes and triumphs".[28] He was especially sore to find that the Working Committee had set out to denounce the socialists without caring to know the meaning of socialism. In his opinion, "the over-mastering desire of the committee was somehow to assure various vested interests even at the risk of talking nonsense".

And, in spite of Nehru's admonitions, Gandhi proposed to him to take over the Presidentship of the Congress and guide its policy. "I would like you therefore to tell me", wrote Gandhi, "whether you will allow your name to be proposed for the crown of thorns" and "take with you such old colleagues as would go with you wholeheartedly".[29] As is well known to history, Nehru accepted the offer and put the Congress on road to elections; and, though declaredly opposed to office acceptance initially, moved in that direction in the provinces under the revised Constitution of 1935. Constitutional advance within the framework of law was a principle of compromise which suited both the imperial and the national vested interests controlling the Congress. Though critical of such interests by Western education and culture, Nehru allowed himself to be guided by considerations of practical politics which did not exclude lure for power. Gandhi, who fitted in well with the formal requirements of the traditional culture, acted as a good cover.

There was nothing unique about what happened after the suspension of the Civil Disobedience movement in 1934. The experience of 1922 was a comparable experience. There was in fact a pattern in Congress policy and its political behaviour to suit vested economic interest. The difference, however, was that while in the absence of a highly magnetized economy and sharply polarized capital conflict its approach remained largely humanitarian in the early twenties, the class-based left forces gained in strength and momentum with increasing industrialization under the organized pressure and influence of the Federation of Indian Chamber of Commerce and Industry established in 1927, the year which marked the surging tide of the trade union movement.

Even so, it was Chauri Chaura that became the raison d'être for the suspension in 1922 of the Non-cooperation and Civil Disobedience movements, involving in the course of its progress questions of both peasantry and labour, which were sought to be examined later officially by the Royal Commission on Agriculture in 1926 and another Royal Commission on Labour in 1929.

The Chauri Chaura incident took place on February 5, 1922, while the Bardoli resolution suspended the movement on February 11. The leaders who were opposed to mass civil disobedience were upper middle-class intellectuals like C. R. Das (Bengal), Motilal Nehru (U.P.), N. C. Kelkar (Bombay), G. S. Khaparde (C.P.), S. Srinivasa (Madras). They all belonged to the learned profession of law and wanted to fight for swaraj from within the Councils. They were the people who stood opposed to revolutionary mass action and cooperated with the Government in putting down industrial unrest and seeking to resolve the indigenous post-war capitalist crisis by a supply of cheap labour. They were in their line of policy supported generally by members of the Congress Civil Disobedience Committee appointed by the AICC at Lucknow in June 1922. It consisted of men like Motilal Nehru, Ajmal Khan, Rajagopalachari, Seth Jamnalal Bajaj, Vithalbhai Patel and Dr. Ansari who expressed themselves against any civil disobedience on a mass scale.

However, when the Council-entry question was raised at the Gaya Congress in December,1922, the "no-changers" remained firm in their opposition to it. C. R. Das, the President, therefore, resigned from the Congress and formed with the help of Motilal Nehru and other supporters a separate Swaraj Party. Its relation with the Congress was, however, no more than a milk-and-water kind of compromise which was reached with Gandhian no-changers in September 1923. It asked Congressmen not only not to do any propaganda against the Swarajists but even to vote and stand as candidates. Those of the erstwhile non-cooperators who had earlier opposed Council-entry but later chose to avail themselves of the permission given by the Congress to contest elections were therefore asked to join the Swaraj Party formally and subject themselves to its discipline. The leading personalities of the Party that so emerged with the implicit consent of Gandhi himself were either the same or comparable to what Jawaharlal described as "the leading figures in the Congress" and jumped to its "front ranks" when the mass Civil Disobedience movement was withdrawn in 1934.

There was thus a pattern in the politics of the Congress. Speaking generally, it consisted of attempts to organize a movement by mobilizing people belonging to every strata of society, especially the more responsive and oppressed ones, to wrest power from the imperialist authority. The object was to see that the power so wrested remains in the hands of its vested interests, more especially of the rising entrepreneurs, political and professional elites. The moment that movement reached a stage where the leadership felt the danger of its control being seized by the revolutionary elements, it applied a brake and proceeded in search of a compromise with imperialism lying in wait for an opportunity of the kind that could save itself and its Indian partners in business and the learned professions, a product of its own social and economic policies. The movement, in consequence, got shorn of its radical elements, converted itself into a party and set out to enjoy the fruits resulting from mass action. This, in a limited sense and on a small scale, started even with the introduction of representative government in 1892, an experience which was repeated in 1908, when the Liberals or the erstwhile Moderates themselves became the Congress and cooperated with the Government in working the Morley-Minto Reforms. The "Nationalists", the party of the lower middle classes, found themselves excluded from the Congress altogether. What Gandhi did was for the first time to involve them in mass politics along with the peasants and workers who reinforced his leadership in recognition of his promises to alleviate their economic ills. The suspension of his mass movement in 1922 was thus an expression of the general pattern of Congress politics. It restored the upper layers of the learned professions and business circles to the importance they wielded in society and government. They carried on with the legislative programmes of the Government until the problems of the economic depression of the early thirties created a situation which called for a political answer to the question, not a mere administrative palliative lying within the scope of legislative action. It was in this context that the Government of India proceeded to submit its views to its home authorities in 1930 on a revised form of government that might resolve the economic crisis and the mass political movement arising from it.

Nature of Economic Depression

The nature of the economic crisis that started in 1929 and continued for some years was clearly explained by the Viceroy himself in a semi-official letter of January 17, 1934,[30] addressed to the governors of all provinces where the agriculturists had become more especially afflicted. The replies which the Viceroy received led him to the conclusion that "although the world economic crisis with its features of low prices and reduced demand had created very serious difficulties, the situation (in India) had not yet become desperate, but that if the present conditions continued indefinitely very serious problems might be set up."

The concern which the Government felt was due to the fact that while the importance of the economic situation called for a policy to take stock of the entire position and consider what action of the Government of India should be to tide over the difficulties, the Congress remained preoccupied with political issues, although there had been, during 1932-33, "a striking improvement" because of a collapse in its civil disobedience movement. "The Congress Party", as the Viceroy's letter added, "is torn with dissensions and without a constructive programme. But we all know how India passes through periods of action and reaction in the political sphere and we should none of us assume that the present period represents more than a phase of reaction–a temporary political calm. Political issues in India have always tended to dominate the scene, but in other countries at present it is the economic issues which dominate politics and although India's special conditions may tend to make us at times forget this, nevertheless our position is essentially the same as that of the rest of the world and it is the economic issue which really matters. Therefore it is on this that we need a policy and we may be quite sure that unless we have it, or unless we can convince the public that we are doing something to tackle the problem, we shall give the political agitators exactly the same force and occasion which they need in order to recreate an atmosphere of political disturbance".

The class which was affected most by the Great Depression was that of the agriculturists, for the fall in prices and lack of markets had enormously reduced the money value of their production. It necessarily meant an enormous increase in the "real burden of the fixed money payments" which they had to make mainly as "taxes, rent and interests" on loans incurred for a variety of purposes, productive or unproductive. The letter added that this was the position generally applicable to all countries. But so far as India was concerned, it said, "the greater part of the strain has hitherto been taken up not so much by the agricultural producers as by those to whom the fixed payments are due, namely, Government, landlords and money-lenders and chiefly by the last two". The result was that while the Government was obliged to make reductions in its dues and payment of rent to landlords was allowed to suffer still more", interest payment on debts ceased altogether. Naturally enough, it was the landlords and the traditional money-lenders who stood to suffer most not only by the cyclic depression in the world economy, but more so by the surging tide of leftism forming part of the nationalist political movement. The suspension of the movement by the Congress in 1934 was, doubtless, a great relief to those who were entitled to "fixed" money payments, but the mass action which had already gained in strength did not omit to leave its leftist mark on the organizational structure of the Congress. The Marxist element of a socialite school of thought had come to stay as an organized counter-force to laissez-faire, even though it differed both in form and content. Its task was, however, enormous. It had necessarily to wage war against imperialism for full freedom as a sine qua non for a socialist order of society; and this it could not do except as part of the Congress, the nationalist organization, which could not perhaps act independently of the business crisis organized in the Federation of Indian Chamber of Commerce and Industry. The socialist forces had in fact to reckon with both imperialism and Indian capitalism emerging as a competitive alternative at home.

This competitive capitalist force would naturally wish the Congress to toe its own line of policy–a trend which has been brought out clearly by H. Venkatasubbiah in his *Enterprise and Economic Change*, a work based on the original papers available in the archives of the Federation in New Delhi. When Sri Ram, for example, made in his presidential address a mild complaint in 1931 that the Congress was committing the country to certain socialist principles of economic policy "without consulting business interests", Gandhi admitted that "the industrial classes were slowly coming within the Congress fold" and that they could "even take over the Congress's reims".[31] All that they needed to do was that "they should regard themselves as trustees of the poor", a condition that was not only vague and undefined but also bereft of both political and legal sanction.

What the Government had actually been seeking to do by way of tackling the economic problem will soon be noticed hereafter. But it is pertinent specifically to note that although essentially a business organization, the Federation of Indian Chamber of Commerce and Industry was intrinsically interested in politics, G. D. Birla of the Federation being specially keen to see that it did not keep away from its political role, for he firmly maintained that *swaraj* was "beneficial" to business enterprise as much as to anyone else. He played in fact a prominent part in one of its sessions held in Delhi in March 1932 to discuss its dual commercial and political role in relation to "non-cooperation" and "direct action" launched as part of the Civil Disobedience movement. The correspondence that transpired between the Secretary of State and the Viceroy[32] in the course of this movement and the Prime Minister's policy declaration of January 19, 1931, make it clear that the Federation was concerned with the restoration of peace in its own interest and prevent the Congress from going red under the influence of communism and revolutionary terrorism. The Gandhi-Irwin Pact and the Congress participation in the second Round Table Conference were the fruits of an effort made by business leaders. It was in fact their interest and the interest of the Congress swarajist leaders that called for the suspension of the entire movement itself in 1934. The person who moved in this direction was the Congress leader, K. F. Nariman of Bombay, a strong supporter of council-entry in the forthcoming elections. It was he who assured the Viceroy that if allowed to meet, the AICC would pass a resolution by majority in favour of withdrawing the whole movement to the satisfaction of the Government.[33] The fact was that while the Congress was anxious to call off civil disobedience without any serious loss of face, the policy of the Government was to save the Congress as the only effective counterweight to communism, a policy on which there was complete accord among industrialists and bourgeois politicians.

Gandhi did the job for all vested interests alone, including the Government and the business circles. By his statement of April 7, 1934, he stopped civil disobedience altogether without any reference to any Congress body. What the Home Department was left to do was to disentangle the Right wing in the Congress from its revolutionary elements and put that section on the road to power by constitutional means, a course of action already referred to above. It created some differences between Gandhi and Nehru.[34] But since both were soft to each other for personal reasons, these did not cause any crisis. The gap between a promised full independence for a new social order as its goal and the acceptance of provincial autonomy in 1937 under imperial safeguards was obvious. The reasons, too, were not far to seek.

Federation of Indian Chamber of Commerce and Industry

Venkatasubbiah's study of the Federation establishes beyond any doubt the existence of a close link between the big business and the Congress leadership, more especially of Gandhi. For in May 1930 the Federation resolved that unless Gandhi attended the Round Table Conference in London, none of its member-bodies should accept invitation to participate in it in their individual capacity. The idea was conceived by Ambalal Sarabhai, though it was G. D. Birla who moved the resolution on the understanding that so far as possible the Federation would avoid active politics. He welcomed the Federation's unanimous declaration of May 1930 because he belonged to the Congress Party which was pledged to boycott the Round Table Conference. Later the Federation however interpreted its resolution of May 1930 as recommendatory and not mandatory. The Irwin Agreement of March 5, 1931, was arranged through the intercession of some leading industrialists, including G. D. Birla. Gandhi joined the Second Round Table Conference.

On the Viceroy's recommendation to the Secretary of State, Purshotamdas and G. D. Birla, too, were invited to participate in the deliberations of the Round Table Conference. On the basis of the Federation's private paper Venkatasubbiah brings out the fact that its delegation acted in collaboration with Gandhi who went by the delegation's brief on the question of the rupee-sterling ratio advocating a return to 1s.4d. in the interest of the Indian national interest conducive to its export trade. On commercial discrimination based on imperial preference in matters of tariff duties, the delegation went by Gandhi's views. "It was based on his well-known personal philosophy that the English, in England and in India, are his friends."[35] This, however, was a view which several member-bodies of the Federation described as equivocal, even contrary to economic nationalism followed by Englishmen themselves. When the delegation's performance was questioned by some member-bodies as inconsistent with the views of its own executive committee, the delegation admitted that "it could not fight foreign interests without the weight of the Congress and therefore could not go further than Gandhi went at the Conference".[36] Even so, as its report said, the delegation had remained firm and "would not agree to anything which curtailed or restricted India's right to pursue the economic policy which she considered to be in the best interests of the country".[37]

From its very inception the Federation in fact acted on the assumption that Indian enterprise could not fully flower without political freedom. It therefore used politics as a means to promote its economic swaraj, a condition precedent. The means it employed to attain its goal was to press for protective tariffs to save Indian industries from foreign competition. Tariff protection was therefore its major plank throughout the twenties and thirties in order to emerge as a competitive economic force used as aid to national politics. The Federation did all it could to promote Indian enterprise. If Indian cotton textiles and steel called for protection against imported goods, it encouraged Indian enterprise in the coal industry developed mainly by British companies in India. In 1931, the Federation even endorsed an appeal issued to the public by the Indian Mining Federation of Calcutta to support collieries owned and managed by Indians. It was in this context that the Congress's *swadeshi* movement had an importance of its own, and though subject to being misused, it served its purpose none the less.

A policy of protective tariff was, however, not without a problem of its own. It could not normally be expected to differentiate between Indian firms and non-Indian firms operating in India. The question was discussed at length by the Indian Fiscal Commission (1921-22).[38] The result was commercial discrimination or, as said before, discriminatory protection extended to certain key industries without prejudice to imperial preference or concession to certain friendly countries. Commenting on the effect of the protection so conceded Sir James Grigg, Finance Member of the Viceroy's Executive Council, said in a speech in the Central Legislative Assembly in 1936 that industrial expansion of India had come through "more and more protection given after less and less enquiry for longer and longer periods".[39] Lord Irwin's private papers reinforce also the view that the Congress and Gandhi were both used by the Federation to promote Indian industrial expansion on capitalist principles of private enterprise for profit-making, monopoly and the concentration of financial power. Based on private enterprise, imperialism, too, was not altogether hostile to the Federation, more especially because it acted as a check on the Congress and saved it from the reddening influences of communism. Interestingly enough, Venkatasubbiah's study revealed that 80 to 90 organized commercial bodies still preferred membership of European Chambers at a time when it was open to them to join Indian Chambers. The imperialist government, however, took a serious view of racial discrimination which clashed with business practice and smacked of political reality. An occasion of this kind arose in 1929 when a Bill for reserving coastal traffic for Indian shipping was sought to be introduced and the Associated Chambers of Commerce of India and Ceylon saw in it an element of racial discrimination. This necessarily became a live issue of politics and the British Parliament tried to justify on this score a provision in the new federal constitution for commercial safeguards to protect foreign interests. The Federation of Indian Chambers of Commerce and Industry reacted sharply and asserted in terms of economic nationalism India's right to pursue its own economic policy, including a policy of economic discrimination against non-national interests. Indeed, the Federation had ever since the early twenties been steadily gaining in strength by a consistent use of the Congress right wing in the advancement of its own economic interests.

Rupee-Sterling Ratio

On the question of the rupee-sterling ratio or exchange value the Federation, however, remained a failure. It could not make any dent on British policy which ignored the views of Indian experts and businessmen who were opposed to the location of currency reserves in England as well as to the unlimited sale of council bills by the Secretary of State with a view to restricting gold imports into India.

The pre-war exchange value of 16d. to the rupee had come to be regarded as permanently settled. Due to industrial expansion in the course of the First World war (1914-18) the rupee gained in strength and its exchange value was allowed to escalate on the assumption that silver would after the war find its own level by a downward trend and return to its pre-war 16d. But the Government fixed the rate at 2 shillings in February 1920 and stuck to it by artificial means until it was given up as an altogether impossible arrangement. The result was a heavy loss to the Indian treasury and fall in export trade.

The question of exchange value was raised again in 1925-26 when on the recommendation of the Hilton Young Commission it was fixed at an intermediate rate of 18d. in spite of the opposition of Indian opinion. Commenting on the revised new rupee-sterling ratio, Sir M. Visvesvaraya, the eminent economist who had earlier acted as Chairman, Indian Economic Enquiry Committee (1925), thus wrote in 1934:[40]

"This has no doubt adversely affected the agricultural population of this country, and particularly those who produce commercial crops for export. The artificial maintenance of this ratio has led to the over-valuation of the rupee, a shrinkage of India's export trade, and a further depression in rupee prices of agricultural produce. Critics are saying that a high exchange is persisted in to help foreign capitalists, importers of British goods, the British officers, British shipping and British insurance interests that send remittances to Great Britain from India. The slight increase in the burden of foreign financial obligations that will follow, if the rupee exchange returned to its true rate, could be more than off-set by the advantages that would accrue to the country by the stimulus of increased export of goods, higher prices and a better trade balance."

The ratio question was debated at length by the Federation of

Indian Chambers of Commerce and Industry at its 1930 annual session which pressed for the setting up of a gold mint in India with gold currency with a view to restoring the confidence of the people in the currency and credit of the country. Purshotamdas, who initiated the debate, made it clear that as a result of the 1s.6d. ratio the Indian "exporter in the world market gets only Rs. 13 and odd annas instead of the standard Rs. 15 for the pound sterling to which he was accustomed from 1900 to 1924". Sir George Schuster, the Finance Member, none the less rejected the Federation's demand for a lower ratio of 1s.4d. although it was well known that the higher ratio so maintained artificially was by means of a regular export of gold from India. When the Federation raised the issue again in April 1931, Schuster argued that the country had since 1927 adjusted itself to the 18d due to the world depression and not to any higher rupee-sterling ratio. Even a meeting with Sir Samuel Hoare, Secretary of State at the India Office in London, bore no fruit. The ratio case was pleaded in the presence of Gandhi himself by G. D. Birla and Purshotamdas. But they all failed to make any dent.[41] The Indian business delegation at the Second Round Table Conference realized the inherent defect of the sterling exchange system functioning in a dependency form of government in India, more especially when the political and economic aims and interests of the two countries happened to be so divergent. This reinforced their determination invisibly to control national politics as a condition precedent to their economic advance. For, as Visvesvaraya shows, Indian businessmen, in the absence of full political control, lost a number of opportunities to buy and stock gold in the world market, especially because of their own country's currency being linked with that of Britain. In spite of the definite recommendation of the Indian Currency Commission that "no favourable opportunity of fortifying the gold holding in the reserve should be allowed to escape",[42] cases occurred where such opportunities were lost to Indian entrepreneurs because of their currency being linked with sterling.

Though allied politically with the Congress and making use of its weight in the promotion of private industrial undertakings, the higher echelons of the business leadership were perhaps still free from active political involvements, more especially in financial terms. For the annual budgetary figures of the Congress even for the periods after the elections of 1936-37 happened to be normally of a limited nature in terms of both income and expenditure. Moreover, while the threat of a second imperialist war had started growing a fight to the finish for independence remained yet unaccomplished. It could not perhaps be done except with the support of the Left which alone could perhaps egg the people on to mass action. The capitalist alliance with the Right wing in the Congress had of course a good case in terms of national politics. But the Federation was not the organization best fitted for anything like a revolutionary or even a radical approach to politics. Its role to act as financiers for political purposes must therefore be kept reserved to the post-Independence period. Even so, its collaboration with the Congress in matters of industrial policy never ceased. The official economic policy of this period was however obliged to take into account the poverty of the rural masses as well as the state of industrial unrest which together gave rise to communism, considered inimical to both capitalist and imperialist interests. The problem of British economic policy was to obviate communist danger by removing mass discontent without any prejudice to private enterprise or even imperial authority.

Measures to Improve Economic Condition

The measures taken by the Government of India to deal with the Indian economic situation between 1920 and 1937 included, for instance, Tariff-Board enquiries, Royal Commissions on Agriculture and Labour as well as Committees on monetary, banking and fiscal problems,[43] throwing light on specific aspects of economic life rather than the integrated picture of the economy as a whole. The tariff enquiries were, for instance, preoccupied with the effects of foreign competition of Indian industrial development and were intended to suggest discriminatory protection to Indian industries.

As the most serious of the economic problems happened to be agrarian, with a crushing weight of rural indebtedness and illiteracy, care was taken not only to appoint a Royal Commission on Agriculture in 1926 to go into the manifold aspects of the agrarian economy and the miserable plight of the peasantry but to precede it with the appointment of an Indian Economic Enquiry Committee a year earlier in 1925 when the Communist Party of India (CPI) emerged in its organized form and established as part of the Communist International functioning under the guidance of Moscow.

The Committee so appointed under Finance Department No. 855-F, dated Delhi, 22 January 1925 [44] with the approval of the Secretary of State was a small body intended primarily to collate and examine the existing material for purposes of an economic survey, to ascertain how the material available could further be supplemented and then to determine what lines an economic enquiry into the resources of the country should take. It consisted of the following gentlemen who had agreed to serve on it:

1. Sir M. Visvesvaraya, K.C.I.E., D.Sc., M.I.C.E, Chairman.

2. Rai Bahadur Pandit Hari Kishan Kaul, C.S.I., C.I.E., Member, and

3. Mr A. R. Barnett-Hurst, B.Sc., Professor, Muir Central College, Allahabad, Member and Secretary.

On the basis of the material already available the Committee was to frame an estimate of the economic condition of the various clauses and to make recommendations not only as to the best manner in which the existing material could be supplemented, but also as to the lines on which a general economic survey could be carried out. As desired by the Legislative Assembly, the Committee was to make a thorough inquiry and submit an ad interim report on the points suggested.[45] These included the economic condition of the various classes; their income; their capacity to bear the existing taxation burden; its manner of distribution; the suitability of alternative sources of taxation and machinery for imposition; the general resources of the country and the economic effects of the recommendations made by the Committee.

The Committee, however, observed that the object for which it was constituted had been misunderstood. It said : "Although the name of the Committee is associated with the term 'Economic Enquiry' we have no concern with any actual investigation into the economic condition of the people. Our task, under the terms of reference, is limited to the framing of a scheme of economic survey after examining the adequacy or otherwise of the material already available. The idea of an economic survey is of foreign origin and of comparatively recent growth in India. The matters to be dealt with in the course of such a survey are partly technical, and the public in this country are unfamiliar with the body of scientific facts which bear upon the issue."[46]

The Committee perhaps took this view of their task because of the inadequacy of the proper statistical data which were of a "side product of various government or other departments produced mainly as a sort of public advertisement of their activity or for departmental use, each acting on its own initiative, the whole un-coordinated and often without technical direction". As the material available in the form of statistics remained unrelated to anything like a theoretic value or background, it could not lend itself to comparative analysis necessary for purposes of "a guide to rational policy".[47] The Committee had therefore no alternative except an exclusive reliance on the methods of empiricism.

Some of the conclusions that emerged from the evidence adduced before the Committee emphasized the fact that the people's traditions and habits were anti-economic. For, speaking generally, "they spend their small savings extravagantly on marriages and litigation, or invest them in unproductive hoards or in the shape of jewellery or ornaments". This was so because "over 92 per cent of the population is illiterate". On the basis of the official publication, *India in 1923*, which the Committee cited as its evidence, "a very large proportion of the inhabitants are beset with poverty of a kind which finds no parallel in western lands". An American export witness told the Committee at Allahabad that "the crop yields of the country are about the lowest of any civilized country he knew of", while the "unproductive debt of the peasants of British India ... is estimated by Mr. M. L. Darling, ICS of the Punjab, at Rs. 600 crores". The marked characteristic of most part of the country was not only the availability of "cheap and docile labour", but also "unemployment among the lower middle classes" which caused "much distress".[48]

The Committee recognized that there were defects not only in the outlook of the people, but also in the economic structure of the country, defects which called for a comprehensive treatment according to the "latest and most approved methods" of statistical analysis based on a coordination of statistical data relating to the economic condition of the people. This precisely was a task which an economic survey should in the first instance seek to accomplish.

Sir M. Visvesvarya, Chairman of the Committee, later produced in 1934 a separate work of his own where he made use of statistical data and covered, within the framework of comparative analysis with reference to advanced nations, a critical survey of Agriculture and Industry, Transport and Power Supply, Trade and Commerce, Tariffs and Finance, Currency and Banking, emphasizing in his *Planned Economy for India* the importance of planning as an instrument of economic development. In the paucity of well-coordinated material for economic analysis he suggested a Ten-Year Scheme for development under an organized structure of planning with a Supreme Economic Council at the Centre as well as provincial and local district councils forming an integral part of the whole organization with the assistance of administrative staff at each level.

The picture which he drew of agriculture was in no way different from that of the Committee of Enquiry of which he had been Chairman. The outstanding features of rural life, as he summed up, were "the excessive pressure of the population on land, the small size of holdings and their progressive fragmentation, the primitive methods of cultivation ... the lack of finance for farm work, the old-fashioned character of subsidiary occupations, the crushing indebtedness of the riot, short employment, universal illiteracy and phenomenal poverty".[49] Some other aspects of his economic survey will be noticed below a little later. Since rural life was relatively far more neglected, the attention of the Government was drawn to it earlier.

Institutional Credit Organization for Rural Uplift

The idea of an organization of rural credit on an institutional basis was first suggested by Manu Subedar, an eminent economist, who, in the course of an interview held on May 17, 1927, discussed it with Sir Basil P. Blackett, earlier associated with Sir Malcolm Hailey in the reorganization of the Central Secretariat in 1922 under the Retrenchment (Increase) Committee of the Government of India. Under a letter of January 21, 1928, addressed to Blackett, Manu Subedar submitted his Note on the Organization of Rural Credit in India for purposes of rural development.[50]

The Note on the Organization of Rural Credit was a scheme for Agricultural Banks, for the most important of the problems of the agriculturist in India was the dearth of capital when he wanted it on reasonable terms. "With the security of his own farm or holding or standing crops", the Note said, "he is unable to secure money at all times and when he secures it, it is on very exorbitant terms," acting as a perpetual tax on the resources of the agriculturist "which he pays in the form of interest on his debts or in the form of a deduction on the price received by him for his produce. The object of the scheme of agricultural banks was in these circumstances to bring down the general level of money rates in India in a manner which should be directly useful to the agricultural districts and the agriculturists. They were designed institutionally to provide capital for such purposes as the purchase of bullocks, sinking of wells, or the purchase of agricultural implements, etc. Besides these requirements on capital account, provisions were to be made in respect of such current purposes as the purchase of seeds and manure or the payment of revenue.

There were, of course, cooperative societies, more directly associated with agriculture. The cooperative movement had of late also made great strides. But its achievements had generally been far short of expectations in so far as an all-round reduction of the rate of interest was concerned. Their total resources too happened to be limited, being estimated at Rs. 48,19,20,000 only. Moreover, its process of selection of persons as members was such that "a man, who might be a good farmer and who might be in difficulties, but who is not socially liked or popular, cannot secure assistance".

There was, in addition, a "new void" created for increasing loanable capital due to a rise in the exchange value of the rupee to 1s.6d. "This rise", as Manu Subedar points out, "is bound to give considerable check to the investment of new capital from England in rupee enterprises and vice versa would give great impetus to the withdrawal of surplus funds and profits from India owing to sterling being made cheaper in terms of rupee. The re-investment of profits earned in India, which has been going on for many years and which is the standard method for India's securing new British capital, will, therefore, be considerably checked. In so far as all this will affect the general rate of interest throughout the country for long-term investment, apart altogether from current bank rates, the agriculturist will also be affected and the tendency will be for agricultural districts to find themselves with less facility than before or with less facility than what they would get if the Government decided to fix the exchange at 1/4d".[51]

The Note made it clear that public opinion in the agricultural districts should be created in favour of agricultural banks not only as an institution where numerous small accumulations of savings, instead of remaining in private pockets or in so-called hoards, could lie with safety and profit in the form of assured interest, but also as an instrument of rural development through loans made available on reasonable terms to the agriculturists. What was necessary, however, was the establishment of their fullest confidence in the solvency of these banks as well as in their power to repay cash as and when required. It was thus recognized that the very first requisite of success was confidence which, as the Note emphasized, "cannot be secured without the intervention of the State". And the State was duty bound to intervene to save the social order from being irretrievably impaired by laissez-faire. The Note thus argued : "If the State has found it possible and profitable for the State to invest fifty crores as the nucleus to generate the confidence, if necessary, in the solvency and stability of the institutions" proposed to be established as part of the agricultural banks, it can go ahead with the scheme at the provincial and district levels.[52]

Of the institutions proposed to be so established, the department of a Reserve Bank was to be at the apex as the final source of security for the Agricultural Banks operating as Government institutions pure and simple. "If confidence is to be the keynote", the scheme pointed out, "the feeling that at any time there should be an unlimited amount of money to pay out to the depositors must be there. Apart from this feeling, a direct responsibility must be laid, to meet the call of the depositors in Agricultural Banks, on those who control the note issue of the future and have the general policy in their hands in currency matters. A further matter of some importance is the general and expert supervision over procedure and audit of Agricultural Banks, which the Reserve Bank can adequately provide."

In view of the difficult and vaguely defined nature of security involved in the realization of loans for agricultural purposes, the direct intervention of the State was suggested as the only alternative to the usurious operations of indigenous money-lenders or *mahajans* as the traditional source of rural credit in India. Indeed, the task, though laudable without any question, was not that easy. In fact, Subedar's Report was by way of mere suggested remedies to mitigate the agricultural crisis resulting from the inadequacy of rural credit. It meant hardly any action which depended on the Government.

The *Report of the Indian Central Banking Committee* (1931) which followed drew the attention of the Government again "to the poverty, indebtedness and illiteracy of the rural population, their low standard of living, the comparatively low production from land per capita of the population and per acre, and the inadequacy of subsidiary occupations to supplement the slender income from agriculture". On the basis of provincial estimates the total rural indebtedness of India was now said to be Rs. 900 crores. The Committee did not even hesitate to admit that in spite of the steady fall in the rural economy "the action taken by the State to mitigate the adverse influences which affect the Indian farmer is inadequate". The Committee therefore summed up the position by saying that "besides the provision of credit the active pursuit of a progressive and constructive agricultural policy is necessary "not only for the sake of the country's economic prosperity", but particularly "for the purpose of stemming the growth of (political) discontent among a large section of the population" by "serious effort" being made "to find a remedy for the chronic indebtedness of the agriculturist so far as it relates to his unproductive debt".[53]

In the opinion of the Committee the most effective remedy for rural indebtedness was "the pursuit by the Local Governments of a vigorous policy of debt conciliation on a voluntary basis". But in cases where the leaders do not agree to voluntary settlement of the debt, it will be necessary to take action to secure a compulsory settlement by means of "legislative enactment", a measure for a "simple rural insolvency" which had been suggested by the Royal Commission on Agriculture appointed in 1926 to provide increased facilities for agricultural research.[54] The Usurious Loans Act of 1918 was sought to be retained, and the Punjab Regulation of Accounts Act (1930) was passed to ensure the maintenance of regular record of accounts of each debtor. But no system of licensing money-lenders was introduced; for the Committee felt that a lasting solution could be found only by the speed of education, cooperative and joint-stock banking and the training of the borrower in the habits of thrift and saving.

Since rural indebtedness was only a part of the problem of rural development, the Committee emphasized the importance of pursuing a progressive and sound agricultural policy which, as the Royal Commission also advised, could not be accomplished in the absence of correct statistical data. In order to provide the Government with the information required for the purpose the Committee recommended "the establishment of provincial boards of enquiry to collect, correlate and analyse all the economic factors influencing the agriculturist". This was done perhaps in the light of the experience gained from the *Provincial Banking Enquiry Committee's Report*[55] which provided information not only on the existing system of rural credit in different provinces, but also on the influence of foreign trade affecting the rural economy.

The Provincial Banking Enquiry Committee's Report which found place in the Report of the Indian Central Banking Enquiry Committee contains very useful information relating to the function and organization of "indigenous banking" as a source of credit not only for the rural economy but also for trade and business enterprise. Together the two Reports make it abundantly clear how in spite of commerce and industry being transferred to the Provinces under the reformed constitution of 1919, their progress remained slow and tardy.[56] While the commercial banks, including the Imperial Bank of India established in 1921, remained loath in the supply of block of even working capital and insisted on attempts to raise private and share capital which was hardly possible in the absence of a foolproof security proceeding from an Indian Reserve Bank with control over currency. The Government showed insufficient interest in measures to stimulate industrialization. Worse still was the step-motherly attitude of the foreign-owned exchange banks which acted as serious constraints on the promotion of Indian export trade as an important source of capital formation. The Indian expert witnesses, including certain leading business men, thus made two general complaints before the Central Banking Enquiry Committee. They produced evidence to show that while "the share of Indians in the foreign trade of India was very small", in matters of "financing that trade the exchange banks had (for all practical purposes) a monopoly.

In addition to these handicaps, as the Central Committee observed on the basis of provincial reports, there were other difficulties which Indian witnesses brought to its notice. It was made clear "that the facilities available for financing India's foreign trade are (no doubt) sufficient. But the agencies which cater for these needs are all of non-Indian origin and the few Indian Banks which at one time or other have attempted to engage in exchange business have never attained even a partial success". The Committee therefore had no way except to observe that it was "not desirable that India should rely for all time on the facilities afforded by non-Indian institutions for the financing of her foreign trade". It was in these circumstances that the well-established Indian joint-stock banks were induced to open foreign branches in the interest of their clients, and recommendations were made not only for the establishment of the proposed Reserve Bank but also for the simultaneous withdrawal of the restrictions imposed on the transaction of foreign exchange business by the Imperial Bank of India.

However, in case the Reserve Bank found it impossible to arrive at a satisfactory settlement with the Imperial Bank, or if the former found that within the stipulated period the Imperial Bank of India was unable to participate actively in the financing of India's foreign trade, the Central Banking Committee advised that the Government of the day should proceed to secure the establishment of an Indian exchange bank.

Indian Business Houses Fight to end Foreign Economic Dominance

A new situation arose when the foreign experts characterized the proposed Indian Exchange Bank as politically motivated and "nationalistic" in character. Six[57] of the Committee's members with high stakes in business enterprise submitted a strong dissenting minute when the foreign experts declined to advocate any Government assistance to the exchange bank so recommended by the Committee. They demanded that "the capital of Rs. 3 crores must be extended and that the whole of the initial capital must be subscribed. The controversy so raised reminded one of a growing clash between laissez-faire and the Keynesian prescription of State intervention as a way out of the capitalist crisis of trade depression. The Committee considered even several other suggestions made by witnesses for the regulation of the operations of existing exchange banks, such as licensing, restriction of deposits, registration with rupee capital as well as training and employment of Indians. It was recognized that "all non-Indian banks wishing to do banking business in India should be required to take out a licence from the Reserve Bank and that licences should be freely granted to banks already established in the country".[58]

The whole emphasis of the Indian business houses was on the attainment of economic swaraj to secure their commercial and industrial advance in competition with foreign interest. Since British economic policy was a policy of compromise with indigenous entrepreneurs, their demands were conceded consistently with the protection of British capital invested in India. Imperial preference in terms of tariff duties was a form of British commercial "safeguards" which the federal constitution of 1935 actually provided after the Reserve Bank of India, which the Central Legislature established in 1934, came into operation on April 1, 1935.

The economic approach of the Indian business houses did not in principle clash with British policy, more especially in relation to the Great Depression which affected the agriculturists most because of the low prices of their produce of raw material for export. In a Finance Department circular[59] addressed to the Governors of provinces for advice to evolve an effective remedy the Viceroy emphasized that in view of an over-all world situation what really mattered was the "economic issue" which called for a policy, and that "unless we can convince the public that we are doing something to tackle the problem, we shall give the political agitators exactly the force and occasion which they need in order to recreate an atmosphere of political disturbance" leading to the Civil Disobedience movement. For the fear was that "political issues in India have always tended to dominate the scene". As already said above, steps were taken not only to seek a remedy to the economic problems but also to resolve the constitutional issues involved therein.

Congress Stress on Politics to Meet the Left Pressure

The radicalism of politics as an instrument of power, which marked the national scene during 1929-33, could not perhaps be avoided in the presence of a foreign rule. It was more so because of the rising tide of communism which had started raising its head under the organized influence of the Communist International established in 1919 as a world force. It was precisely to reduce that pressure which led the Congress to pass its Karachi resolution on socialism in 1931, its object being to stem that tide by any attempt to meet its demand half way in nationalist interest. For it was not only the unconditional withdrawal of the Civil Disobedience movement but Nehru's own subsequent admission[60] which confirmed that the Congress had nothing to do with socialism even after the formation of its ministries in the provinces under the 1935 Act. Sampurnanand, a member of the AICC, in fact described the Karachi Congress resolutions of 1931 as "milk-and-water resolutions which had very little to do with socialism".[61] Even so, when these were interpreted by certain interested groups as meaning confiscation of private property and class war, the Congress Working Committee had to come out with "appeals to all landed and monied classes to help the Congress to the best of their ability", for it had no such "design" at all.[62] After the conversion of the Congress movement into an exclusive Congress Party in 1934 the socialistic content of the Karachi resolution was, however, made full use of by making all kinds of wild promises to remove poverty and indebtedness for purposes of electoral success in 1936-37.[63] It looked like a marriage of convenience for politics to use the language of economics to achieve power. But the declared policy objective of a socialistic kind was not without an impact. The growing controversy over a choice between the Left and the Right in the Congress which began in the early twenties with the advent of Bolshevism and continued through the Civil Disobedience movement of the thirties did not altogether lose its vitality, more especially in the context of the world economic crisis which called for a way out. The idea of planning as an instrument of policy which could be traced to the Reports of the Royal Commissions on Agriculture and Industry as well as the reports of enquiry by several committees emerged in 1934 as a proposal in *Planned Economy for India* by Sir M. Visvesvaraya who had been the Chairman of the first Committee of Enquiry in 1925.

Planning : A Compromise Between Left and Right

A resort to the use of *planning* as an instrument of policy served in fact as a common basis for compromise between the Left and the Right in the nationalist struggle for freedom. A vague term signifying a design or process, no objection was expected from either of the two forces, more especially from the so-called socialists who sought to steer a course in between the two, as depicted in a pamphlet produced by Sampurnanand in 1934–a pamphlet which described Nehru as one of his own category. As discussed earlier in the course of a reference to the reports of Commissions or Committees, planning in concrete terms involved an increasing pressure for the official recognition of the rising demand for State action or enactment for the compulsory settlement of troubles arising in both rural and urban economies as a result not only of the absence of a reasonably satisfactory credit organization, but also of political constraint or restriction, operating as a check on the expansion of business enterprise. The need for State intervention and assistance was in fact being generally felt as perhaps the only panacea for the Great Depression. As said above, even the Viceroy realized the importance of a new economic approach to the problems of that Depression. But since the philosophy of laissez-faire still held the ground, the assistance of the Government to the provinces for industrial development remained more nominal than real. This became clear from the reports of the banking inquiry Committees, both central and provincial. This mainly accounted for a slow pace of industrial development in the twenties and thirties. Tariff protection for Indian industries against foreign competition naturally remained a major plank throughout this period.

It was in these circumstances that the Federation of Indian Chambers of Commerce and Industry, a capitalist organization, invited Nalini Ranjan Sarkar to preside over its annual session of 1934. Comparable to Raja Risheekesh Law, one of the earliest of Bengali industrialists who presided over the Bengal National Chamber of

Commerce for 25 years from 1906, Sarkar, who was later to become Commerce Member in the Government of India, stressed in the course of his presidential address the importance of planning as an instrument of the Federation's industrial policy. Sarkar took the cue from the New Deal in the United States and the measures taken by European countries to counteract the effects of the Depression by means of economic planning which had come to be identified with the Russian form of economic experimentation–a trend which, as Sarkar cautioned, must be resisted. State action, he added, could not of course be ignored. But it must be limited to mere assistance which should be coordinated by the Federation with individual initiative or private enterprise. In other words, State action was not to mean State take-over.[64] It was a mere device to save capitalism from the cyclic disorder or break-down inherent in laissez-faire.

The planning machinery which Sarkar suggested consisted of a Supreme Economic Council with advisory functions in addition to provincial economic councils, both being free from bureaucratic control and functioning as an organized body of experts without any power to supersede the executive and legislative limits of the Government. Sir M. Visvesvaraya who later became one of the original members of the National Planning Committee which Subhas Chandra Bose established as the president of the Congress in 1938 with Jawaharlal Nehru as its Chairman, held, in organizational terms, more or less a comparable view in his *Planned Economy for India*, except in matters of detail where he recommended the establishment of a Development Department and Standing Committees functioning under it in the execution of plans. Moreover, he, was in his comments on the existing Indian economic situation, perceptively critical of British policy, and referred to the various ills that arose from India's "dependency" position. Obviously, he was inclined towards a leftist view of a mild nature, a view, though socialistic, was not opposed to private enterprise or the capitalist economy. Unlike the famous Five-Year Plan of Soviet Russia (1928-32) which covered every phase of national life–political, economic, social and cultural–on an integrated principle, Visvesvaraya's approach was one of an exclusive economic growth, a nationalist approach which differed but little in principle from that of the Federation of Indian Chambers of Commerce and Industry.[65] As Venkatasubbiah's study of the Federation clearly points out, it collaborated with the Congress to win political freedom as a condition precedent to Indian economic progress on capitalist lines. Its interest in planned development, in spite of Sarkar's suggestion, remained none the less dormant till the presentation in 1944 of the Bombay Plan prepared for consideration by the Government by the Indian capitalists[66] for India's economic development. It was at this time that the Government of India established its Development Department to secure the implementation of its own Post-War Reconstruction Plan of 1944.

Political Trends : 1937-47

The political developments began with the establishment of provincial autonomy in 1937 and ended with the partition of India and "transfer of power" in 1947. These have been studied in some depth in two of my earlier works, *The Indian Political Parties* and *India: Her Unity And Division*. And it would serve no purpose to go into these even by reference. All that needs to be said in the context of the present work is to emphasize the role of the big business in India, for the most part Hindu and keen to exploit the whole of the Indian industrial resources in their own class interest. It was perhaps on the strength of their collaboration with the Congress that its leadership assumed a hard line in its political negotiations with the Muslim League and proceeded to act on the principle of one-party rule in the formation of ministries in the provinces in 1937, although the League kept on arguing, not unreasonably, that in view of India's plural society a coalition form of Government was better fitted to enjoy the confidence of all sections. The attitude of rigidity, which flowed from a position of strength on the basis of capitalist collaboration, ruled out any possibility of a compromise with the League which continued to harp on the Communal Award of 1935, condemned by the Congress as an imperialist device to weaken it.

The Muslims, as said above, had a good case and the League sought to exploit it to its own political advantage, irrespective of the interest of the lower orders of society. The strength of the Congress was, however, reinforced in the meantime because of the added influence of the Indian capitalists who had gained considerably from the rapid development of industries to meet the defence requirements of the Second World War. The Bombay Plan was, for instance, an expression of their determination to develop on their own the resources of the whole country for purposes of a self-sustained economy. This increasing concentration of economic power in the hands of non-Muslim entrepreneurs and the refusal of the Muslim League to submit to the Congress, their political patron, not only contributed to the partition of India but also created a situation where a rapprochement between Indian and British business enterprise became a factor in the transfer of power in 1947.[67]

Trends in the Indian Economy

Historically, there were two main trends in the development of the Indian economy. These were governed respectively by the principles of free trade and protective tariff. Because of India's subordinate position under British rule official policy was in general so framed as to give favoured treatment to British economic interest through free trade. As India's economy was in the main agricultural, the defenders of free trade argued that she would be better off if she did not go in for organized industries and concentrated, instead, on specialized agricultural development which could pay for the major requirements of everyday life at a much reduced cost. The free trade school obviously wanted India to continue to supply raw material in return for finished consumer goods imported by British traders and industrialists.

The principle of protective tariff was viewed as contrary to free trade. But the nationalist opinion pressed for it as the only instrument of Indian industrial development, for it looked upon British tariff policy as basically inimical to the growth of the national bourgeoisie, a product of British policy itself. The Government of India, it is true, not only imposed tariff restrictions on imports for purposes of revenue, but also interfered with the operation of free trade as part of its welfare measures in the administration of relief during recurrent famines.[68] But since the recommendations of the Government of India were in this respect often countermanded by the Home Government where they were supposed to conflict with purely British interests, the Indian business communities, as said above, proceeded to use national politics as an instrument of industrialization. The recommendations of the Indian Fiscal Commission of 1921-22 and the establishment of the Tariff Board[69] in 1923 to have them implemented were a recognition, even though partial, of the principle of protection as the main plank of industrial development in India.

Slow Pace of Industrialization

The principle of organized industries on modern capitalist lines was recognized by the first Industrial Commission (1916-18).[70] The Fiscal Commission that followed provided an incentive. Even so, the pace of industrialization remained slow and tardy in the twenties and thirties. For no definitive answer was yet in sight in quantitative terms as to whether India had in the long run gained or lost in terms of economic development by being a member of a free-trade area. All that was emèrging from the reports of the several Commissions or Committees of Inquiry was the need increasingly felt for State action as an instrument of economic development–a trend which remained yet unrecognized due to the continuing resistance of free trade. Naturally enough, the slant remained on the importance of agricultural development and the subsidiary occupations linked with it. Even a progressive economist like Kanu Subedar emphasized the importance of State-owned "agricultural banks" as the best institutional provision for rural credit to relieve the agriculturists from the oppressive conduct of money-lenders. The conference of the provincial governors organized in response to the Viceroy's circular letter addressed to them in 1934 drove in the same direction to provide relief to the farming community on the lines suggested by the Royal Commission on Agriculture.[71] But the Federation of Indian Chambers of Commerce and Industry had its own way, because, unlike the agriculturists, it was a well-organized body of trade and industry carrying on business for profit and concentration of economic power. It was this organization that pressed for the establishment of the Reserve Bank of India as well as provision for exchange facilities to promote India's foreign trade.

War-Time Industrial Development

The development of heavy industries in the course of the Second World War added considerably to the competitive strength of Indian capitalism as an economic force. During the six war-time years, 1939-40 to 1944-45, the annual output of manufacturers averaged about 29 per cent above the last pre-war year, the bulk of this increase being the result of the widening of the war into the Far East towards the end of 1941.[72]

Indeed, Britain was forced to set up in India itself factories to ensure supplies to the army and meet other requirements. Ordnance factories put out during the war ammunitions, rifles, machine-guns, and artillery pieces, while private concerns were entrusted with the supply of landing craft, trawlers, armoured car bodies, machine tools, electric motors, components and spares. This led to many public enterprises being reconstructed and enlarged and hundreds of new factories built to cope with the demand for supplies. G. K. Shirokov, a Russian author, who studied Indian industrial development in some depth, thus wrote : "It is sufficient to note that between 1940 and 1945 the colonial administration increased the number of its enterprises from 191 to 703. The labour force rose from 169,200 to 457,000."[73] According to P. J. Thomas, Economic Adviser to the first Government of Independent India, "The war conduced to the growth of old industries, the establishment of new industries, new plants and new technical build-up, resulting in the expansion of India's industrial structure."

Shirokov points out that war production in India, which constituted the main feature of industrial development in that period, was very much an affair of ordnance factories, forming on the whole a "self-contained organisation in which the entire process of manufacture ... was carried on without outside assistance of any kind". It was only when their capacity proved insufficient that a private industry was called to their aid, more especially in the manufacture of ships and armoured car bodies.[74]

In spite of the war-time industrial expansion of the country, India, however, did not emerge as a producer of capital goods. She could not even reproduce her existing production capacity. This was mainly due to her continuing dependence on imports for machinery, for transport and electrical equipment, for heavy and fine chemicals and other sophisticated industrial inputs. Even adequate technical know-how or provision for training was found wanting at the end of the war. This lack proceeded perhaps from a policy decision taken in 1940 at a conference of Eastern member countries of the British Commonwealth who proclaimed that duplication of war efforts was to be inadmissible.

However, India had by the year 1947 developed considerable potential for industrial development. Though not yet fully equipped with infrastructural facilities, the railways and other means of communication did provide easier and cheaper access to a wider market. And in spite of her inadequate scientific and technical cadre or training facilities she did possess an absolutely large pool of literate man-power which, in the presence of a number of scientific organizations and universities, could be trained to supply the deficiencies. Above all, the economic policy of the Government was by the end of the war firmly committed to a large-scale planned industrial development. It was the experience of war, more especially in terms of defence strategies, that dictated the expediency of State initiative to promote industrialization. The Government in fact issued a statement in April 1945 to confirm its commitment to such a policy. It said that "a vigorous and sustained effort is necessary in which the State, no less than a private industry, must take a part, and the Government have decided to take positive steps to encourage and promote the rapid industrialization of the country to the fullest possible extent".[75]

The economic policy objective so stated was no more empty declaration of intention. It included administrative action as part of the post-war Reconstruction Plan, which called for an administrative structure developing during the war itself. It included the establishment of a Planning and Development Department and subsequently in 1946 the appointment of an "Advisory Planning Board" which proceeded to plan industrial development under both public and private sectors.[76] Though yet frail and inadequate, the structure so emerging served as the basis of post-independence planning.

Approach to Policy Objective

The economic policy objective remained capitalist in its approach, governed in the main by free-trade principles, except with the recognition of the principle of imperial preference[77] which continued with certain changes till 1939. The preferential tariffs with the United Kingdom and the free colonies which provided for preferential rate of duty on Indian exports to Britain and British imports to India formed part of the Ottawa Pact in 1932. The Indian political opposition to imperial preference, however, remained unrelaxed. For Britain took only one-fourth of India's total exports and there was always a fear that other countries might imitiate retaliatory measures against India. The trade agreement concluded with Britain in 1939 preserved India's privileged position in British markets and in addition narrowed the scope of preference granted to imports.

The Indian business communities, which were organized into separate Chambers of Commerce, were the main pillars of the capitalist system. The Industrial Conference of 1915 was a result of their efforts and the first Industrial Commission appointed in 1916 marked the beginning of Indian capitalism as an organized force to compete against British free traders with the support of national politics for self-government. The fiscal autonomy for India provided by the Joint Select Committee of the House of Commons as part of the Government of India Bill, 1919, was an expression of its recognition for that force. The Federation of the Indian Chambers of Commerce and Industry and the Indian National Congress naturally collaborated in their fight against imperialist dominance, the former in fact functioning in the beginning as the economic wing of the All-India Congress Committee and M. K. Gandhi actually attended the Federation's annual session to address it in 1931. The difference, however, was that while the Congress was in the main a political organization of educated elites open to all kinds of influences, both radical and conservative, the Federation remained essentially a business organization, given to economic activity with profit motivation and individual gain. However the approach of the upper conservative elements of the Congress differed but little from that of the Federation, basically capitalistic and prone to profit-making and capital accumulation.

Venkatasubbiah's work on *50 Years of FICCI* makes it clear that "prominent leaders of the Federation" were connected with the National Planning Committee which the Congress established in 1938 to study the problems of industrial development in India. Sir Purshotamdas Thakurdas, the leading industrialist of Bombay who had been instrumental in the Gandhi-Irwin Pact in 1930, was himself a member of that Committee. It is true that the Federation did not take a sustained interest in its work, because its "exercise was meant for the future government of free India".[78] Even so, the Memorandum of the Tata-Birla Plan admitted in clear terms that the plan set out in it was "very largely" due to the "comprehensive" scope of the National Planning Committee,[79] weighted on the side of heavy and key industries for purposes of a self-sustained economy.

Another important trend that gained steadily in strength was a demand for State action or statism to regulate economic policies. The element of planning, which it involved as a remedy to cyclic depression inherent in capitalism, was a common factor in politics. While the Left viewed State interference as the only impartial instrument to bring relief to sufferers through public control, the Right envisaged a prospect of financial assistance to boost industrial investment and production and not to keep demands alive in a state of depression but also to proliferate the same on the basis of individual capitalist initiative as Nalini Ranjan Sarkar had put it in his presidential address to the FICCI in 1934. Little did the Left realize that imperialism was a developed form of capitalism itself and that State action as an instrument of economic policy would mean no more than what might be described as "State capitalism", conducive to the promotion of private enterprise, not only through the development of infrastructure as the British had since long been doing in response to their own colonial investment, but also through the coverage of new fields normally given to private control.

State capitalism or, in other words, the involvement of the State in business enterprise, though immediately intended to boost industrialization, created, in search of development capital, conditions conducive to the growth of Multi-National Corporations functioning as financial pools to promote economic development internationally to forestall the dangers of any slump inherent in the capitalist order of things. The main feature of Indian industry in the colonial period was its close link with foreign, primarily British, capital, essentially monopolistic in origin and operation because of Britain's political hold on India. During the Second World War, the United States took advantage of her difficulties and proceeded to consolidate its position in the Indian market by making use of both the conventional channel and provisions for lend-lease deliveries. The Americans supplied equipment to India, which gave them an opportunity to establish close links with Indian business circles as well as the princely States. It was during the war years that the United States concluded agreements not only with the authorities in British India, but also with private business in Baroda, Cochin, Travancore, Mysore and other native States for the construction of several large factories. The war years in fact saw the emergence of the USA as a nation of investors second only to Britain, controlling, according to the first census of foreign assets and liabilities in India (1948), 71.8 per cent of the bulk of industrial investment as against 6.4 per cent of the USA coming second.[80]

The USA and Britain together devised a plan for a new international monetary system for Reconstruction and Development, which was discussed at length at the Bretton Woods Conference in 1944. It was the Bretton Woods agreements that led to the establishment of the International Monetary Fund and the World Bank. These agreements called for their being ratified before the last day of 1945 by a country desiring to become an Original Member of the Fund and the Bank.[81]

The Federation of the Indian Chambers of Commerce and Industry was immediately interested in these developments of an international financial order which might have a repercussion on the settlement of India's own sterling balance lying with the British Government, an issue which was not without its international bearing. The Committee of the Federation had in fact already been in correspondence on the subject with the Finance Department of the Government of India in 1943. It wanted to know whether there was in the international currency proposals any provision for a free convertibility of India's sterling balances, or for using them to wipe out the balance of payment in her foreign trade or indebtedness. The Indian big business feared that there was perhaps no provision to prevent these balances from being exploited to push foreign goods in the country irrespective of their value or utility. Indeed, their whole object was to have the balances freely converted, so that they could import capital goods and machinery, especially from America, for use as industrial inputs to develop heavy key industries in India. They did not want any consumer goods.

The Indian business representatives were, however, set at rest when at the Bretton Woods Conference the United States Government supported a British proposal to have the Indian issue of sterling balance settled through bilateral negotiations. Lord Keynes who led the British delegation even reiterated that the balance represented a debt generously given and that it would be honourably discharged. It was then that Sir Archibald Rowlands, Finance Member, raised the question of India being admitted as the Original Member of the Fund and the Bank. In a letter written to the President of the Federation, Sir Badridas Goenka, Rowlands suggested in India's own interest that she should ratify the agreements in anticipation of the Central Assembly to which Goenka agreed. G. D. Birla in a brief note simply added that this should have been done with the full consent of those who were likely to hold governmental power in the future.

The correspondence which Rowlands had with the President of the Federation shows that Bretton Woods Conference was the first international conference to which India was invited independently without any reserve, and not as forming part of the British delegation in a subordinate capacity. There was to be no difficulty, technical or even political, in the way of a decision in favour of ratification, especially when the original membership was invested with a leverage in the settlement of any financial or monetary matters of dispute with an international implication. The U.S. Government was in fact anxious to have the Indian big business on its side to win the Dollar Pool of the Fund and the Bank reinforced to be the potential supplier of capital for post-war reconstruction and development on capitalist lines.

As a popularly sustained link between the Left and the Right in the Congress, Jawaharlal Nehru, however, held a facade of State regulation of capital and credit institutions, a facade which not only looked pleasing at first sight, but was also politically advantageous. Although as Chairman of the National Planning Committee he admitted in 1938 that the Congress had "not in any way accepted socialism",[82] he sought to explain the NPC's recommendation for a takeover of banking as proceeding from "some of us at any rate" who hoped to evolve a "socialized system of credit" which, if not to be nationalized, "should at least be under the control of the State".[83]

While Nehru's advocacy in the Congress for State control was more formal than real, the Working People's representatives were really convinced of such control as the only instrument of socialism. On March 10, 1944, they brought out their "People's Plan" under the joint signatures of B. N. Banerjee, G. D. Parikh and V. M. Tarkunde (Convener).

The People's Plan was first received in the Department of Planning and Development, Government of India, which appended a summary for consideration by the Finance Department in September of 1944 itself. The text of the Plan later appeared in the Special Number of *Young Indian*, 1972. I made use of both. The text covered as many as 144 paragraphs as against 99 paragraphs of *A Plan of Economic Development for India*, otherwise known as Bombay Plan of Indian capitalists presented to the Government in January 1944 by Purshotamdas Thakurdas, J. R. D. Tata, G. D. Birla, Ardeshir Dalal, Kasturbhai Lalbhai, A. D. Shroff and John Matthai. While the industrialists gave their highest priority to raising production, the sponsors of the People's Plan emphasized both growth and distribution aspects; for, according to it, the basic problem of Indian economic life was the problem of poverty which could not be solved on the basis of capitalism which emphasized production not for the use but for exchange or market economy for profit. The Plan envisaged that increased production and equitable distribution could alone provide the cure for the evil of poverty.

The sponsors of the People's Plan emphasized the enactment of land reforms by abolishing all kinds of intermediaries between the State and the actual cultivator. They recommended land nationalization to show how this would conduce to increase in the purchasing power of a large majority of people engaged in agriculture–an increase in the purchasing power of the masses which could then be utilized in building up industries. Though in theoretical terms critical of some of the assumptions made in other respects, the Planning and Development Department appreciated the proposed steps towards modernization of agriculture as an effective aid to industrial development, steps especially connected with drastic reforms of land tenure, liquidation of rural indebtedness by an institutional credit system and development of irrigation and scientific agricultural-methods.

The dominant approach to economic policy objective, however, continued to be governed by considerations of private entrepreneurship, a result of development under British rule which, as part of its socio-economic policies, had since long provided for infrastructural facilities, either departmentally or as separate autonomous boards functioning under the authority of the State in varying degrees without interference with free trade privileges. Railways, ordnance factories, transport, communication and irrigation had already come under this category. What the Post-War Reconstruction and Development Plan sought to do was to add to the old list of infrastructure and develop the same as basic industries of national importance under an organized separate public sector, subject to the financial and legislative control of the State. As Shirokov rightly points out, the public undertakings, so created, "serve as the base for expanding the operations of the private sector", the object being to promote the capitalist "class purpose".[84] It was in fact a case of continuity of imperialist tradition, the newly added beneficiaries of infrastructure being, however, the Indian industrialists who had earlier been struggling for fiscal autonomy to rise in competition with foreign counterparts.

Five-Year Planning by the Government : 1944

The Plan of Economic Development for India (1944) known as the Bombay Plan of "Indian capitalists" was rejected by the Government of India who in May of the same year had asked the Provincial Government to prepare their Five-Year Plans for the post-war reconstruction and development. A plan prepared by the Bombay Government was in fact circulated in October (1944) to serve as a model.

An Advisory Planning Board of the Government of India was actually established in October 1946, with E. P. Moon as Secretary and government officials as the majority of members. Its functions were as follows:[85]

(a) To review that which has already been done by the Government, the work of the National Planning Committee, and other plans and proposals for planning,

(b) To make recommendations in the light of this review for

the coordination and improvement of planning,

(c) To make recommendations as regards objectives and priorities,

(d) To make recommendations regarding the future machinery of planning.

Th Advisory Planning Board came into existence in the context not only of the Post-War Reconstruction and Development asking the provinces in 1944 to prepare their Five-Year Plans, but also of the International Monetary Fund and the World Bank established in the wake of the Bretton Woods Conference (1944) which was followed by a statement of industrial policy of the Government of India issued in April 1945. This was an important economic policy statement directly involving the State in the process of industrialization. As contemplated by the Government of India Act (1935), this statement sought to bring under Central control all such industries as were considered "desirable" for purposes of a common policy and goal dictated especially by the exigencies of defence. The statement included 20 such industries. The recommendations of the Advisory Planning Board, established by the Interim Government with Jawaharlal Nehru at its head, added one more (Vanaspati) to the list for Central control.[86]

The question of the extent of State ownership of key industries was of course an important new development. But here again, it was the policy statement of April 1945 that provided the guideline for Nehru's Interim Government of 1946. It was a line of industrial policy which bore no marks of deflection as a consequence of what the Quit India Movement of the Congress had done in 1942. It was a precise policy analysis in terms of India's defence requirements and other valid considerations.

Historically, ordnance factories, public utilities and railways had already been largely State-owned and State-operated. These could not but continue as forming a considerable proportion of the country's total industrial enterprise. The generation of electric power too was then recognized as a matter of State concern. The Policy Statement of 1945 then proceeded to define what it called the basic industries of national importance which, as the defence strategy of both the imperialist wars had suggested, called for nationalization as the best source of national security. These included, for instance, aircraft, automobiles and tractors, chemicals, electrical machinery, machine tools, electro-chemicals and non-ferrous metal industries. All other industries were proposed to be left to private enterprise with varying degrees of control. The case of coal as a basic industry was sought to be treated separately; and so were the cases of ship-building and manufacture of locomotives and boilers run by the State as well as private entrepreneurs. A State enterprise was declared as subject to management through public corporations for experience.

The Industrial Policy Statement of April 1945 as well as the Advisory Planning Board of Nehru's Interim Government both held that the basic industries of national importance which were alike in both of their lists could be nationalized "provided adequate private capital is not forthcoming and it is regarded as essential, in the national interests, to promote such industries". The question of nationalization thus remained open. But, as the Report of the Advisory Planning Board said, "the various industrial panels which, under their terms of reference, were required to report whether on either of the grounds mentioned above they recommended nationalization have so far almost all favoured private ownership". State enterprise was recommended only where in the absence of "an immediate prospect of profit" private capital happened to be shy. "Broadly speaking, therefore, thinking and planning in regard to industrial development has so far proceeded on the assumption that practically the whole field will be left to private enterprise".[87]

The Advisory Planning Board thus resolved to limit the scope of nationalization. It said: "We would give it therefore as our opinion that if at the present juncture the State attempted to take into its own hands the ownership and management of the large range of industries the industrial development of the country might not be very rapid. Nevertheless, it seems to us that it should be our policy to bring under State ownership and management some at least of the basic industries of the country, and that the execution of such a policy should form part of our plans. We recommend, therefore, that apart from defence industries and any industry or branch of any industry which it might be found desirable to start as a State enterprise through the reluctance of private capital to undertake it, the nationalization of the following should be considered: coal, mineral oils, iron and steel, motor, air and river transport."

Indeed, the report of the Advisory Planning Board of Nehru's Interim Government makes it clear that it was in principle not inclined to lend support to the State ownership of industries other than those related to the country's defence. It favoured nationalization, but that, too, in terms of certain limited industries of national importance. Its reason was plain, and simple. "The enlargement of State enterprise", it firmly believed, "will necessitate considerable alteration in the present method of Government administration", geared to the requirements of law and order, a punitive function, not of development, which called for a cooperative bent of mind. The Board therefore emphasized that no State enterprise should be conducted except "through public corporations". The controversy so agitating men's mind was understandable. It proceeded from the State itself being directly involved or committed as an instrument linked with the problems of industrial production and economic development. It was this controversial thinking that led to industries being classified into private and public sectors for purposes of organization, management and control. He also underlined the policy of the Government as regards the various forms of State aid and State control which might be extended to those industries which were left to private enterprise.

Question of Foreign Capital and Management

In spite of active thinking on a variety of State control and management, industries, other than those directly owned by the Government and operated departmentally, remained on the whole as part of private enterprise. In consequence of the Policy Statement of April 1945, the objects of industrialization were of course clearly defined as the maximum exploitation of the country's resources to provide for a high and stable level of industrial employment as well as to make the country fully prepared for defence by removing the potential dangers inherent in India's dependence on overseas supplies for vital commodities required for defence. But no reference whatever was made to foreign aid as an instrument for the attainment of the objects so defined.

As regards the Advisory Planning Board, the panels appointed under it were asked to report whether the capital required for industrial development would be available by public investment as well as "the manner and degree of cooperation with foreign firms considered necessary and desirable both as regards capital and management". On the first question, the finding of the panels was that "the necessary capital will be forthcoming from this country and that foreign capital will not be required for direct investment in industries".[88] The Board endorsed this view, and felt assured that given proper inducements and safeguards, private investors would provide all the capital needed; and in case they failed, "it should be found by Government". This confidence flowed immediately from the gains of the Indian business Houses acquired in the course of the Second World War. These enabled them to buy controlling shares in public limited foreign companies. For while the aggregate share of the Indian business Houses improved from 24.7 per cent in 1937 to 57.35 per cent in 1947, their combined paid-up capital increased from Rs. 15.69 crores in 1937 to Rs. 64.65 crores in 1947.[89] As R. K. Hazari's work on *The Structure of the Private Corporate Sector* shows, the Indian business Houses which gained most were those of the Tatas and the Birlas. Their Plan of Economic Development for India, known popularly as the Bombay Plan, had in fact even claimed that their scheme was "well within the limits of our resources".

What the Advisory Planning Board, however, found wanting was a lack of trained personnel and specialized skill. In the case of highly specialized industries, the Board, therefore, suggested the need to acquiesce in an "Agreement of Management which would leave the control of management in foreign hands for a limited period". It added that in such a case, "if participation in capital is made a necessary condition of association, there should be no objection to it provided that effective control is retained in Indian hands", the Government exercising at the same time a general supervision over the Agreement, so that the Indian personnel could in due course take over the entire management including the technical direction of the Company. "Beyond this", as the Board said, "we are of the opinion that the intrusion of foreign firms in the field of Indian industry should not be allowed".[90]

The rise of Indian business Houses as an instrument of industrial development had thus by 1947 come to assert itself as a competitive force. It was the effect of industry and politics being yoked to wrest economic privileges vested as a rule in foreign British companies or their allies. The strategy which the Indian business Houses employed was pressure for State action involving tariff and fiscal concessions. But it was in the main the compulsions of the two world wars that enabled them build up a sterling reserve which was sought to be employed in the purchase of machinery and equipment for development. Leftist forces doubtless raised their heads from time to time. But the presence of imperialist rule cast the weight of its influence on the side of private enterprise which took further advantage of the infrastructure built up to meet the exigencies of the war on the score of ideology and Statism, pleasing apparently to the adherents of Left politics.

In spite of the official Statement of April 1945 being intended to end laissez-faire, it was in effect the organized pressure of the Federation of Indian Chambers of Commerce and Industry that prevented real incursion into the structure of industrial ownership. It was argued that even where the State owned industries, wholly or partly, there could be no reason why they should not be managed by private corporations or companies, more especially on the score of economy. For it was an admitted truth that management by the State involved "disproportionately higher overhead charges and consequently higher cost of production".

It was perhaps the influence of the Federation that became reflected in the recommendations of the Advisory Planning Board, not only in respect of an emphasis on the side of private enterprise but more so on the exclusion of foreign capital from any participation in Indian industrialization. In its resolution on the Bombay Plan itself the Federation had at its 1944 annual session "noted with satisfaction that acceptance of foreign capital, if necessary, is to be free from political influence and interference of foreign vested interests. India should be free to discriminate against non-Indian interests in the matter of tariff protection if need be".[91]

Even so, it was at this period that a noticeable change appeared in the attitude of both Whitehall and British businessmen who showed an appreciation of the Indian position regarding post-war reconstruction and industrial development. In a letter of January 25, 1945, addressed to Lord Wavell, the Secretary of State, L. S. Amery, even stated that several negotiations were afoot between the U.K. and Indian business Houses for the establishment of joint enterprises in India.[92] Mention was made especially of the Tatas negotiating with the Imperial Chemical Industries and of the Birlas proceeding with an agreement with Nuffield. The Federation's anti-foreign-participation posture was thus no more than a mere show to strike a hard bargain. British interests were in fact prepared, in competition with U.S. investors, to make available to the Federation their knowledge and, in some cases, even their reputation, organization and market facility. In other words, conditions for a multinational collaboration had emerged by the time arrangements were envisaged for the transfer of power in 1947.

No Consideration for the People's Plan

A "People's Plan", as said above, was submitted for consideration to the Government at about the same time as the Tata-Birla Bombay Plan of 1944. It sought to make a distinction between production for use and production for profit or exchange. Its argument was that the fundamental problem of Indian economic life was the problem of poverty which could not be solved except by increased production for use providing for equitable distribution as the only cure for the evil of poverty.

In effect, the authors of the Plan said: "Give us just Rs. 1,600 crores spread over three years, give us power to 'nationalize' land to get rid of the permanent system and the Zamindari system to consolidate the holdings; power to nationalize all new industries and limit the profits by private capitalists of industries to 3 per cent and we promise you the millenium in 10 years."

This People's Plan was, however, rejected by the Reconstruction Committee of Council as impracticable. The advisory Planning Board of Nehru's Interim Government of 1946 took no notice of it. It acted on the lines suggested by the FICCI and the economic policy statement of 1945, but had nothing to do with the socialism which the Plan advocated as its goal.

REFERENCES

1. See *Auckinleck Papers*, Manchester University Library, Item 1152 (May 11, 1946).
2. See Home (Pol.) B. Progs., Jan. 1920, No. 279.
3. See H.N. Mitra, *The Indian Annual Register*, 1923, Vol.I, p. 55.
4. Parl. Papers No. 171 of 1922, p. 293.
5. H.N. Mitra, op. cit., p. 59.
6. Home (Pol.) B. Progs., July 1920, No. 109 (Report from the Commissioner of Police, Bombay), pp. 2-3.
7. See Foreign-Political (External) B. Progs., Nos. 138-142, Oct. 1921 (B. 361); also A appendix I to Home (Pol.) B. Progs., Jan. 1920, K.W. Nos. 283-292,
8. Home (Pol.) B. Progs., July 1920, No. 109 (Report from the Commissioner of Police, Bombay), pp.2-3.
9. Home (Pol.) Deposit (Print) Progs., May 1921, No. 43.
10. Home (Pol.) B. Progs., March 1920, No. 183.
11. Home (Pol.) Deposit Progs., Aug. 1920, No 38, pp. 1-2.
12. See Parl. Papers No. 1586 of 1922, p. 6.
13. Home (Pol.) File No. 82 and K.W. of 1925, Part I (Confidential), para 10, p. 10.
14. See Home (Pol.) File 261 of 1924 & K.W., pp. 1-2; also Philips, *The Evolution of India and Pakistan. 1858-1947* (Select Documents), pp. 254-55, giving an ideal of the financial assistance made available to Indian emissaries for communist propaganda under the guidance of the Comintern in Moscow.
15. See Philips, op. cit., pp. 261-62.
16. Ibid.p. 260.
17. See Home (Pol.) File 262/1 and 262/2 of 1923.
18. See Sir Cecil Kaye (ed.), *Communism in India,* p.30.
19. See Home (Pol.) File No. 18/VII,K.W. XIII (1927).
20. An account of foreign money received by communists in India during 1922-28 is given in Home (Pol.) File No. 18/VII of 1928, K.W. X and XI.
21. Home (Pol.) File No. 18/VII of 1928, K.W. XI.
22. This was admitted by Lord Irwin, the Viceroy. See *Halifax Papers*, I.O. MSS. Eur. C.152/V, p. 56 (Sec. of State to Viceroy, March 5, 1930) and Ibid., p. 85 (Viceroy. to Sec. of State, April 23, 1930).
23. Viceroy to Secretary of State, Feb. 6, 1930, Ibid., p. 27.
24. See Misra, *The Indian Political Parties,* pp. 266-90.
25. Home (Pol.) File 4/4/34, Poll (I), pp. 17-18.
26. Home (Pol.) File 4/7/35-Poll (I) of 1935.
27. See Home (Pol.) File 3/XI/34-Poll (I), pp, 3-4.
28. Ibid., pp. 5-6.
29. Intercepted letter from Gandhi to Nehru, Sept. 22, 1935, Home (Pol.) File 4/7/35, pp. 1-2.
30. See Finance Dept. File No, 16(1)-F/1934. This is an important file which contains not only correspondence on the subject of economic depression and agricultural crisis, but also very useful statistical information and the Resolution of Government adopted at a conference of central and provincial Government representatives held from April 3 to 6, 1934.
31. Venkatasubbiah, p. 4; also see Ibid., pp. 2-3.
32. See Halifax Papers, I.O. MSS. Eur. C.152/V (Feb. 6, 1930, March 5, 1930, April 22, 1930). See also Misra, *The Indian* Political Parties (The Growth of Left Parties and Groups).

33. See Haig to Brabourne, March 13, 1934, I. O. MSS. Eur. F. 97/5, p. 30; also Home (Pol.) File No. 4/4/34-Poll (I),pp.2-3.
34. See Home (Pol.) File No. 4/7/35-Poll. of 1935.
35. Venkatasubbiah, op. cit., p. 16.
36. Ibid., p. 17.
37. Ibid.
38. See Philips, *Select Documents*, pp. 607-09
39. Venkatasubbiah, op. cit., p. 8.
40. Visvesvaraya, *Planned Economy for India*, 1934, p. 183.
41. Venkatasubbiah, op. cit., pp. 11-16.
42. Ibid., pp. 183-88.
43. Indian Fiscal Commission Report (1921-22); Sir Henry Babington Smith Committee (May 1919), Majority Report, 2s. to a rupee; Royal Commission on Indian Finance (1925), Chairman Edward Hilton Young, Report (1926); Royal Commission on Agriculture (1926), Report (1927); Royal Commission on Labour (1929), Report (1931). There were, in addition, committees appointed to report on the problems of rural credit for development involving reorganization of banking and provision for security against loans for rural uplift.
44. This appointment of the Committee was made according to the Council of State resolution of Feb.4,1924, and the resolution of the Legislative Assembly adopted on Sept. 22 of the same year asking the Govt. to dissolve the existing Taxation Enquiry Committee and appoint a committee of non-officials and experts to institute a thorough enquiry on the points suggested by the Assembly.
45. See *Report*, Vol. I, chapter I, p. 2.
46. *Report*, chapter II, p. 6.
47. Ibid., p. 8.
48. Ibid., p. 9.
49. Visvesvaraya, op. cit., pp. 51-52.
50. See Govt. of India, Finance Dept., File No. 17 (110) F. 1931.
51. Ibid., Secs. 10 and 11.
52. Ibid., Sec. 24 indicating the scheme of rural credit at a glance.
53. Govt. of India, Finance Dept. File No. 7-(28)-F of 1931 (Majority Report signed by 18 members, including Report of foreign banking experts)—Summary of Report, pp. 1-40.
54. To provide for coordination between the Central and Provincial Governments an Imperial Council of Agricultural Research was instituted in 1929, the nature of its function in terms of training and research being clearly defined to facilitate coordination with the provinces to which the subject had been transferred under the 1919 Act. See Misra, *Administrative History*, pp. 143-44.
55. See Govt. of India, Finance Dept. File 7-XIX-F of 1930.
56. See Visvesvaraya, op. cit, pp. 57-58. According to 1921 census the total number of persons supported by industries of all kinds was 10.49 per cent of the whole population. The corresponding figure for 1931 was 9.7 per cent. See also *The Cambridge Economic History of India*, Vol. Vol. II, pp. 607-10; also Misra, *The Indian Middle Classes*, pp. 238-41.
57. They were Purshotamdas Thakerdas, D.P. Khaitan, Mukhtar Singh, V. Ramdas Pantulu, R.K. Shanmukham Chetty and M. Jamal Mahomed.
58. *Report*, paras 36-42.
59. No. 16(1)-F/1934, proposing an inter-provincial conference.
60. See Zaidi (ed.), *Economic Planning*, p. 375. In a statement of Dec. 21,1938,

on the subject of Congress policy Nehru observed as Chairman of the National Planning Committee that in spite of its resolution and "approval of socialist theories" the "Congress has not in any way accepted socialism".

61. See Pamphlet entitled "A Tentative Socialist Programme for India" by Sampurnanand in Home (Pol.) File No. 41/1/34-Poll of the abolition of the zamindari system and the State take-over of heavy industries.
62. Zaidi (ed.), op, cit.,p. 65.
63. Ibid., p. 67-69. See also Misra, *The Indian Political Parties,* pp. 310-15.
64. Venkatasubbiah, op. cit., p.21.
65. See Visvesvaraya, op. cit.,chap. XIV.
66. They included Purshotamdas Thakurdas, J. R. D. Tata, G. D. Birla, Ardeshir Dalal, Shri Ram, Kasturbhai Lalbhai, A.D. Shroff and John Matthai.
67. See *Auchinleck Papers,* Manchester University Library, Item 1152 (May 11, 1946) dealing with the importance of leaving "Hindustan" as a friendly country in the interest of British investment as well as free communication through the Indian Ocean.
68. See Misra, *District Administration and Rural Development in India,* O.U.P., 1983.
69. The Board was designed also to implement provisions for imperial preference involved in discriminating protection under the recommendation of 1921-22. These eventually led to the conclusion of the Ottawa Trade Agreement of 1932. Originally, the imperial preference concept proceeded from the offer made by the Indian members of the Viceroy's Legislative Council on March 17, 1913. See Sir Roper Lethbridge *The Indian Offer of Imperial Preference,* London, 1913.
70. See *Report.*
71. See *Report.*
72. See *The Cambridge Economic History of India,* Vol. II, pp. 640-41.
73. Shirokov, *Industrialization of India,* Moscow, 1973.
74. Ibid., pp. 26-27.
75. *The Cambridge Economic History of India,* Vol. II, p. 642.
76. See Govt. of India, Finance Dept. File No. 12(12)-PI/46, Vol. I and No. 12 (12)-PI/46, Vol. II, containing Report of the Advisory Planning Board. See also N.P.F. 12(4)-P/47. The sectoral idea was first suggested by the Government Industrial Policy Statement of 1945 itself. See Philips, *Select Documents,* p. 698-701.
77. See Sir Roper Lethbridge, *The Indian Offer of Imperial Preference,* London, 1913.
78. Venkatasubbiah, op. cit., pp. 22-23.
79. See Philips (ed.), *Select Documents,* p. 697.
80. Shirokov, op. cit., p. 47.
81. See Venkatasubbiah, op. cit., chap. IV.
82. Zaidi (ed.) op. cit. p.375.
83. Jawaharlal Nehru, *Discovery of India,* Bombay, 1965, p. 399.
84. See Shirokov, op. cit., p. 89.
85. See Finance Dept., Planning Branch File No. 12(12)-PI/46, Vol. I.
86. Finance, Planning Branch File No. 12(12)-PI/46-Vol. II, para 52.
87. Ibid., para 56.
88. Ibid., para 58.
89. See S.K. Goyal, *Monopoly Capital and Public Policy,* pp. 45-47.
90. *Report,* paras 59 and 60.
91. Venkatasubbiah, op. cit., p. 52 (resolution cited).
92. Ibid., p. 52.

THREE

The Congress Government Dilemma : Promise-Performance Gap – 1947-67

Jawaharlal Nehru was elected President of the Indian National Congress in 1946. But he was obliged by the Party soon to resign in order to head the Interim Government as the Vice-President of the Executive Council. On the transfer of power in 1947, he became India's first Prime Minister. The Congress Presidency and Prime Ministership, however, remained separate and distinct offices until 1951 when Nehru united both under himself to ensure smooth and coordinated functioning. This centralized arrangement continued till 1954. Between that year and 1963 the organization was sought to be headed by junior leaders looking after its day-to-day affairs under Nehru's own guidance. The period from 1963 to 1967 marked of course a departure, although a new equilibrium appeared to stabilize harmony between Congress Presidency and Prime Ministership. In spite of these changes, the dominance of one-party Congress Government remained unaffected for the first couple of decades since Independence.

Characteristic Feature

The characteristic feature of this period in terms of economic development is the radicalism of the Government's declared policy intent and its preparedness, at the same time, to compromise in practice in favour of continuity. While policy pronouncements were known for their emphasis on land reforms, greater public ownership, strict regulation of private enterprise as well as a just distributive system as a means to mitigate inequalities with the promotion of economic growth, the importance which the big business laid on increasing production as the only way left to alleviate poverty remained in practice unreduced.

Evidence is not found wanting in support of the analysis of the *Indian Economy Since Independence* which says[1] :

"The Congress Party, which has held power over most of the country since independence, has essentially attempted a compromise ... which leans to the radical in declared intent but affords the conservatives ample opportunities to resist implementation of policies. The conservative elements have found it politically inexpedient to oppose promotion of socio-economic justice as a goal of policy. They even acquiesced, under radical pressure, to formulating the Directive Principles, legislating land reforms, accepting a dominant role for public ownership and regulation. But they did so reluctantly and have consistently tried to dilute the policies both at the stage of formulation, and even more, in implementation".

The constitutional-legal framework that emerged in the immediate context of the Congress functioning as an anti-imperialist movement of a radical nature on a national basis served perhaps as the modus operandi for the conversion of that movement into a party apparatus on the basis of class interest. Though seemingly radical, its Directive Principles are little more than declarations of intent with hardly any real sanction behind them. There are, no doubt, mandatory or justiciable provisions relating to fundamental rights, especially touching on property. But the check and balance provided between the Centre and the States as well as among the legislative, executive and judicial wings of government are so interwoven that the weaker sections of society can hardly hope to get the benefit of justice. It is generally the well-to-do who by virtue of their economic power as well as their control of legislature and the administration stand to gain. They alone can afford to go in for prolonged and expensive litigation involved in the administration based on the cumbrous rule of law. The promises held out by law and Constitution cannot but in practice remain unredeemed.

Contradiction at Policy Level-The Mixed Economy Case : 1948

Contradiction existed not only in terms of implementation, but at the policy level itself. The preceding chapter has shown how private enterprise continued to assert itself in spite of the policy statement of April 1945 and the recommendations of the Advisory Planning Board which leaned against laissez-faire in support of State control or public ownership–a line of policy to which the Congress itself had declaredly been committed ever since its Karachi session of 1931. What consistently stood in the way was the influence which the Federation of Indian Chambers of Commerce and Industry had with the top echelon of the Congress leadership.

It was the federation-fed economic situation that Jawaharlal Nehru inherited in 1947. What his AICC did in its meeting held on November 17, 1947, was to have an Economic Programme Committee appointed with Nehru himself as its Chairman, so that the benefits of political democracy might be extended to socio-economic spheres. While the country's political system was to "combine efficiency of administration with individual liberty", its economic structure was to be designed to "yield maximum production without the operation of private monopolies and the concentration of wealth". The structure to be so evolved was to "create a proper balance between urban and rural economies".[2]

The Committee divided the industrial sector into small-scale (cottage) and large-scale (heavy) industries, provided that while the former produced consumer goods on a decentralized cooperative basis the latter engaged in the production of machinery and capital goods in a manner and on a principle not ruinous to any of the cottage or feeder industries. The use of the agency of the State was to be an essential condition for heavy industries, for it was felt that the State alone could best protect small-scale cottage industries against the undue pressure and competition of monopoly capital. The Committee's Report thus said[3]:

"In order to avoid competition between production so reserved for cottage industries and large-scale production the State may bring under its control such competing large-scale industry. Where cottage industry is allowed to operate in the same field as large-scale mechanized industry its output should be protected from the competition of the latter by subsidies or some method of price equalization. This applies specially to cotton textile industry. In this and similar cases, further expansion of large-scale industry should be restricted except where this is considered necessary. In such cases it should be undertaken under State auspices."

Indeed the Committee viewed State agency as obstructive to private monopoly and business concentration. It, therefore, recommended that "new undertakings in defence, key and public utility industries should be started under public ownership". It also emphasized that new undertakings which were in the nature of monopolies or in view of their scale of operation serve the country as a whole or cover more than one province should be run on the basis of public ownership.[4] It was precisely on this principle that the Committee suggested the necessity of bringing private concerns periodically under State control.

The Committee's recommendations were, however, diluted in favour of private enterprise when these were processed by the Government headed by Nehru himself as its Prime Minister. The official Government position enunciated in the form of its Industrial Policy Resolution of 1948 turned out to be a far cry from the views expressed by the Committee in its Report that came out a little earlier in 1948 itself. It reflected more or less a continuity of the existing position, a compromise with private enterprise. In general, the Industrial Policy Resolution provided in 1948 for a mixed economy. The principle of Government ownership and control was accepted in regard to only a segment of the economy confined, as before, to three industries: munitions, atomic energy and railways. In six other fields regarded as key industries the Government reserved for itself the exclusive right to start new ventures. These, for instance, were coal, iron and steel, aircraft manufacture, shipbuilding, telephone and telegraph and wireless apparatus, and minerals. The State was to be responsible for further expansion in these fields except, however, to the extent that it considered the cooperation of private enterprise necessary for the purpose. Nationalization in respect of key industries, as said before, had been permissible under the terms of the policy statement of April 1945. But under the Policy Resolution of 1948, it was to be postponed for a period of at least 10 years. The Government, in addition, guaranteed that in the interim period existing concerns in these industries would remain free from any

State control. In the rest of the industrial field, the entire initiative for development and responsibility for management was to rest on private enterprise. All that the Government did was simply to retain with itself thc right to acquire any undertaking in the public interest and to intervene in cases where the conduct of industry under private control happened to be unsatisfactory.[5] The declared policy statement of the Economic Programme Committee was thus whittled down beyond recognition by the Ministry, Nehru himself being quite moderate in his approach to the Policy Resolution of 1948. A perusal of the First Five Year Plan itself shows that the distinction between the public and the private sector was viewed as one of "relative emphasis" and not as "anything like two separate entities".[6]

It is of interest, however, to note that although geared to development on modern Western methods ever since the First World War, economic growth offered no answer to increasing poverty and unemployment. The First Five Year Plan document of December 7, 1952, admitted it. There had been considerable industrial development, it said, with the growth of large towns and cities, modern transport and communication, modern business enterprise and finance involving the emergence of new economic and social relationships. Even so, the economic development so effected in the last few decades had brought "no significant improvement in standards of living and opportunities for employment, and has perhaps accentuated to some extent inequalities of income and wealth.[7]

The soundness or otherwise of economic development in terms of employment opportunities thus became a debatable issue with the leadership of the Congress Party both outside and inside its Government at the Centre and in the States. While the Gandhians attributed the growth of unemployment to the neglect of the decentralized system of village and cottage industries, pressing demand for the competition of large-scale mechanized industries, the socialists of the Western style advocated large-scale industrial production as the only solution for the mitigation of inequalities and improvement in the employment situation. The Hyderabad session of the Congress in 1953 was, however, weighted on the side of a decentralized rural economy comparable to what was known as the Bhoodan Movement, which calls for a declared policy commitment to village and cottage industries being assigned their own specific plane in the country's economic system. The Congress in fact took its cue from the final draft of the First Plan which laid its emphasis on the expansion and strengthening of the small-scale industries and community development on a comparative basis. Indeed, the fear of the Gandhian school was that while the employment opportunities of capital-intensive plans were all too limited, heavy industries were bound to absorb the bulk of capital investment, thus leaving little for the development of such industries as engaged in the production of consumer goods, the necessity of the bulk of Indian population.

In the controversy that went on between the Congress Party and its Government on the issue of small-scale vs. large-scale industries, Jawaharlal Nehru sought to steer a middle course in the sense that cottage and small-scale industry were to form an essential part of India's main industrial development which was bound to proceed on the lines of heavy capital goods industry intended to subserve the ends of a "socialistic pattern of society", a policy objective which, after his first discussion with the National Development Council in 1954, was endorsed by the Congress session held at Avadi, Madras, in January 1955. Its implication was that the principal means of production should be under social control or State ownership. The objective so approved at Avadi was later incorporated as part of the Government Industrial Policy Resolution presented to Parliament on April 30, 1956.

Public Ownership Case of 1956

The new Industrial Policy Resolution expanded the scope of the public sector by means of a division of industries into three categories, having regard to the part which the State would be expected to play in each. The first category consisted of industries comprised in Schedule A. Their future development was to be the exclusive responsibility of the public sector, of the State itself. Included in this category were all the basic and strategic industries, public utilities and industries requiring large investment, more especially heavy industry like iron and steel, machine tools, heavy electricals and mining. All these were to form part of the public sector in addition to six other fields of public ownership classified under the Policy Resolution of 1948. The second category of Schedule B consisted of 12 industries classified as a concurrent list. These were in the main to be dominant public sector enterprises engaged in the production of machine tools, essential drugs, aluminium, basic chemicals and sea and road transport. The private sector was expected to supplement the effort of the State. But the industries included in Schedule B were generally to be State-owned. It was the State which was expected to take the initiative in establishing new industries in this field. All other industries were in general to be left to the private sector, the third category, where the initiative in terms of organization and management was to remain vested in private entrepreneur. The Resolution also provided for public-private cooperation for purposes of developing reserved sectors.

The Industrial Policy Resolution of April 1956 came out a few weeks before the presentation of the Second Plan based on it. It represented a reconciliation of the differences between the advocates of the small-scale cottage industries and the large-scale heavy industries. This reconciliation was brought about by Professor P. C. Mahalanobis, Chairman of the Indian Statistical Institute and Adviser to the Planning Commission that released his "plan frame" on March 17, 1955. It provided for a basic industries sector constituting the foundation for India's future economic development and a separate decentralized cottage industry sector intended for the alleviation of unemployment and improvement in the flow of consumer goods. The reconciled plan frame of Mahalanobia thus envisaged industrial development to proceed on two planes: a heavy industrial sector based largely on public ownership and a decentralized sector of village and cottage industries calling for increased mechanization as an instrument of greater production.

Though politically designed as an acceptable blend in so far as cottage and village industries were assigned a specific place in the total scheme of industrialization, its conceptual soundness remained subject to question, more especially in terms of financial allocation which, in a state of deficit financing in respect of the Second Plan, called for a capital-intensive approach which dictated the expediency of a resort to foreign aid. Explaining, in December 1955, the financial implications of the Second Plan, Finance Minister C. D. Deshmukh, in fact, made it clear that cottage and village industries were, under its deficit financing, expected not only to be self-reliant, but also to be paying concerns. In other words, these small-scale industries could not look forward to State aid for their development. There was in the circumstances no alternative to reliance on the production of capital goods for export, which necessarily meant inflation in a state of inadequacy in the production of consumer goods and deficit financing to promote heavy industries. The 1956 arrangement was in fact designed to appear Left, though in substance Right. Indeed, it was comparable to the line of industrial policy which the Government of India had adopted for purposes of imperial defence in 1919 – a policy based on the recommendations of the Indian Industrial Commission report of 1918.

Indian and Foreign Capital Collaboration

The pre-Independence view of the Indian industrialists and the Congress was opposed to the use of foreign capital for Indian industrial development. The Indian National Congress had all along called for *swadeshi* and boycott of foreign goods. A resolution adopted by the National Planning Committee in November 1945 stated clearly that "The investment of foreign capital in Indian agricultural, mineral and industrial concerns since the establishment of British rule had resulted in the acquisition by foreign interests of a measure of control over India's economic and political life which has both warped and retarded national development".[8] As said above, even the Advisory Planning Board of the Interim Government warned against the dangers of political influence involved in the infiltration of foreign capital and technology. The Indian business, too, thought in terms of reducing dependence on foreign countries in respect of financial requirements for the development of basic heavy industries. Their Bombay Plan obviously called for resort to internal resources.

Surprisingly enough, however, it was the Government of India who early in 1947 made a policy statement which "welcomed foreign investment selectively on grounds of augmenting domestic savings for industrial development and the need to obtain newer technology". The foreign investment so invited was "assured non-discriminatory treatment."[9]

It was in 1949 itself that the Federation of Indian Chambers of Commerce and Industry realized the importance of lobbying with the leaders of the Congress Party in Parliament in connection with the Industries (Development and Control) Bill under the discussion of the Select Committee in August. Venkatasubbiah's study of the Federation shows that lobbying alone could act as an instrument to accomplish the object of private enterprise, for only "few legislators had seen the inside of a factory", and once the contact was established, it would be easier to have the proposed legislative measure of control enacted in their interest. One of the first things which the Federation President therefore did immediately in 1950 was to arrange a tour of some members of Parliament to certain important industrial centres in the country; a move which brought credit to the achievement of private enterprise against what was said to be "no small odds". Convinced of the benefit of his initiative, the Federation's President in 1950 (Tulsidas Kilachand) later wrote to his member bodies "about the changed requirements of lobbying". It was recognized. he said, "that one of the new tasks which the Federation should undertake if it is to play its due part in shaping the economic life of the country is to establish a liaison between the commercial organizations and members of Parliament. A beginning has been made to approach as many members of Parliament as possible and furnish them with facts and figures relating to industry and trade".[10] The Federation naturally agreed with the Government on the foreign-aid issue.

As Venkatsubbiah points out, on the basis of original correspondence and relevant documents, the Federation had already started establishing liaison with those who counted, in spite of an ideological animation exhibited by the Congress Party. He says, for instance, that at a "reception given to him by business leaders Patel commended the Finance Minister, Shanmukham Chetty, to them as one of their men. There was one unwritten and unspoken proviso, however. Whoever was Finance Minister or Industry Minister –especially one who was not a dyed-in-the-wool, jail-going, Congress Party adherent–must in practice take care not to appear to be pro-business. For the party's hard core always suspected the experts drawn from its fringe or from outside their ranks of pro-business proclivities and therefore corrosive of the party's egalitarian elan, by whatever name described from time to time. The first four Finance Ministers–Shanmukham Chetty, John Matthal, Chintaman Deshmukh and T. T. Krishnamachari – were all suspect in the sense in various degrees".[11]

The 1949-decision to invite the participation of foreign capital was thus a result of an expert advice which was accepted by the Government headed by Nehru, the party boss, popularly acclaimed as a socialist. Committed as the Finance Ministers were to the newly established international system of finance capital as a reinforcement of capitalist economy under the popularly upheld fad of State control, they viewed Nehru's call for nationalization or a socialistic pattern of society as no more than a petty scare in no way intended to act as a curb on private ownership. When T. T. Krishnamachari met the Federation's Committee in March 1954, he assured it that the Government "wanted to carry private enterprise with them. Nationalization was only a scare and that should not deter them. The Government had difficulty in managing even one textile mill".[12] It was in fact for political reasons that the Government and the Congress Party were at the time "talking left but acting right".[13]

It was at the instance of T. T. Krishnamachari that the Federation formally recognized the need for foreign capital and technology in January 1955 when the Avadi session of the Congress adopted the socialistic pattern of society as its goal. Its argument was that if foreign capital had been accepted as an ally of the Government, the best course left open to the Indian business was to accept it as its own ally too. The Federation even proceeded further to extend the operation of foreign capital to consumer goods industries where Indian units were already well established. The object was to make available to the people goods in sufficient quantities and of superior quality. The decision so taken by the Federation was appreciated by C. D. Deshmukh, then Finance Minister.

T. T. Krishnamachari, who earlier had the Ministry of Commerce under him, prompted a high-powered Indian delegation to the United States and Europe under the leadership of G. D. Birla in search of foreign capital in 1957, when he had taken over the Finance Ministry from C. D. Deshmukh. Birla's tour in the USA was arranged to coincide with Krishnamachari's own visit there to secure the World Bank's support for the Second Plan started in pursuance of the Industrial Policy Resolution of April 1956. The Indian capitalist delegation was in fact intended to remove American misgivings about the Congress resolution on socialism, so that a favourable climate could be created for the Indian mission led by the Finance Minister. In fact, the whole object was to attract as much private foreign investment as possible to supplement inter-governmental and Bank loans creating a debt problem in the absence of the old sterling balances. The delegation and the mission both claimed to have removed to a large extent the doubts and suspicions of the American investors about Indian policy on nationalization.[14] Curiously enough, the goal of a "socialistic pattern of society" which underlined the Second Plan was sought to be achieved by means of a collaboration of Indian and foreign capitalist interests under pseudonymous State control, which in practice meant no more than the control of its bureaucracy traditionally geared to punitive functions.

State Entrepreneurship

As my study on *District Administration and Rural Development* has shown the need for State entrepreneurship of the Government's economic function arose from the exigencies of executive action as an instrument of people's welfare against the operation of *laissez-faire*, more especially in the course of the recurrent famines which occurred after the Crown had taken over from the East India Company in 1858. The developing state of a colonial economy in India had, however, created a dichotomous situation. While the Government of India and its civil service were in their reorganized form expected as an imperial force to ensure protection through public utility measures against natural calamities as well as fight against motives of sheer profit and commercial gain their inter-relations with European settlers made both colonial and imperial interests appear as overlapping. The dichotomy so present in the pursuit of economic policy accounted to a large extent for the slow pace of industrialization.

Even so, it was the pressure of the colonial economy for modernization that induced the Government to improve transport and communication as well as to develop the infrastructure necessary not only for the promotion of industrial development but also of the public utility. The major State enterprises in the earlier period were, for instance, railways, posts and telegraphs and ordnance factories. These were administered departmentally, although they were immediately run by autonomous Control Boards for speed and efficiency. To the credit of railways, the locomotive works at Chittaranjan and the coach factory at Perambur are quoted as two of the major manufacturing undertakings of the post-independence period. The river valley projects of the Government are included as part of the same category of State enterprise. L. P. Singh, an eminent retired Civilian, who has studied this subject[15] in some depth includes a number of other enterprises which performed both governmental and entrepreneurial functions. The colonial economy and the Government of India together provided in fact a primary base which Indian industrialists used later to their own advantage.

In spite of a seemingly overlapping nature of inter-relations between the colonial and imperial forces, distinction was never absent. It continued throughout the British rule in India. Considerations for general welfare always called for executive action to bend profiteers to the will of the community for political reasons, although the principles of free trade remained operative as an economic force except in a state of crisis demanding the use of certain palliatives. Normally, the State promoted through its own enterprise and infrastructure the development of key industries considered necessary for both defence and the colonial economy which provided the basic structure for India's modern economic development. This pattern of relationship which had in the past developed between private enterprise and politics was inherited by the Congress Government in 1947 with the only difference that while the Indian business had by then emerged as a distant economic force, the one-party Government of the Congress replaced the imperial authority as a political force.

The greater need for State enterprise in the post-independence period proceeded from the exigencies of industrial expansion as part of the post-war reconstruction plan already announced under the policy statement of 1945 and the weakness of the Indian private enterprise in terms of both financial and technical resources. In the initial stages, the development of the heavy key industries, which the Statement of 1945 had earlier defined, called for an adequate supply of power and raw material which were both found lacking. They did not even hold out the prospect of an assured market and commercial gain. The State's participation was considered essential; for only the Government could enforce a large-scale mobilization of capital, the coordination of industrial construction and the training of technical personnel.

As the Economic Programmes Committee of the Congress pointed out in 1947, another important object of extending the scope of State's participation was to secure the protection of the handicraft industry against the undue and excessive competition of the capitalist enterprise. For it was felt that "the process of primary and capitalist accumulation, if unguided, could lead to painful social conflicts and crises. State entrepreneurship therefore has a definite stabilizing influence on the relations between the different layers of Indian society and on the political atmosphere in general".[16] This was a goal comparable to that of the imperial authority, which the Government of India sought to accomplish as the State's political agency. The Congress Government inherited this conceptual frame to determine its relations with different layers of Indian society, more especially with the commercial organizations.

But because of an ideological overtone which developed in Indian politics under the imperialist rule, there grew a gap between realities and formal professions. "The same politicians sometimes both befriended and attacked businessmen. Their public face on business was different from their private face with it. Ministers also talked to cross purposes.[17] Though at heart supporters of private enterprise, they took care to see that they did not appear to be pro-business. They talked of nationalization without meaning it and even when nationalization was taken recourse to, it did not serve to change the general structure of the country's economy. All that it did was to afford to the Government an opportunity to have its influence. The Imperial Bank of India, the largest commercial bank, was, for instance, nationalized in 1955 and reorganized as the State Bank of India. The Life Insurance Corporation (LIC), the nationalized form of the private life insurance business, came to be similarly established in 1956.

The nationalization of insurance and the Imperial Bank so effected was no more than a method of financial mobilization to meet the needs of industrial expansion under public control. The reason was that "although the field of State entrepreneurship inherited from the colonial and native States administration was quite extensive", the resources thus inherited were nevertheless insufficient on the eve of the First Five Year Plan to meet in terms of quantity and quality the requirements of extended reproduction on a national basis.[18] A resort to the extension of the public sector under the mixed economy resolution of 1948 and a decision to go in for foreign capital and skill in 1949 were two of the measures which ensured continuity not only in terms of the erstwhile industrial policy, but also its modus operandi. Nationalization was brought in simply to help greater mobilization considered beneficial to both public and private sectors.

As the foreign exchange reserves in the course of the Second Plan were being fast drained due to import of plant and machinery in connection with heavy industries and as there was little hope of their being replenished, the Government became still more hard pressed for reliance on foreign credits for the establishment of new enterprises envisaged in the Industrial Policy Resolution of 1956.

But reliance on foreign sources had its own drawbacks. In the first place, it led to instability in the rate of industrialization; for the flow of funds was not only delayed by the complications of procedural formalities involved in the signing of contracts, but it was also determined by the economic situation of the countries extending the aid and their political aims or factors beyond India's control. Secondly, the bulk of foreign aid was given on commercial terms which involved payment of interest. This forced the recipient to use it mainly in profitable industries, so that the investment returns should be high enough to cover all foreign obligations. It necessarily meant a neglect of such key industries in the public sector as held out no such promise for profitability. Thirdly, as a considerable part of payments had to be met in foreign currency, it could not be acquired except by an expansion of exports geared to the market economy–a condition which was hardly consistent with the policy objective of the public sector. Finally, the allocation of foreign aid for particular projects restricted the Government's freedom in the purchase of equipments on a competitive basis. In view of these drawbacks of foreign aid, attempts, as said above, were sought to be made to secure the participation of foreign private capital to avoid debt charges. The growth of multinational corporations proceeded naturally in these circumstances. Their collaboration with local industrialists led to the increasing concentration of economic power in the Indian business Houses.[19] The over-all effect of these developments, more especially of the depletion of foreign exchange, was that the basic industries listed in Schedule B under the arrangement of 1956 continued to be an exclusive concern of the private sector which consumed in its own interest the bulk of the sterling balances to meet heavy payments on the import of capital goods including plant and machinery.

Naturally enough, the Third Plan gave its high priority to the development in the public sector of industries intended for the production of capital goods required for steel making for power generation and distribution, for mining and for chemical plants. The policy of liberal imports was thus reversed indigenously to provide for capital goods need for basic and heavy industries forming part of the public sector. The private sector too proceeded to do the same. It expanded its capacity indigenously to produce equipments for its industries, such as cement and textiles. The new trend so developed in the Third Plan period necessarily called for increasing dependence on foreign assistance to meet the requirements of exchange needed for the production of capital goods in the country itself to ensure the development of a self-reliant economy.

The over-all picture of economic development in the course of the first three Plans doubtless conformed to expectations. The production of steel, cement, fertilizers, drugs, etc., recorded a manifold increase. The production of capital goods required for their manufacture also proceeded largely according to schedule.[20] The *Report on Seminar on Problems of Private and Public Industrial Undertakings* (August 6-8, 1963) organized by the Federation of Indian Chambers of Commerce and Industry pointed out that while India's National income had "increased by over 40 per cent her industrial output had nearly doubled, with the manufacture of new types of capital goods including engineering and chemicals. The result was that the Indian economy had been made "less dependent on imports".[21]

These achievements were recorded in spite of the main twin problems of development and defence purchases abroad which, in the course of war with China, involved heavy foreign exchange outlays and created a situation where the rising level of prices and shortage in foodgrains due to successive droughts added not a little to the problems of capital repayments with interest on foreign credits.

The moot point, however, that arose in connection with the progress of economic development was: who were the beneficiaries? Where had the additional national income gone? The question so raised was referred for investigation to the Mahalanobis Committee on Distribution of Income and Level of Living appointed on October 13, 1960. The Committee was to study the changes in levels of living during the first two Plan periods, the recent trends in the distribution of income and wealth and to ascertain the extent to which the operation of the economic system had resulted in concentration of wealth and means of production.

Concentration of Income, Wealth and Economic Power

The fact that the concentration of income, wealth and economic power had proceeded in the course of the three Plan periods was acknowledged by the Mahalanobis Committee in 1964, although its findings in the first part of the Report remained unrelated to the changes in levels of living. It was surprised to find that in spite of a number of countervailing measures starting with the Industries (Development and Regulation) Act of 1951, concentration of economic power had kept on increasing. It is true that for the three years ending March 31, 1963, the number of industrial licences given to the leading business Houses was only 182 out of a total of 4,211 issued.[22] But, as the Mahalanobis Committee held, the big business complexes had grown more rapidly with powers to control the bulk of industrial activity.

The Committee attributed this concentration of economic power to the economies of scale which led to the growth of big business. But speaking in terms of the social implication, the Committee remained non-committal. It said that "the growth of big business as such ... does not necessarily mean the deliberate adoption of an anti-social policy. There is such a thing as the economy of scale which works in favour of big business on purely economic grounds; and economic considerations are certainly relevant especially in the context of our scarce resources and the imperative need of our making the most economic utilization of these resources".[23] Obviously, the argument was that industrial production in most fields would have meant much greater cost to the country in the absence of large industrial establishments, which alone could ensure economy by making the best use of technology, management and organizational efficiency.

In view of the country's multi-structural economy and its insufficiently developed infrastructure, as said above, it was the public undertakings or State entrepreneurship that actually served as the base for expanding the operations of the private sector. It was the initiative of the Government that not only promoted national enterprises, but also encouraged the development of infrastructure which included power generation, transport, communications, water supply, training of manpower and research. The private sector made full use of these and other public sector undertakings helped the big business build up their economies of scale. Even the bulk of the sterling balances, which enabled them to import plant and machinery, was sought to be spent in their own sectional interest, although, as said before, some eminent Indian economists had expressed themselves against that policy to the annoyance of G. D. Birla.[24]

Among the factors that contributed to the growth of the big business, the financial resources made available to Indian capitalists by the publicly owned financial institutions[25] were treated by the Mahalanobis Committee as by far the most important. It pointed out in clear terms that the growth of the private industrial sector, more especially of the big business, had been facilitated by the financial assistance extended to them by the public institutions like the Industrial Finance Corporation, the National Industrial Development Corporation, etc.

It was not only the assistance rendered to private enterprise that was important. The concentration of economic power proceeded additionally from the commercial banks themselves being free to increase their own holdings of shares in joint-stock companies, as the size of the companies increased. The Life Insurance Corporation (LIC), a nationalized concern, also lent its support to the big business in private industry by its holdings of stock exchange securities. These were all developments which contributed to the growth of monopolies in private enterprise. For, according to the Mahalanobis Committee, "the large companies and bigger enterprises have an easier access to the capital market; and banks, like insurance companies and trusts, besides individuals, have a preference for investing in the shares of large companies. Thus, the operation of the economic system, with its criteria of credit-worthiness and security for lending and investment, tends to support the large and established enterprise against the small and struggling entrepreneur".[26] These were trends which had hardly any relevance to the Directive Principles laid down by the framers of the Indian Constitution.

Monopolies Resulting from Concentration

The Report of the Monopolies Inquiry Commission, which came out in October 1964, made it clear that one of the important consequences of concentration in business was the growth of monopolies invested with the exercise of economic power by big business influencing government policy through heavy contributions made to political parties, more especially to the ruling party.

The Commission doubtless held that the concentration of economic power was not without its own avail. It contributed to the "economic betterment" of the country in the state of the backwardness. But it was not blind to the evil effects of such power on the country's economy. "The most serious of these", it said, "was the emergence of monopoly with its attendant evils–high prices for the consumer, deterioration in quality, and last but not least, keeping out the small industrialist". For "big business" by its very "bigness" often succeeded in eliminating competitors.[27] in other words, the exclusion of small man in business signified increasing imbalance in the distribution of national wealth and income. Even where such elimination by big business resulted in an increase in national wealth and income, the Commission held that the assets of a few already wealthy men increased at a faster rate than those of the many poor. Economic growth under such conditions necessarily meant an increasing gap between the rich and the poor. Concentration created, in fact, a tendency towards investment in directions profitable to big business but not necessarily conducive to the real economic growth of the country in cumulative terms. Foreign collaboration which brought in its train machinery and technical know-how acted as reinforcement to big business as a whole.

B. K. Butt, who recorded a note of dissent, agreed of course that the financial assistance given by private industrialists to the ruling party lent support to the existence of relationship between Government and big business. But, according to him, that alone was not the sole or even the main reason for the influence which big business had on the affairs of the State. The influence so wielded proceeded from the concentrated economic power which "involved control of large resources, and also of large areas of production and of the economy as a whole. Those who have this control are in a position to influence the economic policy in a large measure, irrespective entirely of their relationship with political parties, whether in opposition or in power, or even their relationship with individuals in authority". There was yet another factor that gave rise to influence, and that was "the ability of big business to influence public opinion through their predominance in the Press".[28]

Dutt agreed with the majority who mentioned the power of big business to corrupt. But he regretted their omission to stress the existence of large-scale malpractices indulged in by some of them found guilty of a large quantity of unaccounted money and huge sums involved in tax evasion.

The Industrial Licensing System (ILS)[29] was of course there to control industrial development by regulating procedures involved in the grant of licences. The Swaminathan Committee was, for instance, appointed in 1963 to recommend procedural simplification. The Committee was reconstituted in 1965 after the publication of its report in 1964. The main object was to reduce the number of applications, which was sought to be done by raising the exemption limit or by delicensing a few industries, the former being preferred to the latter. The exemption limit which stood at Rs. 10 lakhs in 1960 was, for example, raised to Rs. 25 lakhs in January 1964 and then to Rs. 1 crore in February 1970. It was then further raised to Rs. 3 crores in 1978 at the suggestion of the Committee headed by G. V. Ramakrishna. This was obviously a trend against the small-scale sector–a trend encouraged and supported by big business in their own interest. The exemption limit was in fact further raised to Rs. 5 crores in 1982.

L. K. Jha, a leading civilian who acted as Economic Adviser to the Government of India for some years in the eighties, shared the views of the Monopolies Commission and attributed the growth of disparities in society not a little to its licensing policy also.[30] He has acknowledged the existence of misdirection in developmental effort, responsible for "making the rich richer and the poor poorer", and said: "The industrial licensing policy came under fire on the ground that it had in fact helped big business to strengthen its monopolistic hold on the key sector of the economy. The public sector financial institutions were accused of contributing to the process. Attention was also focused on regional disparities. The backward areas had continued to stagnate. Industries had continued to gravitate towards those States which were more industrialized, and even within them to concentrate in and around the major cities. Even within the pockets of prosperity which had come into existence, there were stark, ugly contrasts between those who lived in slums and slept on pavements and those who enjoyed luxurious life-styles. Social tensions were getting compounded."[31]

It is surprising that the growth of monopolies took place under the administration of Jawaharlal Nehru himself, a declared advocate of socialism. The performance of his Government and the Congress Party came under fire at the sixty-ninth session of the Indian National Congress which met at Durgapur on January 9 and 10, 1965,[32] with K. Kamaraj as its President, who regretted that poverty continued in spite of the fact that for improving the conditions of the poor they had passed through two Five Year Plans, the third being implemented, while the fourth formulated.

In the course of a resolution moved on the Congress socio-economic policy to remove poverty, Jagjivan Ram, a prominent depressed-class leader, spoke in a spirit of protest on the ground that "only 10 to 15 families" controlled the large part of the country's industrial resources; and since "our policy in this regard" was to enable "rich people" to get "more assistance from the Government", it made the rich definitely richer. He suggested strong steps against profiteers and hoarders of "black money" who had started smuggling "hoarded money out of the country". But he was helpless. For, as he said, "We know the people who have made money through black-marketing, bribery and corruption, we criticize them also at their back, but it is lamentable to note that when we are face to face with them we just forget everything and show them all the courtesy because they are rich and (economically) powerful."[33]

N. V. Gadgil, an eminent economist from Maharashtra, went further still to question the sincerity of the Congress policy decisions. He said, for example, that "year after year" the same kind of resolution on poverty, especially in rural areas, had been adopted by the Congress. But he regretted that there was "bungling from A to Z". K. D. Malaviya from U.P. also shared the same view. He admitted that the Congress had since independence been "drifting away" from its declared socialistic goal. He advised that the policy followed by the Government needed to be radically revised. But there was little hope, for the leaders spoke "with different voices". Even so, he looked forward to "at least" the Fourth Plan being "socialist oriented".[34]

Intervening in the debate on the draft resolution relating to socio-economic policy, Prime Minister Lal Bahadur Shastri agreed with the critics of the administration in some respects, although he treated its over-all condemnation as irresponsible, not consistent with party discipline. Like the Federation of Indian Chambers of Commerce and Industry, Shastri believed in increased production as the only answer to the problem of poverty and therefore emphasized a rapid development of basic heavy industries.[35]

As regards the problem of unaccounted black money, the Prime Minister could not but recognize its existence and growth. The problem had in fact assumed such proportions that the Government was obliged to choose between two evils, namely, letting huge sums of money go underground and writing off a part of it under an ordinance which provided for the waiving of penalty in cases of voluntary disclosures. The Government chose the latter as a lesser evil. But that choice obviously signified its surrender to the rule of monopolies in business which, as said above, kept on growing stronger and stronger in spite of the successive Plans introduced one after the other. It was in fact not the Plans that mattered. As said above, the Congress did not lag behind in promises where it could always afford to be radical from considerations of politics. What, however, really mattered was implementation where, as the AICC proceedings of

January 10, 1965, suggested, it invariably failed. Stress was therefore laid on the implementation of resolutions.

Ten-Point Programme : 1967

The emphasis of the AICC on implementation came in the context of Nehru's death in 1964 which, in addition, not only saw a marked decline in agriculture and industry, but also watched with dismay the reactions arising from the Reports of two of the important committees appointed by the Government to identify the beneficiaries of economic development. The Mahalanobis Committee and the Monopolies Inquiry Commission, whose reports appeared in 1964, were both critical of the concentration of economic power in the hands of a few select business Houses, in spite of the Bhubaneswar resolution stressing in 1964 itself the need for democratic socialism as an answer to the problem of increasing poverty.

Two other factors brought into focus the importance of policy implementation. These were the death of Prime Minister Lal Bahadur Shastri, which occurred at Tashkent in the early morning of January 11, 1966,[36] and the results of the fourth general elections which took place between February 15 and 21, 1967. While Shastri's death meant a serious loss for the Congress of a sincere and honest leader who enjoyed the full confidence of the country as a whole, the marked decline of its popularity as a political party at the elections dictated the urgency of its immediate goal being well defined and its declared programme being implemented to avoid split or even disintegration.

The election result for the Lok Sabha showed in fact a steady decline in the percentage of votes polled by the Congress. In 1957 and 1962, this percentage was 47.78 and 44.72 respectively.

It fell again to 40.73 per cent in 1967. In 1962, the Congress Party had a strength of 361 out of a total of 494 seats in the Lok Sabha. In 1967, on the other hand, that strength fell to 284 out of the total strength of 520. The Congress lost its hold in the State Legislatures of Kerala, Madras and Orissa.

The conditions created by Congress reverses raised several questions in terms of its alternatives, including, for example, an army rule, a coalition government, or even divesting the Congress of its party status because of its top leaders being viewed as part of government rather than members of the organization. These questions assumed added importance, for policy implementation after all formed part of the duties of government itself. In its meeting held on May 7, 1967, and subsequent days the Congress Working Committee discussed the problem of relationship between the organization and its Government. It dismissed the idea of army rule and coalition as no more than ephemeral and proceeded on May 10-12 to define its concept of democratic socialism, its content and measures to implement it. It also discussed the causes of failure and the difficulties involved in the execution of policies. After due consideration the Working Committee adopted its resolution on Democratic Socialism containing the famous Ten-Point Programme.

Briefly, the Ten-Point Programme consisted of the following objectives[37]:

1. Social control of the banking institutions: The Government was to take necessary steps to implement it.

2. Nationalization of general insurance: The Government was to work out schemes to bring general insurance under the public sector.

3. State trading in imports and exports: The Working Committee requested the Government to undertake import and export trade through State agencies and to formulate a commoditywise phased programme to ensure progress in this regard.

4. State trading in foodgrains: It meant an emphasis on the pursuit of a national policy of public distribution of foodgrains, more especially to the weaker sections of the community. The Food Corporation of India and cooperative agencies were to be used for these purposes.

5. Expansion of cooperatives: It envisaged a plan to organize consumer cooperatives to cover commodities at fair prices.

6. Regulating growth of monopolies: Effective steps were sought to

be taken to curb the growth of monopolies and concentration of economic power after the recommendations of the Monopolies Commission had been accepted by the Government.

7. Provision of minimum needs to the community: The Congress Working Committee directed the Government to take steps to provide for the minimum needs to the community. It called for the promulgation of a Socialist Charter for Children ensuring high protein food to them in addition to such other amenities as could be afforded under a phased programme.

8. Unearned income in urban land values: The resolution in this regard envisaged a plan to impose restrictions on individual holdings of urban land in order to prevent racketeering in land values in urban areas. The object was to encourage production investment by putting a curb on "the pattern of conspicuous consumption and wasteful display" of wealth "out of place in a socialist society".

9. Rural works programme, land reforms, etc.: A plan of rural works programme was intended not only to provide opportunities for rural employment, especially for the landless, but also to create certain overheads in agriculture like agro-industries, soil conservation, reclamation of land, afforestation, minor irrigation, feeder roads and cable development. The resolution further emphasized an effective implementation of tenancy laws already enacted and provision for credits against personal security and assets. The plan was also to include minimum wage legislation for agricultural labour.

10. Privileges of ex-rulers of Indian States: The privileges other than privy purses enjoyed by ex-rulers were declared as inconsistent with the concept and practice of democracy. The Government of India was therefore advised to do away with them.

AICC and the Ten-Point Programme
October 28-29, 1967

The Ten-Point Programme was presented for confirmation to the AICC at its meeting held at Jabalpur on October 28-29, 1967. Prime Minister Indira Gandhi was not found wanting in her expression of sympathy for the poor. She was, on the contrary, liberal enough to say that the programme was "incomplete" and that "much more ought to be done to improve the lot of the people". But when it came to implementation, she had hardly any suggestion to make except to generalize that there was nothing new about the Ten-Point Programme except the form in which it was presented. She claimed that the Congress had placed such programmes before the country many years ago.

Though admitting that despite many years of planning the country had remained far from the goal of a socialist society since independence, she asked the new generation of people to suffer more in the hope of an imaginary bright future under her Socialistic Pattern of Society, where State trading, for instance, did not exceed 8 per cent of the total trade of the country in spite of an increase over the past 10 years from Rs. 9 crores to Rs. 241 crores. Even while referring to a distributive system, she said that cooperatives could better be handled by private organizations than by the Government.[38]

Finance Minister Morarji Desai was the person whom the Prime Minister asked to speak on behalf of the Government on the question of social control over financial institutions as an instrument of democratic socialism which the Ten-Point Programme especially emphasized. Nationalization of the banking institutions was a form of social control over which, as Desai pointed out, a good deal of controversy had been going on since 1948, when the Government had first agreed to mixed economy which, according to him, meant no State ownership. Like the Federation of Indian Chambers of Commerce and Industry, he believed that socialism could not be achieved without producing sufficient wealth. His emphasis was on increasing production regardless of the manner in which the benefits of production were sought to be distributed. Indeed, he did not favour nationalization as an instrument of policy although the Advisory Planning Board of the Interim Government had first recommended it in 1946 as part of public sector undertakings.

Desai's argument was that the private-sector commercial banks could themselves be made to work in a manner which might serve the purpose of nationalization and avoid concentration of power by ensuring that credit was given not only to the big industrialists or to those of the influential sections connected with them, but to all those who really needed it for setting up industry or business. He stressed the ideals of the banking institutions and pointed out that the banks, which had so far thought only of the security of the money advanced and the profitability of the concerns which they helped, must change their attitude. But little did he realize that it was not possible for them to change unless the security they wanted was guaranteed by the Government. This precisely was nationalization which the Congress had pledged in its election manifesto but its Government was reluctant to redeem it. The nationalization of general insurance was likewise rejected. As State Trading, it was described as replete with difficulties which needed to be removed before any advance could be made.

The other aspects of the Ten-Point Programme were sought to be met only by generalizations. While the question of minimum needs to the community was, for example, dismissed as unknown and undefined, a number of vague alternatives were suggested to deal with the problem of unearned income and unaccounted money smuggled out of the country. Desai referred to the privileges of ex-rulers but left the issue to negotiations for settlement. At no time did he seek to answer how he planned to implement the Congress pledge to socialism declared and reiterated from time to time ever since the Karachi resolution of 1931. Even the reformist concept of Democratic Socialism embodied in the Working Committee's resolution of May 10-12, 1967, was being scuttled and left to take care of itself, although in so far as the Programme itself was concerned it was accepted without demur.

The leftist members of the AICC were in fact all out to stress the importance of reducing the increasing gap between preaching and practice. Mohan Dharia from Maharashtra deeply regretted that while according to the promises held out by the Organization the Government was to hold the commanding heights of the nation's economy, it was in practice the ever growing gigantic monopolies that ruled the roast. The socialists in general were all keen on implementation and they emphasized that there would be no hope for Congress policies being implemented unless the concerned Ministers' commitment to these policies was not duly ascertained and departmental responsibility enforced. Abid Ali from Bombay went further to add that the word socialism would lose all its meaning if the Government was incapable of providing the people foodgrains and essential commodities at cheap rates. Nationalization, State trading and consumer cooperatives were therefore considered significant, relevant and necessary in spite of Desai's comments to the contrary. It was in fact the leftist elements of the national movement that served as the carriers of socialist ideals. The leadership of the Congress as a political party was essentially an elitist bourgeois entity wedded to status quo rather than change, to power rather than principle. It was political compulsions that alone counted.

Prime Minister Indira Gandhi was aware of the trends moving towards the left. Even so, she would not incur the displeasure of the capitalists who resisted any attempt on the part of the Government to enact measures of industrial regulation and control. In her inaugural address to the 39th annual session of the Federation of Indian Chambers of Commerce and Industry she expressed herself in favour of fewer and fewer controls. In support of her assurance to the Federation in this regard she actually took the opportunity to refer to the removal of controls on steel, pig iron and cement. This was in the presence of a number of her Cabinet Ministers who attended the Federation's annual session.[39]

While winding up the discussion at the AICC session on October 29, she naturally added nothing to what she had already said on the first day except to announce the endorsement of the programmes and tell the delegates that there were no short-cuts to its implementation. It was the responsibility not merely of the Government but also of the organization. The annual report of the AICC for the year 1968 only vaguely commented that necessary information was being collected to find out the extent of implementation.[40]

Organizational Structure : The Managing Agency System

As said in the first chapter, the industrial organization which developed in the wake of the East India Company's administration and continued ever since then till the end of British rule was based on the principle of the managing agency system. Its main feature was, in the first place, a supply of capital by the parent firms and, secondly, multiple directorship in the administration of the industrial units established by the pioneering business House but run by separate companies with functional and legal independence. Each unit was under this arrangement to remain integrated with the parent company and its managing agent in both financial and administrative terms. The peculiar condition which contributed to the growth of such a system in the Indian situation was the great distance of British firms from their home country as well as a paucity of capital supply in India for industrial enterprise. It therefore owed its origin to commerce and went into industry with a sound commercial base from considerations of profit. As the managing agency was in practice hereditary, it fitted in well with the family system of the Indian business Houses. It became their family concern.

Even so, it may be said to the credit of the managing agents that they arranged finance for the concerns they managed at a period when, according to the *Report of the Indian Tariff Board* (1927), banks were unwilling to advance moneys on the security of the assets of a limited company unless the same was backed by the personal security of the Agents themselves. The Tarrif Board therefore suggested that there was no use thinking in terms of an alternative system unless the whole organization of commercial and banking credit in India was changed. This was an opinion before the Board by Sir Purshotamdas Thakurdas, a leading business magnate of Bombay.[41] It is true that the system signified a concentration of business and economic power; for only two firms of managing agents in Bombay controlled at the time in 1927 as many as 23 of the 83 mills. They became exposed to further criticism on the ground that they were unduly conservative; for they were not only cautious but at times even reluctant to embark on new ventures for industrial development. But the year 1927 marked the beginning of economic depression; and since the managing agents were remunerated on the basis of commission on profit, they could ill-afford to take any risk, especially in a period of depression. Economy in cost and efficiency in management were in fact their guidelines to ensure profit. Theirs was a pure business transaction on economic principles. It was not to be mixed up with considerations for what became later known as social responsibility of business enterprise.

According to the Indian Coalfields Committee, the managing agency system was especially advantageous. It united under its control a number of production units for management. It brought together for purposes of employment a technical staff equipped with greater ability and experience. Grouping in fact signified the establishment of a common pool for the supply of a number of common services between coal production units, such as surveying, zamindari work, mechanical workshop facilities, provision of hospitals and medical care. Besides, large benefits accrued to the collieries and the sale of their output. The Indian Coalfields Committee (1946) added that the most important of the benefits which the managing agency provided for the individual collieries under its charge was its "financial backing". During the periods of depression, the Committee said, "many a colliery company would have gone under but for the assistance rendered by its Managing Agents, who, with their own funds, kept the collieries going. Moreover, during the early years of a new production unit, it is the Managing Agent's responsibility to nurse the venture into the profit-earning stage".[42] It was held that the degree of efficiency in management under this system was such that it could not be made available to individual collieries under any other system.

According to the *Report of the Indian Tariff Board*, the managing agents functioning in the cotton industry in 1927 were remunerated on the basis of commission either on profit, or on production or sale. The Indian Coalfields Committee which reported in 1946 confirmed these three modes of payment on commission. It said: "Managing Agents usually receive their remuneration in the form of a fixed monthly sum for office expenses and a fixed percentage on sales or on output or on a similar basis having direct relation to the net profits of the company. The Indian Companies Act (1913), as amended in 1936, provides for the limitation of the tenure of Managing Agents to 20 years and also limits the remuneration of the Managing Agents to a percentage of net profits as defined in the Act."[43]

Apart from stress on profit motivation which meant a virtual neglect of social responsibility, the diversity of business in which the managing agency houses were usually interested accounted for a concentration of industrial power arising additionally from their supremacy of control over technical and managerial skill. Together, these developments called for a control over political operations which, ever since the rise of Indian capitalism in the course of the First World War, were sought to be regulated on its side. It was reinforced during the Second World War which created conditions for multinational collaboration in defence of Indian capitalism. The managing agency system naturally continued even after the transfer of power in 1947.

The amendment of the Companies Act in 1936 introduced an element of uniformity in the functioning of the managing agency system and affected the hereditary nature of the office of managing agents. The establishment of the Post-War Reconstruction Department during the Second World War which envisaged planning and development as an instrument of social and economic policy tended further to tone down the erstwhile supremacy of the managing agency. But the institution remained operative as a centralized mechanism of capitalist control in the hands of big business. In spite of the recommendations of the Economic Programme Committee of the Congress and the Industrial Policy Resolution of 1948 the corporate private sector remained triumphant. The ties of common interest between business and politics led to the proposed State takeover of the existing large concerns being shelved for consideration for 10 years. Provisions were thus first made for a phased abolition of the managing agency system under the Companies Act of 1954 which came into force as a consequence of the second Industrial Policy Resolution adopted by the Government in 1956. Schedule B of that Policy Resolution consisted of a concurrent list of basic industries which were to be partly under the public sector. But, as said above, the private sector control continued over the entire list of such industries. The main industries which remained open to the private sector on account of this departure from the declared policy were aluminium, fertilizers, power, chemicals, pulp, sea transport and synthetic rubber. In spite of the earlier warnings of some eminent Indian economists to the annoyance of G. D. Birla, India's foreign exchange reserves were allowed to be made use of in sectional private interest for the import of plant, machinery and equipment. This was the persistent influence of the managing agency system which underlined the operation of private business organization.

Managing Directorship : On the abolition of the managing agency system under the new Companies Act of 1954 the office of the erstwhile Managing Agent was replaced by a new functionary called the Managing Director. This change in the title of the chief executive of the board of management was understood to have constituted a landmark in the evolution of corporate enterprises in the post-independence period. For no person under the new Act was expected to be a director of more than 20 companies, a curb put on the multiple directorship which constituted one of the main features of the earlier 19th century system. The curb so placed released a movement for broad-based company managements amd giving them a greater sense of participation in decision-making in the enterprise. The whole object was in fact to transform into a broad pattern of institutional nationality the entire norm of industrial management based on restricted family or racial ties.

Broadly speaking, the role of the Managing Agents had been in the past confined to the supply of capital and technical know-how. Their role to raise finance for industry was reduced by a number of new developments, such, for example, as the establishment of State financial institutions for providing loan capital to industry, the stimulus given to industrial expansion under planning, the drawing of more public support to share issues, the growth of State entrepreneurship under the public sector managed by nothing more than boards of management. These new developments were at the time doubtless potential rather than real. Even so, they divested the managing agency houses of their mystique. Under the new corporate arrangement the company boards were still privileged. Many who sat on them inherited their seats. But many more were drawn from the higher executive level of the firm as well as from the ranks of the bureaucracy. When the retired members of the erstwhile administrative services joined company boards, they not only brought with them their knowledge of economic administration, but also constituted a vital link for communication between business and government.

Moreover, the new generation of "hereditary industrialists" turned out to be a different breed in terms of their life-style and outlook on business enterprise. Educated and Westernized, they, unlike their predecessors, brought to bear upon industrial management a new multi-national approach. This was borne out by Lal Bahadur Shastri in the course of an address to the Federation of Indian

Chambers of Commerce and Industry on March 28, 1960.[44] He admitted that the new corporate management had become a more open system in that it facilitated, among other things, understanding with foreign business undertakings which entered into collaboration with Indian firms that earlier used to vie with foreign competitions, more especially for political reasons.

Whether the corporate management introduced on the abolition of the managing agency system under the 1954 reform of company law was better arrangement remained an open question in the light of the Report of the Vivian Bose Commission (1963) which inquired into the affairs of the Dalmia-Jain group of companies. The report cast doubts on the ability of the corporate reform to remove the ills and shortcomings that resulted from it. It was a serious reflection on the image of businessmen. The Federation of the Indian Chambers of Commerce and Industry felt concerned about it; for Shriyans Prasad Jain, one of the three top businessmen who figured in the report, happened to be its President in the very year in which the report appeared. On the failure of the Federation to take appropriate action Tatas and Mafatlals withdrew from it in protest.[45] The image of businessmen showed no improvement.

Indeed, the change effected by the company law of 1954 was more formal than real. The basic principle of industrial organization which conduced to the concentration of wealth and power remained unchanged. The management of a company, it is true, was to be in the hands of the board of directors. But the board itself could be manipulated by a few of the big businesses who held the majority of shares. They could, if they so wanted, manage to stop altogether any participation in the conduct of their business by the general shareholders. The difficulties would not cease even if an elective principle was sought to be introduced in the constitution of the board; for it had the risk of either reducing the board to the level of a political body or bringing to its management a popular figure with little or no experience to manage. As said above, the concentration of economic power and monopoly business went on increasing without any let or hindrance. The State financial institutions established to facilitate the supply of industrial finance as well as the infrastructure built as part of the public sector helped the process of concentration. Together they extended the scope of big business to grow bigger and increased the influence of politics on business. The basic structure of the capitalist economy did not change. It was, on the contrary, reinforced. The greed for money which politics needed and got from business in order to survive and prosper could not but produce its side effect.

Political System as Further Aid to Monopolies

The compulsions of policy in the context of a colonial situation, which called for collaboration between India's elitist and business classes, and the peculiar nature of her industrial structure inherited from the 19th century model of managing agency were together, as said before, responsible for the concentration of economic power and growth of monopolies under British rule. The dominance of the Centre in constitutional terms acted, in spite of its federal form, as a reinforcement to monopoly interests in the post-independence period, which brought freedom to Indian business Houses to expand and operate in collaboration with foreign companies, more especially British, the security of whose business interest had earlier been recognized as an implicit condition in the transfer of power to India in 1947.

The author has, in an earlier work on the *Indian Federal System*, attempted to show how the concentration of power at the Centre was related to regional imbalances which gave rise to conflicts with the States demanding greater autonomy to facilitate their economic development. It involved a periodical review of the Centre-State relations calling for readjustment for developmental purposes in their legislative, financial and administrative powers.

But nothing could be moved so long as the presiding deity at the Centre as well as in each of the States happened to be of the Congress Party disposed to act in league with big business under the influence of Jawaharlal Nehru himself who, though declaredly in support of the public sector, was not opposed to corporate private enterprise. It was only after his death and the Congress debacle in the general elections of 1967 that a wave of criticism against its government began to appear. A Press comment thus said: "Congress Ministers in the States were pretty sure of continuing in power so long as they paid homage to the gods in New Delhi and took care to let off the rural voters lightly in the matter of taxation. State Chief Ministers could, in fact, even disobey the Centre's directives and still bank on the Congress High Command turning a Nelson's eye on such lapses." For, as the comment added, "Nehru was striding the political stage like a colossus" and none could challenge his authority.[46]

The view so expressed about the dominance of the Centre and the Congress Party leadership was later endorsed by no less a leader than C. Rajagopalachari who, after his being the Governor-General and also a Central Minister, said in the course of an address to a conference convened by the Finance Minister that "the Centre was treating the States as its Zamindaris which could not be tolerated.[47] It was of course tolerated when one party ruled both at the Centre and in the States before 1967 when differences between them, if any, were settled at the political level regardless of socio-economic developments proceeding from the emergence of local entrepreneural classes demanding extended scope and freedom to expand–a demand which clashed with the interest of monopoly industrial concerns operating at the national level in collaboration with the ruling party. The dichotomy involved in the Centre-States relations was in fact socio-economic, calling for a periodical review of the Constitution on the principle of decentralization to satisfy politically the requirements of a developing society. But the view taken by the ruling party continued to be purely political, dismissing local demands for extended autonomy as an expression of disruptive forces that must be condemned and suppressed. The federal structure of the Constitution which was essentially based on a unitary system and modelled after the imperialist pattern of the Government of India Act (1935) was sought to be preserved at all cost, although T. T. Krishnamachari, a well-known Congressswallah, took pains to advocate the necessity of a decennial review of the Constitution.[48]

The poor show of the Congress in the general elections of 1967 marked in fact the beginning of demands for the review of the Congress line of policy. It was the Tamil Nadu Government that first proceeded to prepare a case for more autonomy and appointed a Committee presided over by Rajamannar, a former Chief Justice of the Madras High Court, Dr. A. L. Mudaliar, a former Vice-Chancellor of Madras University, and P. Chandra Reddy, a former Chief Justice of the Andhra High Court. The Committee recommended amendment of the Constitution so as to confine the Centre's powers to defence, foreign affairs, currency and communication. It was felt that the case for amendment was important not only because the federal form of the Constitution had initially been woven around a basically unitary system of government in historical terms, but more so because of the predominance of a single party at the Centre and in the States: for several years the Indian Constitution had assumed the overtones of a unitary constitution–a development which seriously clashed with the needs of social and economic goals of the States.

The legacy which the Congress inherited from the British imperialist rule served its bourgeois interest politically. For there was under that rule nothing permanent or sacrosanct about the identity of States. They were no better than the erstwhile Provinces. Their boundaries could be altered and, indeed, the very existence of individual States could be brought to an end by Parliament. The Federal units were thus in no sense sovereign, entitled, as in a truly federal polity, to surrender their authority in their common interest and vest it in a Union. Their legal sovereignty could be said in practice to lie in the legislatures created by the Constitution. But here too Article 249 empowered Parliament to legislate on any matter included in the State List provided that the Council of States by a two-thirds majority authorized it to do so. It meant that the autonomy of individual States, even in their own fields, remained subject to the collective wishes of other States.

The highly centralized political system could with ease be manoeuvred to serve the interest of its equally centralized economic counterpart, the Federation of Indian Chambers of Commerce and Industry. Its annual sessions were without fail inaugurated by the Prime Minister, while the senior and retired bureaucrats who sat on the company boards of corporate private enterprises "helped communication between business and government."[49]

This kind of situation where politics and business came to collaborate with each other was not envisaged earlier by the Constituent Assembly itself which, speaking in general terms, provided for a division of power, resources and functions though not without a regard for capitalist interest. There obviously developed over the years, due to the dominance of a single Congress Party, a vital difference between the original overall national design of the Constitution and the character it came to acquire subsequently in practice during the first phase of its rule based on party consensus rather than on an appeal to constitutional provisions.

The idea of a federal constitution for India, which Sir John Simon, Chairman of the Indian Statutory Commission, had first conceived, was still different and known for its resilience. The Commission had laid down in the report that in view of the plurality of Indian society and the different parts of the country being in various stages of economic and cultural development, its reformed federal constitution must contain within itself provision for its own development. In other words it should not be too rigid and uniform. On the contrary, it should admit of a natural growth and diversity, comfortable to the needs of the time and the ultimate policy objective.

Indeed, Sir John and his Commissioners thought in terms of a real "self-government" applied to "political units of a suitable size", forming part of a federal structure and including "communities at very different stages of development and culture".[50] Consistently with the common interest of India as a whole each political unit, as the Commissioners emphasized, was to be "mistress in her own house".[51]

Contrary to this original concept of a federal polity which the Indian Statutory Commission suggested as a model of self-government for constituent units, the Government of India Act (1935) introduced, from considerations of imperial interest, elements of rigidity and uniformity, concentrating power at the Centre as an instrument of policy to protect British capital invested in Indian business enterprise for purposes of defence[52] and other goals. It was the basic structure of that Act which the Drafting Committee of the Constituent Assembly adopted for its own Indian Constitution.

It is true that the makers of the Indian Constitution were in their efforts guided by national objectives, India (Congress) in place of the Empire, the Constituent Assembly for all practical purposes a predominantly Congress concern. But in the economic field the Indian counterpart of British business interest came to be recognized as the Federation of Indian Chambers of Commerce and Industry.

While the Congress came to be identified as India, FICCI held the entrepreneurial ground as controllers of the country's economy. As said above, they both collaborated with each other. The Bhubaneswar resolution in favour of democratic socialism was no bar till the Congress setbacks of 1967. The Report of the Rajamannar Committee was the first to mark the beginning of protest against an all-powerful Centre and its alliance with business as a reinforcement. The Ten-Point Programme in this context was to stress the policy objective of the Congress which was said to be removal of poverty.

The issue of Centre-State relations as an instrument of economic policy, which the Rajamannar Committee was the first to raise, thus became a live issue agitating men's mind in search of an answer to economic ills arising from the concentration of power at the political level. Prime Minister Indira Gandhi sought in these circumstances to hold dialogues with State Chief Ministers, more especially of non-Congress Governments, whose complaint was that the Centre decided everything and asked the States to take it and go home. While discussing things with the Prime Minister in one of the meetings of the National Development Council, E. M. S. Namboodiripad of Kerala, for example, made it clear that as part of a federal party the States were as much entitled to look into the Centre's incomes and expenditures as the Centre was entitled to look into those of the States. He did not dispute the fact of economic progress during the first three Plan periods. He maintained that progress had doubtless taken place. But the real issue, as he pointed out, was: "Progress towards what?", especially when "the rich had become richer and the poor poorer."[53] This was a contention which had earlier been held by Gulzarilal Nanda of the Planning Commission who in a letter to Prime Minister Jawaharlal Nehru had pointed out that in spite of "considerable industrial development" over four or five decades "inequalities of income and wealth" had actually become "accentuated".[54] In other words, the beneficiaries of economic growth, as the Mahalanobis Committee and the Monopolies Commission reported in 1964, were the higher echelons of the business communities, although their Federation kept on harping on increasing production alone being the only answer to poverty. The controversy so raging around growth versus poverty did not cease. It continued. Its immediate outcome was the Congress Split of 1969.

REFERENCES

1. *Cambridge Economic History of India*, Vol. II, p. 951.
2. *Report of the Economic Programme Committee of the AICC 1948 (Young Indian*: 25 years of Independence, *Special Independence Number* 1972, Documents, D. 98). Besides Nehru as chairman the Committee included Maulana Abul Kalam Azad, Jai Prakash Narayan, N. G. Ranga, Gulzarilal Nanda, J. C. Kumarappa, Achyut Patwardhan and Shankarrao Deo.
3. Ibid.
4. Ibid.
5. See para 15, chap. II of the First Five Year Plan submitted to the Prime Minister by Gulzari Lal Nanda under his Planning Commission letter No. PC (P)/62/52 dated Dec. 7, 1952. Also Stanley A. Kochanek, *The Congress Party of India*, Princeton University Press, Princeton, New Jersey, 1968, p. 165.
6. See chap. II, para 16.
7. See chap. I, para 13.
8. K.T. Shah (ed.), *Report of the National Planning Committee*, Bombay, 1949, p. 230.
9. Venkatasubbiah, op. cit., p. 86. The author, who studied this problem and wrote his *Enterprise and Economic Change*, did so on the basis of the original papers of the Federation of Indian Chambers of Commerce and Industry.
10. Ibid., p. 74.
11. Ibid., pp. 74-75.
12. Ibid., p. 76.
13. Ibid., p. 78.
14. Ibid., p. 87.
15. Mr. Singh was kind enough to consult his manuscript on *Public Control of National Enterprises* which he wrote in 1960.
16. G.K. Shirokov, *Industrialization of India*, p. 126.
17. Venkatasubbiah, op. cit., p. 77.
18. Shirokov, op. cit., p. 127.
19. See S.K. Goyal, *Monopoly Capital and Public Policy*; also *Political Dimensions of Multinational Corporations in India*, a study made in 1984 by the Indian Institute of Public Administration, New Delhi, with the support of the ICSSR.
20. See L.K. Jha, *Economic Strategy for the 80s*, p. 8.
21. See *FICCI, Presidential Address* by Bharat Ram, p. 15.
22. Prime Minister's statement in Parliament on April 23, 1963.
23. *Mahalanobis Committee Report*, p. 35.
24. See Venkatasubbiah, op. cit., pp. 19-20.
25. These included the Industrial Finance Corporation (1948), the State Finance Corporations (1951 onwards), the Industrial Credit and Investment Corporation of India (1955), the State Industrial Development Corporations (1960 onwards) and the Industrial Development Bank of India (1964).
26. *Young Indian* (Special Independence Number 1972), D147 and D148.
27. Ibid., D133.
28. Ibid., D 135.
29. It was introduced under Industries (Development and Regulation) Act, 1951 which laid down Procedures for industrial licensing.
30. Jha, *Economic Strategy for the 80s*, Allied Publishers, New Delhi, 1980, p. 10.

31. Ibid.
32. See Proceedings in Zaidi (ed.), *The Encyclopaedia of the Indian National Congress*, Vol. XIX, 1965-67.
33. Ibid., pp. 40-41.
34. Ibid. See Proceedings, pp. 42-45.
35. See *FICCI on Mahalanobis Committee Report*, New Delhi, July 1964.
36. After Shastri's death the Congress Working Committee met on January 14, 1966, to consider the election of the Congress Party leader in Parliament. According to its decision, the members of the Congress Party in Parliament met on January 19, 1966, and proceeded to elect the leader by secret ballot. Out of 551 members of the Party 526 attended the meeting. Mrs. Indira Gandhi was elected Leader. She got 355 votes as against Morarji Desai who got 169 votes, two votes being declared invalid.
    After the general elections, Indira Gandhi was elected Leader unanimously on March 12, 1967. See Zaidi (ed.), op. cit., Vol. XIX, pp. 483 and 545.
37. Ibid., pp. 555-57.
38. See AICC Proceedings in Zaidi (ed.), op. cit., pp. 362-64.
39. *Hindustan Times* (Delhi), March 13, 1966.
40. See Zaidi (ed.), op. cit., Vol. XX, p. 183.
41. See Philips (ed.), *Select Documents*, pp. 712-13.
42. Ibid., p. 722.
43. Ibid., p. 723.
44. See *FICCI Proceedings of the Annual Session of 1960,* pp. 66-67.
45. Stanley A. Kochanek, *Business and Politics in India*, University of California Press, Berkeley, 1974, pp. 181-82.
46. *Indian Express* (Delhi), March 29, 1968 (Myth of National Unity).
47. See *Assam Tribune* (Gauhati), May 2, 1969 (Dr. Hare Krishna Mahtab on Party Forum).
48. See *Tribune* (Ambala), August 28, 1967, and *Free Press Journal* (Bombay), August 31, 1967.
49. H. Venkatasubbiah, op. cit., p. 93.
50. See *Report of the Indian Statutory Commission*, Vol. II (Recommendations), paras. 23-24.
51. Ibid., para 27.
52. See *Govt. of India (Industries) Confidential A Progs.*, Nos. 7-22. Its letter to all Local Govts. and Chief Commissioners, No. 589-D, dated December 7, 1918, emphasized that "there must be in the immediate future a great industrial development in India"... for "imperial military reasons".
53. See *Patriot* (New Delhi), April 21, 1969 (Economic Relations and the Constitutional Problem by Girish Mathur).
54. Nanda to Nehru, No. PC(P)/62/52, dated Dec. 7, 1952, enclosing chap. I of the First Five Year Plan, para 13.

FOUR

Political Implications of Policy Implementation Game of Power Politics : 1967-1977

After the electoral reverses of 1967, an attempt was sought to be made by the Congress to implement, through legislative enactment, its policy to establish within the framework of democracy a socialistic pattern of society, declared at various Congress sessions from Karachi in 1931 onwards. The 10-Point Programme of 1967 was an expression of realizing the pressing need of implementing some of the most important of its policies. But, as a subsequent Note submitted by a group of MPs to Prime Minister Indira Gandhi showed, the progress made in its implementation even after a couple of years had remained "disappointing"[1] and shorn of any sense of urgency.

In an earlier statement made after the announcement of the 10-Point Programme, Finance Minister Morarji Desai admitted that in spite of considerable economic growth and rise in national income, in the course of the first three Plans, "the per capita income" fell "by 7.7 per cent". Naturally enough, "this reduced the people's purchasing power". Desai referred to the devaluation of the rupee as a step taken in 1966 to boost export trade. But, curiously enough, exports slumped.[2] Certain delegates, who attended the seventy-first session of the Indian National Congress at Hyderabad in 1968, doubtless complained that "some businessmen have bought politicians". That perhaps was the reason why all the actions of the Congress "were rightist", while it always "talked of socialism". Organizationally, the complaint was that while individuals had become bigger than the organization, the organization had acquired an importance much greater than that of the country.[3] The political behaviour of Mrs.

Gandhi, the Prime Minister, was no exception.

In March 1967, Mrs. Gandhi's unanimous election as leader of the Congress Party in Parliament was due to the indefatigable efforts made by K. Kamaraj, Congress President, to bridge the continuing gap between Indira Gandhi and Morarji Desai, two of the contestants for the post of Prime Minister.[4] The Congress President reported to his Working Committee on March 10 that in the course of the talk he had with them both separately and at a joint meeting he emphasized the importance of a unanimous election to counteract the forces of opposition, more especially in a situation where as many as nine State Governments had gone over to non-Congress parties. Though a failure in the first instance to effect any understanding between the two, Kamaraj ultimately succeeded and got Indira Gandhi elected unanimously on March 12, 1967. His personal influence as well as the influence he wielded as a leading Congress figure brought to her the support of the stalwart members of the AICC, including even those who were publicly known for their rightist or conservative views.

Mrs. Gandhi herself had in fact expressed herself in favour of a repeated demand of the Federation of Indian Chambers of Commerce and Industry for reducing controls provided by law to regulate industrial operation and its licensing system. Though fully aware of leftist trends moving steadily in favour of State control of national enterprises, she, in her inaugural address to the Federation in 1966, assured the industrialists that she was an advocate of fewer and fewer controls. As said above, she actually sought to win their confidence by referring to the steps she had already taken to remove controls on steel, pig iron and cement.

Obviously, when Mrs. Gandhi was installed in the office of Prime Minister, she was no socialist. She was an adherent of the established capitalist order in both political and economic terms. S. Nijalingappa, Congress President in 1969, was not wrong when in a letter of October 28 of that year he reminded Mrs. Gandhi that the persons whom she had started disparaging as a reactionary "coterie" functioning in the Congress as "a syndicate" were the same people whose "efforts" had "led to your election as the leader of the Parliamentary Party".

Nijalingappa who had succeeded Kamaraj as Congress President in 1968 made it clear in his letter that it was the Bangalore session of the AICC held in July 1969 which first marked a noticeable change in Mrs. Gandhi's attitude towards senior leaders. It might be, as some people believed, that the change so noticed was attributable to her insistence on Bank Nationalization as part of the Congress resolution to resolve the problem of poverty. But, as Nijalingappa argued in his letter, and perhaps rightly so, that the source of her behavioural change was not obstruction to Bank Nationalization for there were top leaders like Kamaraj, Y. B. Chavan, Atulya Ghosh and many others who advocated the measure much before the Note on the subject she presented to the AICC at Bangalore (a Note reviewed below in this chapter). Indeed, the Congress President's fear was that she wanted to create a rift in the Congress and use her adherents to establish a pattern of "one-man rule in the organization and the government". For he pointed out[5]:

"It appears that everything is permissible and pardonable to those who are recognized supporters of the personality cult that is threatening democracy in the organization. They may have committed serious breaches of our laws like the Income Tax Laws. They may not have submitted the declaration of their assets to the AICC as the rules of the party demand. They may have collected large amounts of money from various sources in the name of the party and not informed the party and accounted for them to the party."

According to the Congress President, it was thus the official influence of a Prime Minister that enabled Mrs. Gandhi to create within the organization a majority group favourably disposed to her. Besides, the slogan for nationalization had come to be popularly invested with a socialistic dimension because of the State control the term involved. In real terms, as said earlier, it meant no more than some increase in the influence exercisable by the Government over the banking industry, more especially in relation to the financial transactions of nationalized banks. Even so, the idea of nationalization, howsoever vague and illusory, was attractive. It lured the emotion-bound leftist elements of national politics who switched over in bulk to Indira Gandhi along with their supporters in the hope that they would manage to keep her on their own track and use her as an instrument of socialist policy. Little did they then foresee that once she was strongly entrenched in her position they would find themselves kept at bay.

Move Towards Congress Split for Self-Assertion
Bangalore Marked the Beginning

The Bangalore session of the AICC held in July 1969 marked the beginning of Mrs. Gandhi's move towards Congress split as a means to assert her independence of the organization which had after Prime Minister Nehru's death emerged as an instrument of control over government.

On July 7, 1969, certain Members of Parliament holding leftist views submitted to S. Nijalingappa, Congress President, a Note[6] on National Economic Policies for inclusion in the official resolution at the Bangalore session of the AICC. They included Chandra Shekhar, Mohan Dharia, Krishan Kant, R. K. Sinha and Chandrajit Yadav.

The Note started with an expression of regret over the utter failure of the Congress Party to implement its promises made in favour of a socialist order of society at various Congress sessions from Karanchi in 1931 onwards. It referred to the context in which the 10-Point Economic Programme was unanimously accepted in 1967 with a resolve to implement it without delay, but regretted again that even after a lapse of two years no progress had been made, no sense of urgency shown. The economic situation of the country had, on the contrary, become more aggravated because of the "growing frustration and despair of the people". The Note therefore sought to provide an outline of a comprehensive policy structure which the Congress governments at the Centre and in the States should pursue as part of their broad and basic objectives.

The Note defined these policy objectives in clear terms. The first guideline which it laid down was "the attainment of a rapid rate of economic growth accompanied by betterment of the living conditions of the weaker sections and not resulting in concentration of economic power or furthering of the disparities in income and wealth in the society". The second principle of policy objective was the removal of inequality in economic relationships, for example, between the employee and the employer, the landlord and the tenant and the labourer, the lender and the borrower. The object was to eliminate the economic exploitation of the weaker sections by those who were dominant in society. It was not to abolish the classes but to regulate their relationships in economic terms through State intervention or action. Last but not least was the introduction of reforms in the country's economic institutions, so that they might serve as "effective instruments of change in the transformation of society towards democratic socialism", a goal laid down by the Bhubaneswar session of the Congress.

The Note stressed the importance of fiscal and financial policies which, as it suggested, "should be so directed as to restrict tendencies towards concentration in the economy, raise larger resources for the development of the public and cooperative sectors, curb exploitation of the consumer by the monopolists and provide support to the new entrepreneurs". It was regretted that the fiscal and financial policies so far pursued since independence had been altogether inadequate to the goal declared by the Congress. It was this failure on the part of the Government in terms of fiscal and financial measures that accounted for "the deteriorating living conditions of the weaker sections of the community in the face of phenomenal growth of a few monopoly Houses".

The Note recommended in these circumstances certain radical policy changes. These included a number of measures proposed to be taken by the Government. Nationalization, for instance, of all private commercial banks and general insurance companies was the first priority. The object was to gain control over the fast growing public deposits with these institutions resulting from economic growth. The financial institutions so nationalized were to be brought under the control of those who had a social commitment and faith in the "philosophy of the public sector," who possessed professional competence to run it with efficiency and with social change and economic growth as the main aims. Another important measure was to impose ceilings on incomes and holdings of urban property. Its object was to make sure that the gains accruing to large estate owners in the urban centres as a result of development through government are duly shared by the community and that there was uniformity in government approach to property in agricultural and non-agricultural sectors. The imposition of ceilings was to apply equally to "unproductive expenditure and conspicuous consumption of the corporate bodies in order to restrict free benefits provided to the company directors and other senior executives at the cost of the public exchequer". The Note also recommended a progressive rate of taxation on the corporate sector as an encouragement to the small-scale industries of the corporate sector. It emphasized that the assistance given to the monopoly Houses by the Government should be converted into equity holdings. The idea was that the economic advantages of the monopoly Houses were duly shared by the public sector financial institutions providing most of the project finance to these industrial Houses. According to the Note special efforts were to be made to finance new enterprises in less developed areas or backward regions.

On the industrial policy, the MPs emphasized the importance of the public sector. They suggested that all new large industrial projects involving more than a crore of rupees should be given only to public or run by competent and experienced men with faith in the ideology of public enterprises which alone should be entrusted with the production of goods of mass consumption. Special efforts were therefore to be made to build up a cadre of professionals best fitted for the job in both technical and ideological terms. The entry of the big business was in fact to be banned in the production of consumer goods which were reserved for small-scale industries. Their Note was directed more especially against the operation of monopolists and foreign capital in India. They recommended expeditious setting up of the Monopolies Commission which was to be manned by persons of integrity and guided by considerations of social justice to ensure that the exploitation of the consumer by the monopolist was eliminated. As regards foreign capital, they were opposed to its entry in the industries already equipped with the technical know-how to encourage genuine Indian producers and avoid unnecessary drain on the national resources. They also took care to warn against inter-corporate investments and loans which conduced to the growth of industrial empires.

In the field of agriculture, the emphasis of the MPs was on the abolition of all kinds of intermediaries between the State and the actual cultivators. They wanted to make the slogan of "land to the tiller" a reality. It was not yet so in spite of several steps towards land reform. Their other important recommendation was to curb profiteering or hoarding of foodgrains by placing in the hands of the public sector organizations the wholesale trade and procurement of foodgrain surpluses. The idea was to reduce the margin of intermediary profit in order to ensure a fair price to the farmer and prevent the consumer from being exploited by private traders. Their recommendation also included provisions for minor irrigation, inputs to increase production, agro-based industries, rural education and care to promote health services in the rural areas.

The Note of the leftist MPs drew the attention of the Congress President towards two other economic problems of a serious nature. These were the growing mass unemployment among educated youth and the regional imbalance arising from uneven economic development, more especially of backward regions. While the first caused frustration and despair among the youth, threatening the foundations of democracy, the second led to the eruption of violence and rise of separative tendencies in the various parts of the country. Both the problems needed to be immediately attended to in the interest of political stability.

The whole approach of the leftists in the Congress was reformist in its nature, based on a call for State interference to regulate the functioning of relationships between the classes with a shift on emphasis weighted on the side of the weaker sections of society for the sake of social justice. It involved no radical structural change, nor even a provision for any effective sanction to make its regulatory suggestions a success. It was mere reiteration of the goal which the AICC had adopted at Bhubaneswar in favour of "democratic socialism".

Mrs. Gandhi's Role at Bangalore

In a separate Note[7] submitted to the AICC at Bangalore on July 8, 1969, Prime Minister Indira Gandhi referred to the views of Chandra Shekhar and other MPs who had stressed the line of economic policy adopted at Bhubaneswar. From a perusal of her Note which formed part of the AICC Proceedings in the same way as that of Chandra Shekhar and his associates, it is clear that she had acted under their influence. It was more or less an endorsement of the recommendations they had made, except for an emphasis on certain technicalities of requirements needed for bank nationalization, or the difficulties involved in imposing a ceiling on urban property or restriction on wasteful unproductive expenditure and conspicuous consumption. It was, on the whole, an appreciation of the proposals submitted by the MPs with a view to reducing the concentration of economic power.

Another influencing factor at Bangalore was a draft resolution on economic policies prepared by C. Subramaniam and Sadiq Ali who submitted it to the AICC there on July 8, 1969. Based on a Report of the Social, Political and Economic Committee the draft resolution reiterated that in spite of certain radical changes which had taken place both in the pre-independence structure of the Indian economy and the standard of living of some sections of the people in India, "tens of millions still live on a subsistence or even lower than subsistence standard whereas a small section of the community has amassed enormous wealth". This small section was a group of a few individual families who delighted in "the flamboyant display of wealth".[8] The Report of the committee, which influenced the draft resolution of July 8, pointed out that "the continuance of such a state of affairs is not only unjust and contrary to the proclaimed objective of the Congress", but that it also leads to a widespread dissatisfaction among the ordinary people who deeply resent the flamboyant display of wealth that is characteristic of life in the higher echelons of society. The manifest inequality is the main breeding ground for the difference "disturbances" which have characterized Indian life during the last few years.[9]

The social control or nationalization of certain banks, which followed in the wake of Bangalore, was by far the most important of the measures taken towards the implementation of what the Congress regarded as democratic socialism. Its declared object was to provide institutional facilities to make credit available for purposes of economic development.

However, what induced Indira Gandhi immediately to react favourably, even though partially, on the side of Chandra Shekhar and some others was not so much her concern to alleviate poverty as to preserve herself politically. For according to the Report of the Social, Political and Economic Committee of the Congress the basic source of threat to her political security was "the breakdown of (people's) confidence in what was announced from time to time as "programmatic statement of the Congress", her own party, "claiming that it stands for social justice, a Welfare State and an egalitarian order". This loss of confidence was responsible not only for her party's poor performance in the general elections of 1967, but for its continuously losing ground in subsequent mini-elections. The restoration of the image of her party with which her own future was linked up thus demanded that "decisive and correct steps" should be taken to put the programme of democratic socialism into practice, "to translate it into real life". It was realized that unless a socialist programme was soon adopted and its implementation effected, there could be no hope of her making any headway in the elections of 1972.[10] The Bangalore decision on bank nationalization was therefore an answer intended to meet the exigencies of a political compulsion.

Open Clash with Congress President

Indira Gandhi's concern for her political future became deeper still on account of differences with S. Nijalingappa, who led the Congress organization as its President. The organizational Chief and the Prime Minister came into open conflict with each other at the Faridabad session of the Congress in April 1969. While the former advocated the cause of monopolists and the private sector, the latter stood opposed to him publicly and lent her support to the group in the Congress inclined towards the public sector and bank nationalization.

In the course of his presidential address at Faridabad on April 27, Nijalingappa, speaking in a vein of regret, referred to the leftists as "a class of people" who, when the Congress assumed office after independence, got into it "without faith in its traditions and programmes". His complaint was that they not only held the Congress responsible for everything that went wrong, but also did everything to decry and slander Congress leaders, especially those in office. "It is these people", he reiterated, "who are contributing to make the Congress weak and also creating the feeling among the people that the Congress had abandoned its ideals and does not mean what it says. It is these few people inside the Congress and other parties outside that have made the common people feel there is something seriously wrong with the Congress organization and its leaders".[11] He was in fact opposed to its being used as a forum and "these people" being given any "quarter" in it. Considerations of politics and future prospect, however, demanded that Mrs. Gandhi should make a common cause with them and other non-conformists in the Congress or outside, who switched on to her from motives of gain and political advantage.

The other national issue of even greater importance was the question of industrial policy involving a choice between private and public sectors. Here, too, the Congress President and the Prime Minister declared themselves at Faridabad itself as belonging to two opposite camps, the former as an advocate of the private sector, while the latter of the public.

The Congress was fully satisfied with the growth of industrialization under private initiative. He was in fact in favour of all big industries being established by private entrepreneurs. He even warned that no big industry should be established in the public sector unless its capacity to produce was duly ascertained. "Simply because an industry is in the public sector", he said, "it does not mean that we should be satisfied with losses and be content with whatever is produced. If production of articles in the private sector can be achieved more economically we can even encourage the private sector. There is a case for reviewing this public sector attempt at establishing large-scale industries". He also felt satisfied to find that along with increasing industrialization, monopoly in industry is growing. It is no use crying hoarse against these monopolistic tendencies", which, according to the Congress President, were conducive to industrial development and a wide "dispersal of industries", beneficial to all parts of the country.[12]

As said above, the Bangalore session of the AICC turned the tide against S. Nijalingappa, the Congress President. It happened not merely because of Mrs. Gandhi's being drawn closer to the left from considerations of political strategy, but more so because of her being the main source of power and patronage as Prime Minister. While the left provided the benefits of a socialist slogan, the non-conformists and waverers in the Congress went by the lure of power, money and position.

The gains of Bangalore, however, did not mean an end of the threat to her political stability. She was soon called upon to face the challenge posed by the Congress President, Nijalingappa, and her Cabinet colleague and Finance Minister, Mr. Morarji Desai, who resigned because he was relieved of his finance portfolio which was taken over by Prime Minister Indira Gandhi herself. None of the two powerful adversaries was prepared to bury the hatchet.

Morarji Desai and Indira Gandhi

The correspondence that transpired between Mr. Desai and Mrs. Gandhi on the subject of resignation from the Council of Ministers shows that it was Morarjibhai who had moved the Congress resolution on the basic economic policy formulated on the lines of the Note submitted to the AICC by the Prime Minister at Bangalore. On the question of nationalization, as Desai has pointed out in his letter of July 17, 1969, and rigtly so, she had herself not been very categorical. She had not suggested nationalization straightaway. She had only said, "either we can consider the nationalization of the top five or six banks or issue directions that the resources of banks should be reserved to a large extent for public purposes". What the Finance Minister had done as part of an observation was merely to repeat his earlier caution about the pace of change in that respect. Moreover, the fact that the Working Committee's resolution on economic policy was unanimous shows that Desai's observations could by no means be construed as opposition to bank nationalization. In her letter of July 16, she too admitted that as "a disciplined soldier of the party" Desai had lent support to the resolution adopted at Bangalore. Even so, she added that "in regard to some of the basic issues that arise, you entertain strong reservations and have your own views about the directions as well as the pace of change. You have expressed your views clearly in the Working Committee and previously on other occasions. I have given thought to the matter and feel that, in all fairness, I should not burden you with this responsibility in your capacity as Finance Minister, but should take directly upon myself".[13] In fact, Mrs. Gandhi took the formal step to relieve Mr. Desai of his Finance portfolio, although she expressed a desire that he should continue to function as Deputy Prime Minister.

On July 16 itself Morarjibhai wrote back to Indira Gandhi to say that she should have given her "colleagues in the Cabinet an opportunity to know what concretely you wish to be done and to invite their reactions before deciding on whether you should change the sphere of responsibility of any of them. At any rate, as far as I am concerned, considering my record of service and loyalty to the Congress Party and Government, I regard it as a matter of ordinary courtesy that you should have discussed your precise misgivings with me before taking the decision that you say you have taken". Desai in fact stressed his point by reminding her that there had been no occasion when he pressed his views for acceptance above the views of the majority where Government decisions were involved. In view of the decision already taken by her, Desai pointed out that he saw no point in his continuing as a member of her Cabinet.

Mrs. Gandhi felt "distressed" at Desai's decision to quit her Cabinet and requested him to reconsider the step and "continue in Government as Deputy Prime Minister". In his reply Morarji said that while he was glad to know that she did not doubt his "loyalty to the party and its leader", he failed to understand the basis on which she had asked him to reconsider his decision to quit the Government. "I am, however, pained to see", he added, "that you doubt my enthusiasm with regard to the implementation of economic programmes adopted by the Party at Bangalore. I may have expressed different views on a given issue during discussions before a decision was taken on it, but once the party or the Cabinet took a decision, I have not only stood by it but defended it, I have done it without the slightest reservation". He therefore saw no reason why he should reconsider his decision, more especially when he was convinced that the Prime Minister was "less than fair" to him in relieving him of the Finance portfolio.

Desai's reply of July 17 contains an interesting reference to C. B. Gupta, a leading Congress politician of U.P. who, on the basis of a talk he had with Mrs. Gandhi, conveyed to the Finance Minister her impression about him. Writing to Indira Gandhi, Morarji Desai thus expressed his inability to understand her stated rationale for his being relieved of the Finance portfolio, for, as he said, "there is something more to it than meets the eye. Guptaji met me this afternoon and told me about his talk with you with regard to me. I was amazed and shocked to hear from him that you told him that I was organising a party (obviously with a view to oust you from leadership). In one breath you have recognized my loyalty to the party and its leader, in another you gave Guptaji to understand that I was conspiring against you. You know it well as anybody else that groupism and conspiracy are not in my grain. Guptaji told you this too". Later, the two leaders met together to discuss their differences which, however, remained unresolved. For when Desai raised the question of his talk with C. B. Gupta, she protested and said that what she had told Gupta applied not to him, but to others. "May I say", Desai wrote back, "that I have asked Guptaji again and he emphatically maintains that your statement was with reference to me "..

This kind of personal bickerings and conflicts went on between the Finance Minister and the Prime Minister in spite of the warnings of some members of the Congress Parliamentary Party who regarded such an attitude as "splitting the party" and "causing irreparable harm" to it. They finally unburdened themselves with the statements they made in Parliament on July 21, 1969. The conflicts did not cease. They led to split. The correspondence that went on between the two for a number of days made it clear that while Indira Gandhi was in her decision guided by a desire to have her position consolidated politically on the scores of ideology, Morarji Desai, like late Vallabhbhai Patel, cared little about class-based slogans and wanted to proceed on the principles of party and Parliamentary government-principles which laid stress on procedural rigidity and respect for majority rule.

Presidency of Indian Republic : A Tug-of-War Between Congress President and Prime Minister

The other important source of threat to Prime Minister Indira Gandhi's political stability was, as said before, Congress President Nijalingappa himself who wanted to have Neelam Sanjiva Reddy elected as President of the Indian Republic after the death of Dr. Zakir Husain. Mrs. Gandhi feared his choice for the highest office in the country which, under the Constitution, was invested with the power of appointment of the Prime Minister. The election to the Presidency of the Indian Republic thus became a tie between the two leaders who had been publicly drawn against each other ever since the Faridabad session of the Congress held in April 1969. Mrs. Gandhi described the Congress President and his group of supporters as "Syndicate" said to be in league with the Jan Sangh and Swatantra Party outside the Congress. In the situation to which she had been reduced, especially since Faridabad, she had no alternative but to declare herself as the champion of the progressive or left forces which, as the continuing trends in the rise of monopoly business Houses showed, she was not.[14]

It was in this political context that the controversy over the choice of the party's nominee for the presidentship of the Indian Republic arose at a meeting of the Congress Parliamentary Board held on July 12, 1969, at Bangalore itself under the chairmanship of S. Nijalingappa. It was naturally a divided Board weighted against Indira Gandhi. Even K. Kamaraj, who had earlier been helpful, even instrumental in Mrs. Gandhi's being elected the leader of the party, now had second thoughts. The Board by a four-to-two majority chose the Lok Sabha Speaker, Neelam Sanjiva Reddy, as the party nominee for the Presidentship of India. The other candidate was Jagjivan Ram, Minister for Food and Agriculture, who lost. Only Indira Gandhi and Fakhruddin Ali Ahmed voted in his favour. The other four members who voted for Reddy were Morarji Desai, Y. B. Chavan, S. K. Patil and K. Kamaraj. Jagjivan Ram and Nijalingappa did not vote. But Nijalingappa's preference for Sanjiva Reddy was not a secret. It was well known.

The announcement of the choice so made was, however, withheld officially for a time; for Indira Gandhi was not happy at the sudden and hasty manner in which the Board had decided the issue. The idea was to consult her before making the announcement, although the die had already been cast and the mind fully made up.

Doubtless, the Congress Working Committee met at New Delhi on July 21 when its President (Nijalingappa) informed the members of the political developments that had taken place since Bangalore. But the decision taken there on the choice of the party's nominee for the presidentship of India remained unchanged. All that the Committee did was to stress the importance of organizational unity and advised the President to meet the Prime Minister for a discussion of differences including even the resignation of Finance Minister Morarji Desai. The meeting suggested, however, did not take place. All that Nijalingappa did was to emphasize, in a letter of July 22, the imperative necessity of a free and frank discussion to remove mutual suspicion.

The Congress President issued in the meantime, on August 1, an appeal addressed to all political parties. He was portrayed as a great freedom-fighter who had held ministerial positions of responsibility in the composite State of Madras and then in Andhra Pradesh before he became the Speaker of the Lok Sabha. He even made a personal approach to some leaders of non-Congress parties with an appeal to them to extend their support to Reddy who had emerged as the Congress nominee for the office of the President in spite of Indira Gandhi voting against him. Between August 1 and 4, Nijalingappa made appeals to all MPs and Members of State Legislatures, to leaders of the Congress Legislature Parties and Presidents of Congress Committees, to the leaders of Opposition parties in Parliament and Members of the Electoral College. The urgency of such a widespread effort was understandable in view of V. V. Giri's standing as an independent candidate after resigning his office as Vice-President.

It was the contingency arising from the candidature of V. V. Giri, a well-known popular leader, that shook the nerves of Nijalingappa and obliged him to make an appeal to the Prime Minister in his letter of August 9. He referred to a meeting of the Congress Parliamentary Party which the Prime Minister had addressed without asking its members specifically to vote for Reddy. "During the last few days", he said, "many Congress MPs who met me spoke to me about what you said in the party meeting and expressed that you should have categorically appealed to them to vote and work for the success of the Congress candidate, Shri Sanjiva Reddy, and that your statement that you stood by the decision of the Parliamentary Board is not sufficient. However, in the light of the persistent comments and interpretations that the newspapers are carrying and the opinions expressed to me by Members of our Parliamentary Party, I feel it will be good if there can be an appeal from you to the Members of the Party as you did at the time of the election of the late Dr. Zakir Husain. I am sure such an appeal from you will add momentum to our campaign and ensure the success of our candidate".[15]

The appeal sought from the Prime Minister by the Congress President never came for the political reason indicated to him in a letter jointly addressed to him by Jagjivan Ram and Fakhruddin Ali Ahmed on August 11. They pointed out to him that considerable suspicion existed in the minds of a large number of Members of the Parliamentary Party "regarding the talks that you had, on your own initiative, with some of the leaders of the Jan Sangh and Swatantra Party", who had decided, "as a direct result of your talks", to extend support to N. Sanjiva Reddy. The main cause of their suspicion, as the letter made clear, was the basis of these talks on the condition on which these parties had agreed to support Reddy. "All kinds of ugly rumours", it said, "are afloat and the situation has worsened because those whom you have approached and their respective parties have openly demanded the removal of the Prime Minister. It is difficult to appreciate the desirability, or indeed the necessity, of these talks by you on a personal level with parties who themselves have an official candidate in the forthcoming Presidential election. Moreover, these parties are opposed to the accepted ideology and policies of the Congress and particularly the nationalization of banks which they have even challenged before the Supreme Court". The Congress President was naturally asked to explain.

From certain interviews I had with some of the delegates who had attended the Faridabad and Bangalore sessions of the AICC, it was confirmed that Mrs. Gandhi's fear of a sudden political setback was not without foundation. It was widely rumoured that if elected, Reddy would be induced to remove the Prime Minister. The exigencies of self-preservation in political terms naturally acted as her guide in the formulation of the public policies which, though formally attractive, conduced to continuity rather than change in any radical sense.

The Congress President denied the allegations made against him. But this did not remove her fear of political insecurity or setback. She issued no "whip" in favour of the Congress nominee, Sanjiva Reddy, when Nijalingappa asked her to do so in his letter of August 12. On the lines of Jagjivan Ram and F. A. Ahmed who, in view of the post-Bangalore political developments, favoured a free vote on the issue of the Presidential election, she expressed her inability to meet the request of the Congress President on the same ground. "I am sure", she wrote to Nijalingappa in a letter of August 13, "you are aware of the strong feelings of Congressmen, Members of Parliament as well as Members of State Legislatures, regarding the steps taken to make electoral arrangements with the Jana Sangh and Swatantra Party in the forthcoming Presidential election. A very large number of members have expressed the view that after these arrangements the basis on which the Party had agreed to the nomination of Shri Sanjiva Reddy has, unfortunately, disappeared". She added that "subsequent developments" had in fact "re-kindled doubts in the minds of many", more especially of Jagjivan Ram and F. A. Ahmed, two of her Cabinet colleagues, who gave an expression to these widespread feelings.

As a trained and sophisticated politician, Mrs. Gandhi did not refer to any threat to her own position, but justified her reluctance to issue any whip in favour of Sanjiva Reddy on the ground of certain fixed principles. "It is a matter of deep anguish to me", she said, "that our colleagues and leading members (like Ram and Ahmed) should have been convinced that attempts are now being made at the highest level in the party to compromise with political parties totally opposed to our principles and accepted programmes. The eagerness with which parties like Jana Sangh and Swatantra have announced their support to Shri Sanjiva Reddy, despite their own official candidate, lends credence to this conviction".[16]

The Congress President repudiated the allegations. "It is unworthy of those who make it", he said, "and it is unworthy of me to comment upon. Apart from my responsibilities as the President of the Congress, my record as a public man would nail the lie to the counter". The fact of his personal approach to the leaders of the Jana Sangh and Swatantra Party and their open demand for the removal of Prime Minister Indira Gandhi was, however, never denied. This precisely was the moot point which brought into focus the main political element underlying the whole behavioural pattern of Mrs. Gandhi. After a brief exchange of arguments and counter-arguments, the two sides issued their appeals to partymen according to their own interest and conviction. While the Congress President asked them to vote for Sanjiva Reddy on party lines as a matter of discipline, Mrs. Gandhi stressed that the issue involved went far beyond the Presidential election and called for a vote on the choice of policies, social and economic. She therefore declared herself in favour of exercising a free vote–a move which the Congress President decried as an act of indiscipline. "It is clear beyond doubt", he told her in his letter of August 18, "that you have deliberately acted against the decision of the Parliamentary Board, disobeyed the order of a competent authority and acted in a way calculated to lower the prestige of the Congress".[17] It was in fact a show-cause notice for disciplinary action which he issued not only against the Prime Minister, but also against Jagjivan Ram and F. A. Ahmed.

The immediate occasion for disciplinary action was the defeat of Sanjiva Reddy and the victory of V. V. Giri in the Presidential election where, in spite of the directive issued to PCCs to ensure that Congress voters were present at State capitals and New Delhi on August 16, 1969, and cast their votes in favour of the Congress nominee, they had not only worked actively against him but sought to obtain the support of Congress voters for V. V. Giri. This was especially so with A. P. Sharma, President of Bihar PCC; Giani Zail Singh, President of Punjab PCC; and Kamalapati Tripathi, President of U.P. PCC. They were all alleged to have carried on propaganda against the Congress candidate, and therefore declared liable to disciplinary action before the Working Committee.

It was in these circumstances that C. Subramaniam took up the cudgels and challenged the authority of the Congress President to proceed with disciplinary action in a situation where his own conduct had been questioned on the ground that he had gone beyond his power in negotiating with the Jana Sangh and Swatantra Party on terms prejudicial to the accepted policies of the Congress. In a letter of August 19, Subramaniam in fact warned Nijalingappa that since he himself was party to the dispute, he could not sit in judgment and declare the Prime Minister and two of her Cabinet colleagues as guilty of a prima facie breach of discipline. This led Subramaniam himself being also gagged for indiscipline and later declared as having ceased to be a member of the Congress Working Committee.

However, the Congress Working Committee which met on August 25 viewd with grave concern the deep fissures which had developed in the Congress Party since the Bangalore session of the

AICC, resulting in Reddy's defeat because of a large segment of the party being disposed to withhold its support from him. The Committee regretted these developments but, instead of going into individual cases of conflict, emphasized the need for unity and called upon the Congress President and the Prime Minister to meet together and resolve their differences, not by treating themselves as heads of two separate and distinct centres of power, but as institutions complementary to each other.

It was in principle a sound resolution. But in practice it remained inoperative from considerations of politics, the game of power. By appeal to some resolution passed a couple of decades back, it was alleged certain leaders of Mrs. Gandhi's group were removed from their position in the organization. C. Subramaniam was, for example, removed from the Congress Working Committee. Kamalapati Tripathi, K. Venkataratnam and a few others were likewise divested of the positions they held in the organization. It is needless here to go into the validity or otherwise of the grounds on which they were removed by the Congress President. What is important here is to stress the inevitable consequence that followed the action so taken by him in the context of the Working Committee's move. Congress split became a certainty.

The Congress President was in fact fighting a losing battle. The success of V. V. Giri in the Presidential election had already been acclaimed as Mrs. Gandhi's success. With Giri as President of India, her position as Prime Minister had already become entrenched. The obduracy of the Congress President went further to reinforce her position, based in practice on the influence of power, privilege and patronage exercisable by virtue of herself being the Prime Minister. It was this influence that led members of the AICC to submit to the Working Committee on October 19 their notice for a requisitioned meeting to consider all the political developments since Bangalore.

In his long letter of October 28, Nijalingappa regretted the unusual practice of the Working Committee members accusing its President and carrying on a campaign of vilification against him, with pressures put on the members of the AICC to go in for a requisitioned meeting to consider what they called his "arbitrary orders" passed for the removal of C. Subramaniam. He was particularly sore about the defeat of the Congress candidate in the presidential election and even expressed regret over the way Mrs. Gandhi "had encouraged and sanctified indiscipline on the basis of a handy untenable story" that he was in league with the Jana Sangh, inimical to her. The Congress President in fact alleged that "there were many reports in the Press that you accepted congratulations on the victory of Mr. Giri and hailed Mr. Giri's victory as the victory you stood for".[18]

The Congress President's letter addressed to Mrs. Gandhi on October 28 makes it clear beyond doubt that the Indian National Congress had virtually split into two groups, one increasingly opting in favour of the Prime Minister from considerations of power and pelf, while the other lending support to Nijalingappa as the head of the Congress organization, separate and distinct from its government. He had the support of such Congress leaders as Kamaraj, Morarji Desai, Y. B. Chavan, Atulya Ghose and others. Those who led the movement on the side of Indira Gandhi included such men as Jagjivan Ram, F. A. Ahmed, C. Subrahmaniam and others of their kind. The main issue involved in their conflict was the choice of a person for presidentship, not in terms of any ideological consideration, but of power to preserve oneself against any eventuality or threat of exclusion. The entire approach was in fact political on both sides. Their open appeal for unity or loyalty to party organization was no more than a mere chimera or bogey. Both sides were, in their efforts to achieve success, guided by no scruple. While the Congress President was believed to be in league with the Jana Sangh, Indira Gandhi's choice for a "free vote" or "conscience vote" was designed as a counterform politically directed in support of a candidate who had the blessing of the Communist Party and the Muslim League against the Congress nominee. With her backing, V. V. Giri won the game as an "independent" candidate. His victory was her own victory.

Nijalingappa thus did not rest satisfied with the several charges levelled against Mrs. Gandhi in his letter of October 28 on the score of indiscipline and unaccounted fund collected in the course of the presidential election. He soon proceeded to remove from his Working Committee two of her close associates, F. A. Ahmed and C. Subramaniam. This led to an immediate split among the members of the Congress Working Committee. Ten of its members met at the residence of the Prime Minister under her chairmanship and declared the action as "invalid" with a comment that both Ahmed and Subramaniam continued to be members of the Working Committee whose balance had been sought to be upset in order to ensure a majority. The other half of the 10 members of the Working Committee met on the same date under the chairmanship of Nijalingappa and declared the proposed requisition of the AICC as absolutely unnecessary. They declared that the implementation of the socialistic programme was the responsibility of government and that the proposal for requisition was no more than an attempt "to divert the wrath of the people from administration to the organisation".

The demand for requisition, however, did not subside, more especially because the governmental machinery of propaganda was on the side of the Prime Minister. Four hundred and five members of the AICC out of the total of 705 addressed a joint requisition to the Working Committee to convene a meeting of the AICC to consider not only the problem of implementation of radical programmes adopted at Bangalore, but also of electing a new Congress President for that purpose.

As regards the choice of a new Congress President, a decision had already been taken by the members of the Working Committee who met at the Prime Minister's residence on November 1, 1969, itself. Their decision was to have a special meeting of the AICC convened on November 22 and 23, 1969, for that purpose. The meeting, which actually took place as scheduled in Delhi, elected Jagjivan Ram as the new President of the Indian National Congress.

The issue involved in the demand for requisition was significant not only in terms of power politics, but also of policy implementation related to it and used as an instrument of propaganda on the score of ideology. The correspondence that transpired between the Prime Minister on the one hand and Morarji Desai as well as Nijalingappa on the other makes it clear that while the former sought to attribute failure in implementation to the leadership of the Congress organization, the latter shifted the blame to the Government and its administration. It was argued, and perhaps rightly so, that in the course of a debate on policy formulation every member of the organization was free to express his or her viewpoint, as it happened at

Bangalore. But once a decision had been taken, all were bound to implement it. Desai's complaint had been that he was deprived of his finance portfolio without being given any chance to *prove* his bona fides . This created a stir and led to unnecessary friction. Nijalingappa, too, was not wrong when he held the country's government and its administration immediately responsible for the non-implementation of policies. Instead of paying attention to administrative reforms, he complained, the Prime Minister proceeded to find fault with the "organization" and took recourse to "requisition" to remove its President on the ground of his being an impediment to policy implementation. Doubtless, the element of political commitment to implementation was of great importance. But this applied more directly to the agencies of government than the party organization.

In his letter of October 28, 1967, he had in fact already stressed the responsibility of the Government for policy implementation. He said: "Though you are the head of the administration clothed with full powers to implement the programmes and fulfil the promises of the party, you seem to think that it is the organization that has to be blamed for tardiness of implementation. You are uneasy when the organisation or even the organ of the Parliamentary Party wants to review the policies or actions of the administration"[19].

Even so, a resort to requisition was acclaimed not only as a move towards "progressive" policies, but also as a forthright endeavour to implement them. The resolutions adopted by the ten members of the Congress Working Committee under Nijalingappa's presidentship on November 2 in New Delhi, however, declared it as "an attempt to find in the Congress organization a scapegoat for the manifest failures of the administration." They expressed themselves whloleheartedly in favour of the nationalization of 14 banks effected in pursuance of the Bangalore resolution of the AICC, but sounded a warning that grave unrest might follow if an attempt was made by the Central and State Governments to shift the responsibility of implementation on to the shoulders other than their own. Nijalingappa therefore requested the Prime Minister "to discuss in depth the concrete programmes which the Congress should formulate and evolve specific measures for their speedy and effective implementation"[20].

From the correspondence that transpired between Nijalingappa and Indira Gandhi on the subject of Sanjiva Reddy's election, it appears that the Congress split took place virtually on November 1, 1969, the date on which the Congress Working Committee was scheduled to meet, but when 10 of its members refused to attend its meeting, and instead met at the residence of Indira Gandhi to resolve that a special meeting of the AICC should be convened on November 22 and 23 to remove Nijalingappa and elect a new President in his place. Obviously, it was an act of indiscipline, motivated by greed for power, though publicly upheld on the score of progressive ideology which she described as a "dynamic leadership inside the government and an organizational leadership that moves with clarity and inspiration" to mobilize the entire people for Indian regeneration in defence of secularism".[21].

And yet when the Congress President had, in his letter of October 28, 1969, accused her of attempting to build up a "personality cult" to collect unaccounted money on behalf of the party from the evaders of income tax, and violators of the income tax laws, she could not cover up the guilt. All that she did in a letter of November 3, 1969, to him was to cite instances of what had been happening in the States, which amounted to a clear admission of that guilt on her own part. She said: "Has any account been rendered by any of the Working Committee members of the funds collected for general and by-elections? Shri S. K. Patil openly admitted that he had collected a large sum of money at the time of 1967 elections. Has this been accounted for? Did this money find its way to the AICC?[22] She naturally argued that she had done nothing wrong in collecting funds in the name of the party without any account being rendered to the AICC. When she said so, she had hardly realized that she was the country's Prime Minister and that any lapse on her part in this regard could not but be viewed as a serious reflection on the Government. As Congress President, Nijalingappa had thus reasons to initiate action against her.

Reasons, however, could not assert themselves in a situation where group politics for power claimed to be the dominant note. In her letter of November 4, 1969, she reminded him once again that more than 400 members of the AICC had called for a requisitioned meeting and that he had no choice left but to face the challenge. The pressing demand for calling a requisitioned meeting led to her being served with a show-cause notice against disciplinary action "even at the risk of splitting the party."[23] For while Mrs Gandhi was terribly allergic to criticism, none would expect the Congress President to be a persona non grata. She asked Ram Subhag Singh, her Cabinet member, to resign and go merely because the Congress Working Committee had, on November 3, passed in his presence a number of resolutions, highly critical of government policies. In a letter addressed to Singh immediately, on November 4, she said, "Since you attended the Working Committee meeting, it would not be unfair to presume that you are a party to the resolutions which we passed there". In accordance with "the recognized practice of government", she added, "you render your resignation from the Council of Ministers".[24]

The splitting of the party was for a short while delayed as a result of the efforts of certain leaders, more especially Abraham of Kerala and Veerendra Patil, Chief Minister of Mysore, at whose instance Nijalingappa agreed to go to the Prime Minister's house on November 7 for lunch to which he was invited. The lunch, however, bore no fruit. While the Congress President had a serious objection to any requisition in the form of a censure against the Congress President and felt reluctant to take back C. Subramaniam on the Working Committee on account of his open revolt, Indira Gandhi did not feel inclined to take back Morarji Desai and some others who had been removed from her Council of Ministers. The emphasis on both sides was on the choice of personalities to give weight to the respective positions they held rather than policies considered necessary in the best interest of the country.

From a circular letter issued by D. Sanjivayya to the members of the AICC on November 11, 1969, it appeared that while efforts at compromise were being made there was no let or hindrance to the requisitioned meeting scheduled for November 22 at New Delhi. A last-minute effort was made to have the charges against the Prime Minister withdrawn and the requisition given up. But it all failed.

On November 12, 1969, the Syndicate, only half of the Congress Working Committee, met in New Delhi. It referred to her acts of indiscipline at the time of the Presidential election and pointed out how in spite of considerable pressure from Congressmen to take action the Congress Working Committee, in its anxiety to maintain unity, condoned all her violations of organizational discipline.

The unity resolution, however, could not produce the desired effect. It was alleged that the Prime Minister launched a campaign against the Congress organization holding its leadership responsible for all the ills the country was afflicted with as well as the failures of policy implementation. It was propagated that the task of implementing Congress policies called for harmony between its parliamentary and organizational wings, which, in other words, signified a desire to impose ministerial dominance, an objective which, as Nijalingappa's Congress Committee alleged, was sought to be achieved by "a signature campaign" launched for ousting the Congress President. "The AICC members, left to themselves, would have thought of no such move, but the picture changed when inspiration came from the top and from persons occupying high ministerial positions".[25] The situation so created by an exercise of ministerial influences at the Centre as well as in the States was in fact unique in the history of the Congress, for never had differences between the Prime MInister and the Congress President been sought to be resolved in the way the former did.

The Congress President removed in the meantime two of the recalcitrant members of the Working Committee who belonged to Mrs. Gandhi's group, and a third of the same group ceased to be its member under the rules. This infuriated the Prime Minister who lost her hold in the Working Committee. She and her supporters, in protest, not only did not attend the meeting of the Working Committee held on November 1 and 2 but held their own separate meetings in defiance of the legally constituted Working Committee. Though politically sought to be justified as a measure of dynamism in ideological terms, hers was under the existing Congress constitution and its rules a clear case of indiscipline motivated by craze for power. It led to a series of complications which, as said above, could not be resolved in the absence of any real commitment to socialism on either side.

But since, in organizational terms, there was a strong case of indiscipline against Mrs. Gandhi, the legally constituted Congress

Working Committee, in its meeting of November 12, 1969, removed her from the primary membership of the Congress for her acts of defiance against its decisions as well as for actively sponsoring the setting up of a rival Working Committee and AICC. It pointed out that in the midst of a continuous chain of unhappy developments since Bangalore in July 1969, it had "to choose between Smt. Indira Gandhi and everything that the Congress stood for and it has rightly decided in favour of the latter".[26]

But far more skilled in the subtleties of politics and invested with the power of patronage as Prime Minister, she outstripped the Congress President, more especially in the peculiar state of Indian social and political developments where the elite went in more for self-interest and opportunism than commitment to principles. Even most of top "freedom-fighters" were no exception. Led by Jagjiven Ram, a number of her supporters issued a rejoinder against the disciplinary action and emphasized the importance of the requisitioned meeting of the AICC, scheduled to be held at Delhi on November 22 and 23 to remove Nijalingappa from the presidentship of the Congress.[27] Jagjivan Ram and his group of Mrs. Gandhi's supporters in fact did the whole job for her in the name of a progressive policy, although it is well known that most of them, including the sponsor himself, were later dropped from her Congress. Jagjivan Ram, however, played a leading role in the tug-of-war for power between Nijalingappa and Indira Gandhi. While the Congress Parliamentary Party lent its majority support in her favour, Jagjivan Ram was rewarded with the presidentship of her Congress (R) which met in Bombay on December 28, 1969.

Congress (R) Bombay Session Policy Announcement

The Congress (R) session at Bombay held on December 28-29, 1969, under the presidentship of Jagjivan Ram did no more than recall its oft-repeated pledge to establish, by an extension of political democracy to social and economic spheres, a socialistic society based on the equality of opportunity and freedom to work. To win confidence and prove its bona fides it reiterated and recalled the stand of the Congress Party made clear at various Congress sessions, viz. Karachi in 1931, Avadi in 1955, Nagpur in 1959, Bhubaneswar in 1964 and the Ten-Point Programme of 1967.

The economic policy statement referred to Mrs. Gandhi's note presented to the AICC at Bangalore, but said nothing about the extent of policy implementation. On the contrary, it admitted that "despite visible changes in the pre-independence structure of the Indian economy certain sections of the community have amassed enormous wealth, but taken as a whole tens of millions still live in conditions of poverty. These glaring inequalities are reflected in a flamboyant display of material possessions, and even more in the exercise of economic power to the detriment of social progress".[28] In other words, economic growth had throughout remained unrelated to social progress or the removal of poverty and unemployment.

However, what the Congress (R) did to deal with the twin problem of poverty and unemployment was merely to express a wish to reaffirm its declared socialist policy which was by no means to affect the basic structure of India's capitalist economy or the concentration of wealth that flowed from it. It envisaged a rapid rate of economic growth, a desire to eliminate the exploitation of the weaker sections of society, maximum production without the emergence of monopolists, the establishment and encouragement of such socio-economic institutions as might consolidate democracy and socialism based on it, and the extended opportunity for employment for a fuller utilization of manpower as the most important productive resources. These were, however, no new suggestions. They had already formed part of the AICC proceedings at Bangalore, though still in a conceptual state.

What the Congress (R) planned immediately to do was to take steps to implement the Ten-Point Programme. These were inclusive of the nationalization of 14 major banks by an ordinance, a legislation against monopolies, and the canalization of the import of many items of industrial raw materials through the public sector. As part of its promise to implement the programme emphasis was in addition laid on the implementation of the following items:

i. Nationalization of General Insurance.
ii. Abolition of the privy purses and privileges of the ex-rulers.
iii. Ceiling on urban property.

iv. Wholesale trade procurement of major agricultural commodities in the public sector and abolition of forward trading of all agricultural produce.

v. The bulk of import trade in the State sector and export trade under public sector.

Of the measures proposed to be taken or actually taken to secure the implementation of the Ten-Point Programme, the nationalization of the 14 major banks was by far the most important. It was an attempt to provide an institutional credit system, more especially in rural areas, to promote the development of agriculture and cottage industry which Manu Subedar, as said above, had first suggested in the 1920s as part of his recommendations to reorganize the Indian banking system for developmental purposes. In the earlier attempts, however, what was stressed was the credit-worthiness of the person, not the credit-worthiness of a project or activity. And since the credit-worthiness of a person was related to his or her property for purposes of recovery, the extension of credit remained restricted to propertied classes. Since the nationalized banks were in principle sought to be based on a suitable system of guarantee by the State Governments, cultivators even with small holdings could be admitted to the credit made available not only to the farming community but also to others possessing entrepreneurial ability. It was envisaged that credit facility covered by a suitable system of State guarantee should in course of time be made available from nationalized banks and cooperative financial institutions also to landless labourers to enable them to take up subsidiary occupations.

Consistently with the policy so formulated for agricultural development, the Bombay session of the Congress Party called upon the Central and State Governments to:

(a) organize special programmes for dry farming,
(b) develop suitable crop varieties for dry lands,
(c) ensure adequate allocation of credit and other inputs,
(d) strengthen all the supporting services, especially cooperatives and agro-industries.

A time-bound programme for land reforms was at the same time declared to win the confidence of the farming community in general. Its object was to make it clear to cultivators that the Congress Party was keen not only to ensure the security of tenure and expedite the settlement of all land disputes, but also to abolish all types of intermediaries and settle surplus land with landless labourers.

On the industrial side, the Bombay session of the Congress Party recognized that the major thrust be "towards stimulating the growth of productive forces". This called for a periodical change in the licensing system and other regulatory measures which, as the Congress(R) claimed, were intended to reduce the concentration of wealth. The Party declared its intention to define the respective areas within which the public and private sectors were to operate and laid down certain conditions to ensure efficiency and economy in the operation of the public sector.

Welfare Policies Politically Motivated

As the policy analysis in the preceding chapter shows, the welfare policies started with the Ten-Point Programme were characterized more by continuity than innovation. These too were largely politically motivated and found wanting in meat. The whole trend was in fact towards increasing production regardless of any social consideration for its pattern and direction of investment, a consideration which might otherwise have regulated productive forces in the interest of the community and territorial defence.

Historically, as pointed out earlier, it was the experiences of the First World War that dictated the necessity of the country's industrial development for purposes of imperial defence; for Indian capitalism, though just emerging and soon after getting organized in the Federation of Indian Chambers of Commerce and Industry (1927) had not yet become an independent economic force. The exigencies of imperial defence were in fact recognized as the basic consideration that led the British Government in India to go ahead with her industrialization on its own in spite of its political constraints. It was this consideration that induced the Government of India to introduce fiscal reforms as incentives to India's industrial progress and the advancement of science and technology. This was a new trend of development which had the support of both the Government and the

Federation of the Indian Chambers of Commerce and Industry.

In the presence of imperialist rule, however, there were questions of currency and exchange or sterling balance and foreign trade restrictions which called for a settlement for purposes of full collaboration on terms of equality between Indian and British business Houses. It took time before some of these were sought to be resolved with the establishment of the Reserve Bank of India in 1934. What paved the way for compromise was the rise of communism and terrorist movement which both viewed as their common enemy. The constitutional change of 1935 and the formation of popular governments in the provinces acted as further incentives to the growth of Indian business Houses in 1937. They took full advantage of the Second World War which enabled them to emerge as a competitive force in collaboration with national politics. It was in these circumstances that the necessity of political settlement with the Congress Party was realized to stave off the capitalist crisis precipitated by the war. The settlement effected in 1947 facilitated the development of multi-national corporations for the advancement of private corporate business on capitalist principles. It was a form of collaboration between foreign and Indian capital directed against the leftist forces, their common enemy. The international financial institutions established in 1944 lent their full support to this new modus operandi as a instrument of capital enterprise. It was stimulated by American entrepreneurs who had just acquired a foothold among Indian businesses in the course of the Second World War.

Another significant development that flowed from the Second World War was the realization of the importance of State initiative and participation in the promotion of basic industries for defence purposes. While retaining the role of private enterprises as an essential instrument of general economic development the statement of 1945 stressed the inevitability of State entrepreneurship for the production of capital goods. For in spite of the war-time industrial expansion, India, due to her continuing dependence on imports, had not yet become self-reliant in the manufacture of heavy machinery, transport and electrical equipments, fine chemicals and other inputs. She could not even reproduce her existing productive capacity as her defence strategy. The development industries geared to defence requirements was thus a goal which the Government alone was considered fit to accomplish. Consistently with this object in view the

Government of India established, as part of a Post-War Reconstruction Plan, its Planning and Development Department already mentioned above. It was this pre-independence development which found expression in the Industrial Policy Resolutions of 1948 and 1956, the latter being weighted more in favour of the public sector than the former.

As the private sector had steadily been gaining in strength under FICCI's leadership, a major policy departure occurred in 1948 itself. Apart from making deviations from the recommendations of the Economic Programme Committee (1948), the takeover of the existing larger concerns desired by the Policy Resolution was shelved for consideration for 10 years. The second departure affected the Industrial Policy Resolution of 1956. It permitted the continuance of the private sector in industries listed in Schedule B, a concurrent scheme. The main industries thrown open to the private sector in Schedule B included aluminum, fertilizers, power, chemicals, sea transport and synthetic rubber. The private sector operated under the organized leadership of FICCI which maintained a close liaison with the Prime Minister invited customarily to address its annual general meeting.

Naturally enough, the country's economic growth was characterized by a steady growth in private business concentration. The period which began with the Bangalore session of the AICC, and the Congress split that followed with a declamatory pronouncement in favour of ideological radicalism, was no exception. The increase in the assets of the private corporate sector was even greater. It rose from Rs. 6,487.08 crores in March 1964 to Rs. 6,990.70 crores in December 1966, while in the period beginning in 1967, the rise recorded was from Rs. 9,670.23 crores in 1969 to Rs. 12,834.90 crores in 1975. According to the *Sachar Committee Report* the top 20 business Houses registered under the MRTP Act recorded a rise in the value of their assets from Rs. 2,430.61 crores in 1969 to Rs. 4,465.17 crores in 1975. But significantly enough, Mrs. Gandhi's victory in the Parliamentary elections of 1971 and the Assembly elections of 1972 was followed by a steep rise in the percentage of increase in the value of the assets of these big business Houses. This percentage rose to 68.6 between 1972 and 1975.[29] They were perhaps rewarded for their contribution to her electoral success. The declared policy of welfare and alleviation of poverty was thus more of the nature of political propaganda than reality.

The Mahalanobis Committee (1984) regretted that in spite of countervailing measures the concentration of economic power in the private sector had steadily been growing. The *Monopolies Inquiry Commission Report* of 1964 as well as R. K. Hazari's *Structure of Private Corporate Sector* both recognized this growing trend. But above all were the opening remarks of the Congress President, Dr. Shanker Dayal Sharma, himself who, in the course of his presidential speech made at the AICC session at New Delhi on June 1, 1972, admitted the existence of "the dominating heights held by monopolies" in spite of a recognition of the increasing importance of the public sector. He pointed out that although the declared policy of the Congress was the establishment of a democratic socialist society, it was regrettable that "the 75 monopoly Houses control 53 per cent of the assets of the non-banking private corporate sector. Innumerable commissions and enquiries have proved that the monopoly Houses are not production-oriented but operate on the principle of maximum profits with minimum production, along with black money operation, pre-emption of licences and collaboration agreements with foreign firms". All these were the result of "the industrial licensing policy, the pricing policy and the absence of trained and conscientious managerial cadre".[30] The Congress President therefore stressed the recognition of an effective curb on monopolies as a national demand.

The nationalization of the 14 major banks had been acclaimed as a radical measure calculated to make loans available for purposes of agricultural inputs and employment-oriented small-scale industrial undertakings. The Congress President, however, pointed out that the State itself encouraged the growth of monopolies; for State loans were in general advanced to monopoly Houses and in spite of the recommendations of an "experts" meeting" the loans so advanced were not converted into equity capital. The result was that the State did not acquire ownership and management control commensurate with its shareholdings in these monopoly companies.

Dr. Sharma was in fact critical of nationalization itself which benefited big business more than anybody else. He did not identify it with socialism, although he held that there could be no socialism without it. He said: "Nationalization is certainly an indispensable requisite for future socio-political changes, but it cannot by itself bring about a raise in the productive forces unless accompanied by an economic policy whose aim is to promote economic progress through material stimulation of labour and production and an efficient coordination of the State and private sectors."

Indeed, it was in terms of a progressive economic policy that bank nationalization was more of a failure than success. Since the nationalization of the 14 major banks in 1969, very little discussion took place at the policy-making level to evolve ways and means to utilize nationalized banks as an instrument of regulating the financial operations of top industrial Houses, the main beneficiaries of nationalization. It is true that nationalized banks extended the scope of larger credit facilities for the development of agriculture and small-scale industries. In terms of percentages, however, the change remained more marginal than real. The nationalized banks were utilized as a source of larger loans to big business, a development which, in the absence of a regulatory agency, contributed to the concentration of economic power.

Though it was recognized publicly by the Congress President that no nationalization would by itself succeed unless accompanied by an economic policy geared to socialism, the resolution, which the AICC adopted at Gandhinagar (Gujarat) in October 1972, continued to emulate the model set by the Industrial Policy Resolution of 1956, weighted in favour of the private sector and attuned to the production of capital goods for a self-reliant national economy in terms of a defence strategy in the context of the Bangladesh war against West Pakistan. Its whole approach was towards the promotion of economic growth on the basis of the Industrial Policy Resolution of 1956 which the resolution considered to be central to the Congress conception of the future pattern of growth. It reiterated that there could be "no question of modifying or abridging the principles underlying the Industrial Policy Resolution of 1956 with a view to enlarging the scope of operation of private enterprise".[31]

The open recognition of the importance of the public sector, however, remained declaredly unabated; for the economic policy objective adopted at Gandhinagar stressed the need for "reducing concentration of economic power". But the way suggested to accomplish it was "to remove impediments in the way of augmenting the productive capacity of our economy", operating "to the disadvantage of new (private) entrepreneurs whom it is the object of our policy to encourage".[32] Consistently with the policy so announced, the Government was urged to accelerate the development of scientific and technological competence. The private sector was, in other words, sought to be benefited by the industrial infrastructure built up by public resources.

The whole trend of economic policy thus conduced to the concentration of wealth and economic power; and yet the Parliamentary elections of 1971 and the Assembly elections were contested and won by the Congress on the basis of a declared programme of "Garibi Hatao", a slogan which ensured the homogeneity of Mrs. Gandhi's Government at the Centre and the success of her party in most of the States.

The slogan so raised was evidently unrelated to performance or even honesty of purpose; for, as the proceedings of the AICC held in Delhi on May 14, 1972, pointed out, "The absolute number of people below the poverty line today is just as large as it was two decades ago", in spite of economic growth and some rise in per capita income. "And these people living in abject poverty", the proceedings added, "constitute between two-fifths and one-half of all-India citizens. Available projections suggest that if one were to rely on growth alone without directly tackling the problems of unemployment and income distribution it may take another 30 to 50 years for the poorer sections of the people to reach the minimum consumption levels. It will neither be feasible nor desirable to contemplate a waiting period of anywhere near such a duration". Naturally enough, the AICC, more especially its President, Dr. Shankar Dayal Sharma, assumed the existence of conflict between growth and social justice in all earlier Plans, a conflict which was sought to be "premised on arguments which assert that whatever surpluses can be mobilized from the richer classes are needed for investments primarily directed at raising the future rate of growth". The AICC recognized that there "might have been some justification for this view in the initial years of planning. However (as its Note added) the economy now has reached a stage where larger availability of resources makes it possible to launch a direct attack on unemployment, under-employment and poverty, and also assure adequate growth".[33]

The AICC session at Gandhinagar, which in October 1972 called for a resort to economic policy based on the Industrial Policy Resolution of 1956, recommended the establishment of a public distribution system that might cover certain essential commodities of mass consumption like wheat, sugar, edible oil and standard cloth. But the step, a mere eyewash to start with, remained a failure in the absence of Government control over their wholesale trade as well as the existence of dual market beneficial to private trade. The inflationary pressure which had already started building up as part of a capitalist crisis could not but assume a serious proportion unless remedied by an economic policy geared to public control over investments, not so much for profit as for use.

Policy distortions, however, continued in spite of the resolutions of the AICC and the determination of Dr. Shankar Dayal Sharma, its President, to have them put into practice. He regretted his failure again at the New Delhi session of the AICC held on July 19-21, 1974. "We have", he said, "won freedom for our nation and have given it a democratic system. But our pledges to our people are yet to be fulfilled, namely, to win for them their economic freedom". On a rough estimate, he added, "more than Rupees 12 to 13 thousand crores had been pumped into the countryside since independence for purposes of development. But, as had been pointed out on many occasions, the benefits did not trickle down to the poorer sections of the people. The bigger landowners and the substantial cultivators had benefited the most". This applied equally to business enterprises; for Dr. Sharma warned that it would not be possible to deal with the crisis of rising prices "unless the private sector was correctly and firmly dealt with" and "a strict surveillance over bank credit to the commercial sector" duly maintained.[34]

It appeared from the remarks of Dr. Sharma, President of Mrs. Gandhi's Congress group, that the capitalists had created "artificial marginal scarcity by deliberate under-utilization of productive capacity and reaped huge profits from it. Production could not be accelerated by forcing the private capitalists to stop monkeying with production. Fuller utilization of the installed capacity of the public sector undertakings was also not made. The result was the present distortions in the country's economy".[35]

Surprisingly enough, the problem of shortages occurred in the essential and basic consumer goods, not in the luxury goods meant for the affluent sections of society. And the distortions creating these shortages took place in spite of the Planning Commission which was invested with the determination of priorities. An important factor to explain the anomaly was that while the public sector had generally on its boards of management representatives of influential and leading industrialists of the private sector functioning as advisers, private industrialists were officially left with discretion to make deviations from Plan priorities. Moreover, as price control in India remained an executive function, it operated informally at the discretion of the bureaucracy and the business Houses.

In his *Economic Strategy for the 1980s*, L. K. Jha, Economic Adviser to the Government of India, has sought to analyse the causes of inflation in terms of budgetary deficits and monetary expansion as well as the non-monetary factors, more especially applicable to Indian conditions. He says that an increase in money supply due to either deficit financing or expansion of bank credits at a pace which is faster than the rate of growth of goods and services in the economy must generate upward pressures on the price level. But the basic cause of deficit financing itself and the consequent decline in the purchasing capacity of money which is closely related to the laissez-faie economy is more or less passed over. On the non-monetary side, stress is laid on the monsoons leading to shortfalls in agricultural production, with its "all-round shortages of basic foodstuffs, oilseeds, cotton" which in turn "set off declines in supplies of agro-based industrial products such as oils, sugar, vanaspati, cloth, etc." He goes on to add that if for any reason production in any particular sector suffers a setback in a developed country, it can make good the shortage "by higher impacts". His argument is, however, vague for reasons best known to him as to why India could not go in for a similar remedy to ward off the widespread distress caused by inflation on the eve of the Fifth Plan. "A poor country like India", he argues, "cannot easily afford to follow suit." "Inevitably", therefore, it "must face rise in prices of basic essentials", for any decline in prices arising from imports had perhaps the risk of reducing profits to the disadvantage of big business. He lends in fact implicit support to what followed the Industrial Policy Resolution of 1956. He views it as necessary and inevitable, although he shifts his emphasis on the production of consumer goods in the 80s.

Power Grip Reinforced Constitutionally Under Ideological Cover

Though presumed declaredly as ideologically radical and progressive, the general trend of Mrs. Gandhi's economic policy, as found in actual practice, was essentially conducive to the concentration of wealth and economic power, in spite of the 25th Amendment to the Constitution which sought to remove the growing concentration of wealth in a few hands, impose a ceiling on income and expenditure, and take other measures to introduce radical socio-economic reforms.

The Congress Party and the Prime Minister tried to explain away their failure on the oft-repeated ground of "Right reaction" and "Left adventurism" being responsible for all the ills that existed. This, however, provided no answer to increasing unemployment and widening income gap proceeding from the concentration of economic power encouraged by the Government itself. The increasing pressure of popular discontent arising from inflationary conditions tended to add fuel to the fire. The issues involved, in fact, posed a serious problem of choice. For if it went against the interest of the private sector, more especially against the interest of the big business who satisfied the money requirements of the Congress Party and its leaders for both personal and political purposes,[36] it might undermine the entire power structure of Mrs. Gandhi. A similar development might as well ensue if the existing situation of general economic discontent was allowed to drift. It might bring into focus even revolutionary possibilities, highly prejudicial to the existing economic system based on a compromise of private and public sectors, the latter benefiting the former through its infrastructural facilities. Her decision was in these circumstances to uphold the cause of big business to ensure not only her inner policy continuity, but also her own continuity in power. For both were considered mutually inclusive.

Mrs. Gandhi sought to resolve her policy dilemma in two ways. The first was to modify the earlier Ten-Point Programme with an emphasis on rural welfare. It added other items to reshape it into what came to be known as the Twenty-Point Programme. The new Twenty-Point Programme laid stress on improving agricultural production, on the distribution of surplus land, on the fixation of minimum wages and agricultural land ceiling. Its emphasis was on the implementation of schemes for integrated rural development, including housing, primary education, removal of adult illiteracy, welfare for women and children, especially in tribal and backward areas, family planning on a voluntary basis, rural electrification and rehabilitation of rural bonded labour. The Programme was in addition intended to liberalize investment procedure and streamline, in the interest of private entrepreneurs, industrial policies to ensure timely completion of their projects. Its object was also to supply technological inputs to promote cottage industries. It aimed at the improvement of the working of public enterprises. The Programme was not exclusive of an important item to continue strict action to check black money and put down smugglers and hoarders.

These, however, were no innovations. They formed part of the several recommendations made from time to time earlier for agricultural and industrial development. It was the second constitutional step to bolster up her power mechanism that was especially significant in economic and political terms. Its object was to concentrate, under a "socialist and secular" cloak, the entire executive power of government in her own bands in order to facilitate the concentration of economic power in the hands of big business. This in fact was the basic feature of the economic policy under Congress rule since Independence itself. While the declared intent of its policy radicalism was advantageous to it in political terms, the vested or conservative elements considered it politically inexpedient to put up resistance because of its leadership being generally indifferent towards implementation. They did not mean business. They meant politics.

It was indeed the lukewarm attitude of Congress leaders towards policy implementation for political reasons that led the top private business to acquiesce under pressure to the enactment of even the Constitution (25th Amendment) Act of 1971, an Act which inserted

Article 31C in Part IV of the Constitution dealing with the Directive Principles. The Article so inserted raised for the first time the status of these "principles" which earlier had been subsidiary to Part III of the Constitution dealing with Fundamental Rights. Article 31C now provided that both the Legislature and the Executive should in future not merely pay lip-service to the Directive Principles, but that they should be made the basis of all legislative and executive action in the matter of the governance of the country. The steady rise of monopolies, however, made it clear that the Amendment so enacted was no more than lip-service. The vested interests knew this well and did not feel concerned about policy radicalism.

Bus this could not be so with the Government which had to deal with the rising tide of unrest caused by uncontrolled inflationary conditions. It proclaimed a state of Emergency in July 1975, which kept alive Parliament for the enactment of a far more stringent and perhaps the longest amendment of the Constitution intended essentially to preserve the existing economic order to ensure her political stability. This was the Constitution (42nd Amendment) Act, 1976, passed by the Lok Sabha on November 2, 1976, and the Rajya Sabha on November 11, 1976.

By far the most characteristic feature of the 42nd Amendment Act was asserted in the area of constitutional amendments which were sought to be placed beyond the purview of any judicial review, including that of even the Supreme Court which was earlier deemed to have assumed the role of a Third House or a "Super-Legislature", nullifying the amendments made by Parliament. It gave primacy to all the directive policies over the Fundamental Rights, including the right to property, and amended Article 31C in a manner which, for purposes of an ideological propaganda, openly asserted that no law giving effect to any of the Directive Principles was to be deemed void on the ground of its inconsistency with any of the rights conferred by Article 14, 19 or 31. Thus the Directive Principles which started as subordinate to the Fundamental Rights came "to make the latter subservient, the rationale being that the welfare of the community can supersede the welfare of the individual thus proclaiming the theory of public good over the individual rights. The Fundamental Rights shall henceforth cease to come in the way of Government efforts to improve the condition of the masses".[37] In its amended form

Article 31C was described by N. A. Palkhiwala as a monstrous outrage on the Constitution damaging its very heart and basic feature. This was sought to be done to bring about a socio-economic revolution which, as we all know, never proceeded beyond the limits of paper.

What actually appeared and formed part of the experience of Opposition parties and organized bodies of dissidents or the people in general was display of the forces of constitutional autocracy which the 42nd Amendment released and provided a constitutional sanction for the repressive measures taken during the period of Emergency.

Without making any alterations in the text of Part III of the Constitution on Fundamental Rights, the 42nd Amendment diluted the overall importance of these rights by adding a new provision. This was Article 31D which enabled Parliament to make a law to prevent or prohibit "anti-national activities" or the formation of "anti-national associations". It provided that "no law providing for the prevention or prohibition of anti-national activities or the prevention of formation or the prohibition of anti-national associations shall be deemed to be void on the ground that it is inconsistent with or takes away or abridges any of the rights conferred by Articles 14, 19 and 31, despite anything contained in Article 13".[38] Article 31D was in fact very widely worded to embody provisions for oppressive measures directed against those held responsible for "threatening the security of the State". These were ambiguous words which were subject to being used as a powerful engine of oppression. They enabled the executive to ban almost any organization or condemn any individual.

In the sphere of Centre-State relations also the 42nd Amendment made no less serious changes to strengthen the Centre's control over the States. The Centre could under these changes deploy armed or other forces for dealing with any grave situation of law and order in any of the States under its own instruction and its own direct superintendence without the control of a State Government. Obviously, it meant a serious erosion of the federal structure, which was further affected by the amendment of Article 352 dealing with the proclamation of emergency.

A Sophisticated Political Design

It was claimed and propagated that the object of the Constitutional amendment so effected was to bring about a socio-economic revolution by a concentration of power in the hands of the executive government at the Centre, a measure said to be essential for a revolutionary change. For the existing arrangement of the judiciary being invested with powers to review Parliamentary enactments was held to have delayed the entire process of change on the score of Fundamental Rights.

The amendment, however, was a sophisticated political device to enable Mrs. Gandhi to continue in power and her big business supporters to keep on raising the level of their assets as *officially* recognized inputs of economic growth. According to a secret report of the Intelligence Bureau of the Ministry of Home Affairs in 1977 (Janata Government) there existed in fact a close liaison between the top business circles and the leaders of the Congress Party who were involved in the collection of "black funds" for personal and party purposes. "The merchants of Chawri Bazar, Delhi", as the Bureau pointed out, "are reported to have paid Rs. 50 lakhs to save the locality from the bulldozers. S/Shri Yashpal Kapur, Bansi Lal, R. K. Dhawan, P. C. Sethi, Rajni Patel, Kuldip Narang, H. K. L. Bhagat, D. D. Puri (ex-M.P.), P. N. Mathur, ex-Chairman of the BIC, Kakatkar of the Indian Cotton Mills Federation, industrialists like K. K. Birla, R. P. Goenka and others were the main collectors of black funds from various firms. The same source, which provided us with a list of firms to whom receipts were given for advertisement tariff for AICC souvenirs, has also supplied us with a list of as many as 1,151 concerns which have together paid, under the table, a sum of Rs. 112,81,85,000 (one hundred twelve crores, eighty-one lakhs and eighty-five thousand). This list does not include the names of some firms from whom Shri Rajni Patel collected money in Bombay. The income-tax authorities were asked whether it would be possible for them to unearth these payments on the basis of lists and details to be supplied by us. They however expressed their inability".[39] The report in fact makes it clear that this operation had already been in progress during the Emergency in 1975. Altogether gone were the days when the AICC used in earlier years to publish its budgetary statements showing its annual income and expenditure for general information.

The report of the Intelligence Bureau pointed out that the first breakthrough came in June 1977 when they seized a number of bank accounts of the AICC. These were held in the name of the Central Election Committee but operated chiefly by P. C. Sethi who withdrew money as he pleased. Yashpal Kapur who had a separate cash deposit of Rs. 6,50,000 in the name of the Central Campaign Committee managed his Canara Bank account as he chose to do. It was this breakthrough that led the Intelligence Bureau to find out the sources of the black money which the nearest trustees and adherents of Mrs. Gandhi utilized for either personal ends or party work. It extended the scope of inquiry beyond New Delhi, and brought to knowledge both the names of the firms which made the payments and of the persons who did the collections. The names of such persons as Swaraj Paul, Amin Chand Pyare Lal, Bansi Lal, Rajni Patel, R. K. Dhawan, R. R. Dhawan, K. L. Dhawan and several others of their kind figured in this context along with the firms who fed the coffers of the Congress.

It is thus clear that socio-economic revolution was not the goal of the 42nd Amendment of the Constitution. The goal was to suppress popular agitation against rising prices and deepening economic crisis–a development which constituted a threat not only to her political stability but also to the economic system which lent support to it. It was in this continuing context that a little later in 1979 Mr. Justice V. R. Krishna Iyer, in a speech on "India's Imperatives and Options", recommended a "shock" treatment to rejuvenate her political system which had shown signs of decay because of its being used for partisan ends or ulterior purposes in the course of the emergency. He spoke of "the disillusionment among all sections of the people because of the suicidal political operations", and added that the common people in the country were so desperate that they might venture to overthrow the system itself in the hope that something good might emerge from such an action".[40]

While addressing the Staff College at Hyderabad Mr. Justice H. R. Khanna expressed more or less a similar view about the Centre which was responsible for the enactment of the 42nd Amendment in

1976, although its effect was later neutralized by two of the succeeding constitutional amendments enacted by the Janata Government. Referring to the Emergency, Justice Khanna naturally regretted the absence of any provision to check a situation where the Centre "misbehaved" and acted independently of the judiciary. The Constitution had explicit provisions to rectify such a situation in respect of the States, but there were none for the Centre. The only check was a sense of basic regard for the recognized norms of political morality, the vigilance of the people and the pressure of public opinion.

Justice Khanna was especially critical of the manner in which the powers vested in the Centre were abused. He asserted that despite all provisions of the Constitution for a strong Centre fissiparous and secessionist forces could by no means be checked by "bungling and party-mindedness" of some individuals and parties. He thus emphasized the need to ensure that no section of the population had any cause to entertain the feeling of being subjected to oppression, injustice and discrimination. According to Justice Khanna, this principle of social justice alone could conduce to political stability, not the use of emergency powers provided under Articles 352 and 356.[41]

The Second Split

The Constitution (42nd Amendment) Act of 1976 was no less than a constitutional despotism foisted by the Centre under Mrs. Gandhi to achieve her ulterior political purposes. The Left forces both inside and outside the Congress felt disillusioned; and despite her money power she was defeated in the general election of 1977. After her defeat and the Janata Party's rise to power, the AICC, still without the letter I in parentheses, met in New Delhi at Sapru House. Those of her followers who had earlier fawned on her but now thought that she was on the run were in for a surprise. They were in fact shaken by her defiant midnight speech which acted as a harbinger of the second split on the new year day of 1978. It marked the beginning of the present day nomenclature of the AICC.

Appendix to Chapter IV

Report of Intelligence Bureau

TOP SECRET/PERSONAL: INTELLIGENCE BUREAU (MINISTRY OF HOME AFFAIRS)

1. As desired, I am giving below the result of the probe by the I.B. into the huge unaccounted funds under the control of the ministers and dignitaries of the previous government.

2. The first breakthrough came early in June 1977 when we ran into five separate bank accounts of the AICC. Two accounts (No. 503, Syndicate Bank, Barakhamba Road and No. 530, Canara Bank, Connaught Circus Branch) were on behalf of the Souvenir Committee and were operated by Shri P. C. Sethi. A third account in the name of Central Election Committee was opened on 1.2.1977 by Shri P. C. Sethi also at the same branch of the Canara Bank. Sums were transferred from Souvenir Committee accounts to Central Election Committee accounts. On 4.9.76 Shri P. C. Sethi opened four fixed deposit accounts for Rs. 5 lakhs each at the Syndicate Bank (Barakhamba Road Branch, A/c Nos. 935 to 938). On 7.5.75 Shri Yashpal Kapur opened an account with a cash deposit of Rs. 6 1/2 lakhs in the name of the Central Campaign Committee (A/c No. 331, Canara Bank, Connaught Circus Branch).

3. On 23.3.77 Shri P. C. Sethi closed the four fixed deposit accounts at the Syndicate Bank and withdrew Rs. 20 lakhs besides the interest worth Rs. 40,000.

4. A scrutiny of the remaining four accounts indicated that while a sum was paid to the Provincial Congress Committees towards election expenses the bulk of the amounts were withdrawn in favour of (a) Self, (b) Confidants, (c) firms many of which appear to be bogus. Crores of rupees were thus siphoned off in this manner. In this connection the CBI registered a case against Shri P. C. Sethi and others on 16.8.77. Salient features of the extent of misuse of the

funds are given in Appendix 'A'. On the basis of the CBI (FIR) the Income-tax authorities conducted independent enquiries and have been pressing K. S. Bhatia, Smt. K. L. Bhatia, Sudhir Sarin, Yashpal Kapur, and Smt. Kailash Kapur to produce returns. We have also assisted the Income-tax authorities in these enquiries which are still incomplete.

5. At Bombay, Shri Rajni Patel collected funds for several causes and opened bank accounts which could be operated by a few of the chosen group of trustees comprising S/Shri Rajni Patel, V. D. Mengde, Ajit H. Mehta, D. V. Chopra, Kamla Raman, R. C. Ankleswaria, Murli S. Deora, and Prabhakar S. Pai. Trustees of the Flood and Famine Relief Committee withdrew an amount of Rs. 10,31,278 themselves. On 20.9.75, a sum of Rs. 12,50,000 was transferred to Silver Jubilee Independence Committee Fund. From this fund a sum of Rs. 21 lakhs were also paid to Tripura, Bombay, Orissa, Gujarat and Uttar Pradesh PCCs (Provincial Congress Committees). Amounts ranging between Rs. 200 and 800 were paid to confidants. From the Silver Jubilee Independence Celebration Fund an amount of Rs. 2,72,630 was drawn under "Self". Large amounts were given as donations to various institutions including Krishna Menon Memorial Society (Rs. 5 lakhs), Qaumi Ekta Fund (Rs. 2 lakhs), Kotwal Sarkar Nidhi (Rs. 25,000), and also to some individuals. In the personal account of Shri Rajni Patel in the Union Bank of India, Bombay, large sums (over Rs. 1 lakh) were credited from time to time. Shri Patel also raised around three crores of rupees for the Nehru Centre Fund. The information regarding this was passed on to the local CBI and Income-tax authorities.

6. M/s Amin Chand Pyare Lal & Co. and Swaraj Pal, the brother of Amin Chand, came to our notice for extensive siphoning off of funds to the former ruler (Mrs. Gandhi) and their confidants and also for acting as custodians. M/s Amin Chand Pyare Lal & Co. also came to notice for purchase of several jeeps which were handed over to the former ruling party even without formal registration, payment of tax and insurance. On the basis of our information, the CBI registered a specific offence against this firm. During the CBI search we supplied accurate information about the place where the suspicious accounts were secreted away. These were recovered during the search. We also supplied to the CBI full details about the various firms run by

the two brothers (Amin Chand Pyare Lal and Swaraj Pal). We supplied to them the lists of subsidiaries of different firms, names of directors and telephone numbers of the main operators. Incidentally, apart from the Birlas and Goenkas, this is the third business house connected with the former rulers.

7. The CBI had independently registered a criminal offence in connection with the huge collections in the name of the AICC Souvenirs. From a source close to Shri P. C. Sethi, we got a list of the parties which were given receipts totalling Rs.8,91,83,123. Some of the receipts were signed by Shri Sudhir Sarin. One such receipt (photostat copy) is enclosed for information (Appendix B). We supplied some valuable information needed by the CBI during the investigations of this case. It is also significant that all the moneys received for advertisements in the AICC Souvenirs have not been properly deposited in the books. A/c No. 503 was probably opened in the Syndicate Bank in 1974. Besides the AICC, many PCCs made independent collections for the Souvenirs.

8. We came across information regarding special favours shown to some firms by the Commerce Ministry for some "considerations". In one case, Shri Vasant Sathe, M.P., had personally urged (31.3.76) the then Commerce Minister for reopening of the case regarding extension of the export permit in favour of M/s Ferro Alloys Corporation, Tumsar (Maharashtra). Though by a notification the Chief Controller of Imports & Exports had banned export of chrome ore w.e.f. 6.8.75, two extensions were given to the firm as a special favour in April 1976 and some time later. The relevant file in the Commerce Ministry contains a letter by Shri Vasant Sathe, M.P. The matter was brought to the notice of the Secretary, Shah Commission. It is learnt that this matter was entrusted for enquiry to an income-tax officer. Since nothing was known about the further disposal of the case, material on the following nine concerns has been passed on to the Secretary, Ministry of Commerce:

1. M/s Ferro Alloys Corporation (Tumsar, Maharashtra).
2. Paramount Engineering Company of Kanpur.
3. Ganesh Prasad Movies.
4. The Fancy Corporation of India.
5. Madhusudhan Gordhan & Company.

6. Concorde International Ltd., New Delhi.
7. ORWO Pvt. Ltd., Bombay.
8. Asian Cables, Calcutta.
9. Raman & Demn, Bombay.

9. The following persons were reported as financiers of Shri Bansi Lal:

1. Amir Chand Singla, Chandigarh and Delhi.
2. Phool Chand Devrala, Calcutta.
3. Madan Lal Suresh Kumar, Calcutta.
4. Ganpat Rai Rasivasi, Calcutta.
5. Srinivas Hada, Calcutta.
6. Prabhu Dayal Dabriwala, Calcutta.
7. Ghanshyam Goel, Calcutta.
8. Ram Niwas Hamarwalal, Calcutta.
9. Surjit Singh Atwal, ex-M.L.A., Jallundar.
10. Panch Hazari, ex-M.P. and ex-Chairman of the CCI, Chandigarh and Delhi.
11. Shyam Sunder, Proprietor of a TV factory at Faridabad.
12. Pushpa Dutt, Bhiwani.
13. Prabhu Lal Bhokra, Bombay, Delhi and Calcutta.
14. Prahlad Rai, Delhi.

Shri Bansi Lal and his sons own huge properties. Lands worth three lakhs of rupees were purchased in May 1976. In June-July, 1977 Shri Bansi Lal had a balance of Rs. 87,000 in bank accounts, and his son Surinder Singh, Rs. 10,000. Shri Surinder Singh and two of his colleagues ran an account in the name of the Youth Congress at the Central Cooperative Bank, Bhiwani. After the elections, a sum of Rs. 3 lakhs was withdrawn in cash and later a sum of Rs. 18 1/2 lakhs was transferred to another account in the Allahabad Bank, Delhi. Information regarding this was supplied to the CBI and also the Haryana Police.

10. A couple of months ago, we took a stock of the persons and firms which came to notice for (a) providing finances through black money during the period of emergency, (b) continuing to supply funds even after the defeat of the former (Congress) government, and (c) acting as custodians of the funds at the present juncture. This

information was supplied to the income-tax authorities.

11. Influential ministers like those in charge of industry, commerce, railways and chemicals and fertilizers and selected officers from these ministries used all levers of power to extract money from big and small business. Threats of income-tax raids and demolition of premises were freely indulged in order to extract funds. Flexible excise rebate and favour in grants of permits and licences were utilised on a grand scale to knock out money from the producers and industrialists. The merchants of Chawri Bazar, Delhi, are reported to have paid Rs. 50 lakhs to save the locality from the bulldozers. S/Shri Yashpal Kapur, Bansi Lal, R. K. Dhawan, P. C. Sethi, Rajni Patel, Kuldip Narang, H. K. L. Bhagat, D. D. Puri (ex-M.P.), P. N. Mathur, ex-chairman of the BIC, Kakatkar of the Indian Cotton Mills Federation, industrialists like K. K. Birla, R. P. Goenka and others were the main collectors of black funds from various firms. The same source, which provided us with a list of firms to whom receipts were given for advertisement tariff for AICC souvenirs, has also supplied us with a list of as many as 1,151 concerns which have together paid, under the table, a huge sum of Rs. 112,81,000 (one hundred twelve crores, eighty-one lakhs and eighty-five thousand). This list does not include the names of some firms from whom Shri Rajni Patel collected money in Bombay. The Income-tax authorities were asked whether it would be possible for them to unearth these payments on the basis of lists and details to be supplied by us. They however expressed their inability.

12. In June 1978. we received information about the almirah buried in the farm house of the ex-PM (Mrs. Gandhi.) Extensive enquiries were carried out in order to find corrboration to this information which was supplied by a female labourer who was employed at the time (March 1977). It was found that most of the labour was from outside Delhi with little idea about either names or places of residences. However, some delicate enquiries indicated that the information could not be rejected out of hand. The results of the enquiry have been placed before the Home Secretary, the Cabinet Secretary and the Income-tax authorities.

13. Unfortunately, the tactless handling of the sources who gave the above information, by the Income-tax authorities, have caused panic among them and extreme embarrassment to us. It may kindly be

appreciated that for want of effective follow-up action by those who are authorised to do so our sources are reluctant to confide in us any longer. Some of the officers who have enthusiastically and tirelessly done a lot of leg work to collect the information are suffering from a feeling of frustration. Under the circumstances, some effective executive action may be considered.

Sd/- V.V. Nagarkar
Joint Director

MHA (Shri T. C. A. Srinivasavaradan)
Cabinet Secretariat (Shri K. Mukherjee)
DIB D.O. No. 1(9)/77 (8)-1892-1893,
dated November 18,1978

REFERENCES

1. Zaidi (ed.), op. cit., Vol.XX, p.543.
2. Ibid., PP. 34-35.
3. Ibid., P. 38.
4. Zaidi (ed.), op. cit., Vol.XIX, pp.532-33; also p.545.
5. *Nijalingappa to Indira Gandhi,* Oct,28, 1969. See Zaidi,(ed.), op. cit., Vol.XX, p.637.
6. See Zaidi (ed.), op. cit., Vol.XX, pp.545-51 (Appendices).It is also printed in Special Independence Number of *Young Indian*, 1972.
7. Zaidi (ed.), op. cit., Vol.XX, pp.553-56
8. Ibid., p.551.
9. Ibid., p.529.
10. Ibid., p.530.
11. Ibid., pp.259-60.
12. Ibid., p.267.
13. Ibid., p.561. The correspondence between Finance Minister Morarji Desai and Prime Minister Indira Gandhi may be seen at pp.561-81 including their statements in Parliament.
14. See S.K.Goyal, *Monopoly Capital and Public Policy*, pp.52-63, showing rising trends in concentration in the private corporate sector even after 1969 when Congress split took place on the ground of promoting socialism.
15. Zaidi (ed.), op. cit., Vol.XX, pp.589-90.
16. Ibid., pp.599-600.
17. Ibid., p.618.
18. Ibid., p.630.
19. Ibid., pp.633-34.
20. Ibid., pp.653-54.
21. Ibid., p.667.
22. Ibid., p.664.
23. Ibid., p.675.
24. Ibid., p.676.
25. Ibid., p.695.
26. Ibid., p.697.
27. After the removal of Nijalingappa C. Subrahmaniam was elected Interim President who continued until Jagjivan Ram took over as President at the Congress (I) session of Bombay on December 28, 1969.
28. Zaidi (ed.), *The Foundations of Indian Economic Planning*, p.245.
29. See India, *High Powered Expert Committee on Companies and MRTP Acts*, Delhi, 1978, p.251.
30. Zaidi (ed.), *The Encyclopaedia of the Indian National Congress*, Vol.XXII, 1972-73, p.156 and p.158.
31. Zaidi (ed.), *Economic Planning*, p.292.
32. Ibid., p.293.
33. Ibid., p.271.
34. Zaidi (ed.), *The Encyclopaedia of the Indian National Congress*, Vol.XXIII 1974-75, pp.24 and 30.
35. Ibid. p.23.
36. See *Indian Express* (Sunday Edition), April 11, 1982, showing black money bank accounts of Congress leaders for personal and election purposes, based on the secret reports of the Intelligence Bureau, Government of India.

37. *Supreme Court Journal*, 1978 (11), Vol. 59, p.22.
38. Ibid., p. 20.
39. *Express Magazine*, April 11, 1982, p.1. See Appendix to this chapter, taken from *Indian Express* (Sunday Edition), April 11, 1982.
40. *Hindustan Times*, September 23, 1979.
41. Ibid., September 23, 1979.

FIVE

Recent Trends in Policy-Making : More Concentration of Wealth

As already said, Indira Gandhi had, in July, 1975, introduced two of her important measures, namely, the Emergency and the Twenty-Point Programme, the well-known sweetener which however failed to click and bring victory to her in the general elections held in March 1977. She was routed in spite of her strength of money power and the constitutional despotism operating under the Constitution (42nd Amendment) Act, 1976.

Commenting on the economy and electoral politics in India during this period of inner conflict and controversy, Justice K. C. Khanna thus made his apt observations relating to the pre-1980s background. "The economy, with nearly half the population constantly living below the poverty line since independence", he said, "has been relatively stagnant while the society has been on the move. The electoral process itself has generated new opportunities, new expectations and new social pressures. Communal, caste and regional antagonisms have intensified as a result. Until 1977 the Congress was voted again and again back to power at the Centre because its leadership alone had the prestige, the authority, the skill and the countrywide organization necessary to keep these conflicts within manageable limits. Even so, it is significant that in no election could it secure more than half of the votes cast and, of the votes it did poll, almost again they were cast by the Muslims, the Harijans and the tribals, the three communities who could look to it for social justice."[1]

The period which began with 1977 was, however, marked by the emergence to the fore of two other forces. The first of these two forces was the "increasing criminalization of politics and the proliferation of secret arsenals" which meant "that the government, whatever its political hue or intentions, can no longer provide protection to the life, limb and property of the whole communities in certain areas and certain situations when they need it desperately. Personal security, not exploitation, is now their immediate concern. This phenomenon was first evident during the Janata-Lok Dal raj when the marked tilt of the government in favour of the thrusting backward castes brought its intentions into question.The outbreaks of communal and caste violence, however, have increased manifold since the return of the Congress to office at the Centre and most of the States in 1980". The result was that the beginning of the 80s was marked by popular suspicion in the Party's ability to stem the tide of violence and, in some areas, even the sincerity of its intentions.

The second, an important development, was a noticeable erosion of the moral authority of the Centre which until the mid-seventies paid more or less due respect to the limited administrative and political autonomy provided for the States under the Constitution. This kind of relationship shored up the Centre's constitutional powers "with moral authority and enabled it to deal effectively with conflicting pulls and pressures from the States". An important result that flowed from a respect for constitutional autonomy was a steady growth of a second line of political leadership, necessary not only for national integration, but also for an efficient and clean administration. According to Justice Khanna, however, the rise of Sanjay Gandhi (Mrs. Gandhi's son) "as a major centre of power" in New Delhi in the mid-seventies marked a watershed. "During 1975-76 the erosion of the autonomy of the Congress-ruled States, at both ministerial and party levels, was limited only by the central leadership's caprice or capacity to interfere".[2] The Janata rule did nothing to restore federalism to its normal functioning. The dissolution of Assemblies in nine of the Congress-ruled States was a clear proof.

Far from improving, the situation deteriorated even further with the Congress back in power in 1980. "The Central leadership of the Congress", as Khanna rightly pointed out, "has tended to treat the legislative and organizational wings of its own party in the States as vassals of no consequence. It has never hesitated to foist on them inept nonentities as Chief Ministers or PCC chiefs, to change these nominees much too frequently and to make them dance to its tune even in trifling matters. All this has in no way strengthened the

Centre. In fact,it has significantly weakened both the Centre and the States and badly bruised regional egos in the bargain. The victories of the Telugu Desam and the Janata-Kranti Ranga combine in the Assembly elections of January 1983 in Andhra Pradesh and subsequent by-elections in the Northern States is a pointer. So is the reinstatement by popular demand of Mr. N. T. Rama Rao's Ministry in Hyderabad after the bizarre toppling drama played out at tremendous cost by New Delhi".[3]

The caste-based Indian society was by itself authoritarian, tradition-bound and prone to centralized despotism. What had tended in the past to impart to it an attribute of mildness was the influence of Western education, rule-bound administration and liberal political system. Though advanced politically, the radical elements of the nationalist movement sought to build up their anti-imperialist agitation on the basis of social reaction which identified the national struggle for independence as organized attempts to restore to vigour the functioning of India's traditional cultures and social systems which, speaking generally, were in practice mutually exclusive. It was these reactionary elements in the Congress that started asserting themselves in collaboration with vested interests in commerce and industry after the death of Lal Bahadur Shastri, the last of the old generation of leaders held in respect for their honesty of purpose and open commitment to a middle-of-the-road policy reflected officially in the Industrial Policy Resolutions of 1948 and 1956. What contributed to the reinforcement of the Indian private sector was the growing influence of the multi-national business corporations, especially the U.S. and U.K., who operated as part of a world financial system which lent support to India's centralized trends in both business and politics.

Though in practice weighted more on the side of private enterprises, the Industrial Policy Resolutions of 1948 and 1956, as said before, had sought to strike a balance between private and public sectors. The second was further ahead of the first in terms of its emphasis on the public sector. But in terms of formulating the principles of State policy both were far ahead of the Bombay Plan of 1944 which was more conceptual than pragmatic. Its planners indicated the distant goal but made no attempt to build the road to it? The first major enunciation of post-Independence State Policy

Resolution of the Government set out two separate lists of industries, one for the State, and the other for the private sector, in addition to a common list for both. It was specifically laid down that whatever further development of the principal basic industries like iron and steel, coal-mining, shipbuilding, aircraft and manufacture of telephone, telegraph and wireless apparatus, etc., was envisaged, it should be only in the State sector, their development being the responsibility of the State, with exclusive State preserve in rail transport as well as in arms and ammunition and atomic energy.

The rest of industrial enterprise was left open to private entrepreneurship with a condition that in case of certain industries of key or national importance the State would be free to step in and take over from the private enterprise when the latter would be failing to meet the requirements of recognized standard and efficiency.

Consistently with the object of the policy so announced, an Industries (Development and Regulation) Act was passed in 1951. It prepared a schedule of as many as 37 industries from out of the three lists, and brought them under the purview of the Act to ensure a regular supply of statistical data for purposes of regulating production, including control over licence, capacity and prices. If any industry failed to supply information or to carry out the instructions of the Government, it rendered itself liable to disciplinary action. The Act also provided for a Central Advisory Council as well as Development Councils to aid and advise in the formulation of policies. It provided even for a direct take-over of an industry found to have defaulted despite warnings.

It was in this context of demands for increasing public control over industrial policy-making that the revised industrial policy was promulgated in April 1956 with a reinforced emphasis on public control over key and basic industries for purposes of self-reliance in matters of defence and the production of capital goods. The Industrial Policy Resolution of 1956 represented in fact a clear shift in policy. The small-scale and consumer industries were sought to be amalgamated with heavy undertakings where the former happened to lose their separate identity. Evidently, the whole trend of industrial policy which began with the 1956 Resolution was towards the concentration of economic power because of the continuing dominance of private enterprise in practice.

Change Under Janata Rule

It was this trend towards the concentration of wealth or the rise of monopolies which the Janata Government seemed to have attempted to modify or set at naught as a measure to reduce the gap between the rich and the poor. In 1978, for instance, the question of take-over of certain key industries like steel, aluminium and agro-industries by the State sector was forcefully advocated by a certain important section of the Party or school of thought. Even the then Union Minister of Industry and Steel lent his support to the proposed shift in policy.

However, the views so expressed represented neither the policy of the State nor of the Janata Government. The opinion expressed was nonetheless significant; for it led to a national debate on the subject of economic policy in general. It was in this background that the policy declarations of the previous Congress Government came to be invested with new dimensions and meanings involving controversies over the widening of the yawning gaps in the employment situation despite economic growth.

Though a mere expression of opinion, the policy statement of 1978 nonetheless enumerated five immediate objectives underlying State policy on industrialization, namely, maximization in the growth of the consumer goods industries, optimization in the development of human and material resources, acceleration in the growth of industries with relatively wider employment potential, making industrialization serve social ends, and prevention of monopoly-power in industrial development. There was no controversy over the desirability of increasing employment opportunities and finding adequate food and consumables for them. But controversies arose around the means to achieve the ends. While the monopolists stressed economic growth as the only remedy, the policy statement of 1978 sought to invest growth with a social purpose.

The guidelines which had been provided by the Industrial Policy Resolution of 1956, however, continued to operate in favour of private enterprise. For even though in the distribution of industries the 1956 arrangement had taken some of the industries from the private schedule to State schedule, "the total investment opportunity and the extent of industrial entrepreneurship available to the private sector were in fact enlarged".[4] Moreover, during the formulation of Five Year Plans and their implementation a whole range of new concepts grew around the original mixed economy concept which allowed both State and private sectors to flourish side by side under the 1956 policy framework based on the principle of what was declared as "guided socialism". Cumulatively, the whole framework got weighted more on the side of private enterprise than public undertaking.

Return of Pre-1977 Policy

Consistent with the policy statement of 1978, the Janata Government had planned to act on the principle of decentralization, involving changes in the centralized pattern of the 1956 framework conducive to the large-scale private sector. It supported, for instance, the compartmentalization of the tiny, small-scale industries. But as the protagonists of heavy industries argued, they would prefer to weave all of them together to achieve a balanced and fast industrial growth. It was this line of argument which found favour once again after the breakdown of the Janata Government in 1979.

Apart from the removal of compartmentalization, several other concessions [5] in favour of large-scale industries were made as part of a policy statement of July 1980. The declared object of these concessions was to ensure healthy expansion, modernization and promotion of exports. A more liberal income-tax concession was, for instance, provided for the benefit of big business under Section 72-A of the Income - Tax Act. The existing guidelines were, in addition, further liberalized to encourage the voluntary merger of sick units with healthy units. The statement also made it clear that the take-over of the sick units of the Government would be more an exception than the general rule. Another liberalization was in relation to excess capacities creating conditions for the growth of black money. The statement resulted in the regularization of such capacities on the ground of replacement and modernization of equipment. The regularization so permitted operated on a large scale, for it was argued that it would not be in the public interest to permit licensing procedures and rules to stand in the way of maximizing production.

The large-scale sector was favoured with yet another important concession. It consisted of the extension and simplification of the facility of automatic expansion which was until then permitted to 15 specific industries. In the name of fuller utilization of capacities, this facility was sought to be extended to all industries specified in the First Schedule of the Industrial Development Act, 1951. It was also laid down that capacity could be enhanced if advanced technology so demanded. This applied 100 per cent to export-oriented industries. The Janata Government's scheme of district industrial centres was given up and replaced by a few large-scale "nucleus plants" which were proposed to be established in backward areas capable of generating ancillaries and small-scale cottage industries.

The concessions so provided were a clear indication of a departure from the policy statement of 1978 when the Janata Government was the ruling force. In spite of these concessions to large business Houses, the Congress (I) Party in Parliament claimed that it "shall not permit the growth of monopolistic tendencies on concentration of economic power and wealth in a few hands". On the role of the private sector the statement of July 1980 talked only in vague and broad terms, assigning to it a role within the framework of the State's socio-economic policy which remained subject to all kinds of interpretation to suit the interests of major business concerns.

Naturally enough, the announcement of this industrial policy statement in Parliament by the Minister of Industry, Charanjit Chanana, on July 23, 1980, did not prove to be a good augury to the Government. The Opposition staged a complete walk-out as a protest against the policy, although the element of misunderstanding on both sides was not entirely absent; for several members sharing a leftist view made serious complaints that the specific points they raised about concessions to multi-nationals had remained altogether unanswered.[6]

It is not that tiny and small-scale industries did not find any place in the policy statement of July 1980. It had agreed to raise the investment limit of the former from Rs. 1 lakh to Rs. 2 lakhs, while in the case of the latter from Rs. 10 lakhs to Rs. 20 lakhs. The trouble, however, was that these categories had remained uncompartmentalized, subject to being absorbed as part of the large-scale undertakings themselves.

The main thrust of the policy statement of 1980 thus consisted of concessions to promote the enlargement of the large and heavy industrial units. The regularization of the excess capacity, the liberalization of the licensing system and the automatic expansion facility were all directed towards the encouragement of monopoly and large business Houses, more especially the multi-nationals, a highly organized sector, which took full advantage of the financial and other facilities made available to increase the pace of industrialization. The extension of these facilities to large units in the priority sector and the establishment of several nucleus industrial centres in industrially backward areas were all steps towards the concentration of economic power. The infrastructural facilities made available to private entrepreneurs by the State sector made such concentration still easier.

According to a comment of the *Business Standard* the policy statement of 1980 and the subsequent rise in prices were no more than an "Aid For Monopolists". Dr. Ashok Mitra, Finance Minister of West Bengal, described it as bungling by the Centre under Mrs. Gandhi. Calling her policies a total "surrender to black-marketeers and profiteers", Dr. Mitra said at a Press conference, "the Prime Minister, in an effort to raise more funds from big business and her other allies, had been squeezing the common man with inflationary measures". He condemned the latest hike in the prices of petrol, diesel, kerosene and fertilizers–a development which escalated the over-all prices of all essential commodities. The Press and public opinion were particularly critical of her policy to encourage foreign investment to help monopolists in the country who were being provided not only with tax reliefs, but also subsidies and other fiscal benefits.[7]

Indeed, what Mrs. Gandhi had started doing after the fall of the Janata Government was a clear attempt to revert to the industrial policy followed prior to March 1977. Writing towards the closing week of February 1980, the *Financial Express* thus reported: "The Janata Government's tilt to the small-scale sector and its restrictive approach to the large industries are being given a quiet burial".[8] The thinking of the new Congress (I) Government was that employment generation did not necessarily depend on decentralized industrial units or the creation of the so-called employment-oriented centres in the districts. Its conviction was that large-scale industries could also create employment opportunities, although their indirect contribution to this was much more than the manpower they directly absorbed. The new Government which came to power after the defeat of the Janata Party acted in fact for the restoration of the pre-1977 industrial policy. That precisely was the reason why it hastened to make in Parliament in July 1980 a policy statement which compared well with the policies pursued before the Janata's accesion to power. As said above, its characteristic feature was an extension of a whole series of concessions to the large-scale private sector, more especially to the multi-nationals who made use of their fiscal concessions to promote the interests of big business and the creation of black money leading to the growth of inflationary conditions.

Mrs. Gandhi had been particularly keen to invite foreign capital which reinforced the private corporate sector and its influence on official policy-making. According to an *India Weekly* report of June 16, 1979, the multinationals operating in India utilized nearly Rs. 2,200 million of the country's foreign exchange per year. This was confirmed by an expert conducting a study on "foreign capital in India".[9] Of the foreign exchange so utilized, they spent 85.71 per cent for importing raw materials from their patent concerns abroad at exceptionally high prices. The dividends remitted at the same time were, however, a mere 4.45 per cent of the total foreign exchange used by them. The study showed that the net assets of the multinationals had been increasing at a fast pace. In 1976, for example, the total assets of 171 subsidiaries stood at nearly Rs. 16,267.7 million against Rs. 8,967.7 million of 243 subsidiaries in 1966.

Another important feature of the multinational industrial investment was its pattern of production. The products were, for instance, designed essentially to catch a large section of the urban upper income groups of the Indian society. The result was that the Indian markets got flooded with such luxury goods as happened to meet the demands of the affluent sections, while the common man had to go without his essential consumer goods, except at high prices. India could, for example, feel proud of her production units for stereos, tape-recorders, air-conditioners, refrigerators, cosmetics, high quality textiles and luxuries. But planning remained more or less a failure when it came to the production of cheap cloth, vegetable oil, pulses and so on. As said earlier, there were deviations in spite of planning, because priorities were determined by monopolists in spite of the MRTP Act, 1970.

It was not only the influence of foreign capital and its multinational business corporations in India that added weight to Mrs. Gandhi's political statement of July 1980. It is true that the statement made in Parliament led to a total walk-out by the Opposition. But the concessions extended to large Houses remained operative. There was no going back. The other powerful influence which immediately operated in favour of the private corporate sector was that of the Planning Commission itself. It was D. T. Lakdawala, Deputy Chairman of the Planning Commission, who sought to spell out in capitalist terms his proposed strategy for the 1980s–a strategy which called for the exploitation of opportunities to attract foreign capital through trading with the Gulf countries, more especially in the context of the uncertainties inherent in the international economic sense of that time.[10] He wanted the Government to avail itself of all export possibilities to the developed world capable of providing capital for India's economic growth, which, according to him, had not yet been able to make any dent on the employment problem, especially in view of the linkage between the organized industry and the rest of the economy being weak in the Indian situation.

Private Sector on the Offensive Against Public Sector

As already pointed out, the public sector had started gaining in importance ever since the policy statement of 1945. Apart from its social objective, it was the experience of the two world wars that dictated the necessity of rapid industrialization. The Industrial Policy Resolutions of 1948 and 1956 naturally recognized that importance of the State sector and in principle sought to assign to it a commanding height in the country's industrial policy, although the allocation of spheres as well as the implementation remained more or less heavily weighted in favour of the private sector. The concurrent list, for example, remained in practice a sphere of the private sector itself. It was this system that operated until March 1977 and returned to life again under Mrs. Gandhi's policy statement of July 1980, with several additional concessions favourable to what Ashok Mitra described as "profiteers" and "black-marketeers".

Not satisfied with the concessions already extended, the private sector proceeded to launch even a direct offensive against the public sector. According to Press reports the initiative taken was through "an important general secretary of the AICC (I)" whose remarks about the country's industrial policy were taken seriously as invested with official weight and importance. The sum and substance of his remarks was that since the private industrial sector had over the years acquired considerable capabilities as well as maturity, "it should be entrusted with larger and greater tasks". In other words, steps should be taken "to redefine the allocation of spheres between the private sector and the public sector as given in the 1956 Industrial Policy Resolution and flexibly implemented since than".

It was argued that the public sector had come into existence to do what the private sector was either not capable of doing or was at the time not mature enough to undertake. But since the situation had over the decades changed and the private sector had become fully equipped in terms of capabilities and maturity, there was no reason why the relative roles of the two should not be changed in favour of the private sector.

Doubtless, it was admitted that the public sector had shown better growth performance and in difficult and challenging fields. During 1956-66, for example, the growth rate of industrial capital formation in the public sector was 14.6 per cent as against 7 per cent of the private sector.[11] But it did not keep on growing as the private sector did. The argument therefore was that the public sector should no longer be deemed as qualified for a better role.

This, however, was an altogether fallacious logic; for the consideration underlying the Industrial Policy Resolution of 1956 was not that of "capability" or "maturity". Coming as it did, in the immediate context of a socialist perspective of the Avadi resolution of 1955, the basic objective of the 1956 industrial policy was, as said above, governed by a two-fold consideration, namely, social welfare and defence strategy, both being considered outside the real aim of profit-motivated private sector, although it took advantage of certain policy relaxations made executively in practice to meet the demands of political expediency. Relaxation had in fact already become a ruling force on the side of the private sector in the immediate context of the Economic Programme Committee of the AICC (1948). As already pointed out, its recommendations in favour of a decentralized economy were revised and made to suit the requirements of the large-scale business and heavy industrial undertakings, which marked the beginning of multinational corporations in India.

Indeed, under a policy of mixed economy or a side-by-side existence of the public sector and the private sector, the latter, with the official tilt in its favour, benefited more than the former. For private enterprise not only learnt from the technologically most sophisticated industrial establishments set up in the State sector and gained steadily from the progressive advancement of infrastructural facilities made available to it at the cost of the public exchequer, but also made full use of its ingenuity, ceaseless drive and uncompromising commitment to profit regardless of all social consequences.

In the context of an expanding private sector the growth performance of the public sector seemed to indicate a downward trend. It was, however, the better growth performance of the public sector itself that had in the earlier period gone towards contributing to the might and maturity of the private sector proceeding from a good deal of the public resources, efforts and expertise made available to it as part of the scheme of mixed economy. The cooperation between the two sectors in the earlier decades was in fact a form of concession to the private sector; for, as said above, the allocation of their respective spheres was neither strictly made nor properly implemented. That perhaps was the Congress concept of socialism which, in the name of the public sector or State entrepreneurship, strengthened the private sector's capabilities and its maturity. It was in fact a pseudo socialism, antithetical to what might be called public weal.

Based as the rise of the private sector was on the functioning of the Congress brand of socialism in the cloak of the mixed economy providing official backing in return for money bags in support of electoral politics, the resulting black economy became its main source of strength to enable it to reinforce its claim to superiority over the public sector. The various concessions extended by Mrs. Gandhi's Government under its policy statement made in Parliament on July 23, 1980, were an expression of its growing strength, the strength of black money and socially retrograde industrial growth. These in fact were developments which portended a big potential assault on the public sector.

The apprehension arising from an organized form of the private sector against the public sector may not be dismissed as purely imaginary. For the Federation of the Indian Chambers of Commerce and Industry actually put forward a demand for a complete take-over of power as an integral part of the private sector, a bold step indeed to have this basic and key industry under the Federation's organized private control. It is of interest to note that the FICCI's demand for such control with the Government's comment on it appeared in *Business Standard* only a couple of days (September 19,1983) after the news about the reported "offensive" against the public sector had been flashed in *New Age* in September 17, 1983. It is clear that the private sector had about this time started thinking in terms of its being an alternative to the public sector.

The FICCI's demand for a total take-over of the power industry was actually discussed at a one-day workshop on "Energy Supply and Industrial Growth", organized by it at New Delhi. It was inaugurated by P. Shiv Shankar, Union Energy Minister, who, however, ruled out the possibility of the private sector being allowed under the existing conditions to play anything more than a peripheral role; for he doubted whether the private sector would be able to mobilize resources of the magnitude required for setting up power plants. He made it clear that he was in principle not opposed to the private sector and that he would certainly consider its proposals "on merit". What he wanted to know was whether it could mobilize resources adequate enough to satisfy the requirements of power plants. In the given circumstances, he was not even prepared to accept any proposal for a joint sector that might involve "any major changes in the Industrial Policy Resolution of 1956 to accommodate the entry of private industry in the power sector".[12] No proposal involving resource constraints was in fact officially acceptable to the Government in a field constituting its exclusive responsibility under the policy resolution of 1956.

The 1956 Policy and Employment Question

Apart from being a step forward marking continuity, the 1956 Industrial Policy Resolution could be said to be a joint contribution of Jawaharlal Nehru and P. C. Mahalanobis who had a large following in the Planning Commission. They believed that the best way to economic self-reliance or freedom from the colonial past was to set up a string of heavy industries to make steel and electrical machinery, heavy engineering equipment and the like.

Money of course appeared as a problem. But Mahalanobis emphasized that if the technological aspects were properly taken care of, resources could be found. He sought to carry conviction with his followers in the Planning Commission that if one produced steel and machines to produce machines, the resulting increase in the share of investment goods in GNP would automatically mean a higher savings rate, because "you can't eat steel".[13] The assumption so made was supported at the same time by two arguments, the possibility of the Finance Ministry taxing more to raise money and foreign aid to bridge the exchange gap.

Obviously, the basic principle of the industrial policy so devised was directed towards the production of capital goods. Power plants, for example, were basically capital intensive as were the railways. Coal mining and oil drilling were no different. Machine-making and heavy engineering were likewise capital intensive, and so were steel, heavy rentals and other related industries. The Government was to take care of these big things, while the others like the small-scale, cottage and medium industries were to take care of the rest.

Things went on merrily until the conditions of drought in the course of the Third Plan period and two of the wars with Pakistan and China, involving heavy expenditure on relief and defence, exposed the unsoundness of the assumptions on which both Nehru and Mahalanobis had proceeded to act. When money ran out for big projects, a resort to more taxes and foreign aid remained the only alternatives which meant a new trend of rising inflation. In effect, it meant that both of them bad been wrong in the formulation of their industrial policy.

The weakness of that policy became in due course apparent more especially in terms of its employment capabilities with economic growth. There is no denying the fact that a major transformation did take place in the Indian economy since 1956, and the country is now in a position to produce a large variety of industrial goods, including some being even highly sophisticated in technological terms. The proportion of industrial output to total output which stood a 13.5 per cent in 1950-51 rose to 15.15 per cent in early 1960-61 and then again to 18 per cent in 1965-66. But the situation here remained static for reasons already stated and it was not until 1977-78 that the manufacturing sector regained a share of 18.7 per cent in the total national income. In spite of this breakthrough in the manufacturing sector under the Industrial Policy Resolution of 1956, the average rate of growth of national income, however, remained extremely low at 3.7 per cent per annum from 1955-56 to 1978-79; and a substantial proportion of the labour force in India still remained unemployed.[14]

This was the result of an undue emphasis on capital-intensive industries considered essential for a high rate of growth. It determined the entire priority pattern of investment allocations to such industries on the assumption that the growth of industrial output was related to employment, a function of the trend in industrial production. During the First Plan period, for instance, investment in the public and private sectors incurred on basic capital and intermediate goods industries worked out to Rs. 254.7 crores, while the consumer goods industries which were supposed to be labour-intensive could get an amount of Rs. 33.3 crores only. In the Second and Third Plans, too, investment in the consumer goods industries did not exceed about 8 per cent of the total investment in the industrial sector. The Fourth and Fifth Plans also assigned to this group a lower priority. In the public sector alone, such industries as iron and steel, engineering, chemicals, petroleum, mining and minerals normally accounted for 70 to 90 per cent of the total public sector investment during all the past Five Year Plans.[15]

It was this phenomenal growth of the public-sector investment in the heavy capital-intensive industries that affected the growth of employment potential of the economy. For the emphasis remained on the production of capital goods and export earnings. "When an inter-industry comparison in respect of the increases in the installed capacity of production in various industries was made for the period 1955-56 to 1977-78, it was observed that the capacity of production in aluminium, fertilizers, electricity generation and sulphuric acid expanded by more than 1,000 per cent. In machine tools, diesel engines, electric motors, power transformers, and tractors, it increased by 1,000 to 3,000 per cent".[16]

Increases in the capacities of labour-intensive consumer goods industries, on the other hand, continued to be low. These, for instance, included cotton textiles (2.5 per cent), sugar (217 per cent), footwear (75 per cent) and matches (18 per cent). In the case of soap, there was even a decline in the overall capacity of production when compared with the 1955-56 position. This naturally reduced the weight of consumer goods in the total industrial output from 48.7 per cent in 1955-56 to 31.03 per cent in 1977-78, a shift in the industrial structure which adversely affected the growth of employment.

It is thus clear that shortfall in employment proceeded from a policy emphasis on investment in basic capital and intermediate goods industries and not on consumer goods industries capable of absorbing a much larger mass of labour force with a relatively lower amount of fixed capital investment. A survey report showed, for example, that industries like beverage, tobacco and tobacco products employed 25 persons by investing Rs. 1 lakh in fixed capital. Cotton textiles came next employing 18 persons. It was followed by food products (16 persons). Chemicals and chemical products, on the contrary, created employment for the smallest number of persons. For every Rs. 1 lakh of fixed capital investment it created employment for only 2 persons. These were followed by basic metals, alloy industries and iron and steel (3 persons); water works and supply (3 persons); rubber, plastics, petroleum and coal products (3 persons) and paper and paper printing and electrical machinery, appartatus and appliances and parts (each 6 persons).[17] Consumer goods industries thus provided more employment to the people at the same cost of investment when compared to basic and capital goods industries. It was, however, the continuing policy emphasis on defence strategy since the First World War itself that weighed more heavily on the side of basic capital goods industries. The Industrial Policy

Resolution of 1948 was the first concrete step in the direction of defence preparedness after independence. It was an expression of the earlier policy continuity which was further confirmed by the 1956 resolution, with a tilt on the side of the public sector in response to Avadi, a call for left politics operating in practice to strengthen monopoly Houses.

State of Economy in early 1980s

The characteristic feature of the Indian economy in recent years, more especially from the early 1980s, has been a deliberate and noticeable move in search for foreign capital to obviate any depression resulting from its low investment trends. The liberalization of the import policy was intended precisely to attract foreign investors, multinationals, potential suppliers of goods and services, more especially from the aid-giving countries, and non-resident Indians, settled abroad, who took greater interest in search of opportunity for trade and investment.

Not long before the budget statement of 1983-84, there was a general consensus in favour of steps being taken to tap the enormous resources–running into billions of dollars–of non-resident Indians (NRIs). For the cost of such funds was comparatively lower than commercial borrowings or raising loans in the Euro-currency or petro-dollar markets. It was therefore preferable. Also, these funds were not likely to be withdrawn for a long period. They could thus be usefully employed in the interest of the Indian economy.

Faced with an unprecedented resource gap, Pranab Mukherjee, Finance Minister, responded positively to an almost unanimous call for the use of NRI resources. In his Budget statement for 1983-84, he announced sweeping tax concessions to non-resident Indians. Income tax was, for example, reduced to a flat rate of 22.5 per cent, inclusive of surcharge. Complete exemption was, in addition, proposed from wealth tax and gift tax. As against this, Indian entrepreneurs were obliged to pay income tax at the rate of 67 per cent in addition to a compulsory deposit of 18 per cent of their earnings. This was not all. They were also subjected to deterrent rates of wealth tax, gift tax and capital gains tax.[18] The distinction so made by the Finance Minister between the two categories of Indians for purposes of industrial investment created a new situation. The basic issue involved was how best to bridge the resource gap. Their differences of approach created a serious controversy over the economic policy and raised questions in support of their respective arguments which reflected on the state of the Indian economy in the early 1980s. This controversy evolved around Swaraj Paul, a London-based non-resident Indian industrialist, with high financial stakes in DCM and Escorts, two of the Indian companies controlled respectively by Bharat Ram and H. P. Nanda.

Swaraj Paul and His Case

As already pointed out, Swaraj Paul's rise to fame in business circles rested on his proximity to the family of Indira Gandhi. He had not only lent financial support to her during her election campaigns of the post-Emergency period, but also remained at her side through a period of her political eclipse that followed her defeat at the polls in 1977. He had in fact thoughtfully cultivated the politically most powerful clan in the country.

Swaraj Paul's subsequent fame flowed from his bid to buy the shares of some prominent industrial concerns in India, namely, DCM and Escorts. He said in an interview in Bombay that he had made his investments on the suggestion of Mr. L. K. Jha,[19] a former Governor of the Reserve Bank of India and then Governor of Jammu and Kashmir at the time when Paul became controversial with Indian industrialists and their organized body called the Federation of Indian Chambers of Commerce and Industry. He added that he had also consulted the Attorney-General of India before issuing instructions to brokers to buy shares in the two Delhi-based companies. He said that taxation in India was not as high as publicized by vested interests. "The only thing is that here in India these people go away without paying taxes, while in other countries people do pay taxes. Here they are used to two colours of money–black and white."[20]

The concessions extended to non-resident Indians and Paul's own investment in two of the well-established Indian companies in Delhi which followed soon at the instance of L. K. Jha created a stir in the Indian stock markets turning them into an arena of international speculation. The purchase of shares of important companies started with a bang, share prices shot up to unprecedented heights. Between January and May of 1983, the share price of DCM moved from Rs. 32 to Rs. 105, while that of Escorts from Rs. 39 to Rs. 82. The paid-up share of Bombay Dyeing, on the other hand, rose in the same period from Rs. 25 to Rs. 66, and then soared to Rs. 99 by mid-June. The other companies which attracted non-resident investments, with their share prices moving upwards, included Reliance Textiles, Hindustan Lever, Tata Chemicals, Glaxo Laboratories, Modi Rubber and Kelvinator India.

Whether the boom in the stock market was conducive to economic growth and real capital formation remained a debatable proposition. But the boom, instead of being viewed as an object of rejoicing, caused in top business circles a feeling of insecurity. They foresaw in the purchase of their shares an obvious management take-over bid by the non-resident investors.

This fear psychosis proceeded immediately from the bulk purchase of Escorts and DCM shares by Swaraj Paul. This purchase was said to have completely upset the shareholding structure of these companies. The result was the beginning of trouble for Paul; for, contrary to his wishes, Escorts refused to register the transfer of these shares, and DCM followed suit. What other companies did was to intensify their demand for the scrutiny of all share transfer applications in order to enable them to refuse their registration.[21]

These developments in the attitudes of Indian companies clashed with the original idea of the legislation which envisaged that remittances from people of Indian origin settled abroad would be sufficient to pay back not only the IMF loan of Rs. 5,500 crores, but generate resources adequate enough to accelerate the pace of development. It was expected that in view of a lower political risk, assured reasonable return and phenomenal growth in the organized capital market non-residents would come forward openly and make large-scale investments in Indian industries. The liberal tax incentives were therefore initially welcome. But the subsequent reaction of indigenous business tended to block the way and raised a serious policy controversy which brought to the surface how the State-controlled financial institutions were being used primarily to strengthen, sustain and promote the private sector[22]–a development which was exposed not only by Swaraj Paul, but also taken notice of by M. V. Kamath in an article entitled, the Relevance of Swaraj Paul and published in the *Telegraph* on August 12, 1983.

In spite of the Indian industrialists' opposition to share transfer, the Government of India proceeded to amend the Company Law Act of 1956 which had invested a board of directors with powers to reject applications for share transfer without giving any reason. Under the amended provision of the Act, the stock exchanges of the Ministry of Finance were, in a letter of its Minister, Pranab Mukherjee, asked to advise companies not to refuse transfer of shares lodged with them "to non-resident Indian investors save and except in exceptional circumstances when it is felt that the transferee is not a desirable person from the larger point of view of the interest of the company as a whole".[23]

The amendment thus made it difficult for boards of directors of companies to refuse share transfer without assigning the reason for it. The only reason provided under the directive of the Government for such refusal was that the transferee was not a "desirable person". But as this condition could not be established without a probe, it could effectively be challenged in a court of law and the company possibly sued for defamation. The other possible reason that could be advanced to justify refusal was that investment by the non-resident investor was in violation of the Foreign Exchange Regulation Act. But once his eligibility was cleared by the Reserve Bank of India, no board of directors could stop share transfer. Even so, the Finance Minister's directive to his stock exchanges could not be said to be completely free from vagueness. It left some discretion with the companies to decide the issue as they liked.

It was this laxity that Swaraj Paul brought into focus in an interview with a staff reporter of the *Telegraph* in Calcutta and used the occasion to make certain comments which are of immediate relevance to the functioning of the Indian economy. While commenting on the Centre's directive to the stock exchange chiefs, Paul was critical of the manner in which the companies were invested with far too much right to decide as to who was a desirable investor and who was not. Doubtless, he felt that the step taken was in the right direction. But his regret was that the Government was not asserting itself as the largest single share-holder, but was playing into the hands of the private companies. Under Section 619(B) of the Companies Act, it was argued, those companies where more then 51 per cent of the equity shares were held singly or jointly by the public sector undertakings had to be treated as "deemed government companies", subject to a regular annual audit by the Government. "It is significant", however, as Paul was reported to have said, "that the Comptroller and Auditor-General of India (C&AG) has failed to report on most of these "deemed government companies", despite the explicit duty of the C&AG to audit the annual accounts of all Government companies. Of the 53 companies under Section 619(B), the C&AG admitted, only 35 had sent their annual accounts for 1982. Furthermore, according to the *Company News and Notes* (of the Department of Company Affairs, GOI), 115 companies fall under Section 619(B) and not Just 53 as claimed by the C&AG."[24] Obviously, the attitude of the Government remained soft towards the private companies which, in their own interest, made full use of the financial resources of the public sector undertakings without being subject to government control.

A still more important disclosure relating to the private sector which Swaraj Paul brought to the notice of the Press was that the companies not reported by the C&AG to Parliament did not come under the jurisdiction of the Public Accounts Committee. "Thus, a large part of public investments in the private sector remained outside the domain of public accountability. Now it appears that the C&AG does not consider companies to be "deemed government companies" if a single public sector institution does not hold a dominant majority of shares".[25]

Indeed, the fear of the private industrial concerns was that since the State-controlled financial institutions or the "deemed government companies" held at the time large blocks of shares in many business concerns and controlled about one-fifth of the total capital in joint stock companies,[26] the non-resident investors could, in collaboration with them, take over the management of these concerns if only the two sides happened to reach an understanding between themselves.

Indeed, the fear of the private industrial business was not ill-founded. For private business in the Indian context inevitably meant family enterprise. The two could not be separated. There was no such thing as a private, non-family business. Writing about the nature of business organization in India, M. V. Kamath rightly pointed out: "If individual A starts a business it is inevitable that A gets his sons B, C, and D and perhaps his sons-in-law E and F to help him run the risk and then, as his enterprise succeeds and replicates itself, hand over charge to non-family executives",[27] the kind of an alternative arrangement involved in Swaraj Paul's plan. As regards accountability to shareholders which that plan emphasized, it was generally recognized that shareholders remained content to get good dividends and bonuses and cared little about the form or nature of the organization. They left the actual administration of the companies with those who initially started them.

As for the financial institutions themselves, they generally did not interfere. They in fact supported the existing family management system, for example, of DCM and Escorts, two of the private companies with 45 per cent and 50 per cent of their respective shares being contributed by financial institutions, publicly owned and managed. The fear of these and other private companies was, however, not altogether without foundation. There had been a few cases where financial institutions had actually unloaded their holdings on better price considerations, as Srivastava and Sahni cited in their article of August 5, 1983. Their very discretion to dilute their shareholding acted as a constant threat and affected the efficiency of the units. It was in the context of this discretionary authority given to financial institutions that the buying spree by non-resident Indians had given rise to a great deal of uncertainty among the leaders of the private corporate establishments who feared their managements being lost to them in case of an alliance or understanding between the publicly owned financial institutions and the non-resident Indian investors who wanted family-oriented industrial management to go. Their argument was that since the bulk of the shares of private corporate units belonged to these government-supported institutions, there was no sense in recognizing such units as the extensive concern or domain of certain families, regardless of accountability to actual shareholders. This was a line of argument which clashed with the interests of traditional business Houses, such as the Birlas or Tatas,

Srirams, Charatrams or Nandas represented in the Federation of Indian Chambers of Commerce and Industry which constituted an organized front against Swaraj Paul and his adherents.

Consistently with the general feeling against Paul and to dispel the corporate sector's fear, Pranab Mukherjee, Finance Minister, announced a limit of 5 per cent on investments by non-residents in an Indian company. The limit so fixed was not to be exceeded except with the prior permission of the Reserve Bank of India which accordingly announced modifications in the operation of the existing scheme of portfolio investment in equity shares/convertible debentures by non-resident Indians and their overseas corporate bodies. Under the revised rules which were to remain valid for three years with effect from May 2, 1983, a designated bank could purchase equity shares or convertible debentures on behalf of its non-resident constituents on a repatriation basis without the special approval of the Reserve Bank of India.

Despite the limit of 5 per cent, however, serious misgivings arose in the minds of Indian entrepreneurs who reiterated that any tilt by the financial institutions on the side of the non-resident investors, even with 5 per cent equity participation, was bound to jeopardize the management structure of many of the Indian companies. The Indian industrialists thus regarded themselves as sandwitched between the non-resident investors on the one hand and the financial institutions on the other. They viewed the new situation as a state of insecurity arising from their being asked to contribute to "growth" within the concept of majority control or the control of the majority shareholders as against family control. Their argument was that "no (Indian) entrepreneur at the present rate of taxation is so resourceful as to have the majority equity holding and at the same time continue to contribute the bulk of capital required for setting up new projects or expanding or diversifying existng business operations".

It was further argued that even the existing norm of 20 per cent contribution by the promoters for starting a new project was only notional in character. Any company which wanted to expand had no choice but to go to the financial institutions which more often than not converted 20 per cent of the loan into equity. This diluted the promoter's holding further. Therefore, minority or family control continued to be the general rule operating in the existing circumstances. It was thus emphasized that since the country needed growth and that too at a fast pace, there should be no controversy over the extent of shareholding".[28] The Indian entrepreneurs in fact pleaded for protection against non-resident investors, more especially against Swaraj Paul who viewed the private corporate sector as no more than family concerns and claimed an immediate take-over of the management of DCM and Escorts on the ground of the bulk of their shares being already purchased by his group of companies. But since Bharat Ram of DCM and H. P. Nanda of Escorts regarded themselves as owners of their respective concerns independently of the extent of shareholding supposed to be under their control, they refused the transfer of shares so purchased by Paul's group of companies.

It was here that the question of the accountability of Indian business Houses to shareholders, including the financial institutions of the Government, was raised by Swaraj Paul–a question that brought to light the evils of the existing business organization where these Houses were, without any regard for social justice, arrogating to themselves the bulk of the benefits of "growth" proceeding from the investment of public money through the financial institutions. M. V. Kamath's article entitled The Relevance of Swaraj Paul thus acquired its due importance in a context where the large business concerns, instead of being answerable to shareholders, were behaving, though rationally, as an instrument of economic growth, tending to exhibit the stamp of a single family and treating its business as a private fief, antithetical to the concept of a corporate organization calling for accountability in its totality. This accountability precisely was what Swaraj Paul emphasized but found completely absent in the Indian situation. He was, in other words, strongly opposed to any single family being allowed to remain for ever invested with the management of a business House, although he did recognize that in any democratic country it was the individual–the founding father–who initially happened to set the ball rolling. Corporate management was, according to him, not to be a family monopoly at all.

The relevance of NRIs' remittances as an instrument of India's economic development could in fact by no means be denied. Swaraj

Paul was a mere expression of that instrument. According to a report of an economic survey by Subrata Banerjee, there were at this time about 10 million people of Indian nationality or origin scattered all over the wide world, more especially in the United States and the United Kingdom. They included technocrats, scientists, managers, businessmen, financial experts and workers, both skilled and unskilled. Many of them were fairly wealthy even by the standards of advanced capitalist countries. The remittances from non-resident Indians in 1980-81 amounted to Rs. 45 billion of which Rs. 10 billion were in bank deposits. This was considered to be no more than peanuts when one took into account the assets built up by non-resident Indians abroad.[29]

Obviously enough, non-resident Indians could be a very rich source of capital investment for development, especially when the extent of investment happened to be low and inadequate because of the various political and economic constraints that made the mobilization of domestic resources increasingly difficult. For while the sources of long-term and low-internal loans were steadily drying up, the export market had already started shrinking. Moreover, if capital investments were to include managerial skill, technological know-how, modern machinery and equipment, non-resident Indians could make their contribution in every single area the country needed.

Despite substantial concessions and incentives provided by the Government, there had been no appreciable investment from non-resident Indians in Indian industries. It was in these circumstances that the Ministry of Finance, Government of India, extended a number of important concessions to the London-based Indian industrialist, Swaraj Paul, who was, however, required to establish his bona fides as a condition precedent to the use of the concessions extended to him. For the possibility of black money being laundered back into the country through non-resident Indians could not be ruled out under existing conditions. This was particularly so because of Indian capitalism being very much family-oriented. It was easy to become a non-resident Indian. What one had to do was merely to spend 10 months in a financial year in a foreign country. A probe was therefore considered necessary under the revised rules to make sure that no black money was sought to be laundered.

What aggravated the NRI controversy and reinforced the fear psychosis in Indian industrial circles was, however, a bulk of additional tax concession as well as exchange facility made available to Paul's companies on terms unequal to the residents of the country. Jahar Sengupta, President of the Associated Chambers of Commerce and Industry, thus observed that if non-resident Indians could bring in Rs. 500 crores, they could, under these conditions, take over "all the top 200 companies in the country". He was not opposed to NRIs being invited to invest in Indian industries. But he stressed that this was not to be done on unequal terms. He added that a government "worth its salt" must not hesitate to investigate whether black money which was sheltered somewhere was "being transferred as NRI investments".[30]

Sengupta likewise expressed his doubts about the role of financial institutions having a grip over the fate of the private sector units. He pointed out that the Associated Chambers of Commerce had formed a study group headed by the Chief of the Economic Affairs Sub-committee to prepare a report to be examined by the Narsingham Committee intended to look into the whole gamut and role of financial institutions. Evidently, there existed a fear of an entente between these financial institutions and the non-resident Indians who wished to acquire a hold over Indian industries. It was viewed as an inevitable threat to the security of the traditional business Houses in India. The NRI controversy in which Swaraj Paul was openly involved was in fact treated as a clear move to "destabilize well-run companies".[31]

Mrs. Gandhi Supported Swaraj Paul

In the controversy that raged over non-resident Indian investments, it was remarkable that Prime Minister Indira Gandhi cast the weight of her influence on the side of Swaraj Paul who had applied to the Reserve Bank of India for the transfer of his Caparo investments lodged with DCM and Escorts. Paul won his case with the Government when in terms of a clarification issued by the RBI in the evening of September 17, 1983, his investment in these two companies was declared as eligible, in spite of the fact that, contrary to the ceiling of 5 per cent put on non-resident investment made after the policy announcement of May 2, 1983, Paul's investment in DCM and Escorts had exceeded that limit and that too with retrospective effect.

Before the RBI issued its Press release on September 17, the matter had reportedly been discussed a day earlier, on September 16, at Cabinet level where Mrs. Gandhi gave a bit of her mind and suggested a directive for the guidance of the RBI Governor, Dr. Man Mohan Singh.[32] RBI clarification in the form of a mere Press release was the result of the political directive received by the Bank. According to this directive the Reserve Bank was now to clear the Rs. 1.07 crores which had earlier been blocked out of Paul's total investment of Rs. 13 crores for the purchase of 12.95 per cent of the equity in DCM and 7.29 per cent in Escorts. Since both the investments were under the said directive declared as cleared on the ground of eligibility, the 5 per cent ceiling imposed on May 2, 1983, was no more to apply to these investments of Swaraj Paul's Caparo companies.[33] According to the clarification, the Government made it clear that it had been its "original intention" that overseas companies could invest under the non-resident investment scheme even if they (investments) were "indirectly but ultimately" held to the extent of 60 per cent by non-resident Indians.

The clarification added that each overseas company could make an investment of up to 1 per cent of the capital of a company "irrespective of whether the ultimate ownership is in the hands of one or more non-resident Indians." It meant that an individual could make an investment of more than 1 per cent indirectly through a number of companies. This precisely was what Swaraj Paul had claimed.

The overall ceiling of 5 per cent on non-resident investment applied only to investments made after May 2, 1983, the date on which the Finance Minister made the announcement. But since Swaraj Paul's claim was that all his investments were made before this date, they were considered eligible. The constraint imposed by the date so announced by the Finance Minister to restrict the percentage of non-resident investments thus did not apply to Paul's case.

At a Press conference held on May 13, 1983, Finance Minister Pranab Mukherjee talked of his earlier announcement relating to a ceiling of 5 per cent of paid-up equity capital, including repatriable as well as non-repatriable investments by individual persons as well as companies, and stressed his point that investment beyond 5 per cent by non-resident Indians was not to be covered under the liberalized policy except with the "specific approval of the RBI" under the Foreign Exchange Regulation Act (FERA). He made it clear that "investments above the limit will be considered as any other form of foreign investments and will be subjected to the rules and regulations governing such investments".[34] In reply to a question, Mukherjee had, however, said earlier that those who bought more than these ceilings would be required to off-load the excess share. This statement of the Finance Minister was at the time welcomed by Indian industrialists.

But the new clarification issued in a Press release of the RBI on September 17, 1983, caused a stir. For under this clarification the Government made it clear "that it was their original intention that the facilities of direct and portfolio investments in shares/debentures of Indian companies and deposits with public limited companies be available to overseas companies, partnership firms, trusts, societies and other bodies in which the ownership beneficial interest is indirectly but ultimately held to the extent of at least 60 per cent by non-resident individuals of Indian nationality or origin".[35] The use of the three key words "indirectly but ultimately" thus saved Swaraj Paul's investments. The RBI was in fact forced by Indira Gandhi to help Paul by its clarification through a Press release. For if what its Press release said was the Government's "original intention", why was this not made clear when the policy was announced first on May 2, 1983, or when the Finance Minister himself explained it later on May 13. Whatever the inner motive of Mrs. Indira Gandhi, the clarification issued in the evening of September 17 after the Cabinet's political directive of the previous day exonerated the RBI to some extent. The Government made its "original intention known" to the business circles, and the RBI dutifully issued its clarification in the best interest of Swaraj Paul.

According to M. V. Kamath, Swaraj Paul was in fact being let loose to humiliate the Prime Minister's opponents. Writing about his investments in Escorts and DCM, Kamath thus commented on Mrs. Gandhi's mode of functioning: "The Nandas and Bharat Rams, it should be clear, are paying for the crime of supporting Maneka Gandhi and George Fernandes. They have been singled out by the Congress (I) leader who has put her greatest sycophant, Swaraj Paul, on the job of stalking the prey. The open punishment that is being meted out to Nanda and Bharat Ram is not likely to go unnoticed by their brother industrialists. The message is clear: elections are near. Congress (I) coffers need to be filled and who dare go to 1 Safdarjung Road (PM's residence) empty handed?"

Kamath added: "It is not that Mrs. Gandhi needed Swaraj Paul to make industrialists cough up the cash but that the Prime Minister wanted to publicly humiliate those whom she considered her opponents. It was (for example) not enough that she would not trust Morarji Desai. He had to be humiliated by having his portfolio taken away from him. It was not enough to chastize Yashwantrao Chavan. He had to be made to wait before being admitted into the Congress (I) fold like a supplicant. In the matter of designing special forms of humiliation and mental torture, the Prime Minister has no need to take lessons from anybody".[36] Kamath in fact used Swaraj Paul as an illustration to show that he was not speaking just for himself. He was speaking for Mrs. Gandhi who wanted that the person who was sought to be destroyed must in the first instance be defrocked, humiliated and proved to be hardly of any consequence. The manner in which she directed the RBI to help Swaraj Paul in his attempt to single out Nanda and Bharat Ran and humiliate them publicly for their support to her opponents was in fact a clear expression of her public conduct.

As suggested above, Swaraj Paul's case was even more important as an indicator of increasing concentration of wealth arising from the growth of private enterprise which the financial institutions of government not only faciliated but also accelerated. These financial institutions served in fact a dual purpose. Many of the industrialists had not only "vastly expanded their business" with their support, but also remained at "the total mercy of the government", filling the coffers of the ruling party as and when needed.[37] Indeed, the public financial institutions still "have a great stake in almost every leading private sector company. If any of these companies try to be too clever, the financial institutions could always be used by the Government to tell them where to stop".[38] Obviously, there existed a reciprocity of interest between Indian industrialists and the leadership of the Congress Government. The NRI concessions in terms of tax relief and exchange facility had a similar story to tell, namely, the story of the expansion of private corporate business with increasing relaxation of restrictions after 1979, the end of the Janata Government. The case of Swaraj Paul represented a mere specimen. No probe was ordered into NRI companies in spite of the growth of black money.[39]

Mrs. Gandhi's restoration to power after the fall of the Janata regime witnessed in fact increasing signs of international investing companies interested in search of new opportunities for trade and commerce in India. These included bankers, multinationals, potential suppliers of goods, equipment, services and know-how, governments of aid-giving countries and others keen to invest in India. The non-resident Indian investors belonged to one or the other of these categories. There were reasons for this incipient change of attitudes and perceptions which form no part of this work to examine in any depth. But the fact that they proceeded from a more liberal import policy remains undisputed. The policy so adopted by India in the begining of the 1980s provided new opportunities for exports from the developed countries, and these opportunities were particularly welcome to them in view of the recessionary conditions of their economy at the time.

As M. S. Patwardhan rightly confirms in his review of the Indian economy towards the second part of 1983, the liberalization of import policy called for a corresponding relaxation of restrictions on foreign trade, an immediate concern for multinationals or even non-resident Indian investors. The Indian economy had been, for example, rather heavily regulated since the Second World War. This proceeded from an emphasis on the public sector as a Directive Principle of State Policy. The first few years of the 1980s, however, witnessed a marked trend towards relaxation.[40]

Apart from taxation, these relaxations applied to three major legislative enactments, namely, (a) Foreign Exchange Regulation Act (FERA), (b) Industries (Development and Regulation) Act (IDRA), and (c) Monopolies and Restrictive Trade Practices Act (MRTP).

Under FERA, the foreign shareholding in companies might range from a maximum of 40 in most cases of the earlier systems to 51, 76 or even 100 per cent, depending upon the level of their exports and technology. For 100 per cent export operation, for instance, 100 per cent shareholding might be permitted. As a general rule, foreign companies might enter or expand their activities in fields which were characterized by high exports, high technology or high priority sector which was usually capital intensive.

The IDRA applied to any company with an investment of more than Rs. 5 crores or about $(US)5 million. Permission was under this enactment required to set up a new undertaking or substantially to expand an existing undertaking. The procedure was cumbersome and time-consuming, more especially because of the poor infrastructural facilities of the backward, more especially tribal, areas to which the Act often applied.

The Monopolies and Restrictive Trade Practices Act Control v. Relaxation

The Monopolies and Restrictive Trade Practices Act, 1969, came into effect in June 1970. Consistent with the demands of political compulsions, the statement of its objects called for control over the concentration of economic power and restriction on unfair trade practices, the first signifying a company's draft on the resources of a community as well as a market share of its products, which together meant monopoly economic power.[41] The major restrictive trade practices, on the other hand, were those practices that arose out of collective price fixing, collusive tendering, withholding or restricting of output, collective boycott, tie-up sale, exclusive dealing, price discrimination, predatory pricing, restrictions on manufacturing process and transfer of technology.[42] A curb on monopoly as well as restrictive trade practices was thus designed under the MRTP Act to salvage the helpless consumers from the greed and rapacity of monopolists in both industry and trade.

Doubtless, the declared object of the Act was praiseworthy. But since the concentration of wealth, as said before, kept on growing, it was doubtful whether the legislation accomplished the object of its enactment. The Act, for example, provided that any company which controlled by itself or along with interrelated companies more than Rs. 20 crores of assets became a "monopoly house", subject to punishment if it sought to expand without a clearance from the Company Law Department, even though its share in production happened to be too small for it to exercise any influence on prices or profits. In the textile industry, for instance, no individual company controlled more than 2 per cent of the production. But because the company controlled as a whole more than Rs. 20 crores worth of assets, it became a monopoly House required to rush up to the bureaucracy for any expansion.[43] The Act was therefore held responsible for the slow growth rate. Moreover, the legally defined limit of Rs. 20 crores became an obsession or dogma with increasing loss in the value of money under growing inflationary pressures. It meant a cause for corruption and failure of the enactment. Assets went on increasing through backdoor means.

The MRTP Act was sought to be amended by the Sachar Committee in 1977. It made several recommendations. The Government accepted some of them without any follow-up action. In order declaredly to curb concentration of economic power to satisfy the requirements of politics the Government of India introduced in December 1983 the MRTP (Amendment) Bill which widened the eligibility criterion to bring under its ambit more enterprises. It incorporated basically the suggestions of the Sachar Committee and recommended certain amendments on the basis of the experience gained on the working of the Act and in the light of judicial pronouncements.[44]

The failure of the MRTP Act and its amendments proceeded in fact from a widening gap arising from a declared commitment to an economy based on control for reasons of left politics, and the actual pursuit of a policy based on increasing liberalization in both the domestic field and foreign trade, considered necessary for status quo ante as a condition for financial security of the ruling Congress (I) Party and its political stability.

The gap so developing steadily between Mrs. Gandhi's declared socialistic ideology and its reality became specially apparent with her restoration to power when the import policy of her Government was openly liberalized and industrial production accelerated by relaxing restrictions in the beginning of 1980. As said above, the regulatory framework of the MRTP Act was onerous particularly for the companies with an investment of more than Rs. 20 crores as well as those having a dominant position in a particular product. There was a great deal of relaxation under the new policy, although its implementation had still to catch up with its intentions. Even so, MRTP-FERA companies were not only permitted but actually encouraged to set up new industrial units. Offshore borrowing was allowed more freely. Imports of capital and non-consumer goods had started on a much larger scale than ever before under a regulatory arrangement. The import of know-how became highly liberalized. Price control on cement which had remained operative for more than 30 years was lifted in respect of 40 to 50 per cent of production.[45] This however did not cover everything. It just marked the beginning of a process of liberalization to speed up the growth rate of the economy in collaboration with the capitalist world and the tax concessions extended to the private corporate sector.

And yet in the same breath, the MRTP (Amendment) Bill, introduced in the Rajya Sabha in December 1983, talked of a controlled economy, which the Sachar Committee had earlier emphasized, and sought to bring more of industrial enterprises under its purview. It also enlarged the scope of the Act to regulate the unfair trade practices.[46] This was no more than policy distortion to which the country had become accustomed under Mrs. Gandhi's leadership and the influence of Indian big business.

Big Houses as Beneficiaries of Politics

Under the political shelter provided by the Government, it is the big Houses that benefit most not only from their ordinary business transactions, but more especially from their heavy tax arrears which they utilize to multiply their assets. Their after-tax profits in fact grow bigger and bigger.

According to the assessments made up to 1981 and some cases up to 1982 but in most cases only up to 1978, the tax due against 111 companies amounted, for example, to Rs. 10,738.66 lakhs. All these companies had above Rs. 10 lakhs each to pay in tax arrears. Even so, the Government treated them with consideration and courtesy, while the poor peasants of drought-stricken areas were severely treated for the recovery of petty sums due towards rent or tax.

The heavy defaulters of the business world remained in fact untouched. Even the MRTP concerns had huge amounts outstanding against them, although they were highly profitable and never reported "sick" were but showing big profits year after year. These companies also held back payments to make all possible use of the funds so accumulated.

Various Birla concerns were especially known for default even relating to the above Rs. 10 lakh category. The result was that they had to pay Rs. 975.82 lakhs on this account. This figure related to the assessment made up to 1981 at the most, and up to 1978 in some cases. The ACC, Vickers Babcook owed the Government Rs. 269.12 lakhs; the Bajaj group, Rs. 123 lakhs; the House of the Singhanias, Rs. 895.39 lakhs on taxes with Rs. 632.18 lakhs lying unpaid by the J.K. Synthetics Ltd. and Rs. 263.21 lakhs by Raymond Woollen Mills Ltd.

The Tatas who claimed to be "clean" industrialists could by no means be said to be any better with Rs. 370.09 lakhs outstanding against them. The Tata Iron & Steel Company had to pay Rs. 196.11 lakhs as tax dues.

The tax arrears of the Kamanis amounted to Rs. 469.25 lakhs, while their Kamani Engineering and Electrical Ltd. had as much as Rs. 408.4 lakhs outstanding against it. The Modis, on the other hand, had Rs. 123.65 lakhs as their tax arrears, while the Sriram group owed the Government as much as Rs. 312.46 lakhs. The arrears outstanding against Soorajmull Nagarmull amounted, on the other hand, to Rs. 250.30 lakhs.

The tax jumpers also included the jute Press, R. N. Goenka's Indian Express with Rs. 89.06 lakhs in taxes, while Sahu-Jain who controlled Bennett Coleman & Company Ltd. had to pay Rs 31.50 lakhs.[47]

These big business Houses that controlled the country's economy were in terms of industrial organization families who benefited most from the public financial institutions which enabled them to build up their own private assets without anything in the nature of social obligations in return. Their only obligation is to have certain representatives of the Government on the board of directors of each of the companies financed officially. In other words, their assets were built up with public money but privately by their families in return perhaps for an implicit obligation to fill the coffers of the ruling party.

Big Houses Opposed to any Control

Interested basically in the promotion of monopolies and restrictive trade practices, the big business Houses were opposed to all ideas of control, more especially to the licensing policy and the Monopolies and Restrictive Trade Practices Commission which were in principle intended to act as the watchdog to promote competition within a legal framework providing for rules of procedure and punishment to check violation. As the framework so provided under an Act of government caused delay due to a bureaucratic state operation, it was viewed as smacking of control, prejudicial to profiteering. The Indian Chambers of Commerce thus stood firmly opposed to any proposal to enlarge the coverage of the MRTP Act as suggested by its projected amendment of 1983. On the contrary, it emphasized the inadequacy of the existing limit of Rs. 20 crores for determining the value of assets of an MRTP company. In view of the country's inflationary situation, the Chamber even insisted on raising its applicability limit.[48]

However, K. K. Birla, head of the Birla concerns, soon intervened and sought to put an end to the controversy raging over the MRTP (Amendment) Bill. In a well-reasoned and statistically-supported address to a Rotary Club meeting held on April 15, 1984, in New Delhi, he strongly pleaded that the MRTP itself must go, because it had become "superfluous" and impeded industrial growth. He admitted that the original objective of the Act was to check any misuse of economic concentration of power. But there was no chance of such misuse. For the financial institutions had their nominees on the boards of various companies and it was therefore not possible for an entrepreneur either to manipulate or misuse his power to the detriment of public interest.

What Birla emphasized most was the element of delay caused by the MRTP Act. He cited the case of the fertilizer industry and pointed out that while a fertilizers project from the stage of conception to its implementation took nearly 84 months in India, it did not exceed 18 months in Japan. The slow growth rate of the Indian economy was in fact attributed partly to the MRTP Commission. According to him, the performance of industry over the year showed, for this and other reasons, a backward trend. While the average industrial growth was, for example, 6.1 per cent in the 1950s, with a marginal rise to 6.3 per cent in the 1960s, it fell drastically to 4.2 per cent in the 1970s. In the first four years of the 1980s the rate of industrial growth averaged only 4 per cent. The bright spot in the progress of the economy as a whole was the spectacular increase in foodgrain production which was likely to touch 144 million tons in 1983-84.[49]

Apart from the functioning of the MRTP Act, the important factors responsible for the slow industrial growth were, according to K. K. Birla, lack of demand and consumer spending as well as the poor marketing efforts of the business community. The rising wages and levels of taxation without a corresponding increase in productivity and labour efficiency were said to be the other causes.

The basic remedy suggested in the course of his address was the removal of all forms of control, statutory or otherwise. His assertion that full freedom to private enterprise had no risk of any misuse of economic power was based on his argument that public financial institutions had their nominees on the boards of various companies. But little did he foresee the consequences of a situation where the financial institutions themselves happened to be in league with a private concern. The involvement of the Life Insurance Corporation, a State-owned body, in the financial affairs of Swaraj Paul's Caparo group of companies was a clear example of policy distortion. The Corporation in league with Paul had served a notice on the Escorts to convene a requisition meeting of the shareholders belonging to Swaraj Paul's group. For Paul had with the support of the LIC purchased the majority of Escorts' shares and wanted H. P. Nanda, its Managing Director, to have these shares transferred–a plan for take-over which the Company rejected and refused to register the proposed transfer of shares as the LIC desired. The Bombay High Court which heard the case in its writ jurisdiction, however, stayed the call for the requisition meeting. The operation of a public financial institution was thus not above board.[50] It would not perhaps be a travesty to say that in spite of the Sachar Committee's recommendations the MRTPC acted more as a show than as an instrument of control to protect the consumer's interest.

Control Relaxation, Black Money and Corruption

The idea of State control as part of economic policy in a colonial situation had its origin in the Bolshevist influence on nationalist movements soon after the Russian Revolution of 1917. Politically, the Congress non-cooperation movement presented its organized resistance to such influence. But since State control was recognized as a necessity in terms of the economic interest of the Indian business community, the Congress adopted a middle-of-the-road policy to secure, in spite of British monopoly of trade and commerce, exchange facilities in order to enable that community to acquire a position of respect in the field of foreign trade. A study of the Central Banking Inquiry Committee shows that the Indian business community kept on pressing for State regulation of trade and industry, more especially in respect of fiscal autonomy and exchange management. The Congress (Karachi) resolution of 1931 was in this context no more than the Indian bourgeois demand for an equality of opportunity in the joint Indo-British exploitation of Indian resources. Its call for socialism implied merely legislative regulation and joint control of the Indian economy against the operation of free trade, weighted heavily on the side of the colonial system.

The Congress and the FICCI (Federation of Indian Chambers of Commerce and Industry) were in fact both for control as an anti-imperialist instrument. The reaction of the British Government in India was in keeping with the reality of the anti-imperialist forces released by the First World War. The establishment of the Reserve Bank of India in 1934 and the constitutional change made under the Government of India Act (1935) were two of the immediate results of collaboration. The principle of control as part of State policy was sought to be recognized under left pressure and accommodated within the framework of private enterprise which was still dominantly British.

The Indian industrial entrepreneurs who had been pressing for planned economy as a form of State control emerged as an economic force during the Second World War. The Labour Government of C. R. Attlee who had been aware of the limitations inherent in any imperialist war recognized the importance of the Indian demand for freedom of choice between control and relaxation. But as no government could afford to ignore the lessons derived from war, his British Government in India stressed, in a policy statement issued in April 1945, the importance of India's large-scale industrialization required to meet the exigencies of her defence strategy. As pointed out earlier (in the second chapter), the statement made it clear that the country's defence requirements could by no means be met singly either by the State or a private industry. It called for a vigorous and sustained effort on the part of both. It was thus in the context of defence strategy that the sectoral idea of the Indian economy being organized into "public" and "private" categories was first mentioned in the policy statement of 1945. Since defence remained the country's main preoccupation, the sectoral idea continued and formed an integral part of the Industrial Policy Resolutions of 1948 and 1956, although with the passage of time the private sector gained in weight and importance even within the framework of the two.

Doubtless, there were provisions for control and regulations relating, for example, to foreign exchange (FERA), monopolies and restrictive trade (MRTP), development and regulation of industries (IDR), dividends, nationalization, agreements with the government, GNP growth, and opportunities for foreign investment. But as the Bombay High Court judgement in Swaraj Paul's case shows,[51] the system of control so provided operated from considerations of political strategy and financial gain. It was a serious reflection even on the public sector which had remained exempted from the operation, for example, of the MRTP Act.

The Janata Government appreciated the need for control which the Sachar Committee had emphasized. But then came, in 1980, a plethora of concessions to the business community on the plea of boosting the economy and checking inflation. These were in effect a New Year gift to black-marketeers who were said to have piled up unaccounted money unofficially estimated at ranging between Rs. 20,000 crores and Rs. 25,000 crores.[52]

The concessions so extended to big business by Mrs. Gandhi in 1980 were not without their earlier counterparts under Jawaharlal Nehru. One of his first acts as Prime Minister was to allow the owners of black money earned during the Second World War to use their wealth in the purchase of British industries and trading concerns in India at rock-bottom prices. This created a base for monopolies and illegal trade practices. It was a new development which the election manifesto of 1951 admitted. It said that "inequalities have been accentuated during recent years largely in consequence of illegitimate gains from black-marketing, tax evasion, certain forms of speculation and other anti-social activities". The Congress manifesto which Nehru himself had drawn up thus said that "these evils should be curbed with a strong hand". It was a clear admission of increasing poverty in towns and villages proceeding simultaneously with economic growth in terms of large-scale industries and production of capital goods. It was in this context that the Congress laid stress on a socialist pattern of society as its goal in 1956. But, as the report of the Mahalanobis Committee of 1963 showed, the country, instead of socialism, witnessed the rise of monopolies and restrictive trade practices. These, of course, were sought to be dealt with by the MRTP Act introduced in 1970. But the evils of black money kept on growing nonetheless. The Sachar Committee appointed in 1977 confirmed it. The industrialists, traders as well as the black-marketeers, who had sized up the calibre of national leaders, were not "taken in by threats of those in power". For Nehru's own earlier declaration after his release in 1945 that in independent India blackmarketeers would be hanged from lamp-posts had proved to be no more than an empty threat.[53]

When defined in legal terms, black money is said to be that income on which tax is evaded by not reporting income-generating activities or sources to tax authorities. The income so generated or secured remains unaccounted. The activities generating unaccounted income may, however, be legal or illegal. When a doctor, lawyer or contractor conceals a part of his earnings obtained through perfectly legal activities, it is unaccounted or black money in terms of the law governing incomes. Black income is also generated through illegal activities like smuggling, adulteration, black-marketing, bribery or any other activity unknown to legally established, relevant or competent authorities. The sources of such incomes are never disclosed or owned individually or institutionally for fear of illegality. The money received from foreign sources for political activities or seemingly non-political services is included in the same category. Any part of the income concealed, or the money acquired illegally, may be permitted to find its way into the black or "unofficial economy" when converted into assets or used to carry on illegal activities.

According to the Direct Taxes Enquiry Committee (headed by K. N. Wanchoo, an erstwhile Supreme Court judge), black money increased through such fraudulent devices as gross under-invoicing of exports and over-invoicing of imports. These processes accounted for the growth of illegal and clandestine foreign exchange held abroad in various forms. The operation of the black money is in fact said to be inclusive of exports by ghost firms and non-realization of the price in India, the proceeds being used in a clandestine manner. The foreign exchange received from non-resident Indians settled abroad has often been a source of illicit transactions responsible for the growth of the black money and the parallel economy supported by it in the form of unauthorized factories working in different parts of the country, extensive cornering of stock, hoarding, smuggling, black-marketing, adulteration, fakes and imitations as well as the sale of spurious stuffs regardless of any consideration for prescribed standards.[54]

The tendency of big business to evade payment of taxes is also reflected in fake receipts of donations for religious and charitable purposes. An interesting case of misuse of the Income Tax Act by the DCM group of companies, for example, came to light in the course of a debate raised in Parliament about the fraudulent manner in which payment of income tax was sought to be evaded by these companies. The Finance Minister, Pranab Mukherjee, told the Lok Sabha that as a result of searches made by the Income Tax Department it was discovered that a total sum of Rs.1.21 crores of bogus donations had been debited in the books of the various companies of the DCM group as well as other concerns and individuals.[55] On November 26, 1983, Mukherjee confirmed that searches had been conducted in the offices and residential premises of Dr. Charat Ram, the DCM Managing Director, as well as some other executives. As a result, bank drafts and FDRs of Rs. 85.20 lakhs in addition to incriminating documents were seized in this connexion. The Finance Minister acknowledged the discovery of a "bogus cheque" of Rs. 40 lakhs which had been made out for Aparna Ashram, run by Dhirendra Brahmachari. The money so debited in the books of the companies formed part of the black money which leaked into their assets. It was part of this black money that found its way, if necessary, into the coffers of political parties, more especially of the ruling party. The Lok Sabha, however, did nothing beyond expressing a sense of complaint that the Minister said nothing beyond what had already appeared in the Telegraph.

Black money, it is true, is a global phenomenon. But the characteristic feature of the Indian scene is that it is generated for the most part through illegal operations, not infrequently manoeuvred under political protection and bureaucratic corruption. The authorities charged with checking smuggling, for instance, are unable to discharge their duty, because they are either themselves corrupt or unable to resist the political pressure brought to bear on them by smugglers who are utilized by politicians for running their own activities in the race for power.[56]

There are variations in the estimate of the size of unaccounted incomes and of the assets held illegally. Kaldor's estimate of block income in 1953-54 was 6 per cent of the GNP. It rose to 9 per cent in 1968-69. The relaxation of control which followed the fall of the Janata Government marked a steep rise in the percentage of this estimate, varying within a wide range with the topmost figure being as high as 50 per cent of the GNP. "According to the best judgement available to me", he says, "the figure is 30 per cent, which with our present GNP would work out to an enormous sum – something of the order of thirty-four thousand crores at current prices." Leaving aside differences in qualification, a recent judgement of the Supreme Court provides a general indication of the magnitude, boldness and ingenuity of black money operations. This is what the Chief Justice of the Supreme Court had to say in the case of Sanchaita Investments (of Calcutta). "The partners of the firm have become millionaires overnight, clerks and chemists that they and some of their agents were in 1975, today they own properties which will put a prince to shame. "Rags to riches" this is how one may justly describe the story of quick and easy enrichment. There is no question that this vast wealth has been acquired by the firm by generating and circulating black money."[57]

The black money so generated did contribute to economic growth with the special concessions extended to the businesses in 1980. But that growth remained for the most unrelated to the alleviation of poverty. The First Five Year Plan, for instance, stressed the need for capital formation as an aid to growth by restraining consumption and increasing the rate of saving. It necessarily favoured a rise in profit income conducive to capitalist enterprise with an emphasis on the production of capital goods. There was no scope for poverty alleviation in such a framework.

It was Professor Mahalanobis who provided a sectoral outline for investment planning based on the division of the economy into two sectors, consumption goods and capital goods.[58] It was a growth model for a capital intensive large-scale industry which laid emphasis on the percentage of total investment going to capital goods industries. In other words, the higher this percentage, the higher would be the income generated in the long run for purposes of industrial investment. The source of growth was the allocation of resources to produce them. It was assumed that an increase in output resulting from a given allocation of resources in favour of capital goods would largely be saved and reinvested in the production of more capital goods thereby strengthening the productive base of the economy for a self-generating and self-sustaining process of growth.

Within the capital goods sector the machine-making industries were given a higher priority to make the country increasingly independent of imports in this respect and to provide the machinery needed for setting up new plants for the manufacture of such basic goods as steel, cement and other material as also to meet the requirements of machinery for hydro-electric projects, railways, and other transport equipment. The production of consumer goods was not excluded. But the emphasis was on the heavy machines to produce basic goods and equipment to accelerate the pace of industrialization independently of imports. This was an approach to investment planning and its outline in terms of priority that

Mahalanobis devised for the Second Plan, and the Industrial Policy Resolution of 1956 adopted in principle. The concurrent list included in addition to the public and private sectors remained, as said before, a private sector affair for all practical purposes. The over-emphasis on the capital goods in the public sector and the profit-dominated approach of private enterprise were both incapable of resolving the problems of poverty and unemployment. And yet, it was the model of the Second Plan that persisted since 1956.

It is true that while preparing the draft of the Second Plan, Mahalanobis did not ignore the employment aspect which was related to the problem of poverty. He divided the consumer goods sector into three parts, namely, goods produced in factory, household and small-scale enterprise. But this did not essentially modify the functioning of the Plan in practice, because the investment allocated to the capital goods sector and its priority retained its predominant position, with a first claim on the entire Plan outlay. What was left over was to be allocated to the three parts of the consumption goods sector. It was thus no more than a residual approach to the problems of unemployment and consumption, a crucial aspect of the strategy of planning that remained unresolved ever since the policy framework of 1956. The growth aspect of the policy continued to dominate the employment or poverty aspect. The two remained for the most unrelated. The Third and the Fourth or even the subsequent Plans did hardly anything radically to make any substantial change; for they called for a drastic redistribution of income which, in the absence of political will, was considered independent from considerations of practical politics. The emphasis laid on the growth aspect of the economy under the relaxation of control introduced by Indira Gandhi in 1980 reinforced the importance of the capital goods sector all the more. Apart from the increasing inflationary pressure on prices, it tended to intensify the problem of poverty and unemployment. It was in these circumstances that the Government of India proceeded in the early 1980's to bring into focus the significance of what it called the New Twenty-Point Programme[59] providing for easy financial assistance for self-employment and alleviation of poverty through labour-intensive household and small-scale enterprise as well as for animal husbandry and agricultural equipment.

The extent to which economic growth can be attributed to black money remains yet to be ascertained with precision. But its contribution to corruption and debasement of ethical norms is widely known. The Santhanam Committee stressed the importance of Ministers of the Government being recognized as public servants and suggested several other preventive measures to check corruption. But, as L. P. Singh, a former Home Secretary to the Government of India, has pointed out, these were "either not accepted, or, having been accepted, were not put into effect with resolution. In the meantime, the growth, accumulation and power of black money, and the ramifications of the black economy have assumed far more disturbing proportions, widely debasing ethical norms, and eating into the vitals of our socio-economic and political system".[60]

Justice G. D. Khosla, an eminent jurist and former Supreme Court judge, held a similar view of conditions arising from the growth of black money. "There is corruption in all walks of life", he said, "and we cannot wish it away or diminish its menace by seeing corruption as part of a global phenomenon. Corruption is also due to a hunger for political power. Every issue is being politicized, including the Courts, which is very distressing. I cannot blame any individual for this. The judges themselves have shown the inclination to be influenced."[61]

The politicization of every issue of public affairs proceeded, however, from an increasingly closer union between politics and big business, reflected for the most part in the inflow of black money in elections ever since the 1950s. It went on growing bigger and bigger, involving political parties, smugglers, tax-evaders and unscrupulous fortune seekers willing to supply funds out of the black money which remained free from public disclosure or audit. It satisfied both personal greed of individuals and electoral necessity. The amounts involved in recent elections were vastly bigger than they used to be in the 1950s or even the 1960s. The money power exhibited in the elections of 1977 marked in fact a sudden jump which for the first time broke all previous records.

From an analysis of the concessions extended to big business since July 1980 and the dominance of the money power that followed, it is clear that recent trends in policy making were an added contribution to the concentration of wealth and economic power. It is true that the relaxation of controls and measures to liberalize the economy have contributed considerably to the acceleration of the process of growth. But, as K. K. Birla publicly admitted, this growth was not reflected proportionately in demands for consumer spending.[62] This acted as a constraint for industrial goods, which plagued many industries. Growth thus remained unrelated to the promotion of job opportunities for the alleviation of poverty. And, as said above, the New Twenty-Point Programme was devised to promote these opportunities, more especially through integrated plans of development calling for people's participation as the Seventh Plan envisaged.

Appendix to Chapter V

PRIME MINISTER'S NEW TWENTY-POINT PROGRAMME

The New 20-Point Programme is as follows:

1. Increase irrigation potential, develop and disseminate technologies and inputs for dry land agriculture.
2. Take special efforts to increase production of pulses and vegetable oilseeds.
3. Strengthen and expand coverage of integrated rural development and national rural employment programmes.
4. Implement agricultural land ceilings, distribute surplus land and complete compilation of land records by removing all administrative and legal obstacles.
5. Review and effectively enforce minimum wages for agricultural labour.
6. Rehabilitate bonded labour.
7. Accelerate programmes for the development of scheduled castes and tribes.
8. Supply drinking water to all problem villages.
9. Allot house sites to rural families who are without them and expand programmes for construction assistance to them.
10. Improve the environment of slums, implement programmes of house building for economically weaker sections and take measures to arrest unwarranted increase in land prices.

11. Maximize power generation, improve the functioning of electricity authorities and electrify all villages.
12. Pursue vigorously programmes of afforestation, social and farm forestry and the development of bio-gas and other alternative energy sources.
13. Promote family planning on a voluntary basis as a people's movement.
14. Substantially augment universal primary health care facilities and control of leprosy, T.B. and blindness.
15. Accelerate programmes of welfare for women and children and nutrition programmes for pregnant women, nursing mothers and children, specially in tribal, hill and backward areas.
16. Spread universal elementary education for the age-group 6-14 with special emphasis on girls and simultaneously involve students and voluntary agencies in programmes for the removal of adult illiteracy.
17. Expand the public distribution system through more fair price shops, including mobile shops in far-flung areas and shops to cater to industrial workers, students, hostels and make available to students text-books and exercise books on a priority basis and to promote a strong consumer protection movement.
18. Liberalize investment procedure and streamline industrial policies to ensure timely completion of projects. Give handicrafts, handlooms, small and village industries all facilities to grow and to update their technology.
19. Continue strict action against smugglers, hoarders and tax evaders and check black money.
20. Improve the working of the public enterprises by increasing efficiency, capacity utilization and the generation of internal resources.

REFERENCES

1. *Times of India*, September 21, 1984, p.6.
2. Ibid.,p. 6.
3. Ibid.,p. 6.
4. *Financial Express*, March 7, 1981 (Shaping Industrial Policy II by S.K. Ray).
5. See *Economic Times*, July 24, 1980 (No Deviation from 1956 Industrial Policy Resolution by Special Correspondent).
6. Ibid.
7. See *Business Standard*, July 12, 1981.
8. *Financial Express*, Feb. 23, 1980 ('77 Industrial Policy to Return by K.S.Ramachandran).
9. See *Mainstream*, June 16, 1979.
10. See *Financial Express Bureau*, Nov. 10, 1979.
11. See *New Age*, Sept. 17, 1983.
12. See *Business Standard*, Sept. 19, 1983.
13. *Financial Express*, June 16, 1984 (Farewell to Mahalanobis? by T.C.A.Srinivasa-Raghavan).
14. See *Economic Times* (B),July 21, 1980 (Industrial Sector : *Impact of Policy on Employment* by M.Y.Khan).
15. Ibid.
16. Ibid
17. Ibid
18. See *Business Standard*, Aug. 5, 1983 (Will Corporate Growth Be A Casualty? by J.C.Srivastava and S.K.Sahni).
19. In *Telegraph* of Aug. 12, 1983, M.V.Kamath, in his comments on the Relevance of Swaraj Paul, described L.K.Jha as "India's economic Czar" and "one of those faceless men who reportedly advise the Prime Minister on economic matters and occasionally make important-sounding pronouncements which seldom are translated into high policy. No one has yet adequately defined Mr. Jha's powers. But he is there."
20. See *Telegraph*, Aug. 4, 1983 (PTI, Bombay, Aug 3).
21. See *Business Standard*, Aug. 5, 1983 (Will Corporate Growth Be a Casualty? by J.C.Srivastava and S.K.Sahni).
22. See *Daily* (an article on "Code of Company Take-Over A Must"), IIPA Corporate Section Press Clippings, OGO/Dy/830829/21 19/AR.
23. *Economic Times*, Aug. 11, 1983 (A Staff Reporter on Changes in Co. Law Act under way).
24. *Telegraph*, Aug. 11, 1983 (Swaraj Paul on Directive of Govt. by a Staff Reporter,Calcutta).
25. Ibid.
26. See *Business Standard*,Aug.5, 1983 (Will Corporate Growth Be A Casualty? by J.C.Srivastava and S.K.Sahni).
27. *Telegraph*,Aug. 12, 1983 (The Relevance of Swaraj Paul by M.V.Kamath).
28. J.C.Srivastava and S.K.Sahni in *Business Standard*, Aug. 5, 1983.
29. *Daily*, June 7, 1984 (The Non-resident Indian Connection—An Economic Survey by Subrata Banerjee.
30. *Financial Express*, Aug. 21, 1983 (Report of Special Correspondent).
31. Ibid.
32. See *Business Standard*, New Delhi, Sept.19, 1983 (PM takes a tough line, S.C.Anantharaman).
33. *Business Standard*, New Delhi, Sept. 18, 1983 (Special Correspondent—

Caparo Investment Cleared by RBI).

34. *Business Standard*, New Delhi, Sept. 19, 1983 (PM takes a tough line).
35. *Business Standard*, New Delhi, Sept. 18, 1983 (Caparo Investment Cleared by RBI by Special Correspondent).
36. *Telegraph*, Calcutta, Sept. 7, 1983 (Swaraj Paul Speaks for Mrs. Gandhi by M.V.Kamath).
37. Ibid.
38. *Business Standard*, New Delhi, Sept. 19, 1983 (PM takes a tough line by S.C.Anantharaman).
39. See *Financial Express*, Bombay, Aug. 21, 1983; *Business Standard*, New Delhi, Aug. 6, 1983 (No probe into NRI Cos. From a Staff Reporter.
40. See *Economic Times*, May 7, 1983 (Foreign Investors: A Review of Indian Economy by M.S.Patwardhan).
41. See *Financial Express*, Madras, March 19, 1984 (Divergent Views on MRTP Act utility by FE Bureau.
42. See D.P.S.Verma, *Restrictive Trade Practices in India*, Himalaya Publishing House, Bombay.
43. See *Hindustan Times*, March 27, 1984 (The Return of 1969 by H.D.Pai Panandikar).
44. See *Economic Times*, Feb. 20, 1984 (MRTP (Amendment) Bill 1983: I-Vital Provisions and Consumer Protection).
45. See *Economic Times*, May 7, 1983 (A Review of Indian Economy by M.S.Patwardhan).
46. *Economic Times*, Dec. 25, 1983 (More Teeth to the MRTP Act to safeguard consumer interests by Special Correspondent).
47. See *New Age*, March 25, 1984 (Big Houses, Big Tax Arrears).
48. See *Financial Express*, Calcutta, April 13, 1984 (From Special Correspondent on Raising Applicability Limit). See also *Economic Times*, Calcutta, April 14, 1984 (Trade opposes proposals to amend MRTP Act).
49. *Business Standard,* New Delhi, April 16, 1984 (MRTP Act must go, says K.K.Birla).
50. See *Business Standard,* Nov. 10, 1984 (Text of Judgement in Escorts Case).
51. See *Business Standard,* New Delhi, Nov. 10, 1984 (Text of Judgement).
52. See *Business Standard,* New Delhi, Jan. 15, 1981 (Political Diary by Ranajit Roy—Black Money Rules the Roost).
53. Ibid.
54. These are some of the distinctive features of the black economy, which the former Home Secretary to the Government of India and Governor of Assam and Nagaland, L.P. Singh, I.C.S. (retd.), mentioned in his Amarnath Jha Memorial Address to the L. N. Mishra Mithila University on the subject of Morality in Public Affairs.
55. See *Business Standard,* New Delhi, Dec. 13, 1983 (Staff Correspondent on Misuse of I-T Act by DCM).
56. See *Patriot,* New Delhi, May 31, 1981 (Tackling Black Money by Girish Mishra).
57. Cited by L.P.Singh, I.C.S. (retd.) in his "Amarnath Jha Memorial Lecture" at L.N.Mishra Mithila University. I was favoured with a copy of his unpublished lecture.
58. See P.C.Mahalanobis, "Some Observations on the Process of Growth of National Income" in *Sankhya,* Vol.XIV, Part IV, Sept. 1953.
59. See Appendix to this chapter.
60. See L.P.Singh, "Amarnath Jha Memorial Lecture" on Morality in Public Affairs, p. 13 of the typescript.

61. *Telegraph*, Calcutta, Jan. 10, 1984 (The dawn of 1984).
62. See *Business Standard*, New Delhi, April 16, 1984 (MRTP Act must go).

SIX

The Indian Administrative Service as Policy-Implementing Agency

The Indian Administrative Service, which came into existence in October 1946, was the creation of Sardar Vallabhbhai Patel, then Home Minister of the Interim Government. As a result of joint consultations with the heads of Provincial Governments, it was modelled after the Indian Civil Service, an imperial service which Britain had earlier established to run her colonial administration in India.

There has of late been a good deal of controversy over the IAS personnel being used as the policy-implementing agency for purposes of socio-economic development. It is argued that officers brought up and trained in the cultural tradition of a colonial administration and wedded to the Weberian approach to public administration with its emphasis on hierarchy, procedural rigidity, status and regard for rule are not fitted for the task of development, more especially when their main concern remains geared to law and order or the collection of revenue in the districts. It is suggested that development administration calls for an attitude of mind, bold enough to take risks on the spot and decide matters without worrying about procedures, rules and regulations. It would be appropriate here in this chapter to find an answer to this controversy by a reference to the principle which underlined the organization of the Indian Civil Service and the objective which that all-India civil service was made to accomplish.

Conceptual Basis in General

The conceptual basis of modern organization, including administrative or political organizations, was derived largely from Max Weber's organizational analysis forming part of his exposition of basic sociological concepts.[1] He used terms like *Verband*, the German equivalent of the English term organization which was in general identified by sociologists as "corporate group" to which admission is limited and governed by rules, and social relationships within the group are ordered and enforced by the action of specific individuals whose regular function is to maintain that ordering. This organizational or corporate group concept is inclusive of an administrative or governing element or authority called chief or head occupying a directing position and exercising the functions of the administrative staff. The set of rules which governed corporate action was considered basic to the concept of organization. These rules formed part of a system of order which Weber preferred to call an administrative order, regulating not only the action of the administrative staff, but also that of the members in their direct relations to the corporate group.

Pre-Independence Position

The study of the Indian Civil Service for the pre-independence period brings into perspective a reflection on the problems of administrative reform, introduced from time to time, to meet the exigencies of changing circumstances. The East India Company's government started, for instance, with the Covenanted Civil Service, the predecessor of the Indian Civil Service. It belonged to separate presidency governments with no commitment to an all-India obligation in terms of political or administrative discipline. It continued till 1878 when, from considerations of all-India integrated imperial interest, it was formed into what came to be known as the Indian Civil Service. The changes that invested this service with qualities of independence and uprightness of conduct had started taking place ever since the enactment of 1793, a result of far-sighted political vision of Lord Cornwalis. These were reinforced by subsequent provisions to safeguard its rights and privileges in terms of disciplinary matters, salary, pension, leave and other conditions of service. In keeping with the contract-based conceptual foundations of its bureaucratic structure, changes were from time to time introduced in matters of its education, training and probation, so that the service might be able to meet the call of time. Functionally, too, the structure did not remain unchanged. Its function kept on expanding with expansion in the function of the State to satisfy political demands, not only normative but also positive, not only general but also developmental.

Evolved out of a competitive capitalist society, the conceptual foundation of the Indian Civil Service was in principle based on the Weberian model of a bureaucratic organization, the term bureaucracy signifying both a type of administrative organization and a system of government or form of rule, the former representing its technical aspect, while the latter its political. Both aspects were united and functioned as a single entity under British rule in India. Technically, the bureaucratic organization was viewed as an impermeable hierarchy or structure, with a whole complex body of rules governing recruitment, education, training, conditions of service, business procedure, and so on. Politically, on the other hand, the officials or bureaucrats acted as rulers themselves. They could as well coexist with elected executives, remaining at the same time conceptually connected in all cases with the exercise of authority as power elites.[2]

Legal authority alone was, however, treated by Max Weber as "rational", not charismatic or traditional. According to him, the most important characteristic of modern organization was derived from law, a contractual concept. Those who happened to be elected were essentially excluded. In fact, bureaucracy was to Weber a collective term for a body of appointed officials. Certain other features were additionally annexed to what he considered to be legal authority.

The set of five characteristics which were so annexed to the Weberian concept of modern bureaucratic organization were[3]:

1. That a legal norm can be established by agreement or by imposition with a claim to obedience on the part of the members of a corporate group or organization.

2. That the law is a system of abstract rules covering all possible cases of conduct within the organization, the administration of law being the application of these rules to particular cases.

3. The fundamental source of authority in the legal type is the authority to the impersonal order of an officer holding a specifically legitimized status under the rules with powers to issue commands.

4. That the person who obeys authority does so in his capacity as a member of the corporate group and what he obeys is only the law.

5. That the members of the corporate group, in so far as they obey a person in authority, do not owe this obedience to him as an individual, but to the impersonal order. In other words, there is an obligation to obedience only within the sphere of the rationally delimited authority which, in terms of the order, has been conferred upon him.

The Indián Civil Service was thus conceived as a bureaucratic corporate organization of power elites, signifying an impersonal order based on a legal foundation, where obligation to obedience flowed from considerations of law and legally delimited authority, not from any personal regard for an individual, tradition or charismatic entity. This concept of legal authority, which underlined the structure and functioning of the Indian Civil Service, was indeed revolutionary in terms of its influence on Indian society, where obligations to obedience and social relationships were supposed to be governed by considerations of caste and religious differentiation. The scope of legal operation and therefore of State action was thus initially bound to be limited, chiefly confined to measures of security, the normative function of a State. It extended to socio-economic spheres only slowly and gradually, with the spread of Western education and technological advancement, considered necessary even in terms of the rulers' own interest. While Indian reformers sought to prepare the ground socially under the influence of Western thought, the early Western-educated leaders of the Indian National Congress, an elitist political organization, sought to be associated with control over the lever of power to accelerate the process of change.

Apart from the five basic features of a corporate body, based on legal authority, there were, according to Weber, eight fundamental forms of rational legal authority that went into the making of bureaucracy as a corporate administrative organization. These were:

(1) discharging official functions on a continuous rule-bound basis; (2) a specified sphere of competence and of distinct functions based on a systematic division of labour; (3) the principle of hierarchy, with a lower office under the control and supervision of a higher one; (4) trained personnel for the conduct of business; (5) complete separation of members of the administrative staff from the ownership of the means of production or administration, with a clear separation likewise in principle of the property belonging to the organization and controlled within the sphere of office, and the personal property of the official available for private use; (6) a complete absence of appropriation of official position by the incumbent; (7) the formulation and recording in writing of all acts, decisions and rules; (8) and the ideal type being the purest form of legal authority or "imperative coordination". The Indian Civil Service as a rational and corporate administrative organization was supposed to have embodied these forms in both substantive and procedural terms.

The Indian Civil Service had by Lord Lytton's time become an all-India civil service, mainly for two reasons. The first was political stability and territorial security of India as a whole, while the second was the progress of plantation industry to feed the colonial economy and trade. Both called for a kind of elitist civil service which, by virtue of its higher education and training, might be action-oriented in terms of the requirements of field for policy formulation at the headquarters. In the Indian situation the conceptual foundation so laid on the Weberian model was considered to be all the more essential because the bureacracy itself happened to be the government responsible practically for both policy-making and administrative action. With the growth of representative government it was this bureaucracy that assisted Ministers in policy formulation, but care was taken to see that the policy so formulated represented the "general will" and no partial or party interest.

The elitist and rational concept of the Indian Civil Service that grew on a non-partisan basis to preserve the country's territorial integrity and promote its economy on a free trade principle was reinforced by the recommendations of the Aitchison Commission (1886-87) which came into force in 1892.

The scope of the inquiry by the Commission was limited. It did not extend to any report on the systems of competitive examinations, probation and training already in force in the various departments, nor on the prevailing conditions of service, salary, leave and pension already settled on principles generally recognized as part of a rational bureaucratic structure. What appeared to the commission as a matter of immediate concern was to lay down conditions under which Indians should be employed in the posts ordinarily reserved for members of the covenanted service–as the Indian Civil Service was then termed–and also to form regulations relating to the admission of Indians and Europeans to those branches of the uncovenanted service--the existing provincial and subordinate services–which were directly engaged in the executive and judicial administration of the country. The whole burden of the Aitchison Commission was in fact to suggest measures to secure for the natives of India higher and more extensive employment in the public service. Apart from their extended employment, for instance, in the Indian Civil Service, it sought also to raise the standard of recruitment and training for the Provincial Civil Service to an extent that might create some scope for promotion to the superior civil service without any sacrifice of efficiency or integrity of character.

The central point of the recommendations of the Aitchison Commission was the division of the public service into two parts, the first being imperial recruited in England, while the second provincial recruited in India. The conditions of appointment in regard to pay, leave and pension of officers belonging to the two services were to be fixed on independent grounds, not necessarily related to each other. There was to be a third service comprising the lower administrative appointments called the subordinate service. With respect to the imperial and provincial services the Commission emphasized that their members should be put on a footing of equality, and when they occupied similar offices, they should be graded together in the official precedence list. These proposals which were developed mainly with reference to the civil service on rational principles were to be applied also to services connected with the special departments; for the division into imperial and provincial categories, which obtained in the civil services and in the police, applied also to the education, medical, agricultural, civil, veterinary, forests, telegraph (engineering), public works and Survey of India departments.[4]

Care was, however, taken to see that the standard of recruitment and conditions governing appointment to the Indian Civil Service were in no way compromised. The Aitchison Commission's approach to administrative reforms was, doubtless, political, synchronous with the introduction of representative principles in the government under the Indian Councils Act of 1892. Even so, the elitist character of the Indian Civil Service remained unaffected. The recruitment of officials in England was to be substantially reduced to admit of increase in recruitment in India. But the exact language used by the Commission with reference to the Indian Civil Service was that it must remain "a corps d'elite" and that its standard of recruitment must under no circumstances be lowered even when some of its higher posts are set free for political reasons and transferred to form part of the Provincial Civil Service. The emphasis was that the Weberian foundations of the superior civil service must at all cost be preserved to serve as an example for other services to emulate.

Forces Against Bureaucratic Rationality

The rise of forces against bureaucratic rationality proceeded immediately from a virtual non-implementation of the Aitchison Commission's recommendation. The problem of Indianizing the public service which the Commission had sought to resolve did not cease because of its extremely slow pace.The annual average number of passes at the several universities in India, which was nearly 2,000 during 1864-73, rose to 5,403 in the decade 1878-88 and then to 9,165 during 1889-94.[5] The rate of educational progress had thus increased nearly five times in about 30 years, whereas employment in the public service increased only by 12 per cent, and that mainly in the subordinate branches.

Yet the Home Department Resolution of May 24, 1904, justified the action of the Government of India on the ground that the higher ranks of the all-India services, though open to Indians under an Act of Parliament, "must nevertheless, as a general rule, be held by Englishmen" because "the rule of India being a British rule and any other rule in the circumstances of the case being impossible, the tone and standard should be set by those who have created and are responsible for it".[6]

This was a kind of thinking which even a liberal leader like Gokhale resented. In a budget speech of 1903, he made a frontal attack on British policy and said: "This question of appointment to high offices is to us something more than a mere question of careers....This is to us a question of national prestige and self-respect."[7]

The report of the Royal (Islington) Commission, which came out in 1916, also noted with regret the failure of the recommendations which the Aitchison Commission had made. "I have had no hesitation in coming to the conclusion," Lord Islington himself admitted, "that the recommendations of the Aitchison Commission have failed in their desired object. So far as appointments made in England are concerned experience has shown that the chances of Indians are inconsiderable, and the Aitchison Commission itself rightly regarded the London door of admission as a supplementary source. Their most important recommendation that recruitment in England for the Indian public service should be substantially reduced as a necessary step towards steadily increasing the scope for Indians has not been carried out. In fact, the reverse has taken place in the more important service".[8] The Report of the Islington Commission refers in fact to several cases where differentiation between Indian and European members of the public service were noticeable not only in their salary, pension and conditions of service but also in terms of social status and racial discrimination. These were all lower dimensions of politics which, speaking professionally, were unrelated to the basic rationality of the bureaucratic organization.

Indeed, what plagued the organization was not its conceptual foundation. It was a combination of politics, arising from a failure of the Aitchison Commission's recommendations, and new economic force of Indian capitalism that emerged in the course of the First World War and proceeded to compete with British firms to gain a footing in foreign trade, a virtual monopoly of British business. As already pointed out earlier, this appeared as an alliance between the Indian bourgeois politics and the newly emerging big business, a development which became first manifest at the Industrial Conference held in Bombay in 1915. The situation so developing simultaneously in politics and business was thus clearly invested with racial trends, highly prejudicial to the essentially rational concept underlying the bureaucratic organization of the Indian Civil Service. But since the bureaucracy in India happened to be both an administration and government, its conceptual integrity was sought to be saved and protected through a series of remedial measures. The just, impartial and corrective view that Islington took in this regard was also a great help to eminent civilians like Sir James Meston, William Morris and Sir Harcourt Butler who had shaped the course of events in a manner that maintained a balanced approach to both politics and business.

It was in the context of these developing political and economic circumstances that the importance of the Industrial Commission appointed in 1916, the Indian Policy Announcement of August 20, 1917, the Montford Report of 1918 and the Government of India Act of 1919 could best be appreciated as measures of reform[9] taken one after the other in quick succession to save the public service from being accused of either political or economic predisposition. The protective tariff introduced under the recommendations of the Indian Fiscal Commission of 1921, the order of the India Council to hold from 1922 onwards a separate competitive examination for the Indian Civil Service in India at Allahabad and the appointment of the Lee Commission in 1923 to act as an ad hoc public service commission were all other measures intended not only to protect the Indian economic interest but also to supervise the conduct of the ICS examination and to see that no member of this all-India civil service was dismissed by an authority subordinate to that by which he was appointed. It clearly meant that in spite of the ministerial control introduced in the provinces in the transferred field under the reforms of 1919, the security of an ICS officer as well as his conditions of service remained unaffected politically to enable him to serve as a non-politico instrument of government. A regular and separate Indian Public Service Commission was actually established in 1926 to ensure political neutrality and control recruitment and conditions of service for the all-India and Central Services recruited in India on that principle under the recommendations initially made by the Lee Commission as an ad hoc body.

The functioning of ICS officers as members of Government had of course its own advantage. They brought a wide range of their field experience to bear upon policy-making at the headquarters. Their intellectual culture and cultivation of mind enabled them to take a cumulative view of any policy issue, which tended to invest decisions with foresight and make them pretty lasting, representative of the general will and not the interest of mere one group or the other which elected politicians or Ministers often prefer to promote. The colonial situation in which the white bureaucracy was obliged to function as part of their political necessity was, however, a serious handicap, involving widespread national movements for what was called "freedom" or independence which called for an elective system of government or constitutional advance based on the skilful management or manoeuvre of votes by means fair or foul. There the bureaucracy had hardly any honest choice but to resign or submit to the inevitable, which would have meant a complete loss of its basic qualities of character.

Happily, however, the process of constitutional advance and the final transfer of power was, on the whole, marked by an exercise of a remarkable degree of restraint and foresight on the part of India's political authority in England. Apart from the problems of defence against foreign intervention, the administration of the country was faced with tremendous odds in terms of her internal affairs divided politically not only as Right and Left groups in the Congress Party, but also as Congress and Muslim League, two of the main political segments of her plural society. So far as the inner politics of the Congress Party was concerned, the pressure of the Left, which was headed by Subhas Chandra Bose, tended to oblige its Right wing to assume apparently a radically anti-imperialist posture which not only made a negotiated settlement of differences impossible, but drove the party to a perilous resort that came to be known as the "Quit India" movement. On account of the power-motivated recalcitrant attitude of both the Congress and the League, a situation developed which made the state of political confusion still more confounded. Even so, the Government and its administration as part of the country's sovereign authority never relented. It remained firm and continued to carry on its business without fear or favour. Considerations of politics did not stand in the way, because the Government remained clear in its policy and showed no reluctance to meet the demands of politics within the framework of internal security and territorial integrity. The August Offer of 1940, the Cripps Mission of 1942 and the Cabinet Mission Plan of 1946 were all evidence of attempts to arrive at negotiated settlements of political issues regardless of attempts at violence committed in the course of the Quit India movement or on other occasions of a breach of the peace for political reasons. My researches on *India: Her Unity And Division* have clearly shown that in their resolve to transfer power British policy was at this period guided by a broad perspective of Commonwealth which envisaged India's territorial unity as a condition precedent to the security of British Communication right from the Red Sea through the Indian Ocean to Burma, New Zealand and Australia. What blocked the prospect of unity was, however, the failure of the Indian leadership to settle the communal question–a failure which proceeded from a spirit of jealousy and greed for power rather than any devotion to religion.

Administratively, the bureaucracy, both European and Indian, acquitted itself professionally well to win a war against fascism, a war which led to considerable expansion in the function of the State in terms of productive activity and its public control without anything of the nature of political bias in one way or the other. This was more especially noticeable in the administration of the districts, the headquarters of executive administration. It is important to note that the war had created a situation of emergency putting to test the efficiency or otherwise of the entire civil administration in terms of the State's normative and positive functions. The quality of its performance in that state of emergency was an index of success attributable to superior civil service based on intellectual culture and cultivation of mind for the different task of managing men and affairs, the basic function of the public service, requiring a capacity for an overall analysis and balance of judgement, an independence of mind and firmness of character.

And since it was the district administration where direct contact with the people was sought to be established, its importance increased with increasing expansion in the function of the State. This functional expansion, however, did not call for the creation of increasingly separate civil services. The leadership of the Indian Civil Service as an instrument of executive administration remained intact. What changed was the district as a unit of administration which steadily grew to be part of a people. In the reorganization of the district administration the object kept in view was not a mere consideration of its being administratively convenient. It was to be regarded as an essential part of the organization of the community. It assumed this position as it came to correspond "to certain fundamental characteristics of the people". The District Officer provided relief against petty tyrannies; it was his duty to look to the whole agricultural condition of the district, to help projects for improvement, to administer famine relief, to help projects for improvement, to administer famine relief, to recommend suspension or remission of land revenue, to preserve peace among agricultural classes, and, in short, to secure the welfare of the whole community living in the district.[10] These were functions which remained traditionally attached to his office. By virtue of his higher liberal education of a superior order, his historical position, his position and status in the superior civil service of the country the Collector-Magistrate alone could best represent the policy and might of the Government in its totality and act on its behalf for all general purposes in the district and its development. Except in matters of purely judicial administration, the district officer naturally held the key position in the district.

The history of the Indian Civil Service makes it clear that it was not merely geared to the law and order problem of the district. It is true that while the leading members of the service were on account of their initiative and drive considered best suited for executive administration, more especially in a plural society that calls for a national and secular impersonal approach to public administration, cadre supplied equally successful personnel for the judiciary as well as for the "special departments" of the Government dealing with accounts and audit, imperial customs and public works, inclusive of developmental functions intended to meet the demands of rural population. The general practice was that often an initial experience acquired in the field of general civil administration extending over six to eight years a civil servant could be trained for a special job calling for a special aptitude of mind as well as skill. He was assigned to it according to his choice without any prejudice to the prospect of his rise in the scale of the service to which he belonged. What the Government was required to do was also to provide an adequate salary and to ensure a regular rise in the service to which the officer elected to opt. And this the Government did by creating a hierarchy of graded promotions at an all-India level. This was an arrangement which had the advantage of uniting the experience of a "generalist" administrator with the skill of a specialist, an arrangement which could lend itself to extend application by a suitable modification or even diversification of the syllabuses built around a common core of higher liberal education.

My study on *District Administration and Rural Development in India* has made it clear that constituted as Indian society is, there was no case for any structural change in the office of the Collector-Magistrate. Far from his powers being reduced, the introduction of representative or responsible government called for these powers being all the more reinforced to maintain a balance in a society known for its mutually exclusive elements and the existence of traditionally dominant castes economically. The development tasks which became the responsibility of popular Ministries since the constitutional reforms of 1919 called for a further reinforcement of his power to give protection to the weaker sections of society.

But since socio-economic protection against the vested interests of Indian society was a politically involved affair, the white bureaucracy was seriously handicapped because of its imperial connexion and steadily depleted strength due to progressive Indianization. The Indian members of the civil service, unlike their European counterparts, besides being recruited from a higher social category, could hardly remain unaligned to one group or the other in terms of caste, creed or religion. Politics and the peculiar constitution of society both united to erode the rational concept of the Indian Civil Service. Europeans became subject to attack on racial grounds when the mass of the people were driven into opposition against them from 1919 onwards. The result of the movement for the Indianization of the public service was not very different. And if the civil service could resist the impact of the irrationality of politics on administration, it was mainly due to the immunity it enjoyed against the act or criticism of any legislature in India.

This, however, did not mean any absence of accountability on the part of the civil service. In a research paper published in the July-September 1983 issue of the *Journal of Indian Institute of Public*

Administration I have discussed in some depth the evolution of the concept of Administrative Accountability to Law, legislative enactments and the rules made thereunder showing how in the absence of adequate security and rational approach to postings and transfers the successor Indian Administrative Service seemed to have started bending to politics, its conceptual rationality getting blurred at the same time though continuing with individuals and men with integrity and character.

Structural Soundness of the ICS Continuing

The Interim Government of India with Jawaharlal Nehru as Prime Minister created, on the model of the Indian Civil Service, its successor, Indian Administrative Service, in October, 1946. Like its predecessor, it was to be an all-India elitist civil service recruited on the basis of higher university education and competitive examination with provisions for a period of training and probation. The change effected was in its nature immediately political, the appointing authority being the Government of India, while its control vested in the Ministry of Home Affairs.

Prior to the establishment of a separate Department of Personnel and Administrative Reforms as part of the Cabinet Secretariat on August 1, 1870, the administration and control of the public service were the immediate responsibility of the Ministry of Home Affairs in the Government of India. This responsibility did not extend to purely Provincial Services which continued to be under the exclusive control of the Provincial Governments. It applied to the Central Services as well as to certain all-India Services organized and maintained jointly on behalf of the Central and Provincial Governments. The day-to-day administration of the various services was of course the concern of the individual Ministries. The responsibility of the Ministry of Home Affairs was limited to the regulation of matters of general applicability to all the services as well as the maintenance of common standards of recruitment, discipline and conditions of service generally. In addition to these matters of common concern, the Home Ministry had a second purpose to fulfil. That was the maintenance of stability against the forces of internal disorder. Though a primary business of Provincial or State Governments themselves, it was deemed essential for the Central Home

Ministry also to keep in touch with such developments as tended to affect security in the country as a whole.

There was, however, nothing novel about these measures of reform except that after the transfer of power these were adopted by a popular Ministry instead of being introduced under the authority of a Department of Government. What was new was a third dimension or reason for the Home Ministry control over the public service which, if accepted by the Cabinet, would have marked a substantial departure from the organizational principles of the Indian Civil Service. It was Prime Minister Nehru who raised this third dimension to secure the realization of his projected goal of what he considered to be socialization. His was a two-pronged suggestion which, while questioning the importance of competitive examinations as the basis of recruitment, raised the issue of suitable personnel being made available for long-term future plans in the context of the expanding activities of the Government at various levels. Obviously, his frame of thinking was opposed to the Indian Administrative Service being recognized as the answer to the question he had raised in his Note of May 14, 1949.

The Note of the Prime Minister referred to "progressive socialization" as a principle of State Policy and invited the attention of the Home Ministry to "the question of numbers" as well as "the question of quality" of recruitment in order to enable the State to "spread out more and more in what has been considered private domain". He added that if the projected goal of State Policy were to succeed, "a great deal of character and integrity would be needed", and "more examinations are not quite enough". His argument was that instead of competitive examinations the desired quality of character and integrity could be ensured by a system of early selection and special training similar to that provided for the Defence Services, where younger men were recruited and rigorously trained. He thus suggested that some such recruitment and training should be adopted for the Indian Administrative Service also. It is true that Nehru did not want that existing competitive examination to be discontinued immediately. "Perhaps this is the most feasible method", he commented. But he made it clear that this should continue only "till a better method is evolved". All that he wanted was "to try both methods at the same time, that is, the competitive examination and the training of younger people who might subsequently sit in the competitive examination also".[11] Obviously, this was an evidence of Nehru's confused thinking on an important issue of the public service which was not without a bright record of its own achievement in the past.

The suggestion of the Prime Minister was examined by R. A. Gopalaswami, then Officer on Special Duty, who enjoyed the status of Secretary in the Ministry of Home Affairs. He regarded Nehru's proposals as open to objections on both theoretical and practical grounds. His main objection was that earlier selection and special training would involve both time and money for a kind of education which students generally acquired on their own at the universities. It was, in addition, feared that the projected training for the Administrative Service on the model of the Defence Services would impart a regimented attitude and create aloofness from the general public, breeding exclusiveness, highly undesirable in a democratic State. Sardar Patel, the Home Minister, argued with Gopalaswami and recognized the soundness of his arguments. It was even further realized that in spite of the defects that can be pointed out in respect of the general education which our universities give, it would be too ambitious to expect that the institutions built up by the Government would be in a position to impart a higher standard of education or even education of a more liberal nature than is available anywhere else in the country. On the other hand, whatever may be the standard of teaching in a Government institution or the nature of subjects taught therein such an institution would certainly suffer from the disadvantage that it would be an exclusive one, meant only for the future members of the Government services. The boys under training will not have the opportunity to mix with boys of their age of different types and calibre not selected for the services.[12]

These precisely were the principles which underlined the structure of the Indian Civil Service also. The Council of Ministers who adopted them for the Indian Administrative Service were no inferior persons. In terms of intellectual calibre and cultural standards, they were by all means comparable to senior members of the civil service or the *competitionwallahs* as they were at times euphemistically called. Besides the Prime Minister, their list included such persons as Sardar Patel, Rajagopalachari, N. Gopalaswami Ayyangar, C. D. Deshmukh, B. R. Ambedkar and John Matthai, who differed little in their education equipment and experience of public affairs from the top echelons of the public service. The Council of Ministers naturally upheld the recommendations of the Islington Commission which had already emphasized the importance of the existing system of recruitment by competitive examination and considered it by far the best in terms of the country's requirement for both efficiency and quality of character.

As said above, the second question which Nehru had raised in his Note of May 14, 1949, related to the availability of suitable personnel likely to be required for long-term future plans because of projected expansion in the functions of the State and the activities of the Government at all levels. This was, however, a question which was being already dealt with in the Ministry of Home Affairs as part of its immediate concern and responsibility. Nehru was perhaps unaware of it due obviously to what might be said to be a lack of coordination at the Cabinet level. The size of requirement for suitable personnel for an expanding economy formed part of the problem of recruitment by open competition itself. It was not an independent issue.

The rule of law and adherence to procedural provisions to ensure it were in fact two of the main features of British administration in India. Both were related to administrative morality which, in turn, it was believed, depended on the standard of intellectual competition for recruitment to the Indian Civil Service. This was a system of open competition introduced in 1855 in accordance with the recommendations of the Macaulay Committee. It replaced the earlier system of patronage under which the directors of the East India Company or their friends nominated their candidates for admission to the Haileybury College for training before being sent out to India as covenanted civil servants. Although the conditions of nomination to Haileybury were such that quality of the service was on the whole not allowed to suffer, the scope of selection remained limited and could not hope, for obvious reasons, to maintain the highest standards in the long run. It was the Macaulay Committee that exposed the inherent weakness of patronage and brought into focus the importance of a competitive system. It was made clear that the quality of an intellectual competition was closely related to the standards of morality in the public service and that if the Company was serious about getting rid of corruption by raising the moral standards of its public servants at superior levels, it could not be accomplished except by an open intellectual competition of the highest standard. The importance of this principle of recruitment was realized all the more when the covenanted service was changed into an all-India service by the Secretary of State, Lord Salisbury, in 1878. In the context of these earlier discussions and development on the subject, it was indeed surprising that Prime Minister Nehru should have, under ideological obsessions, chosen to suggest the inadequacy or weakness of the competitive system and recommend an early "selection" and prolonged training for "socialisation" on the model of the defence services. He perhaps did not care to realize that "selection" was comparable to "patronage" which, in a plural society like that of India, remained subject to greater misuse and corruption.

The non-party Interim Government of 1946 was naturally guided in the choice of a new all-India comparable service by the experiences of history, the functioning of the Indian Civil Service in terms of its both general administration and the administration of "special departments" demanding specialized knowledge. The Indian Administrative Service which emerged as the alternative in the form of a centrally-controlled all-India service was organized on the model of the ICS–an alternative which, it was believed, could alone ensure efficiency, impartiality and freedom from local and communal bias, party allegiance or political influence. It was in fact Sardar Patel, the Home Member, who stressed the importance of a politically free and non-committed administrative service which, on the pattern of the ICS, would put the Centre into close touch with the local realities, facilitate liaison between the Centre and the provinces, and ensure uniformity in the application of administrative norms and standards. Provincial administration, on the other hand, would on its part acquire a wider and integrated outlook by using the best material nationally available for higher posts. This was an objective which, as the Home Member reiterated, could by no means be achieved except by an administrative staff centrally recruited and controlled in a manner which might ensure security of service necessary for independence of conduct and advice.[13]

In the creation of the Indian Administrative Service which emerged in spite of the non-participation of the Provinces which later formed part of Pakistan, the Government of India was guided by a desire to build up an elitist cadre of civil servants. Like Sir Ashley Eden, C. P. V. Williams, Joint Secretary to the Government, actually used in the course of a Note the old term corps d'elite to describe the officers of the new service, who were to be recruited on the same model as the Indian Civil Service. The Centre was to be staffed by these officers. But if the Central Government was to draw its administrative officers from the provinces, as it must, it was necessary to provide for a common standard of acceptability at the Centre, which in turn implied a uniform system of recruitment, uniformity in pay, disciplinary provisions and other conditions of service. And these could not be secured except by the Federal Public Service Commission, an independent body designed to free this public service from political subservience to the party in power. Even the Central Government was not to interfere except in rare cases where a provincial government happened to reject the advice of the Commission. Like its predecessor, the new Service was to function as an administrative staff, separate and distinct from the political apparatus of the Government. The latter might come and go, but the former must go on for ever. Even Prime Minister Nehru's Note of May 14, 1949, as said above, could not alter the position of the service so created, in terms of both structure and function.

Dr. Ambedkar, the founding father of the Constitution of India, also recognized the validity of the principles under-lying the Indian Administrative Service so created in place of the Indian Civil Service. He described the new administrative service as of great strategic importance in that it was designed to man all superior posts, both normative and positive, and to maintain throughout the country a uniform standard of administrative efficiency and morality, both being necessary for natural integration. These were the principles which were duly incorporated into the Constitution of India itself.

It is true that the situation which followed the end of the Second World War, more especially the partition of the country on religious and communal grounds, witnessed in practice a sudden decline in the quality of officers. There were several reasons for it. This decline, for instance, proceeded from a large-scale recruitment required to make up the deficiency in the ICS cadre arising in the first place from the stoppage of recruitment during the war period and, secondly, from the termination by the Secretary of State of the Services of his officers. A large number of Muslim civil servants, on the other hand, joined Pakistan on the partition of India. A considerable number of war-service candidates were thus sought to be appointed to the newly created service. The fall of standards was equally attributable to emergency recruitment from the open market as well as from among temporary servicemen. It was even later decided to select those who had competed for the ICS between 1940 and 1943 but could not be selected because of the limited number of vacancies. Cumulatively, all these developments contributed to a decline in the quality of administrative officers.[14]

However, the soundness of the administrative system, which had over more than a century evolved, matured and passed the test of time in both structural and functional terms, could not summarily be questioned, soiled or sullied. Though geared primarily to law and order, it dealt in the early 1930s with the problems of currency and finance, banking and foreign trade. It was the requirement of special departments that led to the constitution of a Commerce and Finance Pool consisting, in the main, of ICS officers including members of certain other all-Indian services dealing with audit, accounts, customs and income-tax. The Pool contained a requisite number of promising ICS officers with the knowledge of specialized discipline and aptitude of mind. They were for some years after joining the Pool treated as probationers and then given assignments to equip themselves for higher responsibilities in their field of specialization. On being confirmed in the Pool, they were all treated alike independently of the service to which they initially belonged. Their promotion was determined by considerations of merit, not seniority. A select number of posts was therefore earmarked for them in the then departments of finance and commerce or in the offices working under those departments.

As L. K. Jha rightly points out, "the Pool, in the early years after independence, provided the personnel to fill some of the key posts in the economic field, including those in some newly created ministries, such as industry and food".[15] Jha, however, omits to mention that the principle which underlined the organization of the Finance and Commerce Pool had already been in operation. The proceedings and report of the Central Banking Inquiry Committee, which led finally to the establishment of the Reserve Bank of India in 1934, made it sufficiently clear that the problem raised by Jha had already received the attention of the Indian Industrial Commission, 1916. It started engaging the attention of the Government of India ever since then.[16]

In the post-independence period, recruitment to the pool, however, did not continue for long. It was discontinued because of the jealousies created, for its IAS members were assured of a permanent position at the Centre or in the Central Government, while others were obliged to return to their States after their tenure at the Centre was over.

As an Economic Adviser to the Government of India, however, he did not cease to hammer at the "need for building up a body of economic administrators, "though unlike the recruits of the Finance and Commerce Pool of the earlier years, his new proposed incumbents were supposed to satisfy the needs of both the Centre and the State Governments. His exclusive emphasis on the importance of economic administrators is an evidence of his thesis that they can function independently of the elected elements which, though found wanting in rationality, especially in a plural society, Weber rightly considered conceptually liked up necessarily with the bureaucracy, the rational or rule-bound part of public administration, including its economic or developmental side. This is clearly an error of judgement which Jha perhaps failed to realize for obvious reasons. His suggestions for reform in the "procedural field" of administration are, of course, useful, more especially in respect of the horizontal and vertical movement of files. His criticism of the personnel policy of the public sector management is also equally worthy of attention. Higher posts in the public sector should not generally be held by civil servants on deputation, more especially by those who cannot get promoted in their own cadres and remain biding their time till openings in their own fields become available.[17] But his reference to what he calls "duplication of the civil service culture"[18] is dubious, betraying a lack of historical perspective.

Jha has in fact failed to recognize that public administration, economic or otherwise, is an integrated concept. Its frontiers, though in general diffused, are, however, immediately and closely connected with society and politics. Organizationally, Weber identified this concept as based on hierarchy, status and rigidity to the adherence of rules, concerned mainly with the maintenance of law and order. The Weberism model was time and again held by some unsuited to the task of development calling for willingness to take risks and on-the-spot decisions without worrying about procedures, rules and regulations. But no organization worth the name can exist or function without rules or procedures. The Weberian model itself is not exclusive of the elective element, conceptually connected with bureaucratic analysis which though rule-bound is not impervious to considerations of politics. These can by no means be set aside in applying that model within the framework of its procedural rationality. In other words, in the context of India's plural society and her multi-dimensional politics, any attempt to go in for anti-Weberian model of administrative agency for policy implementation or debureaucratization would indeed be dangerous. It would mean an exercise of a degree of discretion by men in authority, making confusion worse confounded. Procedural complexities, it is true, do cause delay and obstruct progress. But the basic source of the evil is to be traced largely to the peculiar constitution of Indian society and politics rather than the Weberian model of bureaucracy.

In an interesting study in 1982 on *Bureaucratic Values in Development*[19]. R. B. Jain and P. N. Chaudhuri focus on the district level of administration in three different fields, two of these being concerned with developmental activities, while the third with non-developmental. The method of investigation used was empirical, conducted in the States of Punjab and Madhya Pradesh. In their attempt to distinguish between the developmental and the non-developmental tasks, like the collection of revenues or the maintenance of law and order, the authors were solely guided by their concern to compare the value system and approach of officials performing the different tasks assigned to them.

The mode of the inquiry so conducted, though empirical, reinforces the earlier analysis of the bureaucratic structure built up on the Weberian model in the course of more than a century before the transfer of power in 1947. The study has clearly demonstrated that the values imported by the colonial bureaucratic system in organizational terms do not necessarily obstruct the process of development. The authors have in fact confirmed that the agricultural and industrial progress that has taken place in Punjab since independence has been achieved through its hierarchical bureaucratic organization governed by a well-regulated system of rules prescribed for the discharge of industrial responsibilities on the principle of impersonality practised by the officers of the Government.

Another important finding that has emerged from the study of the joint authors is a continuing bureaucratic tradition of training officials to respect their political masters as well as observing a system of rules in order to maintain a high standard of administrative morality and integrity of character. This is a characteristic feature of bureaucratic behaviour which never acted as a stumbling-block in the way of development, in spite of its being a heritage of the pre-independence period. Their findings have in fact given no indication in support of the view that the non-observance of a rule or a compromise with one's integrity would accelerate the process of development.[20]

The study has actually made it abundantly clear that the pace of development is never accelerated by debureaucratization or by any resort to what might be described as an Anti-Weberian model of bureaucracy or instrument of policy implementation. What the result of inquiry strongly emphasized was that development depended on the capabilities of the administrator responsible for it. And as the district officer was invested with an overall charge and responsibility, the attainment of the goal in both developmental and non-developmental spheres was a function of the initiative and drive he was expected to command as the leader of entire civil administration under his charge. As the successor of the Indian Civil Service, the IAS officers were therefore put in charge of district administration.

Generalist v. Specialist Controversy in Administrative Reforms

Why was a generalist ICS officer alone considered best fitted for a position of control under British rule in India? This was not without reason. According to British tradition, an open and cultivated mind produced under the influence of a higher degree of free and liberal university education alone could ensure not only an integrity of character but also ability to unravel and understand the many-sidedness involved in a policy decision. Training in skill or specialized education where the emphasis laid was bound to be in its nature unilateral could not accomplish the ends of public administration which called for a multi-dimensional mind to disentangle the issues of a problem involved in it. The education required for the purpose was not to be confused with erudition or learning by rote. The object was to provide for intellectual education to promote knowledge and equip mind conceptually to understand men and affairs with detachment. These were attributes of character which British tradition stressed as necessary for controlling for purposes of an efficient and clean public administration. Key executive positions were therefore held invariably by members of the Indian Civil Service. Though Indian conditions at the time of transfer of power were not congenial ideally to fit in with the earlier standards of recruitment, the creation of the Indian Administrative Service in 1946 was in principle intended to follow the ICS model itself.

Surprisingly enough the Chairman of the Economic Administrative Reforms Commission, Mr. L. K. Jha, had, before the publication of the above study, made a futile suggestion in 1981 to break with the traditional methods of recruitment to the public services. His was an attempt to have a new specialized service for economic development created as an alternative to the existing administrative Service, although in his *Economic Strategy for the 80s,* published a year earlier, he had expressed himself in favour of a body of economic administrators, not by creating another service".[21]

In his Frank Moraes Memorial Lecture delivered in Madras, Jha called for a "radical departure from past traditions" in the methods of recruitment to the public services, including the Indian Administrative Service.[22] Under the arrangement which he suggested the competitive examinations were to be held after the plus-two course to pick up at a younger age "brighter students with higher promise" for government jobs. They were to continue their studies in "special institutions" for a three-year degree level course which would equip them for their duties in public service.

In the course of his lecture Jha took care to avoid any reference to specialization, but pointed out that the education imparted to students would be "of a kind relevant to public service in subjects like economics, politics, history, general sciences and languages". His proposed scheme further provided that after two years of such a course there would be a second examination. They were to be allocated to different services on the results of this second examination. Students were thereafter to be exposed to a greater degree of specialized training comparable somewhat to that given to probationers. It was argued that "most government jobs do need much more of specialized study and training than can be provided by the training they receive as probationers". And the Indian Administrative Service was no exception. Its courses of study, like those of an economic service, were thus sought to be so structured that they might be "capable of adoption by business and industry as well".[23] Obviously, this was a clever device to substitute, from the back door, the specialist for the generalist as an alternative administrative arrangement to accelerate the pace of economic development, an object naturally expected of a Chairman of the Economic Administrative Reforms Commission.

Little did Jha realize that the efficiency and integrity of an IAS officer were both a function of the political system with which he was linked up even conceptually, a system which could hardly ignore the plurality of the society in which it came to function, and the confused character of the country's developing economy which shaped the course of its policy directive. While democracy lent itself to a variety of religion and caste-based pressure groups in society which politicians encouraged in their own interest, the economy was sought to be divided into private and public sectors to satisfy the demand of mutually exclusive ideologies. Together, these developments not only caused confusion in policy-making, but rendered highly problematic the task of the bureaucracy, the IAS officers, who, unlike their predecessors under British rule, were shorn of all political functions of policy or decision-making. Political interference since independence became in fact an every-day experience for them. While resistance to political masters involved risks of disciplinary action, submission lent itself to the charge of corruption. This was the state of the dichotomy to which the bureaucracy became generally reduced on the transfer of power, especially since 1956 when the Coalition Cabinet made room for party rule. Jha happened to be altogether silent about the effect of politics on bureaucracy.

The *Financial Express* of December 4, 1981, described Jha's recommendations to break with past traditions as an attempt to establish "a new mandarinate", comparable to pedantic Chinese official bureaucracy intended to fit in with the requirements of development. His argument was that the irrelevant educational system of the country had given rise to what he called "qualitative imbalance" between the type of manpower supplied by our educational institutions and the type of skilled personnel required by our expanding economy. Jha proceeded to correct this imbalance by means of administrative reforms creating demands for skilled personnel, not by means of restricting education and training only in subjects relevant to public services, a thing which he could not do. He perhaps characterized the educational system as irrelevant because it imparted education to students even beyond the scope of the requirements of government.

His idea was not exactly new. As said above, Prime Minister Nehru had made in 1949 a comparable proposal for the education and training of younger students in socialization on the model of defence services. Like Jha's emphasis on development the educational purpose there, too, was specific and well defined but one-sided, though not vague or irrelevant. As regards the importance of competitive examinations as a principle of selection, Nehru gave due recognition to it. Even so, his note of May 14, 1949, was rejected outright by his Cabinet because the education and training proposed to be imparted to students in special defence institutions of the Government amounted to a denial of the benefits of an open liberal education which a university alone could provide and make available for purposes of an intellectual disciplining of mind, necessary for policy-making and understanding in higher positions of government.

Administrative Improvement Calling for Policy Change

There is in the country at present an all-round clamour for administrative reforms to correct what is generally described as bureaucratic maladies. It is true that bureaucrats holding positions of control at various levels of administration cannot altogether escape responsibility. They have much to answer for. But the important question is whether maladministration is all of their making, more especially when the right political environment for efficient functioning and the sound framework for a coherent and consistent policy formulation are both found more or less non-existent in a situation where the tendency is more and more towards centralization in development planning as well as administration in spite of the country's federal constitution providing against the concentration of wealth, opportunity and economic power.

This tendency towards centralization, which as seen before has been clearly discernible in the formulation of economic policy, is reflected in the development of a series of political crises concerning Centre-State relations in the past, the most being that of Punjab and Assam. I have studied this problem in some depth in my previous work on *The Indian Federal System*. It is quite enough for this analysis here to point out that the imbalance caused in these relations due to the dominance of a single Congress Party rule for more than a couple of decades is reflected in what is politically recognized as one of the ominous portents in constitutional terms. It calls for a change of policy on a decentralized principle first pointed out by the report of the Royal Commission on Decentralization (1909) and then by Sir John Simon, Chairman of the Indian Statutory Commission, who recommended a federal structure with a clear proviso laid down in the first volume of its report that federalism must remain subject to change, so that it may accommodate the varying demands of its units according to the nature and extent of their social and economic developments. This precisely is where the Congress has failed. Constitutional provisions apart, it remains a major task of the Civil Service at present and in the years ahead to so reorient administration as to restore as well as to ensure a viable federal balance.

The concentration of economic power in the hands of big business Houses is another important development which accounts for the growth of black money and corruption. As indicated before, its root cause has been narrow politics. A political solution which Parliament alone could and still can provide was and still is a must to remedy the growing evil. But it has taken hold of the country's political system itself and shaking it off seems to be more or less prohibitive. The only hope, however, is the administrative system which is still good, an organization capable of being sensitive to the needs of the common people because of the wider perspective and quality of education which the IAS officers generally command. What is needed for their better, greater performance is the security of their service and freedom from interference on extra-administrative and non-professional grounds. What the Civil Service needs is encouragement in the execution of a clear and well-defined political directive as well as a development programme with clear realizable and measurable targets, no utopia or grandiose social and economic schemes broadcast for political purposes to promote party interest.

No clarity of a political directive or a well-defined development programme in national interest that flows from it is perhaps possible in a state of growing complexity, and interdependence of a modern industrial society unless it is either based on class concept in economic terms or related to a mutually conceived and accepted compromise among major political parties functioning under a democratic constitutional set-up. Since both are absent in the Indian situation, there is no alternative to dependence on the integrity and ability of the Civil Servants who can not only take a long-term view of policy decisions but also have experience of their success or failure in operational terms. This is an approach to administrative reforms that applies equally to a situation where, as in India, there is, generally speaking, no cut-off point between policies controlled by politicians and administration carried on by the Civil Service. There is an interaction of ends and means, for both are involved in policy-making and problem-solving. By virtue of their education and experience, civil servants should not only be free to advise politicians, but they should in fact be encouraged to do so in national interest. The case of R. A. Gopalaswami, an officer on special duty in the Ministry of Home Affairs, who advised against the acceptance of Prime Minister Nehru's Note on certain proposals for administrative reforms, is a good example to illustrate the importance of the principle suggested.[24]

The absence of a cut-off point between the policy-making instrument of government and the policy-implementing agency of administration calls for a strict adherence to the Weberian model of national bureaucracy, for there is an active operational link between the appointed and the elected wings of administration. The Santhanam Committee, appointed in 1952, pointed out the dangers of corruption involved in this kind of relationship between the two wings unless Ministers were able to set the correct examples in moral and social spheres. Suggestions were therefore made to establish conventions, so that officials should not directly approach Ministers and Legislators for promotion, redressal of grievances or escape from disciplinary action.

The first phase of the post-independence period which covered nearly a decade till 1956, was, as said above, a period of Coalition Ministry at the Centre, known for both talent and character. Cases occurred in the States where even Ministers of Government were not allowed to escape punishment.[25] It was followed by new conditions in both economic and political terms. While spurt in the economic functions of the Government and the artificially created economy of shortage from the beginning of the Second Five Year Plan contributed to the growth of a new class of smugglers and black-marketeers, the dominance of the Congress Party rule in the country and the centralization that followed whetted the desires of political leaders to whittle the ICS and its successor service, IAS, down to size. It was not only the impregnability of the Civil Service that was affected by the rise of big business Houses in spite of the policy resolution of 1956. The new developments "prevented a rise in the status and emoluments of the entire techno-managerial classes in the country, promoted a brain drain and hastened the deprofessionalization of the existing members of this class by making them increasingly dependent on "perks" given by their employers and on bribes.[26] The problem of administrative reforms at present is in fact how best to raise the real income and importance of the public services to the level of what prevailed before 1957, the beginning of the Second Five Year Plan. No perquisites can resolve the problem except a radical change of policy.

The Industrial Policy Resolution of 1956 was geared to the promotion of the public sector. But, as seen in earlier chapters, the economy remained weighted on the size of the private sector which favoured a curb on imports. The inflationary pressures and the resulting forces of corruption released by the economy of shortage were reflected seriously in the functioning of the political system. It has become customary now for political leaders to make use of musclemen to capture booths and to coerce voters into endorsing the candidate who hired them. Attempts are also being made to search out officials or men in authority who might be of help to him in return for a quick promotion or other benefits. This is not altogether a new trend. It proceeded from the use of black money for election purposes. The cases of Swaraj Paul and others who had helped the Congress(I) in the general elections of 1977 are very much on record.

The only hope that still exists is some standard of efficiency and administrative morality of the IAS and, to an extent, of members of the IPS who keep under check and curb the forces of corruption and disorder. Both of these attributes of the public service have since independence been affected qualitatively; and this in no small degree proceeded from the misuse of ministerial powers of transfer and posting, producing a demoralizing effect. Its general tendency was in fact to cause pliancy in administrative behaviour, highly prejudicial to independence of judgement and impersonality of public conduct. Cases were not found wanting of public servants being allowed to stay on far beyond the permissible limits of their tenure or frequently transferred from one station to another to suit the convenience and interest of Ministers or Legislators. No ICS officer under British rule would ever have imagined such a thing to happen against the principles of tenure appointment.

Realizing the dangerous implications of a steady decline in the efficiency and moral strength of the IAS and the allied services, the Prime Minister, as part of the Congress Centenary celebrations session in Bombay, was obliged to make a new policy declaration to boost the moral fibre of the bureaucracy by a promise to restructure the organization so as to restore its vigour by means of regulating transfers and postings as well as by other steps on a principle independent of political consideration or ministerial interest.

Under the new scheme[27] of administrative reforms, State Governments are to ensure that a District Officer has a minimum of two to three years of tenure and is not to be transferred under any political pressure; for numerous complaints are made on the ground that a Collector was transferred before he could even know the topography of his district.

Indeed, this scheme was prepared by the Personnel and Administrative Reforms Ministry of the Government of India, directly at the instance of the Prime Minister who perhaps took lessons from his experience of Punjab and Asam. It envisaged specialization by the fresh IAS recruits not only in the course of probation but also in the several positions assigned to them in the first 11 years of their service. Emphasis on adherence to the principle of tenure proceeds in fact from the importance of acquiring specialized experience in different positions. It has thus been laid down that a freshly appointed IAS officer is not to have more than three postings in the initial 11 years of his service including two years of his probationary period. These postings are to be in field regulatory departments like home, law enforcement organization, general administration and welfare departments, education, health and family welfare. The officers so posted are supposed also to acquire, through training courses, a reasonable experience in matters dealing with finance, commerce and industry.

To ensure adherence to the principles of tenure posting, the system of confidential reports is sought to be changed. Instead of these reports being written by the superior officers of all categories of public servants, provision is made to have the job done on the principle of their "data-based performance". The object is to see that an officer's title to promotion is not prejudiced by an exercise of discretion by his superior boss but remains subject to his performance in the area assigned to him either in the field of development or of general administration geared to law and order.

The Ministry of Personnel and Administrative Reforms had laid stress on the importance of refresher courses in view of the good results that followed the introduction by way of an experiment of one-week refresher courses for IAS officers by the Ministry. A projected four-week training course is therefore expected to show better results. It is believed that in the course of these four weeks there would be an interaction between senior and junior officers, an interaction which would necessarily expose them to new ideas for the improvement of administration.

The Government of India is in fact so serious about the refresher course that even its most senior officers are not expected to be spared. Since the idea is to see that junior officers are benefited by the experience of the senior members of the public service, even the Cabinet Secretary of the Union Government is to be obliged to undergo the inconveniences of a four-week refresher course, where the subjects proposed to be covered include computer training, behaviour training, financial management as well as management in the sphere of water and power.

Among the measures in the direction of administrative reforms, positive steps have already been taken for reducing delays and cutting red tape. Old manuals going back to the 19th century under British rule are, for instance, being revised and updated. It is laid down that a file, unless it is very important, need not go to the Secretary or to the Minister's level. An officer of Deputy Secretary's rank has been given powers to deal with files relating to ordinary matters. Administrative tribunals have in addition been set up to deal with cases which had earlier to go to High Courts for adjudication in an appellate jurisdiction. Thousands of such cases are being withdrawn from High Courts and settled administratively without any prejudice to the powers of those courts.

Delay Still Causing Administrative Malaise

Delay remains, however, a really difficult problem to deal with. It not only impedes the progress of developmental undertakings, but lends itself to corruption in the form of what the Santhanam Committee of 1962 described as "speed money" payable for expedition in the horizontal and vertical movement of files in all offices. It is not that the controlling officers are not aware of what happens around them. But they remain either unconcerned or cannot help it.

On June 22, 1984, Prime Minister Indira Gandhi, who also knew the implications of delay, directed the Cabinet Secretary to work out a system by which "single-window clearance" could be effected in all matters where the Government had to deal with the public, including industrialists concerned with investment proposals.

The directive so issued was the result of a meeting the Prime Minister had with 42 Secretaries of the Union Government.[28] She told them that in the working of the Government there was a lack of coordination between various Ministries as well as within the Ministries themselves. In the absence of this coordination, the people had to go from one place to another and from one person to another several times to get a clearance. This was a state of administrative malaise proceeding from delay in the transaction of public business. It was true of industrial investment proposals received from resident as well as non-resident Indians. In the course of her meeting with Secretaries she laid stress on the delays occurring in various stages and pointed out that these had been a major factor in cost escalation, especially in the public sector. She drove it home by quoting the private comments of Japanese and U.S. entrepreneurs that what was done in a day in other countries was done in a month in India. She urged the Secretaries therefore to streamline administrative procedures so as to expedite decisions.

Mrs. Gandhi admitted that civil servants had a key role to play in the implementation of government policies as well as in the preservation of the country's unity and integrity. She, however, deplored that the original formula of 50 per cent of civil servants coming from outside a State had become considerably diluted and that the proportion of outsiders had come down substantially. In some States, outsiders were even being removed from key positions. The object of the original formula of 50 per cent of a State's IAS cadre being from another State was consequently defeated. It tended to be monopolized by what came to be known as the sons of the soil, who could not be insulated from undue local influence or pressure. It not only signified corruption but a loss of efficiency lending itself to delay in the execution of a task assigned. For when top officials got stuck in a State for too long a period, they tended to develop vested interest, particularly when they happened to belong to that State. This has been the general tendency responsible for the erosion of the basic all-India character of the IAS. The result has been that Chief Ministers and even Ministers have managed to have their favourites among civil servants and the rapport between Ministers and officials has come to be developed on a personal and extra-bureaucratic consideration, a deprofessionalized trend that breeds corruption and causes delay from a relaxation of accountability.

There is a wrong belief in some circles that it is the Weberian model of rule-bound bureaucracy which accounts for delay; for files, under the centralized rules of administrative business, have necessarily to move both horizontally and vertically before they are cleared and decisions made. This contention has been met in an article on "Evolution of the concept of administrative accountability" published recently in a special number of the *Indian Journal of Public Administration*. I have in a historical context dealt with the conceptual implications of administrative accountability to law and law-based rules, both substantive and procedural– a development intended to reduce the area of discretion as a means to make relief and justice available against the arbitrary proceedings of men in authority or those having power and influence in society. This was the concept of a rule of law as opposed to custom which recognized status. It was a sound principle of modernization. But the trouble was that while the rule-of-law concept had emerged as a function of educational and economic growth in the West, the exigencies of a colonial situation in India, as the article shows, called for the induction of that modern principle in a society which for the most was still governed by custom and influenced by traditional values and social relationships. It is wrong therefore to find fault with the rules designed to act as a leveller in social and cultural terms. The fault lies with the culturally underdeveloped state of the bulk of human agencies employed in the implementation of an administrative principle of rule that remains still unrecognized by the status-bound Indian society as a whole, more especially by those who control the lever of political power and exercise ruling influence in the formulation of socio-economic policies. The actual controllers of the administrative machine, not the machine itself, are to be blamed.

Need for Stress on Policy Clarity and Implementation

It is true that the State-controlled expansion of economic functions is bound to cause some delay because of an increase in the organizational hierarchies involved in their actual implementation. Even so, delay proceeds more from an absence of clarity in policy matters than the so-called rules governing the functioning of hierarchies or the movement of files, horizontal or vertical. On socialism, for example, the Indian National Congress passed a resolution in its favour at Karachi in 1931, a resolution which remained unnoticed until it was revived at Avadi in 1955. The emphasis put on the economy of the public sector as part of a policy of State enterprise under the Industrial Policy Resolution of 1956 was, doubtless, a step forward in the direction of State socialism. But since the economy remained nonetheless heavily weighted on the side of the private sector, socialism remained a daydream and the alleviation of poverty a distant goal. In spite of the Constitution's Directive Principles of State Policy, the concentration of economic power went on merrily in favour of big business Houses. The policy statement of the Government of India made in July 1980 came in the form of an assurance that there would be "no deviation from 1956 Industrial Policy Resolution".[29] But the concessions extended to big business as part of this very policy statement were a clear negation of that assurance. The policy statement of V. P. Singh, the successor of Pranab Mukherjee in the Ministry of Finance, who announced in December 1985 his long-term fiscal concessions to Indian industrialists, is no more than a continuity of the earlier industrial policy which had said one thing in 1956 to emphasize the importance of the public sector but did something else. It proceeded to benefit the private sector for financial gains to ensure electoral advantages. In a state of uncertainty or divided opinions on strategic policy issues no administration could function with speed and clarity of conviction. Implementation was never sought to be related to declared policy objectives.

The policy-performance of the post-independence period is perhaps reminiscent of the wild promises which the Indian political parties were in the habit of making to win popular support against a foreign Imperialist Government. There promises were, however, no policies which called for an appreciation or recognition of realities applicable to a given situation. The widespread illiteracy among the mass of the people was another handicap which acted against nationalist declarations being invested with policy content; for the existence of a foreign British rule in the country had made them easily prone to identify national politics with national policies. The old tradition of politics being understood as policy naturally continued under the glamour of a promise for socialism which the Industrial Policy Resolution of 1956 claimed to evince by its declared emphasis on the economy of the public sector. What lay in store for the common people was, however, the economy of shortage which, as said above, brought in its train the evils of inflation and black money, proceeding from a union of big business and politics.

The growth of black money and Prime Minister Indira Gandhi's all-out support for Swaraj Paul, an ill-reputed industrialist and proprietor of the London-based Caparo group of companies involved in the purchase of all the shares of Escorts with the help of the LIC money, has already been discussed in the preceding chapter. It was a case of corruption where Indian black money was believed to have been laundered back into Indian business through Non-Resident Indian (NRI) agencies. And, surprisingly enough, it was being done with the political backing of the Prime Minister and the financial resources of the LIC, a publicly-owned corporation, which pressed for a requisition meeting to secure the removal of nine of the directors of Escorts. The Bombay High Court, however, intervened. The projected removals were restrained. And although the Supreme Court on appeal reviewed the judgement of the Bombay High Court,[30] Swaraj Paul's financial relations with Mrs. Gandhi and the manner in which the Reserve Bank of India manoeuvred the whole thing under the Foreign Exchange Regulation Act (FERA) created a cloud of suspicion which would need to be cleared at the bar of public opinion, that history alone can unravel in due course. The general impression created by the entire development, as said above, was in support of the view held by the Bombay High Court.

No Alternative to Bureaucracy as Policy-Implementing Agency

The organization of modern government and bureaucracy in India, as we know, proceeded originally in the context of British colonial situation which called for a system of administration informed by Western ideas and institutions, for no European would ever agree to submit to oriental norms and practices. The Western institutions were, doubtless, adapted to local conditions. But it was done not with a view to assimilation, but implementation and imposition. Though socially peripheral, its effect in terms of political and administrative penetration was quite sustained and even conducive to a renaissance in urban centres. Structurally, the bureaucratic set-up introduced and developed under British rule thus continued in spite of the change made in the political complexion of the State in 1947. The Indian Administrative Service, which succeeded the ICS, constituted the top layer of the bureaucracy as before.

Considered conceptually or in realistic terms, this bureaucratic continuity was inevitable. It was in keeping with the Weberian concept of organizational sociology, a concept which applied essentially to all modern organizations, independently of whether they were social, economic or political. Weber in fact held that bureaucracy was an integral part of every planned and organized group activity called administration, and that it was not restricted to any particular system, colonial or capitalist, socialist or communist. It formed as much a part of scientific, technological or even religious organizations as of what is called general civil administration. It would not in fact be possible to do away with bureaucracy in the transaction of human business in any organized field of activity. Its inevitability is universally recognized. Weber's "ideal type", which was conceptually rational or rule-bound, applied especially to administration both normative and positive in functional terms. The Indian Administrative Service which forms an integral part of such administration has necessarily to remain bound by considerations of established legal norms and rules, independently of its functions being either coercive or developmental in nature.

The role of bureaucracy as an instrument of economic development was discussed at length in 1982 at an important seminar sponsored by the Leslie Sawhney Programme. It was observed that in terms of development, both national and international, bureaucracy had proliferated like a huge banyan tree. But "neither the standards laid down by the Chinese Mandarinism nor the reforms suggested by the British Fulton Committee or the voluminous recommendations of the Indian Administrative Reforms Commission could improve its role in the sphere of economic development at the national and international levels". Those who participated in the seminar included professional bureaucrats, management men and economic experts. They expressed unhappiness over the functioning of the bureaucracy in the State-dominated economy, more especially in the Indian context which has given rise to a new class vested interest in "the bureaucrats, politicians, businessmen and trade union leaders".[31] Together, they were described as constituting in a bourgeois centralized set-up a "grand alliance" contributing to the escalation of cost without the community as a whole being in any way benefited by the public sector economy. What, however, was the remedy? The seminar had no answer except to admit that bureaucracy "is inevitable. Reforming it, then, is the solution". But how to reform it? Laying down rules of conduct or reducing the area of discretion by individuals and vesting the same in boards of control are not new. Even decentralization fails to work. Bureaucracy is therefore the only way out. Equipped with skill and administrative experience as well as placed in between the people and their elected representatives in a political democracy, bureaucrats alone can deliver the goods, for they alone have the power to punish or reward according to the performance of men entrusted with the task of development. As the basic motivation of private enterprise was profit, considerations of defence and public welfare left hardly any alternative to a resort to State enterprise or action which could not but rely on its own bureaucracy as its policy-implementing agency.

This view on bureaucracy and development is fully supported historically as borne out by three of my earlier works, namely, *The Indian Middle Classes, The Administrative History of India, 1834-1947*, and *The Bureaucracy in India.* In a colonial situation where a foreign Imperial Government suffered from certain innate constraints in social and cultural terms, it was the highly educated bureaucracy of the covenanted service that Macaulay reconstituted on a competitive principle to act as an instrument of social change through the operation of judicial institutions and the implementation of Macaulay's educational policy. Lord Curzon's initiative to modernize agriculture and relate it to the country's industrial economy was a contribution of the bureaucracy, which is not unknown to history. The economic policy statement of 1945, which led to the Industrial Policy Resolutions of 1948 and 1956, was obviously the work of bureaucracy who did change in response to the call of times, but changed within the framework of law and constitution, an essential condition for political stability.

Though lacking in a historical perspective, the empirical study which V. A. Pai Panandikar and S. S. Kshirsagar published in 1978 on the subject of *Bureaucracy and Development Administration* is really useful and trustworthy. For the application of an alternative methodology of research has made no difference in so far as conclusions are concerned. In any State action, there can in fact be no two opinions about the inevitability of bureaucracy as its only administrative agency. The question of reforming in terms of structure and management has never been in doubt. Indeed, it has been a continuing process. But no reform can succeed if its security in a wider and cumulative sense is sought to be weakened, more especially in a plural society, unevenly organized and treated, where the top layers of bureaucracy are the only hope for redress or relief. The sources of their security are not only salary and emolument, but also prestige and impregnability.

Separation of Politics from Administration Main Problem of Reform

The Indian Administrative Service which inherited the ICS tradition was known for its independence of judgement and freedom from politics. It functioned within the framework of the Weberian model of bureaucracy, which emphasized political neutrality as an integral part of the rules governing its professional conduct. This was an old tradition which, as said before, encouraged a civil servant to express himself freely even against the views of Prime Minister Nehru who also recognized the independence of bureaucratic advance. His Cabinet, a mixed body of talents up to 1956, acted on this principle and accepted the comments of the Secretary to Government who had been highly critical of the Prime Minister's projected plan of recruitment, oriented ideologically in favour of a particular political principle, and a course of training comparable to that of defence personnel.

The Government of India became subject to party rule of the Congress after 1956. But the old tradition continued without much perceptible change until 1966. Noticeable changes, however, started appearing under Mrs. Gandhi who was known for indulgence in politics more than anybody else. Politically, the subservience of the State leadership to New Delhi became a regular feature in the appointment and dismissal of Chief Ministers. It was a clear case of erosion of federalism. There was a general tendency on the part of politicians to establish their superiority by an attempt to whittle down administrators to size and humiliate them. Pliancy in administrative behaviour began to be recognized as more paying than uprightness of conduct. In a comment through the columns of *The Statesman* it was thus pointed out that the civil servants, in the 1972-82 decade, had been "faced with the unenviable task of pandering to the whims of Ministers and serving as accomplices in their murky manipulations, while pretending that administrative integrity remained strong as ever".[32]

Under the influence of politics the Indian Administrative Service was thus being subjected to a process of deprofessionalization–a process which has not yet stopped. It is, on the contrary, escalating. It was in these circumstances that Mr. A. V. S. Reddy, a senior IAS officer of the Andhra Pradesh cadre, judged the mood of his fellow officers correctly in launching a diatribe against political leaders who sought to denigrate civil servants. Ignoring the time-honoured conduct rules, he chose to go much further than the IAS officers who preceded him in registering protest. He not only expressed bitterness against the subservient attitude of some of his colleagues but also censored the conduct of his State leadership for being subservient to New Delhi in the appointment or removal of Chief Ministers. Independently of the rules governing official conduct, he reached beyond a limit against the arrogance of politicians by a decision to launch a movement called "Bharat Desam" and start a newspaper to act as its mouthpiece. The infiltration of politics into administration had thus caused distortion in the bureaucratic structure of the Weberian model envisaging a distinction between its appointed and elected links in functional terms.

If a handful of IAS officers willingly obliged politicians and benefited, the majority of them, it was believed, cooperated out of fear and with a sense of resentment that invariably went with it. Reddy's argument was that in playing into the hands of politicians the IAS officers merely weakened their own position more and more until a point would be reached where they would even find themselves utterly ineffective and bereft of any semblance of authority.

An organized resistance to undue political pressure alone could be the best remedy to the administrative malaise that hinders progress. There are cases where individual officers acted on the strength of their moral conviction. P. S. Appu, for instance, fought a running battle with the Union Home Ministry on a controversy over an IAS probationer. A. K. Chatterjee was another officer who declined promotion in protest against the "utterly subservient role and the insignificant authority" to which IAS officers in Bihar had been reduced.[33] Their action, even if unwillingly taken, had set in motion a process which could have a far-reaching consequence if only the IAS (Central) Association had taken care to have branches established on a firm footing in each of the States to make sure that the security and impregnability of the Administrative Service are in no way eroded in the interest of the country's over-all security and the stability of its entire political system. For the firmness shown even by certain individual officers within the framework of conduct rules did not go in vain. For the first time, IAS officers' associations openly criticized "arbitrary transfers" and denial of their right to provide "free and fearless advice" in their capacity as public servants. A disciplined and coordinated protest against the undue pressure of politics on administrators can alone provide the remedy.

REFERENCES

1. See A. M. Henderson and T. Parsons (tr.), 1.
2. See Harold. D. Lasswell and A. Kaplan, *Power and Society: A Framework of Political Industry*, pp.205-6, 209-10.
3. See Misra, *The Bureaucracy in India: An Historical Analysis of Development up to 1947*, p.28.
4. See Report of the Royal (Islington) Commission (1916), CD 8382, Vol. 1, Chapter III on Organization, p. 403.
5. See Misra, *The Indian Middle Classes*, p.301.
6. Home (Establishment) A Progs., June 1904, Nos. 94-104, p.111.
7. See I.O. Parl. Papers, No. 57 (167) of 1905-6, p.187.
8. See *Report*, Vol. 1, p.404.
9. See Govt. of India, Dept. of Commerce and Industry, A Progs. (Conf.) Nos. 1 to 31, May 1917, Appointment of a Commission to examine and report upon the possibilities of further industrial development in India; Ibid. A Progs. (Conf. Simla Records 9) Nos. 7-22, June 1919, Views of the Govt. of India on the main principles on which the most important recommendations of the Indian Industrial Commission depend; Ibid. Progs. July 1919, No. 15. These are all important files dealing with Indian industrial policies in a historical perspective.
10. See my article on "Evolution of the Office of Collector" in the *Journal of the Indian Institute of Public Administration,* July-December 1905; also my *District Administration and Rural Development in India.*
11. M.H.A. File No. 20/21/49-GS, 1949, No.1, p.1 (Notes).
12. Ibid., p. 13-14.
13. See Home Dept. File No. 32/46-Ests. (R), Minutes of the Conference held on Oct. 21, 1946.
14. See Misra, *The Bureaucracy in India*, p. 306.
15. L. K. Jha, *Economic Strategy for the 80s,* p.17.
16. See some of the earlier Confidential Files of Govt. of India, Dept. of Com. and Ind,. A. Progs., May 1917, Nos. 1 to 31 A. Progs., June 1919, Nos. 7-22.
17. See L. K. Jha, op. cit., chapter II, on the Management Machine.
18. Ibid., p. 36.

19. Uppal Publishing House, New Delhi.
20. See *Business Standard,* June 22, 1983, containing a review of the study by Tridib Chakroborti.
21. L. K. Jha, op. cit., p.17.
22. See *Financial Express*, Dec. 1, 1981.
23. Ibid., Dec. 1, 1981.
24. See M.H.A. File No. 20/21/49-GS,1949, No. 1, p. 1 (Notes).
25. See B. B. Misra, *Government and Bureaucracy in India 1947-76*, Chapter VI on Standards of Administrative Morality.
26. See *Times of India*, May 14, 1984, Prem Shankar Jha on Why Nothing Works.
27. See *Searchlight*, January 13, 1986 (Patna).
28. See *Financial Express*, June 23, 1984.
29. See *Economic Times*, July 24, 1980.
30. See *The Indian Nation*, Patna, December 20, 1985.
31. See *The Statesman*, Oct. 19, 1982 (Bureaucrats and Development, a review of *Accountability in Development: National and International*, Leslie Sawhney Programme, Vikas Publishing House, New Delhi).
32. *The Statesman*, Oct. 18, 1982 (In the Public Interest).
33. Ibid.

SEVEN

Some Conclusions

For a couple of decades after its foundation in 1885, the Indian National Congress remained an elitist movement. It consisted of a class of Western educated men of learning and wealth whom Macaulay had in his minute of February 2, 1835, conceived originally as a class of persons Indian in blood and colour, but English in taste, in opinions, in morals and in intellect.[1]

In his educational despatch of July 19, 1854, Macaulay's ideas were further stressed by Sir Charles Wood, President of the Board of Control, who viewed the creation of such a class as highly important in terms of the development of India's resources and her increasing demand for the consumption of British goods. It was argued that the advancement of European knowledge will teach the natives of India the marvellous results of the employment of labour and capital, rouse them to emulate us (British) in the development of the vast resources of their country, guide them in their efforts and gradually, but certainly, confer upon them all the advantages which accompany the healthy increase of wealth and commerce; and, at the same time, secure to us a large and more certain supply of many articles necessary for our manufacturers and extensively consumed by all classes in our population, as well as an almost inexhaustible demand for the produce of British labour.

As already discussed earlier, this chapter seeks in fact to show that the projected Indian elite and business were considered to be two of the main pillars of the British colonial system of government and economy which had started gaining in importance ever since 1834 when the monopoly rights of the East India Company were abolished and the principles of laissez-faire introduced for the first time. It was believed that while the elitist element would contribute to increasing demands for the import of British manufactures arising under Western influence from an expected change in the country's old and tradition-bound pattern of dress and consumption, the Indian business might provide incentives to the development of India's internal resources to pay for the imports and conduce to the prosperity necessary for the purchase and consumption of foreign goods.

However, since the plantation industry and foreign trade remained for that part in the hands of the colonizers, the Indian elite and business could not but function as separate, and distinct entities, although both formed part of the Congress as a national political organization established in 1885. As an essentially elitist body, it was interested initially in advancing the case of educated Indians for appointment to the superior civil service of the country. In fact, it was not until the First World War period of 1914-18, which saw the emergence of the entrepreneurial element as a competitive capitalist force, that a shift of emphasis in Congress policy became clearly noticeable in the context of the Bolshevik Revolution of 1917. During 1885-1920, it remained more or less an elitist national movement although its movement-party dichotomy could not but bring to the surface from time to time its elitist bourgeois class character.

In the first couple of decades since its foundation, there existed in fact an identity of interest between the leaders of the Congress and the British Government in India. While the former wanted an official recognition for rise in the social scale, the latter wanted a non-official organization to serve as a safety-valve or barometer of public opinion, a popular link under an imperialist bureaucracy. Even a highly imperialist and conservative Viceroy like Lord Curzon regarded the Congress as a body of collaborators and appointed, as a Bombay High Court judge, N. G. Chandravarkar who had been president of the Lahore session of the Congress held in 1900.

The rise of Indian entrepreneurs as a competitive capitalist force in the course of the First World War and the Bolshevik Revolution of 1917 ushered in a new era in the modern history of India–an era highly significant in both economic and political terms. It was at the Industrial Conference of 1915 that Dorabji Tata, the leading industrialist of India, announced for the first time the determination of Indian business to "yoke together" politics and industry in order to force the Government of India locally to organize the production of everything needed for defence as well as for making the country even otherwise self-reliant economically. This announcement not only marked a direct link between the elitist Congress and the country's business enterprise, but also led the Government to adopt measures calculated to satisfy the demands of the national economy. The immediate result was the appointment of the first Industrial Commission to report on the expediency of government participation in industrial development within the framework of laissez-faire.

It was difficult to arrange for the import of machinery and skill during the war. But the introduction of provisional autonomy with commerce and industry as part of the transferred subjects, the appointment of a Fiscal Commission in 1921 to review the tariff structure in keeping with the principle of imperial preference, and the establishment of a Tariff Board in 1923 to administer the policy of protection recommended by the Fiscal Commission were some of the important steps taken to promote India's industrial development without setting aside the structure of free trade that kept in view a solemn regard for imperial preference in case of disputed interest.

Imperialism was thus forced to compromise and come to terms with Indian capitalism, though only half-way: the basic reason was not only the weakness of the capitalist system and its crises precipitated by the First World War, but more especially the victory of the alternative socialist system which the Bolshevik Revolution of 1917 seemed to have reflected. The policy of State participation to promote industrialization in the Indian situation, which the Industrial Commission had been forced to recommend, was obviously a form of socialistic principle inducted within the framework of laissez-faire. It was a device to save the basic structure of the imperio-capitalist system by means of a compromise to provide for the protection of Indian industries consistently with the security of imperial interest.

The Russian Revolution nontheless left its mark on Indian politics, which developed a left wing with determination to fight not only imperialism, but also indigenous capitalism. It was the leftist force in national politics that intensified the country's anti-imperialist struggle for *Purna Swaraj* or independence, considered beneficial to all classes and conditions of the people. But so far as the goal of that independence was concerned, there was no unity of purpose, although a vague use of socialism was generally recognized as a popular and attractive slogan.

It was this vagueness of an undefined goal of politics that was found politically paying to the Congress, though actually responsible for its policy-performance gaps. Its Karachi resolution on socialism passed in 1931 in a state of economic depression naturally caused no concern to native business, the financial sources for the Congress engaged in a fight with the Imperial Government for an exchange control of foreign trade. The Indian entrepreneurs in fact knew that socialism in the local context did not go beyond State participation in such economic activities as did not promise a profitable return.

In the given context of imperialist presence in India and the rising popular sentiment in favour of a revolutionary Bolshevik ideology, the policy of the Congress leadership was to cast the real weight of its political influence on the side of the business enterprise with an open and declared support for the removal of poverty on the scope of philanthropy inherent in the Gandhian interpretation of socialism. This is clear from the papers available in the archives of the Federation of Indian Chambers of Commerce and Industry referred to in Chapter II. It was an attempt to remain "yoked" together with big business without showing any disrespect to Leftist forces.

Though obviously based on self-deception this pattern of the Congress policy was not without its own compulsion. As pointed out earlier, it proceeded from its movement-party dichotomy. While the declared object of its movement was to wrest power from Britain in the interest of all classes and conditions of the Indian people, the object of the Congress Party was to make sure that the power when so wrested remained in the hands of its vested interests, more especially of big business, political and professinal elites.

It appears from the researches based on the original papers of the Federation of Indian Chambers of Commerce and Industry that in the formulation of their political policies even the top leaders of the Congress, including M. K. Gandhi, were guided by G. D. Birla who dominated the Federation as its President. However, the Leftist forces, which had emanated in the wake of the First World War and gained in strength during the Great Depression of the early 1930s, did not fade out. They continued in spite of the Congress alliance with the leaders of industries and kept on pressing for land reforms as well as public control over private enterprise.

In a situation where the task of policy-making had to take into account not only the question of capital *versus* labour but also of national *versus* imperial interests, there was bound to be a prolonged period of political unrest preventing economic issues from being examined on their own merits. Whatever the Congress motive force involved in its non-cooperation and civil disobedience movements directed against the British rule, it certainly delayed India's industrial development on the lines of modern technology and equipment. The average paid-up capital of joint-stock companies showed a downward trend towards the 1930s. The British who had the bulk of capital and skill were being obliged to think in terms of withdrawal rather than any extension of their business. The Indian capitalists who had just been emerging as an independent industrial force were being pestered to reckon with socialism. The result was that the earlier favourable trend of economic development received a positive setback. For instance, the value of imports of machinery and other capital goods, which had by 1921 reached a total of over Rs. 53 crores, fell to nearly Rs.10 crores in 1929-30. In spite of an improvement in trade depression which had just begun, in 1929-30, the import of capital goods did not go beyond Rs.19 crores in 1938. It was only in 1948-49, when the politics of the country had become fully stabilized, that this figure rose to Rs. 78 crores.

Conditions of political insecurity were also reflected in the repatriation of foreign capital, its amount being especially heavy in the 1930s, the year of civil disobedience and political uncertainty. The amount repatriated immediately after independence showed a considerable decline, according to a statement made on June 16, 1952, by C. D. Deshmukh, then Minister of Finance.

In spite of the periodical set-backs attributable to political disturbances, the alliance of business and politics enabled Indian capitalism to emerge as an independent industrial force in the course of the Second World War which afforded extended opportunity for the expansion of Indian manufacturers to meet the exigencies of defence. Apart from textiles, iron and steel, these manufactures included, according to a Government report, hydrogenated oil, transport and electrical equipments, machine tools, basic chemicals, power, alcohol, synthetic resins, plastic, etc., which had until then been almost non-existent in the country. This industrial trend towards the extension of the range of Indian business activities imparted to Indian capitalists a status in no way inferior to foreign establishments. They rose to a position where they could compete with British firms on terms of equality.

The Second World War was of course an important immediate factor in raising the Indian economy to a position of independence by a necessary resort to constraints on imports locally to facilitate war supplies. But there were other factors which were not unrelated to the growth in the national economy. The proceedings of the Tariff Board, for instance, make it clear that even within the framework of imperial preference Indian industries kept on growing till 1939 when the war broke out and made local supplies a matter of compulsion. The entry of the United States into the war as part of a multinational corporate entity was another such factor. It helped Britain to win the anti-fascist war, but did so as a sympathizer of Indian independence which in practice meant a positive collaboration with the growth of Indian industries. The functioning of the U.S. and other collaborators on the Indian soil, naturally, affected the monopoly trade rights of Britain and her political hold over India. Indeed, Britain's exclusive hold over the Centre had already been compromised and the powers of the Provincial Governments under Indian Ministers increased as federal units under the Government of India Act, 1935. The outbreak of the war in 1939, the non-cooperation of the Congress Ministries and the Congress "Quit India" movement of 1942 were all developments which had made British position in India politically untenable.

Even so, Britain did not lose control over the political nerves. Important developments took place in the course of the war itself, in

1944, which saw the establishment of the International Monetary Fund and the World Bank, intended to come to the aid of the capitalist order of society and save it from its financial crisis. It was in 1944 that the leaders of Indian industries submitted a plan of their own called the Bombay Plan. It emphasized the importance of raising the level of production as the only way to increasing employment.

The third development, however, was a "People's Plan" presented by the industrial workers to the Reconstruction Committee of the Council in 1944 itself. As it had been initially submitted to the Finance Department of the Government of India, it could not be considered by the Department of Planning and Development simultaneously with the Bombay Plan of Tata, Birla and some other industrialists whose exclusive emphasis on raising production as the only answer to economic ills had been declared as unacceptable to the Government.

The People's Plan, on the other hand, was found to have been based on certain impracticable and unfounded economic and financial assumptions. There was no difference of opinion when the Plan stressed that the fundamental problem of the Indian economic life is stated to be the problem of poverty. But differences arose when it was assumed that it could not be solved "on the basis of capitalist mode of production". In other words, a distinction was sought to be made between production for use and production for exchange, which meant an emphasis on profit. It was assessed that increased production alone was no remedy unless it was accompanied by equitable distribution to prevent concentration of wealth. The Department of Planning and Development had doubtless objections on economic and financial grounds. But the emphasis laid by the People's Plan on the importance of State control and nationalized undertakings could not altogether be ignored. It left its mark on the industrial policy which soon followed in an official statement made in 1945 to enable the Government of India to bring under its direct control all such industries as were considered important in terms of public interest, more especially of defence.

The statement issued in April 1945 explained the reasons for a State take-over of certain basic industries in public interest. "Under the Government of India Act, 1935", the statement said, "the development of industries is a provincial subject, but is open to the Centre to declare by law that the development of certain industries under central control is expedient in the public interest and thereupon the development of such industries becomes a central subject." As no Act of the central legislature had in the past altered this position, the Government of India was obliged to give reasons for any change it proposed to make in its industrial policy. "The reasons", as the statement pointed out, "are twofold. In the first place, the general economic policy prepared by the Government of India under their own constitutional powers exercises a profound influence over industrial development. It is a matter of history, for example, that the cotton textile, iron and steel and sugar industries have made rapid strides in India largely as a result of the fiscal policy pursued by the Central Government. In the second place, the progress of planning has made it abundantly clear that certain industries must be taken over under central control in the interests of coordinated development. It was indeed contemplated by Parliament, when the Government of India Act was passed, that industries in which a common policy was desirable would be brought under central control."

Consistently with these considerations, the official statement of April 1945 listed 20 basic industries for purposes of central control. The industrial policy so formulated was intended to become the guideline for Nehru's Interim Government of 1946.

Though a projected incursion into the existing structure of industrial ownership to end laissez-faire, it was in effect the organized pressure of the Federation of Indian Chambers of Commerce and Industry as well as its influence with the Congress that stood in the way. This influence was reflected in the recommendations of the Advisory Planning Board which decided to limit the scope of nationalization except in the case of certain basic industries immediately related to defence. In other cases, it resolved, in the absence of adequate trained personnel, to go in for private enterprise on the ground of economy as well as experience to exclude foreign capital from any participation in India's industrial development. The Federation in fact kept on insisting, in its own monopoly interest, on discrimination against non-Indian interests in matters of tariff protection, although negotiations were at the same time in progress between the U.K. and Indian business Houses for the establishment of joint business enterprises in India.

The principle underlying the policy statement of 1945 thus remained tenable, though its application was limited only to a segment of the economy specifically indicated. This, in the first instance, included, under the Industrial Policy Resolution, of 1948, these industries, namely, munitions, atomic energy and railways. There were, in addition, six other fields regarded as key industries where the Government had the exclusive right to start new ventures. These were inclusive of coal, iron and steel, aircraft manufacture, shipbuilding, telephones and telegraph and wireless apparatus, and minerals. Nationalization in respect of all key industries had been permissible under the statement of 1945. Under the 1948 arrangement, however, it was to be postponed for a period of 10 years during which private entrepreneurs were also allowed to participate. The Industrial Policy Resolution of 1948 thus provided for a mixed economy under the pressure politics of FICCI. It was a case of continuity in spite of the recommendations of the Economic Programme Committee of the AICC which wanted cottage industries to have a place of importance in the country's industrial structure.

In fact, as *Cambridge Economic History of India* rightly points out about the Indian Economy Since Independance, the Congress Party essentially pursued a policy of compromise, leaning towards the radicalism of State ownership in its "declared intent", but affording the conservative elements "ample opportunities to resist the implementation of policies" publicly announced. The Socialist content of its Avadi session held in 1955 was amply reflected in the Industrial Policy Resolution adopted by its Government in 1956. It divided the economy clearly into three sectors with an emphasis on the importance of public ownership. But the concurrent sector, which was intended essentially as a field for public enterprise, remained virtually a sphere of private concern. This was in spite of the Directive Principles of State Policy which stood against the concentration of wealth and economic power.

A more dubious step still was the introduction of an economy of shortage which marked the beginning of the Second Five Year Plan. The declared object was to promote a self-reliant economy by imposing constraints on imports. But it led in practice to a rise in prices and provided inducement to such corrupt practices as smuggling and black money.

The real issue which had emerged from the Second World War was in fact one of a choice between laissez-faire and State ownership of key industries. In its policy statement of 1945, the British Government in India went in for the latter as the best course to pursue. But acting under the influence of FICCI, while the Industrial Policy Resolution of 1948 imposed limitations on that approach to industrialization in operational terms, the forces of laissez-faire were sought to be strengthened by an attempt practically to dilute the socialistic content of the arrangement made in 1956 to conform to Avadi's call of the previous year. That is why the promise-performance gap of Nehru's Government has been characterized as a clear case of dilemma, where the declaredly accepted role of public ownership was diluted under pressure politics both at the stage of formulation and implementation.

Under Jawaharlal Nehru and Lal Bahadur Shastri the state of dilemma proceeded either from want of firmness or the incapacity of leadership to resist the organized pressure of big business against all forms of State control. Their politics, however, seemed by and large free from what might be described as part of a collusive conduct. But this could not be said of Mrs. Indira Gandhi who was elected to the office of Prime Minister after considerable canvassing and indefatigable efforts made by K. Kamaraj, the Congress President, who counteracted the forces of opposition in a situation where as many as nine State Governments had gone over to non-Congress parties in the elections of 1967. The delegates of the seventyfirst session of the Indian National Congress which met at Hyderabad in 1968 even complained that "some businessmen have bought politicians", so that all the actions of the Congress "were rightist", while it always "talked of socialism".

Shorn of any claim to superiority in terms of political morality or administrative experience, Mrs. Gandhi sought to retain her hold on power by means of a division of the Congress on declaredly ideological grounds. She, for example, declared herself as firmly committed to the policy of nationalization and proceeded in 1969 to nationalize 14 major banks seemingly to make loans easily available for the purchase of agricultural inputs and the promotion of employment-oriented smallscale industries. But as this study has shown (in Chapter IV), the real beneficiaries were a few top business Houses the value of whose assets recorded a steep rise in the wake of their contribution to Mrs. Gandhi's electoral success in the Parliamentary elections of 1971 and the Assembly elections of 1972. Between 1972 and 1975, the percentage of increase in the assets of the top business Houses registered under the MRTP Act rose to 68.6.

Mrs. Gandhi was perhaps unrivalled among Congress politicians in terms of a capacity for policy distortion. At the New Delhi Session of the AICC held on July 19-21, 1974, the Congress President, Dr. Shankar Dayal Sharma, in fact regretted the continuing trend of policy distortion and pointed out that in spite of thousands of crores pumped into the countryside since independence the benefits could not trickle down to the poorer sections of the people. The beneficiaries of institutional loans were either big landowners or industrial magnates who were responsible for increasing inflation. Sharma thus warned that the price situation would assume a serious proportion unless the private sector was firmly dealt with and a strict surveillance over bank credit to the commercial sector duly maintained. This became clearer still in the case of industrial investment by non-resident Indians, more especially by Swaraj Paul and his group of companies who used Mrs. Gandhi's patronage in the advancement of their own private interests.

Mrs. Gandhi's radicalism of her declared policy objective proved to be highly advantageous to her. It led to a split in the Congress at its Bangalore session in 1969 when she won over the leftists to her side and used them to win the Parliamentary and Assembly elections held a couple of years later. But as S. Nijalingappa, who succeeded Kamaraj as Congress President in 1968, had forewarned, the leftists in the Congress took hardly any care to foresee that once she got strongly entrenched in position as the Prime Minister they would, without fail, find themselves kept at bay. History later proved that the Congress President was not wrong in his forecast. Indeed, Mrs. Gandhi had no dilemma. She knew her mind well and cast her lot on the side of big business. Her resort to ideological radicalism was no more than a mere political strategy which paid her good dividends. That explains a steady rise in the assets of top business Houses as well as a concentration of economic power.

The Janata Government, which came into power in the wake of the general elections of 1977, appreciated the need for control which the Sachar Committee (1977) had emphasized. But then came under Mrs. Gandhi in 1980 a plethora of concessions to private enterprises, including import liberalization, which led to the growth of black money and corruption. The amount of unaccounted money was estimated at between Rs. 20,000 crores and Rs. 25,000 crores. The trend set in 1980 has nonetheless been continuing in spite of the Indian Administrative Service functioning as an instrument of policy implementation to alleviate poverty. For the alliance between elitist politics and national industry which Sir Dorab Tata had envisaged in 1915 became, in course of time, more and more weighted in favour of the latter, so that on the transfer of power in 1947 it began asserting itself as an independent and vested economic force powerful enough to reduce the former to its subservience. Indeed, this subservience of political elitism was the result of a social change that flowed from the dominance of the top Indian business, operating in the post-independence period in collaboration with multinational corporations, more especially British and American, a reflex of productive forces in their ultimate analysis.

See *Selections from Educational Records* (National Archives of India), p. 116; see also Misra, *The Indian Middle Classes*, pp. 103-5.

Index